VISITOR'S
SCOTLAND

David Whyte

MPC
HUNTER

Published by:
Moorland Publishing Co Ltd,
Moòr Farm Road West, Ashbourne,
Derbyshire DE6 1HD England
ISBN 086190 565 2

Published in the North America by:

USA	Canada
Hunter Publishing Inc,	Hunter Publishing,
300 Raritan Center Parkway, CN 94,	164 Commander Blvd, Abincourt, Ontario
Edison, NJ 08818	Canada M1S 3C7

© David J Whyte 1995

British Library Cataloguing in Publication Data:
A catalogue record for this book is available from the British Library.

Colour origination by: ga graphics, Lincolnshire

Printed in Spain by: GraphyCems

Cover photograph: *(Highland Dancers at the Braemar Gathering in Royal Deeside)*
Rear Cover: *(The Piper at Urquhart Castle, Loch Ness)*
Page 3: *(Buachaille Etive Mor and Rannoch Moor)*

Illustrations have been supplied by:
© David J Whyte, The Golf Photo Library Tel/Fax +44 1382 643656
Also by: Western Isles Tourist Board pp219

Acknowledgements:
The author would like to thank the many regional tourist offices in Scotland that helped with researching this book

'To Susie, my wife and travelling companion'

MPC Production Team:
Editor: Tonya Monk
Assistant Editors: Clare Pochon, Christine Haines
Designer: Ashley Emery
Cartographer: Mick Usher
Typesetter: Stella Porter

FEATURE BOXES

How To Use This Guide

This MPC Visitor's Guide has been designed to be as easy to use as possible. Each chapter covers a region or itinerary in a natural progression which gives all the background information to help you enjoy your visit. MPC's distinctive margin symbols, the important places printed in bold and a comprehensive index enable the reader to find the most interesting places to visit with ease.

At the end of each chapter an Additional Information section gives specific details such as addresses and opening times, making this guide a complete sightseeing companion.

At the back of the guide the Fact File, arranged in alphabetical order, gives practical information and useful tips to help you plan your holiday before you go and while you are there.

The maps of each region show the main towns, villages, roads and places of interest, but are not designed as route maps and motorists should always use a recommended road atlas.

Introduction

Situated on the north-west flank of Europe, its craggy, western coastline splintered by the Atlantic Ocean and its eastern shores divided from Scandinavia and the Low Countries by the tempestuous North Sea, the country of Scotland, small in comparison to most, exercises a peculiar hold on the hearts of those that have lived there, visited or simply seen its images on page or screen.

The country's enduring symbols, despite the tourist board's constant attempts to remodel them, are fairy-tale glens, medieval castles, swirling kilts, squealing bagpipes, malt whisky and haggis with the occasional appearance of a great, aquatic monster. In a world increasingly given over to the follies and insensitivities of modern man such kitsch emblems seem to bolster and sustain Scotland's appeal rather than detract from it.

Each year some 4 million visitors arrive to explore the country and there are plenty of practical aspects to maintain their interest. In all of its 30,500sq m (79,059sq km) some 96 per cent of the land is classified as countryside with the majority of that comprising of wild mountains, desolate moors and great inland lochs. Furthermore, the bulk of its 5.5 million population live in the southern lowland belt leaving most parts of the north and south in relative peace.

Wildlife can still be encountered with native species such as red deer, wild goats, wild cats and eagles still present in some more remote areas and in relatively high numbers. But despite its isolation and inherent beauty, the remote Scottish environs still bear the mark of human activity with, for instance, over 9 million sheep roaming and grazing the hills. There is also a perpetual and highly pervasive forestation program that has smothered hillsides with uniform rows of non-native pine, occluding the native species and blanking out the views. Of course, the clearing of Scotland's native woodland took place over many millennia as a result of farming and fuel requirements but the present spruce pine forests bear little resemblance to their forebears. Furthermore, the revenue from these plantations offers little benefit to local economies as modern forestry methods requires few workers and wealthy investors from England's south-east reap the rewards from this profitable and tax-avoiding enterprise.

Scotland is not only known for its scenery and wildlife and the people themselves contribute greatly to the nation's character. Visitors could not find a more kindly nation although to one another they might seem less tolerant. There is still an indigenous attitude that scorns the go-getter or entrepreneur and this has perhaps held modern Scotland back. The birth rate of small businesses for instance, is the lowest by far in Europe. Yet Scotland's earlier inventors made some of the most significant contributions to modern society. The telephone, television, chloroform, pneumatic tyre, postage stamp, bicycle, tar-macadam and penicillin are but a few of the innovations conceived and created by Scottish minds.

In terms of health there has been a tendency for the Scots to slip behind other developed nations. Scotland's population, for instance, bears the worst rates of heart disease and dental problems in the world. This is mostly diet related and it is only in recent years that a more enlightened attitude has entered the collective psyche. It has also lead to a marked improvement in the restaurant industry which, until recently was somewhat less than mediocre.

Despite such problems there is a wind of national pride that seems to be freshening. Politically, there is more support for devolution from a British Parliament based some 330 miles (531km) away in a nation that was, for many centuries, the Scots dreaded foe. While full separation, as advanced by the Scottish National Party, might not appeal to the general populace, some form of self-rule may once again be part of Scotland's future.

There is also a cultural renaissance pushing through the dust of years of indifference. Young people are awakening to their traditions and inheritance and Ceilidhs (Scottish dances) are now as popular in Glasgow and Edinburgh as they have been for years in Tobermory.

preceding page; St Andrews is popular for Scottish Country Dancing conventions, attracting participants from around the world

Tourism is Scotland's biggest industry worth around £1.5 billion to the annual economy. The country's rich heritage along with sports such as fishing, golf or even shopping make it ideal for those prepared to explore or pursue specific activities. But even a simple car or coach tour through the glens stopping to visit some of the great castles or experiencing the magnificent vistas is amply rewarding.

A Brief History

It is impossible to appreciate Scotland without some awareness of its history. There are remnants of the past wherever you visit therefore lack of background information could lead to frustration. There are several key events that are easy to remember and form the main stepping stones in the country's antiquity.

Prior to the Ice Age little evidence of man's existence in this northern spur of the British Isles exists. Dating from 7,000BC the remains of brochs, burial chambers and other stone constructions have been uncovered indicating the presence of early nomadic tribes, probably originating from Asia, passing through Europe and coming into Britain and Ireland. They settled in a climate that was several degrees warmer than we know today or continued to travel, living in caves or temporary dwellings and hunting the plentiful reindeer, elk and wild boar.

The neolithic period 4400-2000BC saw settlement along the Scottish west coast with early travellers using the Atlantic as their main route of transport. Villages such as the remarkably well-preserved Skara Brae in Orkney were probably common throughout the west coast where small groups lived off the land and nearby sea. The Bronze Age 'Beaker People', so called because of the clay beakers found in their single graves, were responsible for the many 'henges' or groups of upright stones found throughout Scotland. These were often formed into a circle such as the Stones of Callanish of the Western Isles or the Ring of Brodgar on Orkney. Most of these date from around 2,000BC.

Between 1000BC and 500BC, Celtic tribes arrived from France via Ireland. They also settled the western coasts of Britain establishing new standards in the design of their dwellings and fortifications while their culture and society flourished. With them came the Iron Age and the advent of new weapons such as swords and shields which subsequently lead to a need for better defensive buildings. The Celts, an enlightened race with fair hair and rich cultural life as well as a talent for metal working and agriculture, introduced fortified timber structures which were followed by stone hill forts some of which are still standing.

At the time of Julius Caesar's first advance into Britain in 55BC the Celts had spread throughout Scotland and were becoming increasingly fractious with one another as demand for good agricultural land grew. Two

Tar-tuan from ancient Gaelic means 'district colour'. Different plants found in the glens and hillsides were used as dying agents and helped to produce the varying hues that were incorporated in the fabric and forming distinctive colour combinations that were exclusive to a clan. Even the water from each area contained unique chemicals that effected the hue.

The existence of tartan was first recorded by the Romans who were impressed by the Celtic or Pictish people's skill in dying and weaving. A system of 'striping' in certain colours became a method of identifying a person's home region and this proved most useful especially during inter-clan battles. The Proscription Acts of 1746 did much to inhibit the wearing of tartan with the exception of the government troops such as the Black Watch. Highland men were forced to wear trousers and, along with the restrictions on owning of any kind of weapon and the playing of bagpipes, much that was Scottish Highland heritage almost disappeared.

Tartan

It was in 1822 when George IV visited Scotland that a new craze for kilts and everything 'Highland' caught on. Tartan makers had a field day following the historic visit, making new tartans and devising new names to accompany them. On the most tenuous of evidence they attributed names to clans and dreamt up an appropriate cloth to satisfy the tartan hungry market.

There was a further resurgence when Queen Victoria became enthralled with her Highland retreat at Balmoral. This caused a minor migration of the upper classes to the Highlands each summer and brought tartan back to the drawing rooms and outdoor picnics of the south. Tartan is now popular throughout the world, mainly in ladies fashions. Men wearing kilts in Scotland is usually on special occasions such as weddings or Highland Games.

There are currently around 700 tartans in existence but the number keeps increasing as new tartans are devised.

The commercial production of Scotch whisky began more than 300 years ago when an Argyllshire farmer derived the drink in a simple device using a similar method to the monks that introduced distilling centuries before. Distilling alcohol from various fruit or grain was brought from China by Arab traders to the Middle East then to Europe, most notably France where Cognac was produced from grapes. The method then travelled from France to Ireland with monks escaping pillage and persecution. They used barley instead of grapes in their process and now the Irish lay claim to having the oldest whisky distillery in the world. And from Ireland as with many other things, it came to Scotland.

In the late seventeenth century a landowner, Duncan Forbes was granted the rights to produce whisky 'from any of the grain grown on his estate' without paying tax. When, in 1784, this 100-year-old monopoly was abolished distilleries rapidly sprang up throughout central Scotland and began to export to England. The English war with France and high taxes forced these small lowland distilleries out of business but the trade carried on using illicit stills. Remote Highland glens were the ideal setting to conceal the cottage industry

Scotch Whisky

that then sprang up and the peat fires and pure water of the glens, used with more traditional methods, produced an even more palatable product.

In 1822, the visit of King George IV once again made whisky widely popular and changes were made in the law reducing excise duties and encouraging legal production. Blending became an important innovation with huge vats in which whiskies were mixed to improve their flavour.

Scotland is divided into regions coinciding with the type of whisky it produces. The distilleries below a line from Dundee to Greenock produce lowland malts which are lighter with a subtle flavour best suited as aperitifs. Whisky produced above the line is considered Highland.

The east of Scotland from Dundee to Royal Loch Nagar produce a whisky whose predominant flavour is malt although much depends on how it is casked. To the west from Speyside to Oban the whisky is very well balanced although there are distinct flavours to be found in the Islays.

Speyside is the modern heart of whisky production with over 30 per cent of Scotch malt whisky coming from this small area such as Glenlivet, Glenfarclas , Glenfiddich or the MaCallan. This is where the illegal trade flourished.

principal groups appeared above the isthmus between the rivers Forth and Clyde and the Romans called them Picts and North Britons. Roman rule had brought long-term benefits to conquered nations throughout Europe but the Picts would have nothing to do with it. Major attempts were made to subjugate them around AD80 by Agricola, the Roman governor but despite plenty victories the Romans retreated south to build first Hadrian's wall between Carlisle and the Tyne near Newcastle then later in AD143, the Antonine Wall between the rivers Forth and Clyde. In due course the Romans withdrew entirely to lend their services elsewhere in their troubled Empire leaving the Picts free to swoop south and cause havoc with lowland dwellers.

A Celtic tribe of Scotti migrated from Ireland in the early fourth century and established themselves on the Kintyre peninsula calling their kingdom Dalriada and bringing with them the precursor to the Gaelic language still spoken in the north-west today. Close behind them came Christianity when St Ninian, a Briton, established the first Christian church at Whithorn in Galloway. St Columba, a Gaelic speaking Scotti, landed in Iona 150 years later and was the main factor in integrating the different Pictish tribes by bringing them to his religion. But it was the Vikings who finally brought an end to the Picts. From AD800 the Pictish people began to lose tenure at the hands of raiding Norsemen and finally most of the Northern and Western Isles as well as large sections of Caithness and Sutherland were under Norse rule.

At the same time, to the south, Kenneth MacAlpine, a Scotti king, united Dalriada and Pictland in AD843 forming the kingdom of Alba later to be known as Scotia and gradually extended his rule to cover the majority of mainland Scotland. This progressed under the rules of Malcolm II and Malcolm III whose pious wife, Margaret, helped bring Scotland's religious life in line with the rest of Europe. It was the son of Malcolm III and Queen Margaret, David I (1124-53) who was responsible for the many monastic abbeys that sprung up throughout the country especially along the Borders. His motivations were not only religious but his monastic communities, largely made up of imported European monks helped increase his communication and control throughout the kingdom. David I's reign saw an increase in Scotland's overall stability and prosperity as he prudently granted royal charters to towns and encouraged foreign trade.

Alexander III was known as the last of the Celtic kings and continued to establish Scotland's affluence. At the Battle of Largs he finally expelled the Norse from the Hebridean islands although the subsequent Lords of the Isles were no real benefit to the national cause preferring to remain autonomous. Alexander went on to forge stronger trading bonds with his old enemies, Norway and England. His untimely death in 1286 heralded the end of this period of growth and with no clear heir to the throne, began an era of bitter conflict stemming from the south. Edward I, having already crushed Wales and determined to subjugate his northerly neighbour commenced a protracted campaign that earned him the title of 'Hammer of the Scots'. He forced Scottish lairds and nobles to sign a 'Ragman's Roll' acknowledging him to be their king and showed little mercy on those that stood against him, exterminating, for instance, most of the population of Berwick-upon-Tweed, then Scotland's main seaport.

It was inevitable that a hero would rise and lead the nation against such tyranny and oppression. William Wallace was a relatively unknown knight who became the leader of the Scottish resistance movement and, in 1297, captured the fragmented country's imagination when he defeated the far superior English army at the Battle of Stirling Bridge. His determination inspired young Robert the Bruce, Earl of Carrick who was actually married to Edward I's god-daughter to take up the cause for Scotland's independence. The pair resorted to guerilla tactics against the might of Edward's army but Wallace was betrayed and horribly executed in 1305. In March of 1306, Robert the Bruce was crowned king of Scotland at Scone and almost immediately become a hunted exile.

Edward I died in 1307 and left his son, the less militarily enthusiastic Edward II to carry on the domination of the Scots but Bruce triumphantly defeated Edward II's army at Bannockburn in 1314 completing his rout of the occupying army. The Scottish Wars of Independence reached an unsteady conclusion in 1320 when eight Scottish earls and thirty-eight barons signed the Declaration of Arbroath, basically a plea sent to the Pope for freedom from English harassment. Although this was a milestone in their efforts, the conflict between the two neighbours continued almost unabated.

The Stewart line of monarchs emerged with Robert II but control over the country was indeterminate leaving a regent, the Duke of Albany, to weald effective power. James II through ruthless means gained back control for the crown from the powerful families that had arisen such as the notorious 'Black Douglases' but the internal power struggle continued through the reigns of James III and then James IV who, on trying to lend support to his French allies against the English, was killed at the Battle of Flodden.

James V's daughter, Mary Queen of Scots, on the death of her father, came to the throne when she was but one week old and instantly attracted the attention of the English King Henry VIII who wished her to marry his 5-year-old son, Edward and bring Scotland under his authority. His aggressive, pre-marital campaign was later dubbed by Sir Walter Scott as the 'Rough Wooing' when much of southern Scotland was destroyed in Henry's attempt to seal the love-match. Instead, Mary was spirited off to France to marry the dauphin, Francis. Mary, versed in the ways of a Catholic France, returned to Scotland some 13 years later on the demise of her sickly spouse and was faced with a country on the brink of religious transformation.

Known as the Reformation and based on Lutheran principles and already supported from a converted England, advocates of the new

Golf

The game of golf is one of Scotland's most famous exports originating here, despite similar claims from the Dutch and Chinese, some 600 years ago. By its physical nature Scotland was perfectly suited to be the cradle of the game. The coastal links, broad areas of unfertile sandy soil and hardy grasses formed when the sea retreated thousands of years ago, can easily be imagined with a young shepherd lad using a suitably shaped branch or crook to knock a rounded pebble over the grassy dunes and into a rabbit hole.

Today, there are some 400 courses throughout the nation, more golf courses per head than any other country in the world. The game is part of the social fabric. The majority of courses are cheap and accessible which allows everyone including youngsters to easily take up the game.

There are the better known courses such as St Andrews, Muirfield, Royal Troon, Royal Dornoch, Carnoustie, Turnberry, Gleneagles and Prestwick, that should be experienced if you are prepared to pay the higher green fees. But golfers find themselves equally rewarded on some of the less exalted tracts and, in fact, locals will tell you that the less famous neighbours are actually better than the sometimes over-played premier courses.

East Lothian is one of Scotland's more famous golfing belts with some of the most inspiring holes in the game. Further north across the Forth Road Bridge is the world's most revered golfing area, the Kingdom of Fife. Within the ancient county are naturally formed links intrinsic to the birth and formation of the game. Continuing along the east coast the region of Tayside includes Carnoustie, Rosemount and Gleneagles while further north is Royal Aberdeen, Cruden Bay and around the Moray coastline to Nairn. The Highlands and Islands are first thought of for their unparalleled scenery but for the golfer this is a bonus to some of the most challenging golf tracts. Favoured courses here are Boat of Garten, Kingussie and Royal Dornoch.

Scotland's north-west is not noted for its golfing grounds although there are several good holiday courses including those on the Western Isles, Skye and the Northern Isles. Travelling south the golfing opportunities pick up again around Glasgow and into

St Boswells Golf Club has one of the finest locations in the Borders

Ayrshire. From Largs to Girvan Ayrshire's coast including Turnberry and Royal Troon could be explored for weeks on end without playing the same course twice. There are also some of the best public courses in Britain in this area. Continue south into Dumfries and Galloway to sample their fine links and parkland courses that are usually quiet. For more information on golfing holidays in Scotland, contact Discovery Golf, ☎ 01382 228861

religion such as George Wishart and John Knox attempted to oust the corpulent, hierarchical Catholic church and replace it with Protestant-arianism. With the Confession of Faith in 1560 the Pope authority was denied and Mass outlawed. The returning catholic Mary Queen of Scots tried to navigate a middle route between the two opposing religions as well as the powerful, land-owning barons whom she relied on for support but this did little to help her turbulent period of rule and she was finally betrayed by her suspicious cousin, Elizabeth I of England. After 20 years imprisonment she was beheaded.

It was her son, James VI of Scotland (King James I of England) that brought the two nations of England and Scotland together in a glimmer of confederacy with the Union of the Crowns in 1603 making him James VI of Scotland and James I of England. But, following his coronation he quickly settled his court in London and came back to his native land only once during his reign leaving Scotland much neglected. The religious issue remained confused through James VI reign and into his son's Charles I who advocated a form of Catholicism, Episcopacy. The results, when he tried to administer this to his Scottish subjects lead to one of the most perplexing and ferocious eras of Scotland's history.

The signing of the National Covenant in 1685 was an attempt to thwart Charles' 'Popery' and it raised Charles to war although the attempt back-fired on the monarch so badly that he ended up declaring war on his own Parliament for their reluctance to back his battle plans. The ambivalence of this period came out when Scots who largely rejected King Charles reforms decided to support him. This lead to the Marquis of Montrose raising an army against the Convenanters but this was small interest compared to the Civil War that had erupted south of the border with the Covenanters and the Parliamentarians waging war against the crown. Finally, divisions between factions caused Cromwell to invade Scotland forcing Charles II into temporary exile. His return in 1660 brought the 'Killing Times; where many Covenanters were put to death for practising their beliefs. Scotland's religious wars finally ended with the reign of Mary and William of Orange and the restoration of the Presbyterian church.

The Union of Parliaments came about in a period when Scotland faced bankruptcy and further war with mounting pressure brought to bear on merchants trading across the border and concern that a catholic Stewart king should regain the Scottish crown. To avoid this the Scottish Parliament voted itself out of existence and elected forty-five Members of Parliament and sixteen peers to sit in the Houses of Parliament in London. The Union failed to bring Scotland any tangible benefits and support of the Old Pretender, James Stewart, exiled in France grew in both Scotland and England.

The first Jacobite uprising took place in 1715 with the Earl of Mar raising the Stewart standard at Braemar Castle and taking Perth shortly after. Mar did not pursue his military advantage and with the arrival of reinforcements the government troops quelled the rebellion. Charles Edward Stewart, better known as Bonnie Prince Charlie returned to his native land from France in 1745 in an attempt to reinstate his father and, with no money and few men to start with, was, in only a short period, surprisingly successful. The conflict ended at the Battle of Culloden when Hanoverian troops crushed the Jacobite corps, slaughtering most of the wounded and hounding to death any that escaped. The aftermath of Culloden was perhaps worse than the event itself when the Duke of Cumberland's troops humbled the Highland spirit by seeking out any remaining supporters and with the Proscription Acts of 1746, banning the wearing or tartan, bearing of arms and the playing of bagpipes.

Culloden heralded a major change in Highland life and the lairds and landlords, once dependant on their tenantry for military support and now unable to raise arms, realised there was more profit to be had in sheep and sporting estates. The relatively large populations resident in the glens and on the islands were forced off their crofts and given little option other than to emigrate mostly to Canada and America which they did in great numbers. It was not until the Crofter's Act of 1886 that Highlanders enjoyed any form of security of tenure but emigration continued from Scotland up until and throughout the twentieth century.

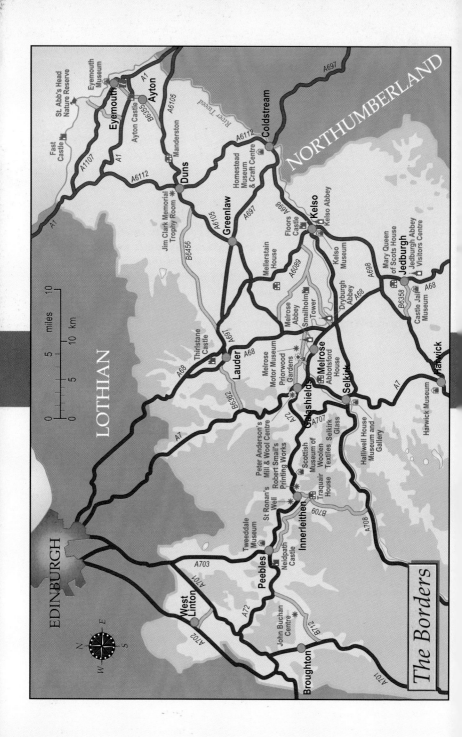

The Borders

1

From the south there are four main routes into the Scottish Borders, each offering a particular introduction to this distinctive region. The upgraded A1 follows the east coast and is the easiest to drive, with long stretches of dual-carriageway and occasional coastal views. The alternative A68 through Carters Bar is undulating and scenic although slightly more demanding for the driver. It crosses the pastoral and hilly heart of Borders country. The A697 through Coldstream is similar and from the west the A7, signposted from the M6 as the tourist route for the Borders and Edinburgh, passes through the market towns of Hawick and Selkirk.

Despite acting as a crash barrier between Britain's two largest countries through many tumultuous centuries, the Borders is now one of the most gentle and peaceful of Scottish regions. Its rolling country roads and picturesque villages, compared to other regions, are quiet even at their busiest times. In the east quilted rolling landscapes are occasionally interrupted by higher elevations such as the Eildon Hills, whereas the west is more remote in character.

The larger towns of Hawick, Jedburgh and Peebles are more influenced by the modern world with super-stores set next to woolly jumper and fishing tackle shops. The river Tweed contributes immensely to the character of the region. The Borders are famous for fishing with salmon beats, depending on the season, available throughout the region. Trout fishing is also available from March to October on some rivers.

The area's history has contributed greatly to local traditions and perhaps even the local disposition. The predominant and persistent factor over nearly 400 years was the aggression between Scotland and its southerly neighbour. Between 1296 and the Union of the Crowns in the early seventeenth century the Borders was a battleground or the through-route to one between the two constantly warring nations. This virtual no-mans-land, as it became, fell into a lawless state and cattle stealing was rife, even amongst closer neighbours. Not until the Union of the Crowns did the wild Borders settle into the peaceful province that it is today.

Eyemouth, a harbour community since the twelfth century, is best reached by leaving the A1 for the A1107. James VI granted the town freeport status in 1597 and it immediately became a flourishing centre for smugglers. Some of the older houses in the maze-like town centre have underground passages and hidden chambers still intact. The cliffs and their numerous caves along the rugged shore-line were also employed for the storage of booty.

Eyemouth epitomizes the seaside resort with its array of shops selling postcards, ice-cream, buckets and spades, and so on. Activities include walking, fishing and diving. The tale of the Great East Coast Fishing Disaster of 1881 in which 23 boats were lost in a sudden storm that took the lives of 189 local fisherman is brought to life in a tapestry at the Eyemouth Museum, located near the harbour.

A few miles north of Eyemouth, off the A1 on the B6438 is the little village of **St Abbs**. Overlooking Coldingham Bay, well-known for its colourful pebbles, its character is unique for this part of Scotland. The tranquil port, once renowned for its thriving haddock and cod industry, resembles a Cornish fishing village, with cottages clinging like limpets to the steep, rocky shore.

St Abbs Head is just north of the village and best reached by parking at the main car park and visitor's centre between St Abbs and Coldingham and following the short path towards the cliffs. It is also possible to drive the single track road past Northfield Steading Farm and Mire Loch, a dammed stretch of water and regular stopping place for small birds at migration time. There is limited car parking just before the entrance to the lighthouse. This dramatic piece of saw-toothed headland is where the Lammermuir Hills plunge into the North Sea, 192 acres (77 hectares) of protected land edged with craggy, volcanic basalt that drops 300ft (91m) to ragged rocks below.

Run by the National Trust for Scotland along with Scottish Wildlife Trust, it is a reserve mainly for sea birds such as kittiwake, shag, guillemot, fulmar and razor bills. These can be closely observed from the road or cliff edges although care must be taken, as no barriers have been

---

preceding page: Smailholm Tower was rescued from demolition by Sir Walter Scott

erected. St Abbs Lighthouse can only be visited with permission from the keeper.

For those that are sure-footed and interested in visiting one of the most dramatic sites for a Scottish castle, take the path northwest from St Abbs Head for about 4 miles (6km) to the impossibly positioned **Fast Castle**. This ruined fortress now only a few stacks of weather-worn stone, perched on a narrow peninsula was employed by ship-wreckers; some say they built it and set lights upon it specifically to lure ships onto the rocks. Sir Walter Scott was so inspired by this ragged promontory and its fort that he employed them in his novel *Lammermoor*.

Crossing the busy A1 again, a few miles southwest of St Abbs and Eyemouth is the village of **Ayton** and Ayton Castle, a distinguished red sandstone building of the Victorian era. This is still a family home but open during the season only on Sunday afternoons or by appointment. It was built in 1846 by an owner who insisted on changing the design as the inspiration took him and the end result is basically Scottish Baronial with a touch of Gothic.

A few miles south, just off the A6105, is one of the finest Edwardian houses in Scotland. **Manderston** is described as the 'swan-song of the great, classical house'. The Miller family, who made a fortune trading with Russia in herring and hemp, spent a large part of it on turning their home into this opulent palace. The architecture, is influenced to some extent by Robert Adam and it has one unique feature that few other houses can boast. The silver staircase was modelled on that found in the Petit Trianon at Versailles. Outside there are 56 acres (22 hectares) of rhododendrons and azaleas, well worth experiencing in late spring.

The nearby village of **Duns** is not an enticing place. Like so many of the Border communities, it was completely destroyed by the English in 1545 as part of the Rough Wooing, Henry VIII's indelicate attempts to encourage Mary, Queen of Scots to marry his son. It is now a residential hamlet with a nature reserve and a 9 hole golf course nearby. At 44 Newton Street on the west side of the village, you will find the Jim Clark Memorial ✳ Trophy Room, in which the trophies, letters and memorabilia of this Berwickshire farmer have been collected, following his fatal racing accident in 1968.

Coldstream has been a crossing place between England and Scotland for centuries with a narrow section of the River Tweed offering a ford, then later, a good bridging point. Apart from the military significance of this crossing, Coldstream once rivalled Gretna Green for run-away English couples who took advantage of Scotland's easier marriage laws of the time. Coldstream is also closely associated with the famous military regiment, the Coldstream Guards and their history is presented in the local museum. The Hirsel estate, just west of Coldstream, houses the Homestead Museum and Craft Centre, an old farmstead building offer- ing a rare glimpse into the common tools and crafts formerly used in this area. The house is closed to the public, although there is a particularly fine golf course on the estate.

A main event in Coldstream's Civic Week in August is the ride to Flodden Field to honour the dead in that battle of 1513. Flodden is about 6 miles (10km) across the border, due south of Coldstream and just off the A697. Here, James IV of Scotland, much against the advice of his lords, lead a gallant army of men to one of the worst defeats experienced by the Scots in their centuries long attempt to secure independence.

Kelso is the most easterly of a string of historically important Border towns. Founded in 1128 by King David I, Kelso Abbey was the most influential ecclesiastical establishment in this area and is a superb example of medieval architecture. The Abbey was reckoned, in its heyday, to be the largest of the three Borders abbeys. Although there is not much left to see today, it took 80 years to build.

Set on the confluence of the Rivers Teviot and Tweed, Kelso is now a well appointed, country-market town. The elegant five-arched bridge over the Tweed dates from 1803 and was built by John Rennie as a model for London Bridge. Closer to the town centre is Turret House, now Kelso Museum, one of the town's oldest buildings. It interprets Kelso's consequential history and its role as a centre for the skinning and tanning industry. King James Stuart, the Old Pretender was declared king in the town's French looking market square in 1715 and his son, returning after his march to London in 1745, stayed at the Cross Keys Hotel which still looks over the elegant Georgian square claiming to be the biggest town square in Scotland.

The flamboyant outline of **Floors Castle** may ring bells for many visitors who will suspect they have seen it before. The extensive castellated parapets and elegant interiors of this, Scotland's largest inhabited house, were the settings for the film *Greystoke* where the jungle-liberated Tarzan, the Earl of Greystoke was seen jumping from rampart to roof. The more romantic may recall the announcement of the engagement of Prince Andrew and Sarah Ferguson on the lawns of Floors. This sprawling eighteenth and nineteenth-century castle and estate is the home and offices of the present Duke of Roxburghe. The rooms seem more intimate and family oriented than most inhabited stately homes as the Duke and his family use them when visitors are away. The family furniture is backdropped with tapestries and surrounded by porcelain and paintings. The building was designed by William Adam between 1721 and 1725 and added to in 1849 by William Playfair.

Another Adam project lies quite near Floors Castle. **Mellerstain House** is well known for its distinctive architecture and refined interiors. The estate existed as far back as the fifteenth century but the present house was commenced by William Adam in 1725. His son, Robert took over and completed the house in 1778 being mainly responsible for everything bar the wings. There are particularly tasteful ceilings and friezes in the library, drawing room and music room and paintings by Allan Ramsay, Gainsborough and Constable. The house is situated 7 miles (11km) northwest of Kelso on the A6089. A famous character, though not the subject of Robert Burns' poetry, was probably conceived in these grounds during

Floors Castle near Kelso is the ancestrial home of the Duke of Roxburghe

Kelso's Market Square claims to be the biggest town square in Scotland

an illicit love affair between a young master of the house and an estate worker. Known as Tam o' Shanter, his exploits were well established even during his lifetime.

Driving through country lanes, it might prove slightly difficult to find **Smailholm Tower** but it is signposted although not very distinctly. A busy farm yard is part of the route, a bit disconcerting for those thinking they are lost but once over the cattle grids and on towards the now visible structure, a single track road provides an impressive approach to this fifteenth-century tower. Fronted by an old mill pond which is garnished with rocks, spearwort and water lilies as well as frequent wildlife visitors such as herons and water hens, Smailholm Tower stands 57ft (17.38m) high on an already elevated outcrop of rock. It is an unusual setting for an extraordinary monolith whose main purpose was to command a wide view over the Tweed Valley and to withstand attack during the Reiver's raids. From the top there is a fine panorama of the Cheviots, the Lammermuirs and east to the Eildon Hills. The tower was in ruins by 1799 and would have remained so or cleared away if not for the intervention of Scotland's most famous author, Sir Walter Scott. He had spent his childhood holidays at the adjacent farm with his grandparents and was quite attached to the old stockade. On hearing of its demise, Scott made a deal with the then owner, Scott of Harden, to write a ballad about the tower providing the farmer made sure that it was saved. The *Eve of St John* was the consequence. Smailholm was also mentioned in Sir Walter's book, *Marmion* and it now houses an exhibition of dolls and tapestries.

Nearby and well signposted, **Dryburgh Abbey** has one of the most romantic settings of all four of the Borders abbeys founded in the reign of David I. Set in a horseshoe bend of the River Tweed it is enclosed by tall trees of several varieties including cedars from Lebanon brought back from the Holy Land during the Crusades. Its pale reddish brown sand-stone was erected and occupied by Augustinian monks from Alnwick in Northumberland in 1140. Again, it was repeatedly ravaged by the English. In 1322, the ecclesiastical centre was nearly lost but financial aid from Robert the Bruce saw it completely rebuilt. Acting for Henry VIII in 1545, Hertford, of Kelso infamy, left it a smouldering hulk. Little now remains of the church but the twelfth- and thirteenth-century cloister buildings are still tolerably intact. The tomb of the Borders' greatest son, Sir Walter Scott, is found here along with that of his biographer, Lockhart, who lies buried at his feet.

Following the B6356 beyond Dryburgh Abbey you come to a walled outlook over the Tweed called **Scott's View**. The prospect, centring on the Eildon Hills, was such a favourite of the author that, whilst drawing his funeral cortege on its way to Dryburgh Abbey, his horses paused of their own accord.

What we see of the village of **Melrose** today was built in the last two centuries creating a delightfully quiet hamlet that is set around its square where four main routes converge. Most visitors come to Melrose to see its abbey lying just north of the square. The Cistercian monks that settled here in 1136 preferred a simple existence and the original Melrose Abbey was a plain building that lay at the heart of their farming province. The ever-threatening English dealt the same blows here as at the other Borders abbeys during the Wars of Independence laying waste the building on several occasions. Reconstruction took place in a much more elaborate style through to the sixteenthth century incorporating, as well as grand arches, towers and huge windows, humorous stone-carved figures such as a cook with his ladle, a mason with his mallet and a pig playing the bagpipes which can still be made out around the top.

Beyond the abbey walls Melrose offers a stimulating Motor Museum with a host of paraphernalia as well as a collection of some 200 cars and motor bikes. To the south of the abbey is a pleasant retreat in Priorwood Gardens where small plant beds contain flowers especially suited for drying.

From Melrose it is possible to hike up the **Eildon Hills**. The Eildon Hill North was once a fortified Pictish settlement and, later, a Roman Signal station. The Southern Upland Way passes near town for the more enthusiastic walker and a good golf course graces the lower slopes of the Eildon's. To get there from the village square, head south up the hill on the B6359. There are many fishing spots in this area primarily on the Tweed and for all fishing needs get in touch with Ted Hunter at the Angler's Choice in Market Square. Permits are obtained through his unique Salmon Letting Computer service which tells, at the press of a button, what beats are available at any given time.

Turning south from Melrose on the A68 you enter the Teviot Valley, fringed by the Cheviot Hills and punctuated by some of the Borders main towns. Situated only 10 miles (6km) above the English Border on a vitally important transit route for armies and supplies **Jedburgh**, so called because of its position on the Jed Water has seen more than its fair share of conflict. Its townsmen gained a deserved reputation for tenacity and aggressive behaviour during the troubled times, no doubt out of necessity.

Founded by David I, first as a priory then elevated to the status of abbey and subsequently destroyed by English armies during the Wars of Independence. Jedburgh Abbey was later reconstructed and now stands imposing above the Jed Water. In the Visitor's Centre the history of this and the other Borders abbeys is thoughtfully explained.

The town of Jedburgh is encapsulated in the central area behind the abbey. It is a busy place, very well kept, with locals and visitors hunting round a colourful array of gift shops and quality purveyors. From the central Market Place you can walk up the hill to Castle Jail Museum. This nineteenth-century reform prison stands on the site of Jedburgh Castle, a fortification that the Scots destroyed themselves to avoid it coming into English hands. It occupied a strategic position overlooking the town and its valley which extends to the south. The jail, maintained in its original condition, gives a good idea of nineteenth-century prison life which does

The impressive red sandstone shell of Melrose Abbey

Abbotsford House near Melrose, built by Sir Walter Scott

not seem as bad as you might imagine. There is a wide grassy area outside to rest before the hike back into town.

The Mary Queen of Scots House and Visitor Centre on Queen Street presents perhaps a rather over-dramatised version of this much exposed monarch's life. The fact is, they are slightly unsure if she even stayed here. More substantiated events surrounding her life did take place around Jedburgh, very possibly in this house, which is well restored to tell the story.

Hawick, pronounced 'Hoik', is set on the banks of the Teviot River. Wool and its products have been Hawick's forte and a great pastime for visitors is 'raking' through the many woollen mill bargain bins for a low-priced jumper. Its main industry was, at one time, hosiery but this has been replaced by more up-market demands for golf sweaters and fashionable woollen fabrics. The history of the town is contained in Hawick Museum and Scott Art Gallery found in Wilton Lodge Park. If it rains you can take refuge in the Teviotdale Leisure Centre with its saunas, steam rooms and swimming pools.

The A7 from Carlisle comes from the west through Hawick and continues on north to **Selkirk** some 12 miles (19km) away. This 'Ancient Royal Burgh' stands high above the Ettrick and Yarrow Valleys which were once alive with the clatter of water-powered textile mills throughout the nineteenth century. There is still plenty of such activity in the production of tweed, tartan and cashmere and most of these items are on sale from the modern factory units found on the outskirts of town or in their mill-shop outlets. Selkirk is also know for glass-ware which can be seen being made at the Selkirk Glass factory also just off the A7.

Selkirk was the first municipality to benefit from King David I's ambitious plan to erect abbeys and priories throughout Scotland. But Selkirk Abbey lasted for only 20 years before it was abandoned by the Tyronensian monks who preferred Kelso's flatter location. The town's Market Place is squeezed into one corner by the lively A7 road which passes through the centre of town. It contains a statue of Sir Walter Scott, county sheriff here for 33 years. At the other end of the High Street is a memorial to the Battle of Flodden of 1513. Visit Halliwell's House, the town's oldest building, for an excellent display featuring Selkirk's ironmongery industry, an important part of its heritage.

Driving north from Selkirk there is a minor road, the B6360, well signposted for **Abbotsford House**, the Tweedside mansion of Sir Walter Scott. Scott bought the old farmhouse of Cartleyhole or 'Clarty-hole' as it was dubbed in 1811, immediately replacing the name and, in stages, building the present house. One of the great architectural charms of the place is its mish-mash of styles.

Incorporated in the building's fabric are numerous inscribed stones rescued from sites across south-eastern Scotland. Scott assembled a large collection of curiosities, items such as a lock of Bonnie Prince Charlie's hair, Flora MacDonald's pocket book, Montrose's sword, Rob Roy's sporran purse and over 9,000 books. It was in Abbotsford that Scott wrote most of his famous *Waverely Novels*.

The **Galashiels** Manufacturer's Corporation's motto encapsulates the community's spirit, 'We dye to live and live to die'. Just off the main shopping area and along Huddersfield Road is Peter Anderson's Woollen Mill, which produces the world's largest range of pure wool and worsted tartans and may be explored by guided tour.

The Borders Wool Centre to the west following the A72, has a collection of rare breeds of sheep as well as spinning demonstrations, a shop and display of fleeces reflecting the importance of wool in the economy of this area. Ladhope Golf Course behind the town to the north has some of the steepest holes in golf, namely the 9th and 10th. If you are staying in this area an interesting diversion leads north either on the A7 or the A68 from Melrose to the village of **Lauder** and its nearby Thirlestane Castle. This has been the home of the Maitland family for some 400 years and displays paintings by Gainsborough, Lawrence, Hoppner and Romney.

The A72 west of Galashiels meets up with some spectacular stretches of the River Tweed once it descends on to its plain. The roadside village of **Walkerburn** has the Scottish Museum of Woollen Textiles which is worth a short stop if you really are interested in wool. Admittance is free and the displays show the history of the wool trade from its early days as a cottage industry to the fashionable business that it has become. There is a large mill shop and a coffee shop.

The next Tweedsdale village is **Innerleithen**, a popular holiday escape for those that know its hidden virtues. Innerleithen was famous for its spa throughout the nineteenth century and was mentioned in Sir Walter Scott's *St Ronan's Well*. A pump room was built by the owner of Traquair House to help capitalize on the fashion, mostly created by Scott's mention of the place, and now there is the St Ronan's Wells Interpretive Centre to further exploit the well's enduring appeal.

Found on the High Street in Innerleithen is a remarkable survivor from the Victorian era as well as a valuable archive of the printing trade. Robert Smail's Printing Works, now run by the National Trust for Scotland served the local community until 1986 with letterheads, posters, invitations and, up until March 1916, a weekly newspaper. Much of the equipment dated back to the commencement of trade and records of every print job carried since the business started in 1866 were still on file when the Trust took over. The 100-year-old printing press was originally run by water and its water wheel had to be restored to put the press in motion again. Today, you can watch the printer preparing the presses and you can try setting type by hand yourself.

Traquair House is signposted from Innerleithen following the B709, One of the most remarkable homes in Scotland it is also said to be the oldest continuously inhabited. The grounds, although not the house which is slightly more recent, have been owned by the same family since as far back as the tenth century. The present Traquair House started as a twelfth-century keep to which was added a fifteenth-century tower and there were further extensions throughout the sixteenth and seventeenth centuries, resulting in an odd but impressive conglomeration of period styles.

One of Traquair House's most famous residents was Mary, Queen of Scots who stayed here with her husband, Darnley, in 1566. Prince Charles Edward Stuart, 'Bonnie Prince Charlie', was a brief guest on his march to London in 1745. The main Bear Gates, as they are called, are said to remain shut, on the owner's pledge to Charles, until a Stuart king or queen once again sits on the British throne. You enter the grounds, therefore, by the side entrance. Through the back there is a working eighteenth-century brew-house fermenting Traquair Ale. There are some craft-shops in nearby buildings.

Glentress Forest, just before the town of Peebles, is known for mountain bike trails through the forest and over the hills of Moorfoot. Bikes can be hired at the Glentress Mountain Bike Centre, bike holidays are arranged and racing events are often staged. The trails go along the Tweed or through Forestry Commission property but the best rides are for those with stamina enough to climb through the forestry tracks and face the hills and dales beyond.

Peebles is a large town by Borders standards with a High Street that is well stocked with an interesting mix of country stores and unusual gift shops. This is also the main parade for the Common Riding of the Marches, a yearly display of the horse-power of the area. Its origins of vigilance in the time of the Border raids and Wars of Independence are more serious. The Tweedale Museum is housed in the Chambers Institute found half way down the High Street. The building was presented to the town by the publisher, William Chambers, already full of art works, casts of famous sculptures and colourful friezes. With the help of money donated by Andrew Carnegie the house was then enlarged to include reading rooms, a library, an art gallery and two museums.

Off Peebles High Street are pends and alley-ways such as Newby Court with craft workers turning wood or making bagpipes both Scottish and Northumbrian. Continue down the alley to overlook the River Tweed which cuts the town in two and is flanked by wide, grassy commons to relax or stroll on. There are several walks through the surrounding hills listed in the *Popular Walks Around Peebles* leaflet available from the tourist office.

Neidpath Castle a mile or so west of Peebles, has an imposing prospect over the Tweed which is best appreciated by walking down either of the river banks and gazing up at its domineering situation. The tower is fourteenth century while extensions were built in the seventeenth century. Inside the front doorway is an arrow indicating the 12 foot (3.66m) width of walls along with a tongue-in-cheek display of trash left by more recent visitors. There is also an interesting little museum.

The north-western corner of the Borders is more elevated, lonely moorland with fewer trees and isolated little communities. **Broughton**, 10 miles (16km) south-west of Peebles following the B712 was the childhood

village of the novelist and governor-general of Canada, John Buchan.
There is a well supplied museum inside a converted church, the John
Buchan Centre, dedicated to his remarkable career as a barrister, soldier,
statesman and creator of fifty books, including *The Thirty-nine Steps*.
Broughton Place is a modern castle that only looks ancient, designed in
the 1930's by Sir Basil Spence and a frequent venue for some outstanding
contemporary art exhibitions. The gallery is only open in summer. A
further 6 miles (10km) south is the Crook Inn one of the oldest pubs in the
Borders and frequented by customers such as John Buchan, Sir Walter
Scott and Robert Burns.

In the north-west corner of the Borders region the quaint village of
West Linton sits off the busy A702 between Edinburgh and Biggar. West
Linton Golf Club offers an excellent challenge. From West Linton the
centre of Edinburgh is only 16 miles (26km) away to the north.

Additional Information

Places of Interest

Broughton
John Buchan Centre
10 miles (16km) south-west of Peebles
Open: Afternoons, Easter to mid-October.

Broughton Gallery
A701 north of broughton village
☎ 018994 234
Open: Late March to late, 10.30am-6pm.
Closed Wednesday.

Coldstream
Homestead Museum & Craft Centre
In the grounds of Hirsel Estate
☎ 01890 882834
Open: All year, Monday to Friday
10am-5pm, Saturday and Sunday,
12noon-5pm.

Duns
Jim Clarke Memorial Trophy Room
44 Newtown Street, Duns
☎ 01361 882600
Open; Easter to end of October, Monday to Saturday, 10am-1pm, 2pm-5pm.
Sunday 2-5pm.

Eyemouth
Eyemouth Museum
Auld Kirk, Market Place,
☎ 01890 750678
Open: Easter to October, 10am-5pm,
Sunday 2-3.30pm

Galashiels
Peter Anderson Woollen Mill
Nether Mill, Galashiels
☎ 01896 752091
Open: Monday to Saturday all year.
9am-5pm and Sundays in June to
September, 12noon-5pm.

Borders Wool Centre
Wheatlands Road off A72
☎ 01896 754293
Open: All year, Monday to Saturday,
9.30am-5pm.

Hawick
Hawick Museum & Scott Gallery
Wilton Lodge Park in Hawick 1 mile
(2km) from town centre
☎ 01540 73457
Open: October to March, Monday to
Friday, 1-4pm, Sunday, 2-4pm. April to
September, 10am-12noon and 1-5pm.
Sunday, 2-5pm.

Innerleithen
St Ronan's Well Interpretive Centre
☎ 01721 720123
Open: Easter to October, daily 2-5pm.

Robert Smail's Printing Workshop
High Street
☎ 01896 830206
Open: 14 April to 22 October, Monday
to Saturday, 10am-1pm and 2-5pm.
Sunday 2-5pm.

Traquair House
B709 off the A72 in Innertheithen
Open: Easter, May to June and September, 1.30-5.30pm. July to August,
10.30am-5.30pm.

Jedburgh

Jedburgh Abbey and Visitor Centre
High Street, Jedburgh
Historic Scotland ☎ 0131 244 3101
Open: April to September, Monday to
Saturday, 9.30am-7pm. Sunday, 2-7pm.
October to March, Monday to Saturday
9.30am-4.00pm. Sunday 2-4pm.

Jedburgh Castle Jail Museum
Open: Easter to September, Monday to
Saturday, 10am-5pm, Sunday 1-5pm.

Mary Queen of Scots House
Open: Easter to Mid-November, 10am-
5pm.

Kelso

Kelso Abbey
Bridge Street, Kelso
Historic Scotland ☎ 0131 244 3101
Open: April to December, Monday to
Saturday during daylight hours and
Sunday afternoons.

Kelso Museum
Turret House, Abbey Court off Bridge
Street, Kelso
☎ 01573 223464
Open: April to October, 9am-5pm.

Floors Castle
North-west side of Kelso
☎ 01573 223333
Open: Late April to late September,
10.30am to 5.30pm

Mellerstain House
Off A6089, north-west of Kelso
☎ 01573 410225
Open: Easter, 1st May to 30th September, Sunday to Friday 12.30-4.30pm.

Smailholm Tower
Off B6404 6 miles (10km) north-west of
Kelso
Historic Scotland, ☎ 0131 244 3101
Open: April to September, Monday to
Saturday 9.30am-6pm, Sunday 2-6pm.

Dryburgh Abbey
Off A68 near St Boswells
Historic Scotland ☎ 0131 244 3101
Open: April to September, Monday to

Saturday, 9.30am to 7pm. Sunday, 2-7pm.
October to March, Monday to Saturday
9.30am-4.00pm. Sunday 2-4pm.

Lauder

Thirlestane Castle
Off the A68 near Lauder, 28 miles
(45km) south of Edinburgh.
☎ 01578 722430
Open: Easter week then May, June, &
September, Wednesday, Thursday and
Sunday only; July to August, daily from
2-5pm except Saturday.

Manderston

2 miles (3km) east of Duns on A6105
☎ 01361 883450
Open: 11 May to 28 September, Thursdays and Sundays, 2-5.30pm.

Melrose

Melrose Abbey
Off the Main Square, Melrose
Historic Scotland ☎ 0131 244 3101
Open: April to September, Monday to
Saturday, 9.30am-7pm. Sunday, 2-7pm.
October to March, Monday to Saturday
9.30-4.00pm. Sunday 2-4pm.

Melrose Motor Museum
Across the street from abbey
☎ 01896 822642
Open: Mid-May to mid-October,
10.30am-5.30pm. Part time the rest of
year.

Priorwood Gardens
Next to Melrose Abbey
☎ 01896 822555
Open: April to October, Monday to Saturday 10am-5.30pm, Sunday 1.30-5.30pm.

Abbotsford House
2 miles (3km) west of Melrose on B6360
Open: Mid-March to October, Monday
to Saturday, 10am-5pm, Sunday 2-5pm.

Peebles

Glentress Mountain Bike Centre
East side of Peebles off A72
☎ 01721 722934
Open: Easter to October.

Tweedale Museum
High Street, Peebles
☎ 01721 720123
Open: All year including Saturdays and
Sundays in April to October, 2-5pm.

Neidpath Castle
A72, 1 mile (1^1/$_2$km) west of Peebles
☎ 01875 870201
Open: Easter to September, Monday to
Saturday, 11am-5pm. Sunday 1-5pm.

Selkirk
Halliwell's House Museum and Gallery
Off main square in Selkirk town centre
☎ 01750 20096
Open: April to October, Monday to
Saturday, 10am-5pm, Sunday, 2-4pm.
July and August until 6pm.

St Abbs
Fast Castle
Off A1107
☎ 01890 771280
Open: Always open but care must be
taken.

St Abbs Head Visitors Centre
Northfield Farm off B6437
Ranger can be contacted on ☎ 01890
771443 for groups and guided walks.
Open: April to October 10am-4pm.

Walkerburn
Scottish Museum ofWoollenTextiles
On the main road, A72 in Walkerburn
☎ 01896 870619
Open: All year, Monday to Saturday,
10am-5.30pm. Sundays, Easter to
Christmas, 12noon-4.30pm.

Other Useful Information

Weathercall for this area
☎ 01898 500422

Emergencies
Ambulance, Police & Firebrigade ☎ 999

Fishing Permits and Information
Angler's Choice
23 Market Square
Melrose, TD6 9PL

Golf
Freedom of the Fairways Passport
The passport allows access to 10 of the
16 participating courses in one week.
For more details contact:
The Scottish Borders Tourist Board
Murrays Green
Jedburgh
Scotland TD8 6BE
☎ 01750 20054

Tourist Information Offices

The Scottish Borders Tourist Board
Murrays Green
Jedburgh
Scotland TD8 6BE
☎ 01750 20054

Coldstream
Henderson Park
☎ 01890 882607

Eyemouth
Auld Kirk
☎ 018907 50678

Galashiels
3 St John's Street
☎ 01896 755551

Hawick
Common Haugh
☎ 01450 372547

Jedburgh
Murray's Green
☎ 01835 863435

Kelso
Town House, The Square
☎ 01573 223464

Melrose
Town Centre
☎ 01896 822555

Peebles
High Street
☎ 01721 720138

Selkirk
Halliwells House
☎ 01750 720054

Accommodation

Hotels & B&B's
Coldstream
Iolar, Victoria Street *
☎ 01890 882607

Duns
Simon and Tracey Ashby B&B *
Broomhouse Mains
☎ 01361 83665

Galashiels
Kingsknowes Hotel **
☎ 01896 758375

Hawick
The Old Forge *
☎ 01450 85298

Jedburgh
Greyfriars Hotel **
☎ 01835 862000

Mrs McNeill B&B, Millheugh *
☎ 01835 862208

Near Kelso
Sunlaws House ***
☎ 01573 450331

Kelso
Ednam House Hotel, Near Market Square **
☎ 01573 224168

Melrose
Burt's Hotel **
☎ 01896 822285

Peebles
Cringletie House **
☎ 1721 730233

Mrs M Teasdale B&B *
4 Langside Drive
☎ 01721 721931

Selkirk
Philipburn House **
☎ 01750 20747

Mr & Mrs Thurston B&B *
Greenwells, Yarrow Feus
☎ 01750 82228

St Boswells
Dryburgh Abbey Hotel ***
☎ 01835 822261

Camping
Melrose
Gibson Caravan Park
☎ 01896 822969

Peebles
Rosetta Caravan and Camping Park
☎ 01721 720770

Jedburgh
The Jedwater Camping and Caravan Park
☎ 01835 24219

Elliot Park Campsite
☎ 01835 863393

Youth Hostels
Kelso (Grade 2)
Kirk Yetholm
☎ 01573 420631

Melrose (Grade 1)
Near High Street
☎ 01896 822521

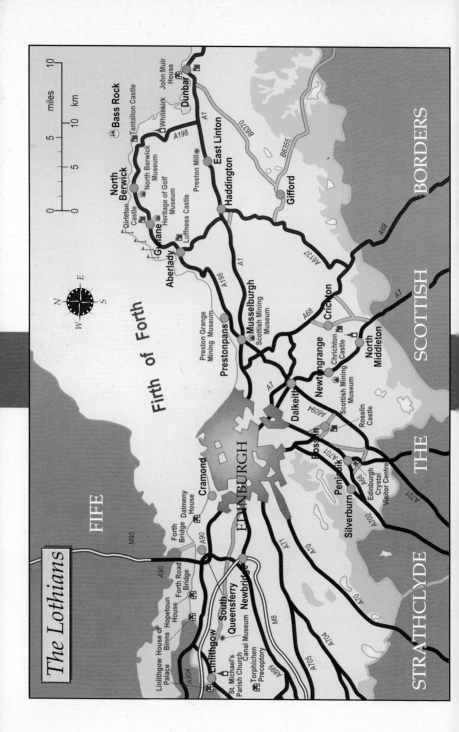

The Lothians

FIFE

Firth of Forth

EDINBURGH

STRATHCLYDE

THE SCOTTISH BORDERS

Linlithgow House of Palace
Blinns
Hopetoun House
Forth Bridge
Dalmeny House
Forth Road Bridge
Cramond
A90
M90
A90
A904
Linlithgow
St. Michael's Parish Church
Torphichen Preceptory
Canal Museum
South Queensferry
Newbridge
M8
A899
A705
A704
A70
A702
A71
A11
A7
A703
A71
Silverburn
Penicuik
Edinburgh Crystal Visitor Centre
A701
A766
A768
Roslin
Rosslin Castle
Scottish Mining Museum
Dalkeith
Newtongrange
A6094
Chrichton Castle
North Middleton
A7
A68
Crichton
A6137
A6124
Musselburgh
Scottish Mining Museum
Prestonpans
Preston Grange Mining Museum
A198
A1
A198
Aberlady
Gullane
Heritage of Golf
Luffness Castle
Dirleton Castle
North Berwick
North Berwick Museum
Bass Rock
Tantallon Castle
Whitekirk
Dunbar
John Muir House
A1
Preston Mill
East Linton
A198
Haddington
B6370
B6355
Gifford

N E S W

0   5   10 miles
0   5   10 km

34

The Lothians

2

Between the Firth of Forth, the Lammermuir, the Moorfoot and the Pentland Hills lies a wide, mainly agricultural belt, the Lothians, with the city of Edinburgh at its centre. With the interior mainly consisting of pastoral land most of the interest in this region is along the coast.

Giant coal bings once blighted the horizon, although the remnants of this once considerable industry gradually disappeared after the1970's.

In East Lothian, the A1 route following the coast is the most popular road for visitors heading toward Edinburgh. It is a fairly direct approach avoiding the narrower and more undulating routes that cross the Lammermuir Hills. In years gone by this was also the route for invading armies who chose to avoid the semi-circle of protective hills not only for ease of passage but for fear of ambush.

Near the shoulder where the Firth of Forth meets the North Sea, the A1087 off the A1 leads to **Dunbar**, the first major town after Berwick-upon-Tweed across the border. Dunbar was often targeted by English aggressors as they moved towards the capital and was severely treated during successive invasions. A popular seaside resort during Victorian times, the cobbled, quayed harbour with its orange piles of fish nets and seaweed-hung lobster creels is the most interesting place to explore. King Malcolm Canmore installed his cousin, the deposed Earl of Northumbria here at Dunbar Castle in the eleventh century, making him the Earl of Dunbar.

Immediately west of Dunbar overlooking Belhaven Bay and the mouth of the Tyne is **John Muir Country Park** taking its name from the founder of the American National Parks system. John Muir was born here in 1838, and it is possible to visit his house in the High Street restored in period style. He later became associated with wildernesses such as Yosemite National Park.

Following the coast involves turning right onto the A198 sigtnposted for North Berwick. About a mile up that road turn left into the village of **Tyninghame** following signs for **Preston Mill** which is another mile beyond. Restored by the National Trust for Scotland to working order its unusual form and ruddy-red building materials are striking.

Back en-route to the coast you come upon **Whitekirk**, built in the ubiquitous red sandstone of these parts which must have been covered in white harling in previous periods to give the church its name. Its history dates back to the sixth century when it was famed for a healing well which is no longer in evidence. The tithe barn behind the church is one of the oldest of its type still standing.

For those seeking dramatic landscapes, the site of **Tantallon Castle**, a few miles along the A198, will not disappoint. Pull over on this quiet approach road to appreciate its strawberry red massive bulk set against the backdrop of the Forth Estuary. Competing for your attention, off-shore, is the great guano-covered volcanic plug of Bass Rock.

The massive square citadel of Tantallon with its 50ft (15.25m) high curtain walls stands precariously at the edge of an abrupt cliff-face. It was the Red Douglases who dwelt within its walls, actually renting it from the Earls of Fife and keeping a well-trained army to maintain their independence. From the car park it is a pleasant walk to the castle frontage revealing more of the castle's defences in the form of as a series of earthworks and ditches designed to protect against James V's cannon when he laid siege here in 1529.

The **Bass Rock**, one of several pieces of volcanic debris scattered around the coastal Lothians, can be visited seasonally from North Berwick. A small, open boat sails round the rock to look at the breeding colonies of gannets, guillemots and puffins. Special permission is needed to land.

The seaside resort of **North Berwick** surrounds another volcanic plug called the North Berwick Law, a 613ft (186.96m) mass that towers above the town as can be appreciated from the High Street and Law Street which you take to access the path that ascends it. At the top, after a steep but short climb, there are wide views of the Lothian coastline with its groups of little islands, no more than perches for shags and cormorants. You can see over the Forth to Fife and south to the Lammermuirs as well as the

preceding page; With the sea on three sides, Tantallon Castle was a formidable stronghold

other volcanic debris scattered throughout the area such as the nearby
Bass Rock or further west, Arthur's Seat and the Braid Hills of Edinburgh.
On the Law itself, caged in a spiky iron fence, is a set of whale's jaw bones
rather gruesomely arranged to form an arch and commemorates this
area's heavy involvement in the whaling industry.

An 'Auld Kirk', now a ruin, stands beside the harbour, a central site in
a peculiar story that is often told about these parts. James VI had almost
been lost at sea just off North Berwick when returning to Edinburgh from
Denmark with his 15-year-old bride. During the storm James thought he
saw a small craft being navigated by three hares, a common disguise for
witches. Suspecting a witch's coven to be the cause of the near disaster he
later visited North Berwick with a party of armed followers and secretly
observed a large gathering of witches performing around the old parish
church near the harbour. At its centre was his cousin, Francis, Earl of
Bothwell, a known dabbler in the black arts and a perpetual pain in
James' side. Disguised as the devil, Bothwell was having his followers
kiss his rear when the king and his party pounced, rounding up most of
the revellers but the ring leader, Bothwell, escaped. There is a small
museum in town situated in a former school with displays on natural
history, archaeology and life in this area.

Following the A198 coast road, the village of **Dirleton** is delightful to
look upon even though there is little to visit apart from an ancient square
of cottages and the skeleton of a castle. Dirleton Castle cannot be seen
from the village square, enclosed as it is by trees, but you can get an
admirable view of it from the by-pass, should you have missed the
turning into Dirleton. At one time, huge circular towers dominated the
landward aspect while the main block at the south-west corner stood
very much as it is. The warm yellow and ochre stones were intricately
placed upon an igneous outcrop of rock creating a high fortified stronghold. The castle was taken by Edward I in 1298 and ravaged by General
Monk as he cut his way through Scotland in the 1650's. If the lawn
reminds you of a bowling green, that is precisely what it was in the
seventeenth century. The beehive shaped dovecot in the grounds offered
shelter for pigeons in the form of 1,100 nesting holes. The birds were
usually destined for the winter pot.

The town of **Gullane** further along the coast oozes golf. If you pull up
and sit a while in the main street you will sense this. There is a small
museum on West Links Road illustrating the area's golfing heritage, and
Gullane is home to Muirfield, the Honourable Company of Edinburgh
Golfers as well as several 18 hole courses.

The shore-line from Gullane Bay to Aberlady consists of a string of high
dunes that offer refuge for wildlife and nature-lovers alike. **Aberlady Bay**
was the first area in Britain to be declared a Local Nature Reserve in 1952
and has become a valuable site for all manner of ducks, divers and grebes.
Access is from the car park at Gullane Links or by crossing the narrow
wooden bridge just off the road beyond the golf courses between Gullane
and Aberlady. Here also are the remains of Luffness Castle, a sixteenth-

century fortress with a thirteenth-century keep and opened by appointment only.

Aberlady is a charming, pantiled roofed village that straddles the main route. There is an excellent Caravan Club camping site in a secluded walled garden just beyond the village. Inland is the antiquated town of **Haddington**, now quite a large and thriving community that serves the prosperous agricultural interior of East Lothian. Over 130 buildings in Haddington are listed as being either architecturally or historically interesting.

Further inland, following country roads such as the B6355, the seventeenth century village of **Gifford** lies in a dip below sheep dotted hills. The village is attractive in an austere kind of way with the village Kirk at one end, the Mercat Cross and Square at the other and a line of frugal old dwelling houses lining its main thoroughfare. There is an excellent 9 hole golf course just south of the village.

Returning to the coast and progressing towards Edinburgh there is a more industrial characteristic to the landscape and buildings. Prestongrange Mining Museum near **Prestonpans** tells the story of 800 years of mining in the area and includes steam engine exhibitions, documents and artifacts of the industry.

Prestonpans gained its name from this enterprise of obtaining salt from great open-air pans but its fame came later in 1745 when Bonnie Prince Charlie gave the Westminster government one of its greatest shocks and put Scotland back in control of the Scots. Charles was already in control of Edinburgh within 4 weeks of his initial landing in the country. It was dawn on a bright September morning when the Highlanders descended on the Hanovarian camp to find its General Cope having a lie-in. The battle of Prestonpans lasted little more than 15 minutes with most of the government troops trapped against a mile long wall at Prestongrange House. The wall still stands although little evidence of the battlefield remains.

Musselburgh is now by-passed by the A1 and the Edinburgh Ringroad system but until recently it took most of the A1 traffic travelling north and south. The race-course at the east side of town is the oldest in Scotland and the golf course it surrounds is one of the first where James IV and James VI are said to have played. The rest of the town centre is uninspiring although the harbour and nicer banks are quite pleasant.

From Musselburgh it is quite easy to explore the area south of Edinburgh fast becoming a dormitory belt for Edinburgh. Referred to as Midlothian this too, was an active mining area until not so long ago. The A6094 leads to the busy market town of **Dalkeith**. At the far end of its High Street is the entrance to Dalkeith Country Park, part of the estates of the Duke of Buccleuch. The extensive grounds contain woodland walks beside the river, nature trails and an unusual 'tunnel walk'. The magnificent red-stoned mansion, Dalkeith Palace is not open to the public but can be appreciated from the outside. George IV stayed here during his State visit to Scotland in 1822.

Dunbar is the first of a number of good golfing venues throughout East Lothian

North Berwick Law towers over the East Lothian town

Just south of Dalkeith at **Newtongrange** is the Scottish Mining Museum centred around the Lady Victoria Colliery, the main pit for this region which was established in 1890. Guided tours of this pioneering operation are offered between April and September. The winding tower operating down the 1,625ft (496m) deep shaft was driven by Scotland's largest steam engine, still on view. The displays bring to life the conditions both at work and at home for the colliery workers and their families.

Taking the A7 south from Dalkeith and turning left on the B6372 leads to fourteenth-century **Crichton Castle**. Its most notable feature is the bizarre Italian Piazza styled forecourt, much out of character with the rest of the building. This is the product of the unstable Francis Stuart, 5th Earl of Bothwell.

Eight stories high **Borthwick Castle** is nearby at **North Middleton**, in fact there is a pleasant 2 mile (3km) walk that links both castles, taking around an hour. This Scots tower house with its distinctive twin keeps was the quarters of Mary Queen of Scots and her husband Bothwell following their marriage. Although 500 years old, it has been much restored and is now a private hotel where, for a price, you can use the same bed-chamber as Mary and Bothwell.

Follow the A6094 from Dalkeith or try crossing west from Borthwell Castle using country roads until you see signs for the village of **Roslin**. Rosslyn Castle, poised on a crag, stands high above the glen carved by the River Esk far below. In the fourteenth century this became the home of the St Clair family, its most prominent member being the fifteenth-century Sir William St Clair. Sir William's excesses were notorious, such was his taste for a sumptuous lifestyle. In his later years he sought amends by building a church and Rosslyn Chapel was the result. Founded in 1446 and never finished following William's death in 1484, the chapel is still quite incredible. The finest craftsmen of Europe were employed. The most famous piece is the Prentice Pillar found on the south side of the Lady Chapel. While the master mason was away in Italy looking for inspiration for his 'magnum opus', a young apprentice, following the design he saw in a dream, set to work. On seeing the finished result the master murdered the boy in a fit of jealousy. It greatly surpasses all the other carvings.

The best reason to visit **Penicuik** a few miles south on the A701 is to see the Edinburgh Crystal Factory and Visitor Centre. There is a large crystal shop and a video presentation. It is possible to watch the craftsmen blow, cut and engrave the world famous crystal but children under 8 are not allowed on the tour.

Returning to the west side of Edinburgh via the city by-pass there are signs for **Hillend Dry Ski Slope**, open all year and once the largest dry ski slope in Europe. Hire equipment and tuition are available.

The west side of Edinburgh is collectively considered West Lothian. Take the by-pass to its terminal roundabout at Gogar and turn right back towards Edinburgh then follow the signs for the Forth Road Bridge. At the Barnton Roundabout carry straight over for the village of Cramond. Now a middle class suburb of Edinburgh, **Cramond** has a long history being a site for a Roman fort and naval harbour dated from AD142. From here the Emperor Severus embarked on his northern campaigns to quell the Picts. The foundations of the fort can still be seen.

There are also remnants of eighteenth-century water mills that worked corn and drove weaving machines although little is now left apart from successive weirs. There is a pleasant walk following the river that comes out at a medieval bridge and finishing off at Cramond Brig Hotel.

It is possible to take the tiny passenger ferry, a rowing boat, across the mouth of the Almond River and walk the 2 miles (3km) or so to **Dalmeny** **House**. Alternatively you can drive following the A90 and turning off for Dalmeny and South Queensferry. The house is 1 mile (2km) east of the village of Dalmeny. Built in 1815 it contains a fabulous collecton of eighteenth-century French furniture, Napoleonic memorabilia, tapestries, porcelain and British portraits.

South Queensferry is a charming little village on the banks of the Forth about 10 miles (16km) west of Edinburgh. At the eastern end where there are good parking facilities is South Queensferry's most prominent feature, the **Forth Bridge**. This rail bridge is unique of its kind and attracts bridge and rail enthusiasts from around the globe.

Built in 1890, it is known as one of the engineering wonders of the world aligned with the Eiffel Tower and the Taj Mahal. A remarkable tribute to Victorian engineering it was the first major structure to be made entirely of steel, with significant amounts of extra steel being employed as a result of the collapse of the Tay Bridge shortly before construction commenced. Its three massive, double cantilevers expand by almost 3ft (1m) from mid-winter to mid-summer.

The Forth Road Bridge, commenced in 1962 to replace the ferries that had crossed between North Queensferry to South Queensferry was opened in 1964. The most important function of the Forth Road Bridge, some might say, is not to take you into Fife but to give a great, elevated platform from which to view the Forth Bridge. The vista from the public footpath is remarkable.

Below the russet rivets of the Forth Bridge is the old ferry landing still used today for pleasure craft. The first public ferry across the Forth at this point was established in 1129 by David I to facilitate communication between his palace at Dunfermline and the south. Pilgrims to Dunfermline and St Andrews were encouraged to use the free service. Now, the *Maid of the Forth* sails from Hawes Pier to Inchcolm Island and its abbey to the north-east throughout the summer. Seals are often spotted from the boat. Below the rail bridge stands the sixteenth-century Hawes Inn that was the starting place of David Balfour's misadventures in Robert Louis Stevenson's book,*Kidnapped*.

Two miles (3km) west of South Queensferry and 12 miles (19½km) from Edinburgh, **Hopetoun House** stands at the end of a wide square, its palatial central structure flanked by gracefully balanced wings. First completed around the turn of the seventeenth century it was soon enlarged by William Adam and his son, John to their oft-repeated and

King Edward I, the Hammer of the Scots used Dirleton Castle as a base in 1298

Linlithgow Palace, birthplace of Mary, Queen of Scots

impeccable standard. It remains the home of the Hope family and Marquess of Linlithgow and inside displays many fine paintings. The 100 acre (40 hectares) landscaped grounds overlook the Firth of Forth the best views of which are found from the viewing platform on the mansion roof. There are stock attractions such as a walled garden, a nature trail and deer park.

Following the A904 west from South Queensferry there are other stately homes and castles to be seen near the south shore of the Forth. The **House of Binns** echoes the seventeenth-century Scottish transition from the fortified house to a more self-indulgent mansion style. General Tam Dalyell (pronouced Dee-el) who sided with the royalists against the Convenanters, was associated with the house. On display, a heavy table was found in the nearby lake having rested there some 200 years, flung, so it is said, by Tam's acquaintance, the Devil when he lost to Tam at cards. Other stories of flagellation parties and glass eating antics give the visitor, let alone his Covenanting enemies, a rather disquieting impression of the general.

Nearby **Blackness Castle** is associated with Linlithgow. Its massively structured sixteenth-century battlements on the north side were built to withstand the barrage of naval guns with narrow chambers allowing defenders to return fire.

The town of **Linlithgow** was once nearly as important as the nearby centres of Stirling and Edinburgh though, beholding today's concoction of bad 60's planning and irreverence for former glories, it is hard to comprehend what possessed past generations of town planners as you drive through the charming town centre and view the concrete blocks at the end of the main street.

Linlithgow Palace is best known as the birthplace of Mary Queen of Scots, born here in 1542 and crowned to the throne a week later. Linlithgow Palace's own history goes back to the time of James I who commissioned the earliest building around 1425. Covering the reign of eight monarchs and two centuries in its progress, James VI finally completed the palace to its illustrious proportions in 1642. Within its five storeys and rather square hulk supported by two unusual flying buttresses on the east side, it is not difficult to imagine what royal panoply furnished the magnificent interior spaces, bed chambers and corridors that remain now in skeleton form. The palace was burned by accident in 1746 by the Duke of Cumberland's troops who were garrisoned there for the night. It is possible to fish on Linlithgow Loch and there are extensive paths around the grounds.

The Great Hall is the building's centre point with its elaborately fashioned fire recess while the inner courtyard is embellished with an octagonal Renaissance fountain. Every Sunday afternoon in August you will find the Linlithgow Festival Trust players re-enacting Mary Stewart's return to her birthplace with great pageantry and costume.

Next to the palace gate is St Michael's Parish Church, one of Scotland's largest pre-reformation churches dedicated in 1242. The church was re-built in the sixteenth century but the addition of the unusual aluminium 'Crown of Thorns' spire, standing out like huge crossed claymores, did not take place until 1946. John Knox and his adherents spoiled the church during the Reformation and Oliver Cromwell used it as a stable.

If you are interested in exploring other aspects of this area there is Beecraigs Country Park south of Linlithgow that offers trails through a variety of woodland as well as a deer farm, adventure playground and fishing loch. There are organised activities such as archery, water sports, angling, orienteering that can be joined by applying in advance. There is also a caravan park with thirty-six pitches. A rewarding walk can be found up nearby Cockleroy Hill through pine woods with unexpectedly fine views as far as Goat Fell on Arran in the west and Ben Lomond to the north. Cairnpapple Hill approached from the Beecraigs Road, beyond the park is well signposted. This rather eerie, ancient neolithic then early Bronze Age burial cist and ceremonial mound still shows the remnants of a standing stone ring as well as the cairned tomb, which can be entered by ladder. In Linlithgow there are often folk evenings held at the Black Bitch Tavern. The Star and Garter opposite the roundabout at the beginning of the High Street offers good bar meals.

The Union Canal in the Linlithgow basin was a short lived success as it took nearly 14 hours to traverse the distance between Glasgow and Edinburgh while the train when it was introduced in 1842 took only 2 hours and at the same price. Short trips on the *Victoria*, a diesel powered replica of a steam packet boat or the *Janet Telford* passenger boat are available from Manse Road Basin, and visitors can gain an insight into the canal's history at the Union Canal Museum.

The beginnings of the St John's Ambulance Brigade or the St Andrews Ambulance Association in Scotland can be traced at Torphichen Preceptory south-west of Linlithgow off the A706. A great order of military monks founded the community of the Scottish Order of the Knights of St John of Jerusalem in 1153. A museum tells the story of the knights both at home and overseas. The M9 carries on west from Linthigow into Central region and Stirling or returns towards Edinburgh.

Additional Information

Places of Interest

Dalkeith

Crighton Castle
B6367 7 miles (11km) south of Dalkeith
Historic Scotland ☎ 0131 244 3101
Open: April to September, Monday to Saturday, 9.30am-7pm. Sunday, 2-7pm. October to March, Monday to Saturday 9.30am-4.00pm. Sunday 2-4pm.

Rosslyn Chapel
At village of Roslin, A703, 7 miles (11km) south of Edinburgh
☎ 0131 440 2159
Open: April to October, Monday to Saturday, 10am-5pm and Sunday 12noon-4.45pm.

Dunbar
John Muir House
High Street
☎ 01368 863353
Open: June to September, Monday to
Saturday, 11am-1pm and 2-5.30pm.
Sundays 2-5.30pm.

Preston Mill and Phantassie Doocot
Off A1 at East Linton or through from
Dunbar
☎ 01620 860426
Open: April to September, Monday to
Saturday, 11am-1pm and 2-5pm.
Sunday 2-5pm.

White kirk
A198
Open: Each day from early morning to
late evening. Sunday worship at 11.30am.

Gullane
The Heritage of Golf Museum
West Links Road
☎ 01875 870277
Open: By arrangement.

Luffness Castle
On A198 west of Gullane
☎ 01875 870218
Open: By arrangement.

Linlithgow
Hopetoun House
Between South Queensferry and
Linlithgow
☎ 0131 331 2451
Open: Easter to September, daily, 10am-
5pm.

House of Binns
Off A904, 4 miles (6km) east of Linlithgow
☎ 01506 834255
Open: Easter and May to September,
daily except Friday. 2-5pm

Blackness Castle
B903, north of Linlithgow
Historic Scotland ☎ 0131 244 3101
Open: April to September, Monday to
Saturday, 9.30am-7pm. Sunday, 2-7pm.
October to March, Monday to Saturday
9.30am-4pm. Sunday 2-4pm.

Linlithgow Palace
Centre of Linlithgow town
Historic Scotland ☎ 0131 244 3101
Open: April to September, Monday to
Saturday, 9.30am-7pm. Sunday, 2-7pm.
October to March, Monday to Saturday
9.30am-4.00pm. Sunday 2-4pm.

Beecraigs Country Park
Preston Road south from Linlithgow
☎ 01506 844516
Open: All year.

Union Canal Museum
Manse Road Basin
☎ 01506 842575
Open: Easter to the end of September.

Newtongrange
Scottish Mining Museum
Off A7 and B6372 junction and north for
2 miles (3km)
☎ 0131 663 7519
Open: April to September, Monday to
Saturday 9.30am-7pm, Sunday, 2-7pm.
October to March, Monday to Saturday
9.30am-4pm, Sunday, 2-4pm.

North Berwick
Tantallon Castle
Off the A198 east of North Berwick
Historic Scotland ☎ 0131 244 3101
Open: April to September, Monday to
Saturday, 9.30am to 7pm. Sunday, 2-7pm.
October to March, Monday to Saturday
9.30am-4.00pm. Sunday 2-4pm.

North Berwick Museum
School Road
☎ 01620 824161
Open: Easter to end of May & June to
September, Monday to Saturday, 10am-
1pm and 2-5pm. Sundays, 2-5pm.

Bass Rock Boat Trips
North Berwick Harbour
☎ 01620 822838
Open: Easter to early October 2-4pm.

Dirleton Castle
Off the A198 west of North Berwick
Historic Scotland ☎ 0131 244 3101
Open: April to September, Monday to
Saturday, 9.30am-7pm. Sunday, 2-7pm.
October to March, Monday to Saturday
9.30am-4.00pm. Sunday 2-4pm.

Penicuick
*Edinburgh Crystal Factory and Visitor
    Centre*
Eastfield, Penicuick
☎ 01968 75128
Open: All year.

Prestonpans
Prestongrange Mining Museum
Morrison's Haven on B1348
☎ 0131 663 7519

Open: Easter to September Monday to
Friday 10am-4.30pm. Saturday and
Sunday 12noon-5pm.

South Queensferry
Dalmany House
By South Queensferry-B924
☎ 0131 331 1888
Open: May to September 2-5.30pm.
Closed Fridays and Saturdays.

Torphichen Preceptory
A706 from Linlithgow and B792 to
village of torphichen
Historic Scotland ☎ 0131 244 3101
Open: April to September, Monday to
Saturday, 9.30am-7pm. Sunday, 2-7pm.
Closed October to March.

Tourist Information Offices

Bo'ness
Hamilton's Cottage
☎ 01506 826626

Dalkeith
The Library, White Hart Street
☎ 0131 663 2083

Dunbar
143 High Street
☎ 01368 863353

Edinburgh Airport
Tourist Information Desk
☎ 0131 333 2167

Linlithgow
Burgh Halls
☎ 01506 844600

Musselburgh
Brunton Hall
☎ 0131 665 6597

North Berwick
Quality Street
☎ 01620 2197

Old Craighall
Granada Service Area
By Musselburgh
☎ 0131 653 6172

Pencraig
A1 by East Linton
☎ 01620 860063

Penicuik
Edinburgh Crystal Visitor Centre
☎ 01968 673846

Accommodation

Near Airdrie
*Mrs Elsie Hunter Farmhouse B&B *
☎ 01236 830243

Direlton
*Open Arms Hotel ***
☎ 01620 850241

Near Dunbar
*Mrs J Tuer **
Whitekirk
☎ 01620 870245

Gifford
*Mrs M B Whiteford B&B *
☎ 01620 810327

Gullane
*Greywalls Hotel ****
☎ 01620 842144

Haddington
*Brown's Hotel **
☎ 01620 822254

North Berwick
*Mrs Ramsay B&B *
☎ 01620 895150

North Middleton
*Borthwick Castle ****
☎ 01875 820514

Uphall
*Houston House ****
☎ 01506 853831

Campsites
Near North Berwick
Rhodes Caravan Site
☎ 01620 893348

Roslin
Slatebarns Caravan Park
☎ 0131 440 2192

Edinburgh

3

The capital of the country is one of the most beautiful cities in Europe often referred to as the 'Athens of the North' due to its fine, Palladian architecture and general air of education and refinement. Having said that, over more recent years 'rather stuffy' Edinburgh was jarred from smug complacency after resting long on its world-renowned reputation. The monopoly over the Scottish cultural crown was quietly hijacked during the 1980's and it now remains an open issue who best represents the country's cultural heart. The challenge comes from the 'Empire's Second City', Glasgow, following its rise to becoming the Cultural Capital of Europe in 1990. Competition, they say, is no bad thing and Edinburgh is now working harder than ever to keep happy its near 2 million visitors a year.

The topography of the town is remarkable with several elevations breaking the city's slate-grey, chimney-potted expanse. Robert Louis Stevenson declared, 'No situation could be more commanding for the head of a kingdom and none better chosen for better prospects'. Edinburgh, like most of the Lothians, is set on the wide plain of the River Forth with volcanic left-overs such as Castle Rock and Arthur's Seat being the most prominent natural heights. Around these hills 'Auld Reekie' grew.

For exploration, it is best divided into three sections, the Old Town, the New Town and the outskirts. Each section would need at least a day to best appreciate, so 3 days should be allowed.

47

The Old and New Town are essentially a walking proposition with most places of consequence within easy distance of one another. Parking a car anywhere near the city centre will be difficult but public transport is very effective both into the centre and to outlying parts.

Edinburgh is a multi-faceted locale with an illustrious and sometimes complicated past so to best appreciate it, it is beneficial to understand a modicum of its history. The easiest method is to make sure you tag on to a tour-guide during visits to historic sites.

Edinburgh's history seems to surround its central fortification and this is the point where much archaeological evidence has been uncovered. The lofty lump supporting Edinburgh Castle is the residue of a volcanic plug that resisted the forces of a huge glacier pushing eastward along what is now the Forth Valley. This formed Castle Rock and the trail of debris to the east now known as the Royal Mile (High Street) was its residue. The strategic position of Castle Rock was long recognized by both the Romans and their main adversaries, the Pictish tribes as well as the powers that followed them.

In the Dark Ages, the area known as the Lothians was invaded by King Edwin of Northumbria and his Angle army. He built a fort on the strategic stone and it was called Dun Eadain meaning 'Fortress-on-a-Hill' later to become either Edwin's Burgh or Eadain's Burgh. A fledgling community slowly developed hugging the skirts of the protective stockade. In 1124 King David I decided to move his court and thus the Scottish capital from Dunfermline to Edinburgh after founding Holyrood Abbey there. From then on the town rapidly grew in importance and size. As animosity grew between the Scots and the English, Edinburgh's strategic importance grew also with its castle being the focal point.

There is only one tenable approach to **Edinburgh Castle** via the eastward sloping Royal Mile and would-be attackers were forced to consider this. In 1313 some resolute assailants under the administration of Robert the Bruce scaled Castle Rock's formidable northern aspect and ramparts to retake the castle from the English. They then dismantled it and Bruce later granted the town a royal charter in 1329 as well as jurisdiction over the port of Leith which lead to greater trading opportunities and wealth. Rebuilt in 1356 the castle became not only a fortress but a royal palace.

A defensive wall was erected around the area east of the castle in 1456 roughly defining the area we now know as the **Old Town**. Through the Renaissance period the small city flourished in a stable era until Scotland's defeat at the Battle of Flodden in 1513. A second wall, the Flodden Wall was hurriedly thrown up after this defeat which was followed by a time of great instability culminating in the sacking of the town by the forces of Henry VIII.

On her return to Scotland, Mary set up court in Edinburgh's Holyrood Palace. In 1603 her son, James VI, with the Union of the Crowns inherited

preceding page; Edinburgh Castle was once protected by a man-made loch, drained in the 18th century and turned into Princes Street Gardens

the English throne and moved his Scottish court to London. In some ways this was the end of the Scottish monarchy as, despite his promises, James only returned to his native land once.

The last significant assault on Edinburgh Castle came in 1745 when the Jacobite forces of Bonnie Prince Charlie once again wrested it, without much resistance, from English hands. The period of the Enlightenment continued and thrived following the upheavals and defeat of the Jacobite Rebellion and throughout the period of peace that followed. New ideas in science, philosophy and literature flourished without the inhibiting presence of nobility. Philosophers and writers such as David Hume, Adam Smith, Allan Ramsay, even Robert Burns were products of this era. James Watt was inspired to invent the steam engine around this time.

Today, outside of London, Edinburgh and its castle are the most popular attractions in the United Kingdom. The castle unfolds the various chapters of its long existence. Being consecutively a stronghold, palace, barracks and prison it is not a beautiful set of buildings compared to Scotland's abundance of more archetypal castles but it is a maze of historic portions in the country's annals.

Entrance to the castle is made at the top of the Royal Mile and into the Esplanade, a wide parade ground that presents splendid views north over the city and south to the Pentland Hills about 8 miles (13km) away. The imposing building you see on the south side is George Heriott's School, built in the mid-seventeenth century as an orphanage and now a private school. During the summer the Esplanade is prepared for nightly pageants held during the Military Tattoo. The castle entrance is guarded by members of the Highland Regiment, the last draw-bridge to be built in Scotland as well as the imposing statues of Robert the Bruce and William Wallace. There are some six gates between the entrance and the Argyle and Mills Batteries designed to keep the English out but now for a cost they are made most welcome. Every day at 1pm (13.00 hours), a salute is fired from the upper battery.

Entering the upper level by Foog's Gate, on the highest terrace stands the remnants of the castle's oldest building and, in fact, the oldest roofed building in Scotland. This miniature chapel was built for Queen Margaret in the late eleventh century or perhaps in her memory by her son, David I.

Entering Crown Square you come upon the Scottish National War Memorial, a commemorative site for the dead of each of the twelve Scottish Regiments of both World Wars and up until recent times. Douglas Strachan designed the sombre stained-glass windows depicting the scenes of battle through the four seasons.

The **Royal Scots Regimental Museum** diagonally across the square contains large rooms crowded with military memorabilia.

The **Great Hall** or Banqueting Hall, built by James IV on the south side of Crown Square was the meeting place of the Scottish Parliament until 1639. Its hammer-beam ceiling, said to be the up-side down hull of a ship, was restored to its former glory in the late nineteenth century after the hall had been used as an army barracks for Cromwell's troops. It was here

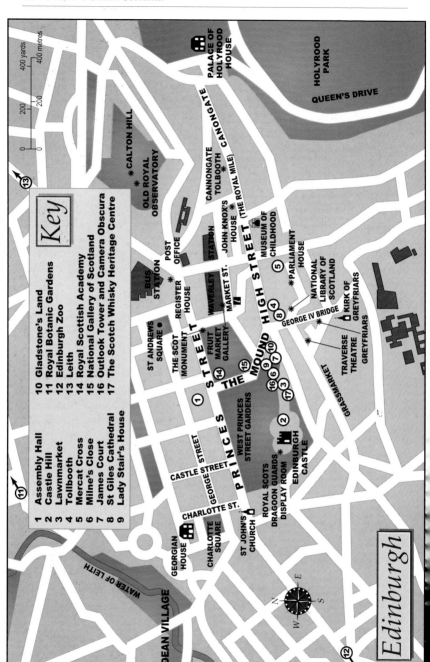

Key

1   Assembly Hall
2   Castle Hill
3   Lawnmarket
4   Tollbooth
5   Mercat Cross
6   Milne's Close
7   James Court
8   St Giles Cathedral
9   Lady Stair's House
10 Gladstone's Land
11 Royal Botanic Gardens
12 Edinburgh Zoo
13 Leith
14 Royal Scottish Academy
15 National Gallery of Scotland
16 Outlook Tower and Camera Obscura
17 The Scotch Whisky Heritage Centre

Edinburgh

The Scottish Crown Jewels or Honours of Scotland on display in Edinburgh Castle

Ramsay Apartments and Gardens were an attempt to bring Edinburgh's professional classes back from the New Town to the Old Town

on an occasion known as the 'Black Dinner' that the 8-year-old King James II witnessed the death of two of the Black Douglases, a notoriously powerful family.

The **Palace Block** on the south-east corner of the castle housed the royal apartments. Mary Queen of Scots gave birth to James I/VI in 1566 in a small antechamber adjoining her own room. Next to this in the centre of the Palace Block is an exhibition surrounding the dramatic story of the 'Honours of Scotland' (Scottish Crown Jewels). The crown, sceptre and sword are the oldest in Britain, having survived the Restoration period.

The crown, which can only be worn again if a Stewart comes back to the throne, is made of Scottish gold and is adorned with 94 pearls, 10 diamonds and several other precious stones. The fascinating history unfolds as you make your way round the exhibition.

The Old Town was built upon a tadpole-shaped ridge with the castle and its rock at its head. As it pushed east, glacial action peeled away the ground around the basalt volcanic plug and left behind a residue of silt and debris. This is now the Royal Mile which as always been the backbone of the Old Town.

Many of the surviving buildings have seen 200 years or more of Edinburgh life. 'Auld Reekie', as it was then known, was a fusion of smog and smells. The Flodden Wall forced the town to grow up instead of out, the high tenements creating a canyon community of great character and diversity.

A tour of Edinburgh's **Royal Mile**, the principal thoroughfare of the Old Town, usually starts at **Castlehill** outside the Esplanade. On the wall before the start of Castlehill is the **Witches Fountain**, a spot where more than 300 women were burned as suspected witches, the last in 1722. **Ramsay Gardens** on the left, an unusual 1890's apartment block includes **Ramsay Lodge** built by the poet Allan Ramsay, father of the famous painter of the same name.

The Royal Mile is divided into four sections, Castle Hill, Lawnmarket, High Street and Canongate. **Canonball House** stands on the opposite side of Castle Hill with an actual canon ball embedded in its castle-facing wall above the stairs leading down to Johnston Terrace. It was said to have caught a stray shot fired at Bonnie Prince Charlie's encampment but, in truth, the ball was placed there to mark the gravitation height of the city's first piped water supply, the old reservoir standing opposite. Next door to Canonball House is the **Scottish Whisky Heritage Centre** which gives a worthwhile sample of the whisky making process blended into audio-visual presentations and historic tableaux. Just outside the Witchery Restaurant is where the 'Murder and Mystery' walking tours of the Old Town meet.

Outlook Tower and the **Camera Obscura** stand opposite, a seventeenth-century house that was converted for this purpose with a mirrored periscope device reflecting the moving images from outside onto a round white table, the quality of which is determined by the clarity of the day. The roof-top viewing area gives some of the best views of the city equipped with telescopes and view finders. There are displays of old pictures of Edinburgh, a pin-hole camera exhibition and a holography presentation. The lower floor houses a small gift shop.

The dark, towering spire of **St John's Church** is the highest in the city and dominates Castle Hill. This was the Highland Kirk in Edinburgh where all the services were given in the Gaelic language, catering to the large number of Gaelic speakers living in Edinburgh following the Highland Clearances. The **Assembly Hall** across the road is the meeting place of the General Assembly of the Church of Scotland and is taken over during the Festival for larger theatrical productions.

Lawnmarket, a wider stretch of the Mile and once a daily fruit, vegetable and dairy produce marketplace, houses some notable buildings. On the left are **Milne's Close** and **James Court**, two courtyards restored in the late 1960's to give an impression of seventeenth- and eighteenth-century Old Town buildings as well as accommodation for Edinburgh's students. **Gladstone's Land** was an earlier seventeenth-century tenement building favoured by the wealthier residents of the Old Town but gradually declining into a slum when the more prosperous inhabitants migrated to the less polluted New Town. **Lady Stair's House** down the close of the same name was built in 1622 and is now a museum to three of Scotland's more famous literary sons, Sir Walter Scott, Robert Louis Stevenson and Robert Burns. Brodie's Close was the home of Deacon Brodie, upon whom Robert Louis Stevenson based his character, Dr Jekyll and Mr Hyde. Brodie was a carpenter and counsellor by day but by night, using wax impressions of the locks of houses he visited in his professional capacity, he returned to rob them.

The heart-shaped stones outside the Parliament Square mark the site of the old city jail and **Tolbooth** and it was here that the head of the Duke of Montrose was displayed following his execution in 1650. Passers-by spit on the stones for luck. Sir Walter Scott appropriated the Tolbooth's main door and incorporated it in his house at Abottsford in the Scottish Borders and also used the Tolbooth as his opening setting in the novel *Heart of Midlothian*.

The imposing Georgian designs of Parliament Square continue behind St Giles Cathedral and it is worth exploring to visit **Parliament House** using the door marked number 11. It may not seem accessible to the public but it is a municipal building open to visitors and well worth experiencing. The Scottish Parliament sat in Parliament House between 1639 and 1707 and is now attached to the Court of Session for the Scottish Law Courts. In the square itself, is Edinburgh's oldest statue, that of the equestrian Charles II. The **Mercat Cross** at the eastern end of the square was traditionally a gathering place for merchants, merry-makers and executions. Royal proclamations were also made here including Bonnie Prince Charlie's declaration of his father as king.

The present **St Giles Cathedral** or the High Kirk of Edinburgh belie the ancient structures that have occupied this spot. The first church dates from around the ninth century and was succeeded by a Norman building which was destroyed by English invaders. Rebuilt in the fifteenth century, this was the base for John Knox's Reformation of the style of Scottish worship from Catholic to Protestant. At the time of Mary Queen of Scots, and having written the infamous treatise, *The First Blast of the Trumpet against the Monstrous Regiment of Women*, he marched down the Canongate to Holyrood Palace to harangue his queen on several occasions. Much to his chagrin, Scotland, France and England were all ruled by Catholic queens at the time.

In 1826 the much neglected St Giles building was refurbished by William Burn unfortunately destroying much of the interesting medieval detail. There is still plenty to appreciate inside especially in the Thistle Chapel. Across the High Street is the City Chambers then Cockburn Street turns off to the left with a variety of unusual and tempting stores.

This part of the High Street is populated with some fine pubs, delicatessens and restaurants. The **Museum of Childhood** contains a riot of artifacts from infancy of the ages but it is curious to note it was started by a patchier.

The Scottish Reformation

The revolutionary Lutheran and Calvinist ideas of the new Protestant religion were already spreading from the continent to Scotland, provoking a ruthless and violent response against this heresy from the established Roman Catholic church. The spread of this new religion, however, was relentless, helped not only by its firebrand preachers, but more significantly by Scotland's already reformed southern neighbour. By the second half of the sixteenth century Protestantism had become the official religion of the Scottish church.

John Knox's House jutting out into the Canongate, is Edinburgh's oldest building dating as far back as 1490. It is uncertain whether he lived here but widely believed that he did. The rooms are rather bare but there are interesting painted ceilings at the top level.

Set at the eastern foot of the Canongate and the termination of the Royal Mile is the Abbey and **Palace of Holyroodhouse**, more commonly referred to as Holyrood. This is the official domicile of Her Majesty the Queen when she is in Edinburgh. The Abbey was founded in 1128 by King David I after he had been injured by a stag whilst hunting. Legend has it that the animal was about to gore him and he reached defensively for its antlers whereupon he found himself grasping a crucifix or holy rood (cross). He therefore founded the abbey for Augustinian monks devoted to the cross and granted a burgh to the canons, Canongate. The abbey, set in a valley, became a more favoured royal residence, sheltered by Arthur's Seat and Salisbury Crags as opposed to the draughty heights of the castle.

The Royal Mile offers shopping for more unusual souvenirs

The Palace Holyroodhouse is still used as the royal residence when members of the royal family visit Edinburgh

James IV was responsible for the creation of the original palace in the early 1500's which was replaced with a more imposing building by Charles II who never had the opportunity to live in it. During the 'Rough Wooing' of 1544 and the Reformation as well as at the hands of Cromwell's troops, both the palace and the abbey took a considerable pounding. Mary Queen of Scots set up her court here and was married in the abbey church in 1655 to Darnley then later to Bothwell. In 1745 Prince Charles Edward Stewart held court in the palace during his brief, victorious stay before venturing south to Derby then back to his ignoble defeat at Culloden.

From the reign of James VI until Queen Victoria the palace stood empty of royal visitors. Tours covering some of the more public areas last 35 minutes and leave regularly. The abbey stands in the grounds of the palace with little more than the nave left to see of this once beautiful building.

Directly opposite the palace is a wide tract of grass and craggy hills. The largest expanse of open ground in the city, **Holyrood Park** is a gathering site for leisure pursuits. Dominated by the volcanic fragments of Arthur's Seat at 823ft (251m), an active volcano about 250 million years ago and Salisbury Crags, there is a winding road that takes you around these hills to **Dunsappie Loch**, a wildfowl sanctuary and easy starting place for a hike up Arthur's Seat. This circular route returns via the Queens Drive or you can take a diversion past Duddingston Loch and into the village of Duddingston. This was the quarters for Bonnie Prince Charlie's Jacobite army whilst he held court at Holyrood.

It was James Drummond, the six times Lord Provost of Edinburgh, who came up with the idea of a 'new town' and urged the council to support it to relieve the chronic overcrowding that had occurred in the warren of ancient closes and alleyways of Old Edinburgh. A competition was announced in 1767 to design the new quarter, won by James Craig, a 23-year-old unknown architect. His plan was to create an entirely residential area consisting of three main east-west streets encompassed by two grand squares at either end and incorporating large public gardens and green areas.

The symmetry of Craig's design was unusual at the time, a grid-iron layout that allowed for ample fresh air and wide, uninterrupted views. The New Town according to Craig's plan was complete in 1830. Using cart-loads of earth dug up from foundations of new town houses a rampart was also created over the now drained Nor' Loch to gain easier access to the New Town. This was imaginatively called the Mound. The Nor' Loch was later transformed into the beautiful Princes Street Gardens which are divided in two by the Mound.

The foot of the **Mound** is graced by two buildings that have contributed much to Edinburgh's epithet of the 'Athens of the North'. Designed by William Playfair in the 1840's and the first stone laid by Prince Albert in 1850, the **Royal Scottish Academy** and the **National Gallery of Scotland** are Grecian-style, Doric temples, opened daily and admission is free. The gallery was completely refurbished in the 1980's and brought back to its original Playfair design. The interiors are carefully designed to augment the themes and colours of the paintings on display and the collection brings together painters of every school and part of the world.

The Royal Scottish Academy holds Old Scottish Masters but is more dedicated to its two main exhibitions of fine art, the Annual Exhibition during the summer and the Festival Exhibition.

On **Princes Street** you enter the **New Town** proper. Of course, the New Town now is over 200 years old and much of Craig's original ideas have been abandoned. The largely residential intent was superseded by financial and professional institutions now occupying most of the buildings in the adjacent George Street and Queen Street while Princes Street has become the main shopping thoroughfare.

At the eastern end of Princes Street there remains an architectural gem, **Register House**, a Robert Adam neo-Classic design of 1770 with the Duke of Wellington on horseback standing before it. The **Cafe Royal**, to the left of Register House is one of Edinburgh's oldest and best known pubs. **Waverley Market** stands between the Balmoral and the Scott Monument above Waverley Railway Station. On its upper level is the main Tourist Information Centre. Below is a spacious shopping mall with several good shops and eateries.

Across the road is the **Scott Monument**, a predominate feature on Princes Street's skyline with a total of 287 steps in all leading to a tremendous view of this part of the city. The monument chiselled from a 50 ton block of Carrara marble was erected in 1844 in honour of Sir Walter Scott.

How did a writer deserve such a monument, one might ask. At the time, Scott's contemporaries felt that he had achieved a rekindling of pride and national feeling which had been lost since the time of Bonnie Prince Charlie. This culminated in a visit by George IV in 1822. Scott used all his creative skills to stage-manage the event incorporating some of the over-romantic images he had used in his highly popular novels. The kilt and the bagpipes were ushered back from their 100-year exile almost as stage-props with George IV even wearing a kilt during the visit. Since then Scott has been largely attributed to the image of tartan kilts and skirling pipes that means Scotland to the rest of the world.

For those that wish to see the city from yet another viewpoint, the climb up **Calton Hill** will be more than adequately rewarded. The hill is seen at the east end of Princes Street and is easily reached by a flight of steps or the road a little further on. The views stretch across Edinburgh in all directions taking in the Firth of Forth, just catching the bridges, across to Fife and a good prospect of Arthur's Seat with Holyrood Palace at its foot. Perhaps the best vista is looking west up Princes Street with its spires, chimneys and many statues. This was Robert Louis Stephenson's favourite escape to view his much loved city. The various Calton Hill structures include the National Monument standing like a Parthenon, started in 1822 by William Playfair. The intention then was to build a full-sized replica of that famous Greek monument but the town ran out of money and it later was nicknamed ' the National Disgrace'. The 100ft (30.5m) Nelson Monument, shaped like a telescope, was completed in 1814 in honour of the naval hero. The Old Royal Observatory to the west of the hill now contains 'The Edinburgh Experience' with details on the city's history from its volcanic birth to the present day using a three-dimensional slide show.

For the architectural enthusiast there is much to see on George Street and Queen Street. St Andrews Square and Charlotte Square stand at opposite ends of George Street like square barbels and contain some of the most exalted examples. **Charlotte Square**, designed by Robert Adam in 1791, a year before his death bringing to it a unity of aspect that some of the New Town developments lacked. The **Georgian House** on the north side has been opened to illustrate the social and domestic life of a nineteenth-century well-to-do family with delightful accoutrements of the period and furniture. **St Andrews Square** at the opposite end has several imposing structures now mostly used by financial institutions.

Returning to Princes Street, there are moves afoot to pedestrianise from the Caledonian Hotel at the western end to the Balmoral in the east. At the moment a malevolent river of traffic has to be negotiated to reach the more sanguine **Princes Street Gardens**. The gardens are an oasis of greenery and unstinting flower displays set in the heart of the busy centre of the capital. During the summer concerts are staged in the canvas covered auditorium. The main north and west railway line fringes the south side of the gardens hidden away from view. At the east end of the gardens is Waverly Station and standing outside are a selection of open-top buses providing enlightening tours of the city.

Many visitors come to Edinburgh specifically for the Edinburgh International Festival held for 3 weeks every year in August when the town is taken over by thespians of every sort who put on more than 13,000 performances per Festival. The Festival was started in 1947 to help shake off the gloom of the post war years and with several names of international stature supporting it, the new festival got off to a good start. The Fringe started at the same time and is now the world's largest arts festival with over 500 performances each day supported by 450 companies. During this time the Military Tattoo is held every night in the Castle Esplanade. A more recent development to try and bridge the tourist gap around the Christmas holiday is 'Edinburgh's Hogmanay' with several attractions culminating in the traditional Edinburgh gathering around the Tron Church on the Mile to bring in New Year.

Edinburgh has a particularly lively pub scene around the centre. Hostelries of interesting historical and architectural significance are included in several trails from the Grassmarket to Rose Street. Pubs have replaced the old coffee houses of Edinburgh's past and are an important element of local culture. Some worth visiting for their atmosphere would be The Last Drop and the Preservation Hall around the Grassmarket, Deacon Brodies Tavern in Bank Street at the corner with the Royal Mile and the Auld Toll Bar just beyond the Toll Cross in Bruntsfield Place. Check out the Rose Street Brewery also, one of the many public houses along this colourful back street.

The areas just beyond the Old and New Towns are peppered with good places to escape from the crowds. Beneath the south side of the castle is the rectangular Grassmarket, once an agricultural marketplace but now dominated by car parking along with some good pubs, restaurants and interesting shops. It can be reached by following Castle Wynd Steps or Victoria Street off George IV Bridge. Here you find a host of little antique or curiosity shops along with the famous Brush Shop, one of the least changed stores in Edinburgh since the 1950's selling brushes of all shapes, balls of string and other household tackle. The cross at the bottom of Victoria Street is where more than 100 Covenanters were hung for following their beliefs. The **Traverse Theatre** stands opposite, one of Edinburgh's several experimental stages. Famous Grassmarket residents were Burke and Hare, grave-robbers who turned to murder as a quick way of providing corpses for the medical faculty. Ironically, Burke's skeleton can still be seen in the Department of Anatomy in the University of Edinburgh.

On George IV Bridge itself stands the **National Library of Scotland**, a huge complex holding every book ever published in Britain as well as many rare manuscripts and letters including the last letter Mary Queen of Scots wrote to her cousin, Queen Elizabeth who had imprisoned her and condemned her to death. There is also the orders that commenced the Massacre of Glencoe in 1692.

Greyfriars at the end of George IV Bridge is the site of a medieval monastery. In 1638 the National Covenant was signed in the Greyfriars Kirkyard behind the pub, declaring the independence of the Presbyterian Church of Scotland from government control. This victorious event was followed by years of civil war, great bitterness and bloodshed.

On the north-west corner of the New Town sheltering under the Thomas Telford's expansive Dean Bridge built in 1829, there is a charming group of buildings called **Dean Village**. Set around the Water of Leith this former milling community has been rescued from decline and transformed into a 'yuppified' ghetto. Many of Dean Village's buildings appear Tudor or early Victorian. From here you can walk following the Water of Leith to Stockbridge, in fact the river runs from the Pentland Hills and into the docks at Leith with walks for most of its length. Stockbridge was another older community, this time being engulfed by the sprawling second phase of the New Town development.

If you wish to wander further afield a pleasant walk over the Water of Leith brings you to the **Royal Botanic Gardens**. These 70 acres (28 hectares) are casually arranged more like a well-tended wood and decorated with rhododendrons and azaleas. The glass houses and pavilion display more exotic vegetation in a steamy, tropical environment. From Princes Street catch buses 23 or 27.

Leith has had a chequered history through the centuries, sometimes riding high in favour as Edinburgh's seaport then, in more recent times, suffering high unemployment and dereliction amongst a jungle of dilapidated tenements. To many locals it remains a separate town but it has recently been embraced by Edinburgh's fashionable faction and become recherché with popular wine bars and bistros blossoming along its attractive water-front.

The south side has several nearly autonomous communities that have their own distinct flavour. From Bruntsfield to Morningside the main road is lined with dozens of interesting shops that would take a few hours to explore.

On the west side of town **Edinburgh Zoo** on Corstorphine Road is reached by bus from Princes Street Gardens. The zoo is one of Britain's best and has over 1,000 birds, reptiles and mammals housed in 80 acres of scenic landscaped parkland at the base of Corstorphine Hill. A 'Penguin Parade' is held daily from April to September at 2pm in the world's largest penguin enclosure complete with underwater viewing.

Additional Information

Places of Interest in Edinburgh

Edinburgh Castle
On the Canongate, Royal Mile
Historic Scotland ☎ 0131 244 3101
Open: April to September, Monday to Saturday, 9.30am-5pm. Sunday, 11am-5pm. October to March, Monday to Saturday, 9.30am-4.20pm. Sunday 12.30-3.35pm.

Edinburgh Experience
(formerly Royal Observatory)
Calton Hill
☎ 0131 556 4365
Open: April to October, Monday to Friday, 2-5pm, Saturday and Sunday 10.30am-5pm.

Edinburgh Zoo
Off Corstorphine Road, 4 miles (6km) west of city centre
☎ 0131 334 9171
Open: All year daily, summer 9am-6pm. Winter, 9am-5pm. Sunday opening 9.30am.

Georgian House
No 7 Charlotte Square
☎ 0131 225 2160
Open: April to October, Monday to Saturday, 10am-5pm. Sunday 2-5pm. Closed during winter months.

Gladstone's Land
Lawnmarket on the Royal Mile
☎ 0131 226 5856
Open: April to October, Monday to Saturday, 10am-5pm. Sunday 2-5pm. Closed during winter months.

Hillend Dry Ski Slope
Biggar Road on the south outskirts of Edinburgh
☎ 0131 445 4455
Open: April to September, Monday to Friday, 9.30am-9pm.

John Knox's House
45 High Street, Royal Mile
☎ 0131 556 9579
Open: All year, Monday to Saturday, 10am-5pm.

Lady Stair's House
Off Lawnmarket on Royal Mile
☎ 0131 225 2424
Open: June to September, weekdays, 10am-6pm. October to May, weekdays, 10am-5pm. Sundays during Festival, 2-5pm.

Museum of Childhood
High Street, Royal Mile
☎ 0131 225 2424
Open: June to September, weekdays, 10am-6pm. October to May, weekdays, 10am-5pm. Sundays during Festival 2-5pm.

National Library of Scotland
George IV Bridge
☎0131 226 4531
Open: All year, 9.30am-8.30pm. Saturdays, 9.30am-1pm.

Outlook Tower and Camera Obscura
Castle Hill between the Castle and
Lawnmarket
☎ 0131 226 3709
Open: April to October, Monday to
Friday, 9.30am-5.30pm. Saturday and
Sunday, 10am-6pm. November to
March, Monday to Friday, 9.30am-5pm.
Saturday and Sunday, 10.30am-4.30pm.

Palace of Holyroodhouse
Foot of the Royal Mile
☎ 0131 556 7371
Open: April to October, 9.30am-5.15pm.
Sunday, 10.30am-4.30am. November to
March, 9.30am-3.45pm. Closed on
Sunday.

Parliament House
Parliament Square off Royal Mile
☎ 0131 225 2595
Open: All year, Tuesday to Friday,
10am-4pm.

Register House
East end of Princes Street
☎ 0131 556 6585
Open: All year, Monday to Friday,
9.30am-4.30pm.

Royal Botanic Gardens
Inverleith Row behind Stockbridge
☎ 0131 552 7171
Open: Daily, 9am to sunset.

Royal Scots Regimental Museum
Within Edinburgh Castle grounds
Historic Scotland ☎ 0131 244 3101
Open: April to September, Monday to
Saturday, 9.30am-5pm. Sunday, 11am-
5pm. October to March, Monday to
Saturday, 9.30am-4.20pm. Sunday,
12.30-3.35pm.

St Giles Cathedral
On the Royal Mile
☎ 0131 225 4363
Open: Monday to Saturday, 9am-5pm.
Sundays in the afternoon.

Scotch Whisky Heritage Centre
358 Castlehill, The Royal Mile
☎ 0131 220 0441
Open: June to September, daily, 9am-
6.30pm. October to May 10am-5pm.

Scott's Monument
Princes Street
☎ 0131 529 4068

Cinemas, Theatres & Galleries
Edinburgh Festival Theatre
13 Nicholson Street-up North Bridge
☎ 0131 662 1112

The Kings Theatre
Leven Street, Tollcross
☎ 0131 229 1201

The Lyceum Theatre
Grindlay Street
☎ 0131 229 9697

The Cameo Cinema
Shows cult films and new releases of note
Tollcross
☎ 0131 228 4141

The Dominion Cinema
3 screens presenting a variety of classics
and important contemporary films
Newbattle Terrace
☎ 0131 447 2660

Edinburgh Art Galleries
For listings of current exhibitions obtain
a copy of the *Edinburgh Gallery Guide*
available at most Edinburgh galleries or
tourist information centres.

National Gallery of Scotland
The Mound, just off Princes Street
☎ 0131 556 8921
Open: Monday to Saturday, 10am-5pm,
Sunday, 2-5pm.

National Portrait Gallery
1 Queens Street
Handsome Victorian building housing
portraits of nobility as well as a
Museum of Antiquity.

Royal Scottish Acadamy
Foot of the Mound on Princes Street
☎ 0131 225 6671
Open: Monday to Saturday, 10am-7pm,
Sunday, 2-5pm.

Scottish National Gallery of Modern Art
Displays international and Scottish art
of the twentieth century.
Belford Road (West End of New Town)
Bus No. 13 from Princes Street.

The Edinburgh Experience
At the City Observatory, Calton Hill
☎ 0131 556 4365

Open: Monday to Friday, April to June, 2-5pm, Saturday and Sunday 10.30am-5pm, July to September daily, 10.30am-5pm.

Traverse Theatre
Cambridge Street, Next to Usher Hall
☎ 0131 228 3223
Open: See local press for performances and times.

City Art Centre
Market Street
Popular internationally touring exhibitions.

The Fruit Markert Gallery
Market Street
More casual exhibition room with a wide variety of exhibitors.

Printmaker's Workshop and Gallery
23 Union Street, Off Leath Walk
Industrious unit churning out work with prints from notables around Scotland for sale in shop.

369 Gallery
233 Cowgate
Contemporary Scottish Art with a penchant for happenings, launches, music etc.

Other Useful Information

'Talking Tourist Guide to Edinburgh'
Calls charged at 39p per minute cheap rate and 49p at all other times.
☎ 01891 775700

Weathercall for this area
☎ 01898 500422

Emergencies
Ambulance, Police & Fire-brigade ☎ 999

Airport
Edinburgh Airport
☎ 0131 344 3136

Car Hire
Edinburgh Airport
Alamo ☎ 0131 344 3250
Avis ☎ 0131 333 1866
Hertz ☎ 0131 333 1019
Courtesy phones for Eurodollar and Budget are found beside Meeting Point opposite Airport Information Desk in airport.

Rail
Edinburgh Waverely Station
☎ 0131 556 2451

Tourist Information Offices

Edinburgh and Scotland Tourist Information Centre
3 Princes Street (Above Waverley Centre)
EH2 2QP ☎ 0131 557 1700

Edinburgh Airport Tourist Information
Airport is 7 miles (11km) west of the city at Turnhouse ☎ 0131 333 2167

Accommodation

The Scandic Crown ***
80 High Street, Royal Mile
☎ 0131 557 9797

The Balmoral ***
Princes Street (East)
☎ 0131 556 2414

The Caledonian ***
Princes Street (West)
☎ 0131 225 2433

Bruntsfield Hotel **
69 Bruntsfield Place
☎ 0131 229 1393

Braid Hills Hotel **
134 Braid Road
☎ 0131 447 8888

Sibbet House *
26 Northumberland Street
☎ 0131 556 1078

Teviotdale House *
53 Grange Loan
☎ 0131 667 4376

Campsites

Little France Caravan Site
219 Old Dalkeith Road
☎ 0131 666 2326

Mortonhall Caravan Park
38 Mortonhall Gate
☎ 0131 664 1533

Muirhouse Caravan Site
Marine Drive, Silverknowes
☎ 0131 312 6874

Youth Hostels

High Street Youth Hostel
Off Royal Mile
☎ 0131 557 3984

Bruntsfield Hostel
7 Bruntsfield Crescent
☎ 0131 447 2994

The Kingdom of Fife

4

During the lead up to 'regionalization' of Scotland's old counties in 1975, the 'Kingdom of Fife' fought hard to avoid being swallowed up by Tayside to the north and Lothian to the south. If anything, this helped to reinforce the area's sense of identity both to its residents and outsiders. Its geographic position is unique and probably contributes to this character, thrust into the North Sea and detached north and south by the rivers Tay and Forth. With such attractive jewels as St Andrews, the East Neuk and historic Dunfermline its potential to draw tourists is now its greatest asset and, as the 'Home of Golf', it has attained almost mythical status with hackers around the world. Historically, like other parts of the nation, it has held the mantle as the hub and focus of political and ecclesiastical life for long periods with Dunfermline and St Andrews being the major centres.

Touring through Fife you notice a distinctive style to much of the architecture especially in the charming coastal cottages. These and most of Fife's older buildings, reveal strong links with the Low Countries, Holland, the Netherlands and Belgium where sixteenth-century trade before links with the Americas were established, was a key element to Scotland's economy. Ships loaded with wool, cloth, timber and fish were sent across the North Sea and often returned with the distinctive red roofing pantiles loaded as ballast.

The views approaching Fife from the road or rail bridges are stirring enough particularly looking down on the village of **North Queensferry** which appears in miniature from the bridge spans passing high above it. To investigate further, leave the motorway or if you are enjoying a rail excursion from Edinburgh, disembark at North Queensferry. The village was the centuries-old northern terminal for the ferry established by Queen Margaret to carry pilgrims to nearby Dunfermline, crossing to and from South Queensferry for nearly 800 years until the road bridge was opened in 1964.

Apart from the wonderful views across the Forth and excellent camera angles of the marvellous engineering feat of the Forth Bridge, North Queensferry's latest attraction is Deep Sea World, a giant aquarium complex housing the world's largest underwater viewing tunnel. Created next to a former quarry, this nautical safari takes you beneath one million gallons of sea water through a sturdy transparent tube to see, at close quarters, most of the creatures you would find in British coastal waters. Wriggling through the rocks and swimming overhead are 100 different species native to Scottish waters including lobster, squid, octopus, eels, salmon and sea trout. A 'people-mover' conveyer belt transports visitors slowly through the main tank while upstairs there are more aquariums, educational exhibitions, a coral reef display and a café.

Follow the A985 from North Queensferry via Inverkeithing. The sixteenth-century burgh of **Culross** (pronounced Koo-riss) is a medieval hamlet set amongst the industrial Upper Forth Estuary. Antiquated cobbled streets, still used today by the modern residents, climb through the hillside village bordered by excellent examples of terracotta pantile and white-harled cottages.

Culross was once one of Scotland's major trading ports due mainly to the enterprises of one man, Sir George Bruce, a sixteenth-century coal and salt merchant as well as a descendant of Robert the Bruce. The 'palace', situated to the left of the main square, was built for Sir George and his family in 1577. Culross Palace was bought a year after the National Trust for Scotland was formed in 1932 for the amazing sum of £700.00. The structure reflected the wealth Bruce had accumulated through his local colliery along with the simultaneous production of course salt.

The Town House or Tolbooth is the rather striking dark stone building overlooking the village entrance. Its clean cut, rather austere sandstone outline is augmented by the double staircase approaching the doorway. Built in 1526, with the tall tower adjoined a century and a half later, this is now the offices of the National Trust in this area and also the town's visitor centre.

James VI had made Culross a Royal Burgh in 1588 but by the late nineteenth century it was too poor even to pull down its own crumbling buildings. This turned out to be the National Trust's good fortune. For

preceding page; King Robert the Bruce lies buried at Dunfermline Abbey instance, the Trust bought 'the Study' along with nine others for a total of £168.00. The cobbled streets climbing toward the Town Square and Merkat Cross reveal a protruding piece of early seventeenth-century architecture, a lofty apartment called the Outlook Tower. This is 'the Study' where the Bishop of Dunblane set out his manuscripts during visits to the then important burgh. Inside are finely preserved painted ceilings and panelled walls along with a small museum exhibiting local objects and maps of the period. Further up the hill behind the grey council houses are the remains of Culross Abbey. In 1217, this Cistercian abbey was founded by monks who were the first to mine the coal along the shores of the River Forth. There is little left of the main abbey buildings but the choir and tower are now the site of the Parish church which itself dates back to 1300 although rebuilt in 1633. Inside you will find an alabaster bust cast in memory of Sir George Bruce.

On Fife's western-most boundary, the town of **Kincardine** is a conven-ient crossing point of the River Forth. Like so many other towns in Fife, Kincardine has many buildings showing a Dutch influence. It also shares with several of the kingdom's coastal burghs an industrial heritage of salt-panning.

Dunfermline was one of the most important ancient Scottish capitals until the time of James VI of Scotland, (James I of England) and the Union of the Crowns in 1603. Lying 2 miles (3km) inland from the Firth of Forth, it is today a main focus of commercial activity for south-west Fife situated near the M90 motorway. Its narrow town-centre streets are usually busy, mainly with local 'Fifers' going about their business, a fairly typical lowland market town but with a particularly rich heritage.

Most of the important areas of Dunfermline can be explored by foot and there is ample sign-posted car-parking near the abbey and its historic precincts. Approaching the town by car from the south under the high railway viaducts your eye is drawn to the central elevation on which sits Dunfermline Palace and Abbey. The words 'King Robert the Bruce' can be seen like an early advertising hoarding, carved in huge stone letters surrounding the balustrade of the nineteenth-century parish church which nestles alongside the abbey.

The largely ruined Dunfermline Abbey and Palace was a great Ben-edictine house built in the time of King Malcolm Canmore (1005-1034) by his wife, Margaret. Queen Margaret was instrumental in the reformation of the nation from Celtic religious practices to Catholic. The present site is a loose arrangement bringing together buildings of several eras, the ruined monastery and palace with their romantic aura standing next to a much restored and more austere nineteenth-century church. Beneath the present knave, the foundations of Margaret's modest little church remain and can be seen through thick iron grills.

Guided talks are provided by enthusiastic and well-informed locals. In the church choir, under the pulpit beneath a great brass plaque, the bones of Robert the Bruce are buried. In 1818 whilst preparing the foundations for the present church, a stone coffin was discovered by workmen who

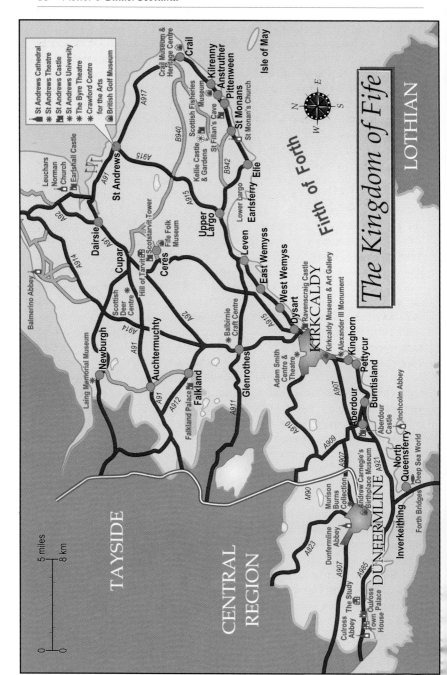

found the skeleton wrapped in lead and covered with gold cloth. Its breast bone had been sawn indicating that the heart, in accordance with Bruce's instructions, had been removed. He decreed that his heart was to be carried to the Holy Land to atone for his murderous accession to the throne. Sir James Douglas was charged with the task but was killed in Spain doing battle with the Moors. Fortunately, the heart was retrieved and returned to Scotland where it is now buried at Melrose Abbey in the Borders while his bones remain in Dunfermline.

For lovers of Robert Burns and his poetry the Murison Burns Collection is found in Dunfermline's Central Library in Abbots Street. A collection of books, pamphlets, prints, portraits, and commemorative bric-a-brac relating to the life and works of the 'Great Bard' is found there.

In Moodie Street, an old weaver's cottage was, in 1835, the birthplace of the great industrialist, Andrew Carnegie. This weaver's son emigrated to America to become one of the world's richest men. And yet in vastly generous but perceptive donations, he gave away 350 million dollars for the benefit of mankind doing great damage to the old fable that Scots were mean. One of his local purchases was Pittencrieff House Museum situated in Pittencrieff Park, locally known as the 'Glen'. The house dates back to 1610 and was purchased along with the marvellous open parkland, by Carnegie in 1902, to display certain items of local history, costumes and art. When Andrew Carnegie was a small boy he was forbidden entrance to this privately-owned estate. He never forgot this, and on his return from America he bought the estate and gave it to the people of Dunfermline so that no child should ever feel locked out as he had. His life is amply illustrated at the Carnegie Museum found opposite his cottage birthplace just beyond the park. The family lived upstairs while the room below contained his father's weaver's workshop.

Returning to **Inverkeithing** it is a rather uninviting municipality, its foreshore spoiled by a rust littered ship-breaker's yard. It was granted a Royal Charter by William I in 1165, making it one of the oldest Royal Burghs in Scotland. In the High street, behind the central square is the fourteenth-century Greyfriar's Hospice which houses a small museum recalling the antiquity of this Royal Burgh. This includes the life of Samuel Greig, born here in 1735 and described as the founder of the Russian Navy.

The coastal route around this part of Fife is the A921 to Kirkcaldy. Five miles (8km) east of the Forth bridges the village of **Aberdour** commences a series of delightful seaside hamlets that skirt the Firth of Forth. First impressions of its long, main street may not convey a great deal but Aberdour has important historical roots. At the far end of town is the entrance to Aberdour Castle. Built on lands originally granted to Thomas Randolph, Earl of Moray by King Robert the Bruce in 1325, the castle comprises three main sections dating from the fourteenth, sixteenth and seventeenth centuries. The walled gardens are its most appealing aspect, ablaze with colourful plants throughout the growing season.

The views across the Forth include **Inchcolm Abbey** on a string of rocky islands as well as the city-scapes of Edinburgh on the opposite shore. A boat runs from Hawkcraig Point near the village out to the islands. Known as the 'Iona of the East', the Abbey of St Columba was established on these islands in 1123 by Alexander I. It is believed that this was St Columbo's base while he converted the Southern Picts to Christianity in the sixth century. During a fishing trip King Alexander's boat was swept out to the islands in bad weather and ran aground. A hermit monk found him and his companions, more dead than alive and cared for them while signal fires eventually brought help. The king had Inchcolm Abbey built in gratitude for his rescue. Although sacked many times by the English and desecrated during the Reformation, the island and its abbey contain some of the best examples of monastic buildings in Scotland.

The main street of **Burntisland** is one of those places that would be attractive with just a little more attention. There are some admirable old buildings that have been restored next to others that remain sadly dilapidated. Help may be on the way from the fourteenth century with the discovery of the treasure ship of King Charles I in the Forth just of Burntisland. Charles I was the patron of the Arts for Britain and his extravagant exhibits of the finest works in Europe lead to amazing scenes in court. Leaving Burntisland during a tour of Scotland to cross the Forth for the port of Leith the ship carrying his baggage, the *Blessing of Burntisland*, overloaded with carts full of plate, gold and valuable tapestries, capsized. Thirty-five of his servants drowned and only two survived. Now the floor of the Forth is being explored for the treasure and artifacts that might remain.

Its more glaring attraction is the Links Fun Fair taking over the wide park area at the north end of the town for most of the summer. Also held here in mid-July, the Burntisland Highland Games is said to be the second oldest in the world. The first church to be built following the Reformation from 1592 to 1595 was St Columba's at the top of the Kirkgate in East Leven Street. The General Assembly of the Kirk of Scotland was held here in 1601, when in the presence of James VI it was proposed that there should be a new translation of the Bible, the Authorized version, published in 1611. The impressive contours of Rossend Castle, which was first built in the early twelfth century, now house architects offices and are not open for further exploration. The present structure dates to around 1554. The most famous incident of the building was the discovery of the poet, Pierre de Chastelard, hiding in the bed-chamber of Mary Queen of Scots who was staying there in 1563. The spirited Frenchman lost his head over the incident when he was dragged off to St Andrews for execution, crying 'Adieu, thou most beautiful and most cruel Princess in the world'.

A mile or so north of Burntisland brings you to a spot that radically altered the course of Scottish history. Beyond Kingswood Hotel and directly below a group of static holiday caravans is the **Alexander III Monument**, the place where King Alexander III, the last of Scotland's Celtic kings, was killed. The king had been in council with his lords in

Edinburgh and had set out in bad weather, anxious to join his new wife who awaited him at the Tower of Kinghorn. As he neared his destination, his horse stumbled on rough ground and fell over the steep cliffs. A prophecy of the event had been made at the king's wedding in Jedburgh 6 months earlier. The country was devastated without its rightful leader and fell into many years of conflict with the consequent power struggles. A Celtic cross marks the spot of Alexander's demise. There is a meagre parking facility long enough for two vehicles.

The wide sands of **Pettycur Bay** stand behind the commemorative cross to Alexander III. The tiny harbour, once a main ferry port between Fife and Leith is now a haven for small fishing boats, the pier walls littered with lobster creels and crab claws. **Kinghorn** adjoins Pettycur and was created as a Royal Burgh in the twelfth century by David I. It is a pleasant little holiday town catering mainly to older Scots who still prefer a week by the coast rather than a package holiday to Spain or Florida. In a pleasant setting, there is a nice section of sheltered sandy beach, some water sports and a short, undulating 18 hole golf course. Sea fishing for saithe and flatfish is possible off Pettycur Pier and Kinghorn Beach. A restaurant worth trying is the Longboat on the road approaching Pettycur Bay from Kinghorn.

The town of **Kirkcaldy** developed from little more than a single street stretching for 4 miles (6km) along the sea-front and thus became known as the 'Lang Toun'. It has since expanded in other directions and is now the largest town in Fife with good motorway and rail-links to neighbouring communities and beyond. The esplanade that shields the town's frontage from wild, winter North Sea waves was built in 1922-23 to help alleviate a chronic shortage of employment. This problem was further allayed when a local man, Michael Nairn, a sail cloth worker, combined jute as a backing and linseed as a main surface ingredient to make a water-resistent facing called linoleum.

Today, the town is trying to make the transition from an industrial to a service and tourist based economy. Kirkcaldy is Fife's main shopping centre with the usual outlets lining the High Street but some of the side streets near the centre are worth exploring. Facing the inner harbour in an area known as the 'Sailor's Walk' is the oldest crow-stepped house in Kirkcaldy, built around 1460. Kirk Wynd running down to the High Street has several antique buildings the most notable being Kirkcaldy's Old Kirk with its Norman tower.

For 5 days in April, Kirkcaldy's Esplanade is closed off to accommodate the 'Links Market', the oldest and largest street fair in Britain dating back to 1305. On a more dignified front, Kirkcaldy is the birthplace of Adam Smith, the illustrious philosopher, political economist, pamphleteer and, in 1776, author of the *Wealth of Nations*. The Adam Smith Theatre ✳ near the railway station puts on shows and plays throughout the year, the main auditorium also being a cinema showing interesting if often dated films. There is a restaurant and bar and no further reference to Adam Smith apart from his bust in the foyer.

The Andrew Carnegie Museum stands in the town of his birth, Dunfermline

Dysart Harbour offers a suprising glimpse into the past, next to the more modern town of Kirkcaldy

The Kirkcaldy Museum and Art Gallery in War Memorial Gardens next to the railway station captures the history and development of the 'Lang Toun' quite well. As well as an interesting archaeological collection there is a display of the famous local Wemyss Ware pottery and a small art gallery with work by Sir David Wilkie, Samuel Peploe, William McTaggart and Lowry. One of Kirkcaldy's historic centre pieces has recently been crowded by a modern housing development but never-the-less Ravenscraig Castle towers dramatically above the shore-line at the east end of the town. Overlooking the Firth of Forth, the ruin dates from 1460 when James II intended it for his first wife. Flanking the castle are a flight of steps leading to the beach which inspired the novelist John Buchan to write his novel *The 39 Steps*.

Dysart, an eastern district of Kirkcaldy, is a little burgh dating back to the sixteenth century. With enchanting wynds and courtyards this small corner is still full of character. Dysart was formerly a busy port trading with the Netherlands. Some replica designs of the old fishing skiffs still ply out into the Forth. The Pan Ha' is a parade of seventeenth-century houses restored by Kirkcaldy District Council and the National Trust. Also restored was the home of John McDouall Stuart. This house, now a museum, dated 1575, was the 19th century explorers birthplace. He was the first man to cross Australia from North to South in 1866. The Rectory Restaurant is situated behind St Serf's Church and is an intimate yet informal place conscientiously run by its owners.

The two villages of **East** and **West Wemyss** lie side by side to the east of Kirkcaldy and acquired their name from the many 'weems' or caves found on this coast. Below McDuff's Castle, these remarkable caverns gave shelter to man as far back as 2500BC. Now quite dangerous and damaged by vandalism, there is a campaign to preserve them. Depicted inside is Britain's earliest picture of a boat as well as various hunting scenes portrayed by craftsmen of Pictish times. The most impressive is Court Cave, so named because James IV once held court there but now this and Well Cave are closed to the public. The local tourist board advises the use of hard hats if you wish to enter Doo Cave or Jonathan's Cave. The ruined McDuff's Castle in East Wemyss was the stronghold of the Thanes of Fife and reputed to be the home of 'MacDuff' in Shakespeare's *MacBeth*. Little now remains of this castle.

Although commenced in the 1950's, **Glenrothes** is still sometimes referred to as one of Scotland's group of seven 'new towns'. It was originally intended to meet the housing needs of Fife's colliery workers but that industry declined soon after the town was commissioned and it subsequently turned its economical attention to more modern industries such as electronics. There is little to see in Glenrothes unless you are interested in rather uninspired 'sixties' architecture. There is, however, a prehistoric henge monument at **Balfarg** and the restored stone circle of **Balbirnie** on either side of the A92 about 1 mile (½km) north of Glenrothes. Balbirnie Country Park with a craft centre and attractive 18 hole parkland golf course is situated in the nearby village of **Markinch**.

Returning to the coast you find the once industrial conurbations of Buckhaven, Methil and Leven. These towns were, until recently, connected with the coal industry and shipbuilding. The most appealing now is the seaside holiday town of **Leven**. Situated on Largo Bay with its sandy beaches, its promenade is punctuated with putting greens, paddling pools and amusement arcades as well as two fine links golf courses. Levenmouth Swimming Pool and Sports Centre just over the bridge coming into town is a modern indoor facility. Away from the beaches and ice cream vans is Letham Glen, a herbaceous adorned park with a pet's corner and nature trail while, on the outskirts of town is Silverburn Estate with woods and gardens a mini-farm or craft centre.

On Fife's eastern-most stretch of coastline is a timeless gathering of ancient fishing villages, little changed and still little discovered judging by the tranquil air of their quay-side streets and alleys. Each has its own particular character and charm, recalling times when they were all thriving sea-ports trading with the Low Countries and Scandinavia. This influence can still be seen in the distinctive Dutch and Flemish architectural styles.

Skirting the shores of Largo Bay are three charming hamlets, Lower Largo, Upper Largo and Lundin Links. With its golden crescent of sand and picturesque little harbour, **Lower Largo** is probably the best known as the birthplace of Alexander Selkirk, the model for Daniel Defoe's *Robinson Crusoe*. A statue of Crusoe, looking expectantly out to sea can be found in the village. The Crusoe Hotel serves good bar meals and offers moderately priced accommodation with uninterrupted views over the Firth of Forth. Slightly inland, **Upper Largo** is a country village with an ancient parish church.

Further along the coast and following the A917, the villages of **Elie** and **Earlsferry** at the eastern end of Largo Bay are really one and the same place. With a mile of wide, sandy beach encircling the harbour area this is one of Fife's most popular escapes. Local windsurfers and dinghy sailors take over the dunes by the harbour and spend the weekend on the water with occasional jaunts to the Ship Inn where live entertainment and good food is laid on. Another good restaurant in town though more formal is the Bouquet Garni on the High Street. Golf is popular all along this coast thanks to the natural links land and Elie or the Golf House Club offers one of the best rounds unless the wind is blowing which it often does. A haven for well-healed retirees, Elie and Earlsferry have an exclusive air giving them the reputation of being Fife's Riviera. The Lady's Tower, a short walk from the harbour was built as a bathing box for Lady Janet Anstruther.

The East Neuk villages are very close to one another and can be covered quite easily in a day. Three miles (5km) north-east along the coast from Elie is **St Monans**. This was a thriving fishing port making its living mainly from herring. Miller's boat-yard by the harbour is one of the oldest surviving boat-builders, established in 1747 and still producing fishing vessels today. St Monans parish church sits close to the sea-edge, a most picturesque, stalky little building with its history going back to the time of David I. Inside, suspended in the transept, is a model of a full-rigged ship and the breaking of the waves on the rocks outside must remind the congregation of the areas long links with the sea.

Pittenweem is the home of the Fife fishing fleet and has a new fish-market and refurbished granary containing the all-important ice-house. The harbour can be a bustling scene with fishing boats landing their catch early in the morning then fishermen sitting on the piers fixing their nets. The occasional brave seal will pop its head up in the harbour looking for scraps. At the start of the eastern breakwater, the Gyles, not open to the public, is a pleasant corner of sixteenth- and seventeenth-century houses restored by the National Trust for Scotland, a good example of the Dutch influence that this part of Fife is known for. Kellie Lodging, the distinctive honey-coloured tower in the High Street has also been restored by the Trust its ground floor occasionally open as an art gallery.

Found in Cove Wynd overlooking the harbour, St Fillan's Cave was a refuge for the seventeenth-century Christian missionary, St Fillan. He lived in the cave and the site became a shrine to later pilgrims. This simple dwelling also gave the town its name. In the Pictish tongue, Pittenweem means place of the cave. The key to the cave is available from the 'Ginger-bread Horse' gift shop and café in the High Street.

Three miles (5km) inland from Pittenweem, near the tiny village of **Arncroach** stands Kellie Castle. This castle was owned by the Oliphant family for two centuries before it was sold to the Earl of Mar and Kellie in 1613. It lay abandoned until taken over and restored by Professor James Lorimer, a distinguished legal expert. On holiday in Fife in 1877 he discovered Kellie Castle on a walk, windowless and deserted, practically a ruin. The professor and his family fell in love with it and acquired it from the Earl of Marr as improving tenants which they certainly proved to be.

The walled harbour of **Anstruther**, known locally as 'Anster' once contained Scotland's main fishing fleet with over 1,000 boats until the onslaught of deep sea trawlers and the demise of the herring stock. There are now mostly leisure boats moored in the harbour but Anstruther still reflects on its fishing past at the Scottish Fisheries Museum found at the head of the harbour. The museum gives a unique insight into the life and work of a fishing community, with the marvellous interiors of a typical fisherman's home. There is also a collection of model fishing boats, fishing gear and equipment, maps and compasses, as well as an aquarium. Behind the museum in East Green is one of Fife's best restaurants, the Cellar, which serves exceptionally fresh and well prepared seafood. 'Anster' also boasts a fine 9 hole golf course, located at the foot of Bankwell Road, behind the Craw's Nest Hotel. This is one of the better hotels in the area where you can enjoy good food with a fine view over the Forth.

Between Anstruther and Crail on the B9171 road is Scotland's Secret Bunker, an underground Nuclear War Command Centre now redundant

East Neuk fishermen still repair their nets on the harbour, Pittenween

The well preserved Kellie Castle near Pittenween is a tribute to the Lorimer family who have restored it over the past 100 years

Thousands of visitors to St Andrews, sadly, might never bother to investigate the town's historic aspects or, indeed, wander very far away from the 19th hole. They have come for one thing alone and that is to 'play golf'.

St Andrews is regarded as the conceptual home of the game despite rather weak counter-claims that it started in Holland. The naturally formed Scottish coastal margin or links land, created over thousands of years by the receding sea, was used by locals as common land for the grazing of animals or drying clothes. Here, by the sixteenth century the game of golf began to take shape and direction. Even before 1457, when the Scottish Parliament tried to ban the game, golf or a distant relative of it, was enjoyed on these links. Mary Queen of Scots was known to enjoy the odd round. It was not until 1895 that a second course to the Old, the New, was laid out by the R&A. The Jubilee course came next in 1897.

St Andrews
The Home of Golf

The sandy peninsula next to the town of St Andrews was gifted to the people by King David in 1123 and, despite once being sold by an unscrupulous and bankrupt Town Council for rabbit breeding, it remains the property of St Andrews citizens. St Andrews golf courses are, therefore, essentially municipal allowing anyone to play providing they can obtain a ballot or tee time and for the Old Course this requires a handicap certificate.

The Royal and Ancient Golf Club of St Andrews, set in its honey-coloured citadel overlooking the 1st and 18th holes of the Old Course, is, along with the USGA, the ruling body of golf world-wide. The men-only clubhouse built in 1854, may only be entered by invitation.

It may be hard for non-golfers to fully grasp the significance of St Andrews to the game of golf but most will enjoy a tour around the well presented British Golf Museum, situated behind the Royal and Ancient clubhouse. The museum has taken a potentially 'stuffy' subject for non-golfers and brought it to life with the use of audio-visual and hands on presentations.

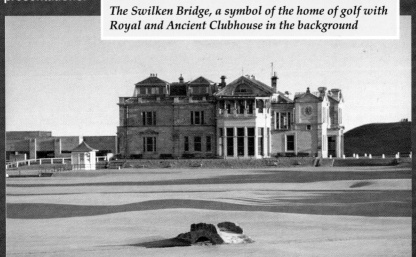

The Swilken Bridge, a symbol of the home of golf with Royal and Ancient Clubhouse in the background

since the end of Cold War aggression. This is where central government and military commanders would have run the country in the event of a nuclear war. The operations rooms of the RAF and Royal Observer Corps as well as dormitories and broadcast studios have all been left as they were during the past decades of tension.

Out of all Fife's East Neuk villages, the village of **Crail** has the most picturesque harbour. From Crail's wide main street, steep cobble-stoned wynds run down to it, this being the older part of the village. Painters and landscape photographers spend hours here. The small anchorage caters mainly for lobster and crab fishing boats and lobster creel-markers are seen in the water all along the coast. The upper streets of the village are more spacious with the Tolbooth at its centre behind which is the small Crail Museum and Heritage Centre giving an insight into the burgh's history. Crail Preservation Society has conserved this and many other fine buildings in the village.

In the summer, boats from Anstruther and Crail run excursions to the **Isle of May** some 5 miles (8km) off-shore. The grandfather of Robert Louis Stevenson built the existing lighthouse but the first lighthouse in Scotland was built here in 1636. The island became a National Nature Reserve in 1956 and is home to a large population of puffins, razorbills, shags, guillemots and kittihawks, as well as common grey seals.

Following the A917 which cuts across Fife's eastward protruding nib, the view from Kinkell Braes gives an excellent preface to the 'Auld Grey Toon' as **St Andrews** is known, overlooking the West Sands and the old harbour with the spires and stumps of the once great cathedral towering over all. In many respects St Andrews is like an island of culture, of ecclesiastical antiquity and of the great game of golf, set in a largely rural sea. Accents are heard from most parts of the globe coming to venerate St Andrews' history or is it the fairways? Fulfilling a life-long ambition to play the St Andrews Old Course has become a modern pilgrimage for many modern travellers while, centuries before, the town had the same magnetism for more pious visitors who came to venerate the site of St Andrews burial.

How the town, indeed Scotland's relationship with the Christian apostle, came about is slightly confused as there are several stories. Legend has it that St Andrew was crucified by the husband of a convertee, asking to be placed on a X-shaped cross so as not to emulate Jesus. Several centuries later, a monk called St Rule, charged with the care of the saint's relics, received a vision to 'journey to the utmost edge of the world' and there place the remains of the saint. St Rule's ship floundered on the rocks just off the site of today's harbour and he scrambled ashore to be met by King Angus who had also received a vision of St Andrew granting him victory over vastly superior forces. Angus gave the monk the land near the harbour to establish a shrine and place of pilgrimage and thus started the town and religious centre of St Andrews.

As you come into town from the south, the most prominent buildings breaking the skyline are St Andrews Cathedral and St Rules Tower.

Massive stone precincts encircle the cathedral grounds which are entered at the top of North or South Street where there is limited parking. The construction of the present cathedral began in 1160 but was not consecrated until around 1318 by Bishop Lamberton in the presence of King Robert the Bruce. It then became the greatest as well as largest church in Scotland with thousands of pilgrims travelling hundreds of miles to receive its benediction. The cathedral must have been a gratifying sight through the medieval period but, in 1559, Scotland's zealous reformer, John Knox stirred his audience so much they ransacked the place of its images, altars and books leaving the cathedral in virtual ruin. There is a small museum in the grounds and the earliest surviving sculpture in Scotland is found there, the St Andrews Sarcophagus, not a coffin but an intricately carved, shrine stone box.

Utilising the cliffs as part of its defence, St Andrews Castle stands on a rocky promontory, a hundred yards away from the cathedral entrance. As the residence of the bishops and later Archbishops of St Andrews it was also used as their palace, fortress and prison. First erected around 1200, the ruins seen today date back to 1571.

There are plenty of interesting shops in St Andrews' Market Street or South Street which form part of a useful circuit that takes in the best stores the town offers. For lunch there are several good places such as the Italian oriented Little John's or the more wholefood Brambles. The best evening meals are found in the Babur, an exceptional Indian Restaurant or travel out of town to the Peat Inn near Cupar for an upscale but worthy repast. In mid-August every year, the length of South Street and part of Market Street is given over to Scotland's oldest surviving medieval market, the Lammas Fair. Stalls and booths are established along with carnival rides during what was once the Celtic Festival of Autumn.

The St Andrews Sea-life Centre, close to the Golf Museum, is ideal for children with many of the species found out in the North Sea as well as more exotic specimens. Another good excursion for children just outside St Andrews is **Craigtoun Country Park** where a mock Dutch village is surrounded by a large boating pond. A miniature railway, dubbed the Rio Grande, runs along the western side of the park and there are play areas with inflatable castles, trampolines, a putting and bowling green and cafes. There are also gardens, glasshouses and flower and shrub beds. Mount Melville House adjacent the park has been purchased by St Andrews Old Course Hotel as the clubhouse for their new, parkland 18 hole golf course. To the north of St Andrews is Guardbridge and Leuchars, dominated by the important RAF base.

The interior of Fife is dominated by the vast agricultural heart of the Kingdom and most of its towns are connected with this activity. **Cupar** is its main town and was once Fife's administrative centre. It is a pleasant stop for a stroll around the town but there is not lots to see. The Ostler's Close bistro/restaurant is worth seeking out just off the main street. Two miles (3km) south of town is an Edwardian country house, beautifully remodelled by Robert Lorimer in 1906, the **Hill of Tarvit**. It was originally built for one of the Dundee Jute barons and among the fine collection of treasures inside are sixteenth-century tapestries, Chinese porcelain and eighteenth-century English and French furniture. The magnificent central hall is encased in panelled oak and adorned with fine paintings of the Dutch school. The gardens are equally impressive and there is a woodland walk leading to a hilltop viewpoint looking north over the Howe of Fife. A mile further south, on the same road, is **Scotstarvit Tower,** known to have been in existence since 1579. It now stands deserted.

Ceres lies 3 miles (5km) south of Cupar just below Scotstarvit Tower. It has appealing pantile cottages surrounding a village green and an ancient cobbled bridge crossing the shallow river. Some of the cottages and the bridge have been there for more than 650 years. The men of Ceres supposedly marched across the bridge on their way to the battle of Bannockburn and on their return celebrated their victory with games on the village green. The games are still an annual event, on the last Saturday in June, with the Ceres Derby the highlight of the day. There is a monument beside the green which recalls the village's proud heritage. Across the Ceres Burn bridge, the Fife Folk Museum is housed in part of the seventeenth-century Tolbooth weigh-house and two adjoining cottages. The award-winning museum displays crafts and trades, costumes, tools and utensils that were commonplace throughout in rural Fife over the past two centuries. Set on the gates just beyond the museum is a genial little statue called *The Provost* said to represent the last ecclesiastical provost of the village.

Three miles (5km) south-east of Ceres on the B940 is **Peat Inn** where an eighteenth-century building houses a restaurant of the same name that has a world-wide reputation. The French-influenced decor is matched by French/Scottish cuisine that is perhaps the best in Scotland. Swinging north and west, the **Scottish Deer Centre** is set 3 miles (5km) west of Cupar on the A91. There are a variety of deer species to be seen during ranger-led tours. There are also indoor and outdoor adventure parks for children as well as a restaurant, winery and well stocked gift shop.

Dairsie, 3 miles (5km) east of Cupar, just off the A91, has a bridge over the River Eden that was built by Archbishop Beaton in 1522. Dairsie Castle lies above the river. Dura Den is an enchanting wooded gorge south of the bridge where a large number of fossils have been found, giving vital clues to the formation of land and life here over millions of years. Beside the Ceres burn you can see the ruins of several linen and jute mills which were once an important part of the Fife economy.

Ten miles (16km) south-west of Cupar and tucked away at the foot of the Lomond Hills is the ancient and beautiful Royal Burgh of **Falkland**. Here stands the great palace of the Stuarts, a favourite residence of many Scottish kings and queens. The palace is in the heart of the town, which is a surprise in itself, showing a remarkable lack of class distinction, rare in medieval Scotland. It was built as a hunting lodge for royalty who came here to hunt deer and wild boar in the surrounding forest. Facing the street, the south front is a splendid example of Scottish Gothic with its buttresses, niches and statues of Christ and the saints. Scotland has few surviving buildings that were in the mainstream of Renaissance architecture, but here is one which ranks among the best. The building shows a strong French influence but there is a flavour about it that is unmistakeably Scottish. Most of the existing palace was built in the early sixteenth-century by James IV and his son James V. The royal tennis court at Falkland was built in 1539, the second oldest in Britain after Henry VIII's at Hampton Court, and is still in use.

The name of the larger village of **Auchtermuchty** is often scoffed at for its parochial enunciation but it is also well known for its musical associations. Scotland's premier accordion player, cherished by many older Scots around the world, Jimmy Shand, comes from here. The Auchtermuchty Folk Festival attracts players from around the country and regular impromptu sessions occur in the lounge bars. The duo, the 'Proclaimers' also hail from 'Muchty'. The High Street is the most interesting architectural area with an elegant early eighteenth-century Tolbooth.

A minor road leads out of town to the north, the B936 signposted to **Newburgh**. Lying on the shore of the River Tay, Newburgh has a long main street and an illustrious history. The aspect of the cobbled sidings and many of the dwellings testify to some antiquity although the outlying areas are rather dowdy. The Laing Museum is the main focus for visitors, established by a historian and banker, Dr Alexander Laing. It displays a fossil fish found in Dura Den and material on the town's past and movement of the Scottish people through the ages. To the east of town are the ruins of the twelfth-century Lindores Abbey. There is little of the buildings left apart from orange-stoned arches and fragments of the once great walls which suffered spoliation in 1559 at the hands of John Knox and his followers as well as local pilfering for other building projects.

The road bordering the wide River Tay heading east is scenic and winding. The city of Dundee comes into view at several points but 3 miles (5km) west of the Tay Rail Bridge is **Balmerino**, known for its abbey, which stands on a hill overlooking the river. It was founded in the thirteenth century by Alexander II whose mother, Ermengarde, widow of William the Lion, lies buried there. Little of the abbey remains today. In 1547 it was set on fire by the English army during the Rough Wooing and in 1559 John Knox and his reformers completed the destruction on their way back to St Andrews after reforming Lindores. Some of the pillars and part of the cloister are still visible and in the orchard is a great Spanish chestnut tree planted by the monks some 700 years ago.

This circular route passes through Newport on Tay and follows the Firth of Tay to Tayport, both now residential outposts of Dundee but with their 'Fife' character still intact. Return to St Andrews via Leuchars and the A919 or continue north over the Tay Road Bridge into Dundee and Tayside.

Additional Information

Place of Interest

Aberdour
Aberdour Castle
A921 to Aberdour
Historic Scotland ☎ 0131 244 3101
Open: April to September, Monday to
Saturday, 9.30am-7pm. Sunday,
2-7pm. October to March, Monday to
Saturday, 9.30am-4pm. Sunday,
2-4pm.

Inchcolm Abbey
On Inchcolm Island on Firth of Forth,
Boats from South Queensferry and
Aberdour
Historic Scotland ☎ 0131 244 3101
Open: April to September, Monday to
Saturday, 9.30am-7pm. Sunday, 2-7pm.
October to March, Monday to Saturday,
9.30am-4pm. Sunday, 2-4pm. Closed
Wednesday afternoon and Thursday in
winter.

Anstruther
Scottish Fisheries Museum
Next to Anstruther Harbour
☎ 01333 310628
Open: All year daily, 10am-5.30pm.
Sundays, 11am-5pm. November to
March, 10am-5pm, Sundays, 2-5pm.

Ceres
Fife Folk Museum
3 miles (5km) south of Cupar
☎ 01334 828380
Open: April to October daily except
Tuesdays, 2.15-5pm.

Crail
Crail Museum and Heritage Centre
62-64 Marketgate
☎ 01333 450869
Open: Easter week, 9am-1pm and 2-
5pm
April to May, weekends only and any
holidays 2-5pm.
June to September, Monday to Saturday, 10am-1pm and 2-5pm, Sunday 2-
5pm.

Culross
Culross Abbey & Palace
7 miles (11km) west of Dunfermline
Historic Scotland ☎ 0131 244 3101
Open: April to September, Monday to
Saturday, 9.30am-7pm. Sunday, 2-7pm.
October to March, Monday to Saturday,
9.30am-4pm. Sunday, 2-4pm.

The Study
In centre of old village of Culross
☎ 01383 880359
Open: April to October, Saturday &
Sunday, 2-4pm or by arrangement.

Town House
Sandhaven at front of village of Culross
☎ 01383 880359
Open: Easter weekend and May to
September, 11am-1pm and 2-5pm.
Saturday & Sunday, 2-5pm

Cupar
Hill of Tarvit
Off the A916 2 miles (2km) south of
Cupar
☎ 01334 653127
Open: Weekends during Easter and
April, May to September, daily 2-6pm.

Scotstarvit Tower
Off the A916, 3 miles (5km) south of
Cupar
Historic Scotland ☎ 0131 244 3101
Open: April to September, Monday to
Saturday, 9.30am-7pm. Sunday, 2-7pm.
October to March, Monday to Saturday,
9.30am-4pm. Sunday, 2-4pm.

Scottish Deer Centre
On the A91 3 miles (5km) west of Cupar
☎ 01337 810391
Open: April to October, 10am-5pm.
November to March, special opening
times.

Dunfermline
Andrew Carnegie's Birthplace Museum
Moodie Street, Dunfermline
☎ 01383 724302
Open: April to October, Monday to
Saturday, 11am-5pm. Sunday 2-5pm,
November to March 2-4pm.

Dunfermline Abbey and Palace
Monastery Street
Historic Scotland ☎ 0131 244 3101
Open: April to September, Monday to
Saturday, 9.30am-5pm. Sunday,
2-5pm. October to March, Monday to
Saturday, 9.30am-4pm. Sunday,
2-4pm.

Murison Burns Collection
Dunfermline Library
Abbot Street, Dunfermline
☎ 01383 723661
Open: Monday, Tuesday Thursday and
Friday, 10am-7pm. Wednesday and
Saturday, 10am-5pm. Closed Sundays.

Dysart
McDouall Stuart Museum
Rectory Lane
☎ 01592 260732
Open: Daily 2-5pm, June to August.

East Neuk
Pittenweem
St Fillan's Cave
Cove Wynd, towards the harbour
☎ 01333 311495
Open: All year, 10am-1pm & 2.30-
5.30pm or collect key from Gingerbread
Horse shop in main street.

St Monans Church
Off A917 at south-east corner of village
Open: All reasonable times.

Kellie Castle & Gardens
On the B9171, 3 miles (5km) north-west
of Pittenweem
☎ 01333 720271
Open: Castle, Easter & May to October,
2-6pm.

Falkland
Falkland Palace and Gardens
In village centre
Between Dysart & Kirkcaldy
Historic Scotland ☎ 0131 244 3101
Open: April to September, Monday to
Saturday, 9.30am-7pm. Sunday,
2-7pm. October to March, Monday to
Saturday, 9.30am-4pm. Sunday,
2-4pm.

Adam Smith Centre & Theatre
Bennochie Road, west of town centre
☎ 01592 260498

Leuchars
Leuchars Norman Church
A919 in village, 5 miles NW of St Andrews
Open: All reasonable times

Earlshall Castle
1 mile E of Leuchars
☎ 01334 839205
Open: Easter and June to September

Markinch
Balbirnie Craft Centre
In Balbirnie Park, Markinch
☎ 01592 755975
Open: All year, Tuesday to Saturday,
10am-5.30pm. Sunday, 1.30-5.30pm.

Newburgh
Laing Museum
Newburgh main street
☎ 01334 853722
Open: April to September, 11am-6pm,
Saturday & Sunday, 2-5pm. October to
March, 12noon-4pm, Sunday 2-5pm.

Newport
Balmarino Abbey
South shore of River Tay, 5 miles (8km)
south-west of Newport
☎ 0131 336 2157
Open: At all times.

North Queensferry
Deep Sea World
Under Forth Rail Bridge
☎ 01383 411411
Open: All year except Christmas & New
Year.

St Andrews
British Golf Museum
Next to the R&A in St Andrews
☎ 01334 473423
Open: Daily, June to October, 10am-
5.30pm. November, Tuesday to Sunday,
10am-5pm. December, Tuesday to
Saturday, 10am-4pm.

St Andrews Castle
Shore-line south of town centre
Historic Scotland ☎ 0131 244 3101
Open: April to September, Monday to
Saturday, 9.30am-7pm. Sunday, 2-7pm.
October to March, Monday to Saturday,
9.30am-4pm. Sunday, 2-4pm.

St Andrews Cathedral
Top of North Street or South Street
Historic Scotland ☎ 0131 244 3101
Open: April to September, Monday to
Saturday, 9.30am-7pm. Sunday, 2-7pm.
October to March, Monday to Saturday,
9.30am-4pm. Sunday, 2-4pm.

St Andrews Sea-life Centre
The Scores behind Golf Museum
☎ 01334 472950
Open: From 9am 7 days a week through
most of year.

Other Useful Information

Weathercall for this area
☎ 01898 500422

Golf
For information on golfing holidays to Scotland contact Discovery Golf
☎ 01382 228861

Cinemas, Theatre & Galleries

St Andrews
The Byre Theatre
Abbey Street
☎ 01334 476288

Crawford Art Centre
93 North Street
☎ 01334 474610
Open: All year, Monday to Saturday, 10am to 5pm. Sunday 2-5pm.

New Picture House
North Street
☎ 01334 473509

Tourist Information Offices

Anstruther
Scottish Fiheries Museum
☎ 01333 311073

Burntisland
4 Kirkgate
☎ 01592 872667

Crail
The Museum Marketgate
☎ 01333 450869

Cupar
The Granary Business Centre
☎ 01334 652874

St Andrews
70 Market Street
☎ 01334 472021

Dunfermline
13/15 Marygate
☎ 01383 720999

Glenrothes
Kingdom Centre
☎ 01592 754954

Kirkcaldy
17 Whytescauseway
☎ 01592 267775

Leven
The Beehive
Durie Street ☎ 01333 429464

Accommodation

Anstruther
Craw's Nest *
☎ 01333 310691

Dunfermline
Pitbauchlie House Hotel **
☎ 01383 722282

Kirkcaldy
Victoria Hotel **
☎ 01592 260117

Ladybank
Redlands country Lodge *
☎ 01337 831091

Lower Largo
Crusoe Hotel **
☎ 01333 320759

Markinch
Balbirnie House Hotel **
☎ 01592 610066

North Queensferry
Queensferry Lodge Hotel **
☎ 01383 410000

St Andrews
Old Course Hotel ***
☎ 01334 474371

Edenside House *
By St Andrews
☎ 01334 838108

Hazelbank Guest House **
☎ 01334 472466

Rufflets Hotel ***
☎ 01334 472594

Wormit
Sandford House Hotel **
☎ 01382 541802

Campsites

Kinghorn
Pettycur Bay Holiday Park
☎ 01592 890321

Kirkcaldy
Dunnikeir Caravan Park
☎ 01592 267563

St Andrews
Craigtoun
☎ 01334 75959

Tayside

5

Dundee is Scotland's fourth biggest city, sometimes referred to as the largest village in the world. This title has, no doubt, been gained by the friendliness of the natives and the fact that, when you walk down the High Street everyone seems to know one another. Dundee's river-front situation is noted for its fine views over the Tay to Fife and an exceptionally rich hinterland of mountains, moorland and farms.

Through the past two centuries Dundee has been a working-class town with large numbers employed in the jute and textile industries. This industrial base has now all but disappeared leaving the town with one of the highest rates of unemployment in Scotland. Despite efforts to brush up its image and attract more inward investment, recent militant action and the further departure of several large companies from the industrial scene is about all that has attracted media attention. Despite this the city retains a certain earthy quality that visitors seem to enjoy.

In the seventeenth century Dundee was considered to be the wealthiest burgh in Scotland making good use of its natural harbour to trade. Its prosperity declined when it was pillaged by the Duke of Montrose's army in 1645 and soon after in 1651 by an army of Roundheads lead by General Monk. The town and its people suffered greatly from the second sacking and did not re-emerge as a robust community until the mid-1800's with the coming of industrial expansion and occupations such as whaling and jute.

The most impressive approach to Dundee is by the Tay Road Bridge built in 1967 to replace the old ferries crossing between the town and Fife to the south. The present town centre extends around a medieval layout with four principal streets or gates leading to the High Street and old market area. The Cowgate, Seagate, Marketgate and Overgate still exist although the Overgate suffered unconsidered sixties re-development which replaced the crumbling old tenements and closes with a concrete shopping tunnel. It remains an architectural eye-sore, set amongst some relatively pleasant Georgian buildings.

Dundee's renown seems to revolve around the delights of the palate with its celebrated Dundee Cake as well as jam and marmalade jams. Its most famous preserve, Keillor's Marmalade, was established in the eighteenth century when a trading ship was stranded in port by storms with a hold full of sugar cane and Spanish bitter oranges. The cargo was in danger of deterioration and was purchased by James Keillor whose wife, using a quince recipe, created the famous 'marmalett' or marmalade. A local company, Mackay's of Carnoustie, is again making Dundee marmalade to the original recipe.

A walk north along Reform Street brings you to another group of distinctive buildings the most impressive of which is the Victorian McManus Galleries containing the city's principal museum and art gallery. The museum building, a splendid Gothic showpiece contains an over-all impression of the area's history from the prehistoric Picts to the Tay Bridge Disaster. There is a recreation of an old pub with an original mahogany bar as well as insights into the town's social fabric. Upstairs, the Albert Hall contains sculptures, silver and displays of furnishings while paintings from Dutch, Flemish, French and British artists as well as frequent contemporary exhibitions are found in the Victoria Gallery.

The dark-red sandstone building opposite the gallery is the headquarters of the D.C. Thomson empire, publishers of universally cherished titles such as the *Sunday Post*, *People's Friend*, the *Scot's Magazine*, the *Dandy* and *Beano* comics and many more popular journals. Across the road is Dundee's oldest burial ground, the Howff, a fascinating place to stroll through if you enjoy tombstones from as far back as 1567. The Barrack Street Museum, in sight to the west, specialises in natural history.

One of the most interesting buildings that survived the many conflicts of Dundee's past is the Old Steeple or St Mary's Tower just west of the City Square, reached by following Barrack Street south through the Overgate. This fifteenth-century tower is a fragment of the largest medieval church in Scotland, burnt down in 1841. The City Churches now surrounding the tower, are nineteenth century.

preceding page; Glamis Castle is the childhood home of the Queen Mother and her family, the Bowes-Lyons

Due to the town's nineteenth-century commercial interest in whaling, Dundee became a centre for ship-building. It was for this reason that Captain Robert Scott came to the town to find a ship for his two Antarctic expeditions. The story of the *Discovery* and Scott's quest to reach the South Pole is unfolded at Discovery Point, where the ship is now berthed, the strongest wooden ship ever built with a hull 75cm at its thinnest point.

In 1911, Scott and his companions died in sub-zero conditions only 11 miles (18km) from sanctuary. The *RRS Discovery* came back to Dundee in 1986 from St Catherine's Dock in London to great fanfare from the town's marketeers.

Further east along the river-front at Victoria Dock lie two other floating ✳ relics, the *HM Frigate Unicorn* and the *North Carr Lightship*. The *Unicorn* is Britain's oldest surviving battleship, a 46-gun wooden war vessel launched in Chatham in 1824 but never once firing her guns in anger. The adjacent *North Carr Lightship* did service off Fife Ness for more than 40 years and is now a museum where you can picture life for the seven-man crew in those cramped conditions for weeks on end.

Heading back towards the railway station at the foot of Crighton Street there is an interesting pub, the Galleon, serving helpings of good pub food. The Deep Sea Restaurant at the Nethergate has been around for decades and serves exceptional fish and chips. Try the Phoenix Bar along the street for more good food and hospitality or the Parrot Cafe for a more demure snack and a mile or so out, the Campbelltown on the Hawkhill for an unsophisticated sample of how pubs in Dundee used to be.

At Camperdown Park on the north-west edge of town there is a Wildlife Centre with brown bears, eagles and Scottish Wildcats along with a good, if rather hilly 18 hole golf course. There is a camping and caravanning park here also. Near Camperdown and well sign-posted is Shaw's ✳ Dundee Sweet Factory, where you can watch confectionery being made. Caird Park, at the opposite end of the Kingsway is the venue for Dundee's ⌐ Highland games in June and has two 9 hole golf courses along with a relatively flat but testing 18 hole course.

For an overall view of the city and its surrounds it is possible to drive 571 feet (174m) above sea level to the top of a volcanic plug, the Dundee Law. In 1831, Scotland's first passenger railway, the Dundee to Newtyle line, ran through a tunnel under this hill, now blocked off. Balgay Hill is clearly seen from here and is the site for Britain's only permanently manned public astronomical telescope at Mills Observatory.

The Tay Rail Bridge was built between 1871 and 1878, designed by Sir Thomas Bouch but the narrow, poorly designed structure collapsed in 1879 giving rise to the death of 90 passengers on board the train which happened to be crossing at the time. The second and existing construction is 2 miles (3½km) long supported by 86 piers. The stumps of the original bridge can still be seen alongside the present piers.

East of Dundee along the river is the old fishing village of **Broughty Ferry**, now a suburb of the city but with its own distinctive character. It is a good place to walk around or visit for a meal and a drink in the evening.

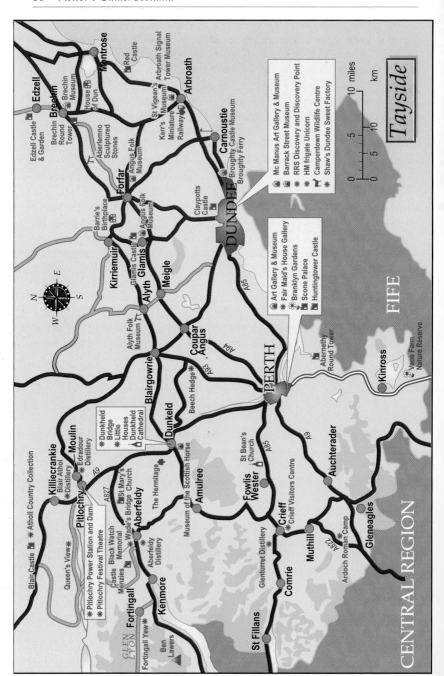

The story of RRS Discovery *and Scott's quest to reach the South Pole is unfolded at Dundee's 'Discovery Point'*

The Ferry has a reputation for many good pubs and restaurants. There are interesting little shops, art dealers and gift outlets on Bruce Street and Gray Street. Along the foreshore there are extensive views across to Fife and up the Tay. Broughty Castle stands at the mouth of the Tay, overlooking the harbour, built to defend the river from Crimean Russian warships. The existing castle is now a branch of Dundee Museums and, on four levels, it tells the story of the local fishing community, and whaling.

For collectors of miniature castles and cottages, the structure at the top of Claypotts Road (junction of the A92 and B978) might look familiar. **Claypotts Castle** is the inspiration for the best-selling model probably due to its stocky but classic castle outline. Built in 1588, its staggered, 3 unit, Z-shape was highly practical, offering comfort and ease of movement to the occupants while making it easier to defend.

Following the coastal route through Monifieth, Barrie Mill, signposted off to the left is a restored and working flour mill. **Carnoustie**, further on, is best known for its Championship golf course, on the itinerary of most serious golfers. There are pleasant walks along the beach here and a leisure centre that offers indoor sports. The A92 coast road north arrives in the fishing and holiday town of **Arbroath**, a major centre for the county of Angus.

Reformation, once again, brought vandalism and neglect to the Abbey of Arbroath. Stones were taken to construct many of the older buildings you see in Arbroath today although interesting portions survive such as the south transept and massively proportioned front entrance. There is a small museum occupying the Abbot's House.

Through later years Arbroath was renowned for its sail-canvas while it became even more famous for smokies or smoked haddock found in nearly forty fishmongers or curing houses around the front where the process of smoking can still be observed. The hot cure method, a traditional technique using kilns or 'smoke barrels' results in a cooked, smoked fish that can be eaten hot or cold. For fish of the battered variety, queues regularly form along the sandstone tenement walls at the front in anticipation of a fish supper from Peppo's, one of the most popular fish and chip shops in Scotland. The harbour is a focus of activity in Arbroath even if it is just to sit and eat a steaming 'poke' of fish and chips.

Along the West Links Promenade you will find the inspiration for many childhood memories of a holiday in Arbroath, the miniature railway. Everything is to scale, tiny sheds, miniature signals and dwarf bridges. Kerr's Miniature Railway has been running for over half a century and has not changed much in that time. Next to the diminutive train station is the terminus for the miniature bus or fire engine.

Next to the harbour is the Signal Tower, now a museum and art gallery with displays on fishing, the flax industry and natural history. The building was a former signalling station for the Bell Rock or Inchcape Lighthouse which, on a clear day, can be seen 12 miles (19km) out in the mouth of the Tay.

It is possible to walk along the tops of the Arbroath Cliffs also known as Seaton Cliffs to the little fishing cove of Auchmithie. These cocoa-col-

oured cliffs are older than 350 million years and many sea-birds can be
seen especially fulmar, gannet and the occasional puffin, fishing off-
shore. The cliffs are unfenced and can be dangerous if you stray off the
path. It is a 6 mile (10km) walk there and back and the path becomes
rather confused on reaching the wooded glade near Auchmithie where
you can find yourself wading through corn fields. Auchmithie is equally
accessible by road and said to be the first home of the smokie, it is perched
on a rugged headland above a wide, pebble beach and ancient harbour.
The 'But and Ben' restaurant here serves some of the tastiest local dishes
such as a smoked haddock pancake done in a cream sauce or, for a really
traditional dish, try their 'tatties, mince and skirly'.

Coming out of Arbroath there is a turning left, off the A92, through a
modern housing estate and down to a fascinating little hamlet called St
Vigeans. **St Vigeans** is quite unlike the other farming villages in these
parts, especially in its architecture. Its centre piece is a small, red sandstone church perched on a steep knoll, the site dating from the twelfth
century or earlier. There is a distinctive row of cottages surrounding the
knoll and one has been converted into a miniature museum. Here, the
remains of a large collection of Pictish standing stones are housed. Many
of the original stones were incorporated as building materials for the
church and surrounding cottages and others are sadly mutilated. The
Drosten Stone is the most notable, a carved cross-slab of the ninth century
with animals, birds and a hooded archer carved in relief.

Back on the coast, the fine, wide sands of Lunan Bay make an ideal
escape. Watching over the sands is **Redcastle**, a lonely, ruined fortification of the twelfth century, first built by King William the Lion as a royal
hunting seat to protect the coast from marauding Danish pirates. It can be
explored by climbing the steep path from the beach or there is easier
access from the minor coastal road behind the castle.

The mouth of River South Esk at Montrose is one of the most important
sites in Britain for wintering wildfowl. Each winter sees over 12,000
pinkfeet and 2,000 greylag geese roosting in the basin after spending the
day feeding on nearby farm-land. There are several hides around the
basin. From the car park at Mains of Dun off the A935 follow a track to
two hides or from the car park at the north-east corner on A935 there is a
hide 500 yards to the south. A warden naturalist may be available.

The town of **Montrose** is a curious combination of maritime and rustic.
The oil industry of the last 20 years has brought benefits while the rich
surrounding farm-land has always been a reason for the burgh's wealth.
There is a large medieval market square in the middle of the main street.
The seafront is a major attraction with a wide beach and coastal links
providing space and plenty fresh air for recreation or relaxation. There
are football fields, play parks and two 18 hole golf courses. Tennis is
available on courts in the town and there is a nearby public swimming
pool and fitness centre.

Three miles (5km) west of Montrose on the A936 is the **House of Dun**,
one of the most original houses designed by William Adam. A rather

The Phoenix Bar in Dundee's Nethergate is one of several good pubs in the West End of Town

Arbroath 'Smokies' are considered a delicacy througout Scotland

severe, Palladian mansion surrounded by a beautiful garden and out-buildings, the house is now run by National Trust for Scotland who have done an admirable job in restoring it from a fairly dilapidated state. The exhilarating eighteenth-century plaster-work found in the Saloon is a particular tribute to the restorer's talent as well as that of the original craftsmen.

Brechin is an important town in this strongly agricultural region of Angus. The surrounding Vale of Strathmore is one of Scotland's most productive farming belts. Visitors come to see the cathedral and tower situated on the banks above the South Esk along Chanonry Wynd. The tower, dating from AD990 is one of only two such round towers in Scotland, the other being at Abernethy in Perthshire. Supposedly, these towers were constructed to offer protection during Viking raids. The library in St Ninian's Square is also the local museum with information on the cathedral and tower as well as details of industry and archaeology around the area.

It is interesting to observe the countryside as you cut across the Vale of Strathmore, north towards **Edzell**. This is prime farming country but it changes as it edges towards the higher ground around Glen Esk. Fishing is popular on the River North Esk with a variety of trout and salmon beats. The village of Edzell commences with the triumphal Dalhousie Arch commemorating Queen Victoria's visit.

Edzell Castle is found along a country road at the north-west end of the village turning left opposite the Panmure Arms Hotel. The castle is an imposing sixteenth-century ruin. The most impressive remaining feature is the walled garden or pleasance where visitors often linger with a sketch pad or paints to capture the grandeur of the garden and castle ruins from this sheltered spot.

The road through Glen Esk following the River North Esk is a beautiful drive through gentle hill-country always changing in its nature as you progress up the glen. The Glen Esk Folk museum, about 12 miles (19km) from Edzell, is a commemoration to life over the past 200 years in the glen and most of the items on display came from local cottages. If they are not too busy, try and get a conversation going with the women running the centre as they are mostly local and have many tales to tell about the micro-culture preserved in this secluded glen.

Returning south on the busy A90, the market town of **Forfar** was once established as a jute and flax milling centre making use of its close proximity to Dundee and the River Tay. Its industry is now more reliant on the production of man-made fabrics as well as firms that serve the agricultural community. The Forfar Bridie, a flat meat pie with or without onions, has a far-reaching reputation with North American Scots. More alarming is the Forfar Bridle, a vicious device used to restrain so called witches as they were burned at the stake. This is on display in Forfar's museum found in the Meffan Institute on West High Street. The inland Forfar Golf Club on the A932 east of town has peculiar swells similar to a links course attributed to jute being stacked in rows to dry in bygone days and leaving marked undulations on what are now fairways. Six miles (10km) north-east of Forfar on the B9134 are the **Aberlemno Sculptured Stones**. The first of these Pictish story books of stone is found in the churchyard behind the village and there are three more further up the hill at the side of the road but be sure to park off the road.

Kirriemuir, only 6 miles (10km) from Forfar on the A926 is typical of Angus towns, little changed over the past century with clusters of deep, red sandstone buildings and a mix of agricultural and textile industries that came to this part of Angus in the eighteenth century. It is most famous as the birthplace of J.M. Barrie, a local handloom-weaver's son and creator of *Peter Pan*. Barrie's birthplace is an unassuming little cottage at No.9 Brechin Road and a Peter Pan statue overlooks the town's square. Despite being offered a resting place at Westminster Abbey in London, Barrie chose to be buried in Hill Cemetery off the Brechin Road, the B957.

The Angus Glens are rugged expanses on the southernmost edge of the Grampian Mountains, little changed over the years apart from the occasional renovation of a cottage, offer easy hikes up to Loch Brandy or, at just over 3,000ft (915m) Mayar, with access to more strenuous tasks such as Jock's Road. The single track road from Clova Hotel to the parking area at the foot of Glen Doll is prone to traffic jams in the summer months. There is a Youth Hostel at Glen Doll, a converted hunting-lodge that is popular with walkers. Fly, bait or spin fishing for sea trout or salmon on a 3 mile (5km) stretch of the River South Esk is also available through the hotel.

Glen Prosen is perhaps less popular than its neighbour but for walkers that enjoy the peace of the hillsides to themselves this airy valley may be preferred.

Due south from Kirriemuir, **Glamis Castle** is the childhood home of the Queen Mother and her family, the Bowes-Lyons, Earls of Strathmore and Kinghorne. Along with a resident ghost, reputedly that of Lady Janet Douglas who was burnt at the stake for witchcraft, this striking citadel has hosted many royal visitors throughout its history. The core of the castle was established in the fifteenth century with most of what you see today built in the seventeenth century. Tours through the castle's rooms are permitted. The works of art reflect earlier periods of life at court with glimpses into the more casual lifestyle of today's royalty. Glamis is also the setting for the murder of Duncan in Shakespeare's 'Macbeth'. In July of each year the Scottish Transport Extravaganza is held here and vintage vehicles from around the world turn up in their antiquated splendour. There is a good restaurant and plenty of space in the grounds to stroll and relax. In the village of **Glamis** is the Angus Folk Museum, a terraced row of agricultural workers cottages restored in 1957 and containing the fascinating bric-a-brac of country life. From Glamis you cross into the eastern edge of Perthshire, dominated by the Vale of Strathmore and lands long associated with Glamis Castle.

Alyth is a pleasant little Perthshire town lying at the foot of the Braes o' Angus. Passing under the old Roman Bridge, the Alyth Burn runs

through the town centre and the park beyond. The tiny Alyth Folk
Museum overlooking the burn, houses a collection of agricultural and
domestic artifacts. Above the town on Barry Hill there is an Iron Age fort,
part of a series of hilltop forts throughout Fife and Angus. Legend has it
that Queen Guinevere was imprisoned here. There is a steep-sided,
wooded valley further up the Alyth Burn called Den of Alyth. This gorge
was carved out during the Ice Age and can be wet underfoot.

Blairgowrie lies at the heart of raspberry growing country and is also
a main accommodation and facilities centre for the Glen Shee Ski Resort
24 miles (39km) to the north. Its fame as a soft fruit producer started in
1898 when a local resident decided to grow wild raspberries as a commercial crop. Today, with its favourable soil and climate, it is the major soft
fruit growing district in the British Isles. The town has a relaxed air with
a selection of woollen mill outlets and pleasant cafés or ice cream shops.
Keithbank Mill and Heraldry Centre is located on the Braemar Road, the
A93, just north of town. There is an engine house and water-wheel still in
working order. A coffee shop is located in the mill's lower section serving
Blairgowrie Cream Teas. A footbridge leads over the River Ericht to
explore Cargill's Leap as well as interesting short woodland walks leading back into town or up to the Knocky, a rise overlooking the town. Well
Meadow in the heart of town is a nice place to sit and watch the world go
by.

Following the signs from Blairgowrie to Braemar using the twisting
and undulating A93, you find Bridge of Cally where the River Ardle and
Black Water converge. This is a good spot for hill walkers and climbers
who set out from the car park. An alternative route, if you are heading
back to the Pitlochry area is along the B950 to Kirkmichael, popular for
day trips or holidays. The Spittal of Glenshee has eating facilities, a hotel
and woollen shop. 'Spittal' was a general term for a hospice or shelter for
travellers particularly on higher ground. Glen Shee is one of the most
popular ski resorts in Scotland. Perhaps not as developed as its European
counterparts, it still attracts thousands of skiers throughout the winter
depending on the weather. The Cairnwell Chairlift at the Pass of
Glenshee is open throughout the summer offering easy access to the
fabulous views across the Grampian and Cairngorm Mountains.

To the south of Blairgowrie, **Coupar Angus** at the western end of the
Vale of Strathmore, is a busy little market town. There was once a flourishing Cistercian abbey here beside the present Dundee Road but only
the gatehouse remains almost merged into the surrounding foliage. The
abbey was built by Malcolm IV around 1164 and was destroyed in 1559.
The site of the old monks chapel is now covered by the parish church but
you can still see the remains of the original piers from the nave. The Jail
Tower, built in 1762, quite nearby the abbey ruins on the A923, is currently being renovated.

Five miles (8km) to the north-east of Coupar Angus is **Meigle**, once
another major Pictish centre. Its old school house has been converted into
a museum that houses thirty Pictish carved stones and four fragments

dating back to the seventh century. The carving on the stones is intricate with one showing Daniel in the Lion's den. Others show swimming elephants, mirrors and combs. The largest stone, according to an American professor and leading Arthurian scholar, may be the burial stone of Queen Guinevere, King Arthur's wife. In Meigle's ancient kirkyard nearby, there lies a large burial mound known as Vanora's tomb where the immense stone is supposed to have marked Guinevere's grave. Passing through Coupar Angus again, the Dunsinane Hill Vitrified Fort is found just off the A94 Coupar Angus-Perth road and reached by a steep path. It is a good example of the many such hilltop forts found throughout Perthshire.

Perth is the communications centre for this part of Tayside and long referred to as the 'Gateway to the Highlands' although the hills are still a fair drive on. The 'Fair City' as it is also dubbed, with its tall spires and shallow River Tay flowing through it is surrounded by two wide parklands, the North Inch, the site of the famous Battle of the Clans in 1396 and the South Inch where today there are various facilities for bowling, boating and field games. There is strong evidence of Roman occupation of this area although the town does not appear in records until the twelfth century. Later it was to become Scotland's capital, much favoured by James I. The walled, royal burgh with its navigable river provided an excellent inland port making Perth prosperous through the sixteenth century.

Perth Art Gallery and Museum presents exhibitions that illustrate the development of local industry particularly whisky which remains very important to the area along with the insurance industry. Silverwork is also on display fashioned by the county's craftsmen of three centuries and there are good depictions of Perth's local history. The Fair Maid's House situated behind Charlotte Street in North Port was the home of Sir Walter Scott's heroine, Catherine Glover and is one of the oldest houses in Perth. It contains a well stocked and popular craft and gift shop. The nearby Church of St John is quite small and unadorned and was the scene of John Knox's most inflammatory sermons in 1559.

The famous Aberdeen Angus Bull Shows are held early in February and October at the Agricultural Centre on the Crieff Road near the outskirts of town. The Perthshire Agricultural Show is held in August and horse racing takes place regularly at Scone race-course. The city of Perth also offers a fine Victorian theatre with an excellent restaurant and bar inside. Shopping is of a high quality and variety and there is a good level of accommodation. B&B's are concentrated on the north side of town.

To the north-east of Perth is Kinnoul Hill, one of Perthshire's best vantage points, reached by either a short drive and half mile woodland walk from the car park (quite steep in parts) or a steady 40 minute walk from the town. The extraordinary view from this precarious vantage point overlooks the east end of Perth, the River Tay and the Carse of Gowrie with distant views north to the Grampians. Branklyn Gardens, (open to the public) at the foot of Kinnoul Hill has been described as the finest two acres of private garden in the country.

Perth Leisure Pool, just off the Glasgow Road, is Scotland's most advanced water-works complete with flumes, wild-water rides, an outdoor lagoon and bubble beds. Further west is Bell's Cherrybank Gardens just off the A9 on the Glasgow Road and part of the whisky distiller, Arthur Bell's head office. It incorporates the Bell's National Heather Collection along with a bright, pleasant café.

The village of **Abernethy** is found by passing through Bridge of Earn and following the A913. It overlooks the upper reaches of the Tay and is a charming, unspoilt conservation village, an ancient Pictish capital in an area of manifold Pictish artifacts.

At the southern entrance to Tayside, **Kinross** is a main town surrounded by several interesting areas. In the town itself is a seventeenth-century Tolbooth and in the High Street a museum devoted to local history, linen and peat. In summer, the gardens at Kinross House offer the experience of a magnificent seventeenth-century formal design with yew hedges, herbaceous borders and rose beds to accompany the wonderful views across Loch Leven. The island and its fortress set in the middle of this famous trout fishing loch was the prison of Mary Queen of Scots. It can be visited by taking the small ferry from Kirkgate Park in Kinross. In 1567 Mary Queen of Scots was exiled to Loch Leven Castle.

Five miles (8km) south of Kinross is a converted farm with displays that interpret the local environment and its animal inhabitants. The area surrounding Vane Farm is a favourite resting place for wild geese and ducks and there are facilities provided to observe these and other animals more closely throughout the year. The Butterfly Farm at Turfhills in Kinross is a tropical habitat for butterflies and moths from around the world. There is also a children's farm, an aviary, café and gift shop.

Going back into Perth and travelling west on the A85 you arrive at **Huntingtower Castle**, a castellated mansion, originally the hunting seat of the Earl of Ruthven. The painted timber ceiling on the first floor of the eastern tower is one of the earliest of its kind done around 1540. Another feature is the dovecote in the garret of the western tower.

Travelling west again along the A85 **Fowlis Wester**, 5 miles (8km) before Crieff, is a charming little conservation village. The thirteenth-century Church of St Bean houses a richly carved, eighth-century Pictish stone while the village square holds a 10ft (3m) high Pictish cross slab bearing a cross on one side and an equestrian scene on the other.

Crieff is situated on the southern slope of an impressive wooded hill, the Knock, on the physical and cultural boundary between the Scottish Highlands and the Lowlands.

Crieff's history includes the town being the administrative capital of twelfth-century Celtic Earls. It later grew to become one of the most famous market towns of Scotland where Highlanders drove their cattle from as far as Caithness and the Outer Hebrides to feed the growing population of the Lowlands. Many were hanged on the kine gallows at Gallowhaugh — now Gallowhill. The Weaver's House and Highland Tryst Museum in Crieff shows the development and skills of the Master

Weavers of Strathearn and the traditional tartans for which they became famous.

The Perthshire Highland Golf Ticket can be purchased at the Crieff Tourist Information Office allowing play on the six participating 9 hole courses throughout a 5 day period and is exceptional value.

Crieff Visitor Centre is a commercial development just south of the town. Here you will find traditional crafts allied to modern technology to produce the internationally known Stuart Crystal. The fascinating process of blowing the molten glass can be watched from the viewing gallery. Across the road is the Crieff Plant Centre, Buchan Pottery and Perthshire Paperweights with a myriad of potential gifts. There is also a modern self-service restaurant which serves a variety of good dishes.

Innerpeffray Library, 4 miles (6km) south-east of Crieff, is a must for book-worms or anyone interested in Scotland's oldest surviving free-lending library which houses 3,000 titles printed between 1502 and 1800.

Drummond Castle, 2 miles (3km) south of Crieff, was originally built around 1490 but destroyed intentionally in 1745 by its owner, the Duchess of Perth, to prevent its falling into the hands of Cromwell's troops. It was then rebuilt in Tudor style and includes a magnificent Italian formal garden. **Muthill** is another conservation village 3 miles (5km) south of Crieff on the A822. It is largely unspoilt with late eighteenth- and early nineteenth-century housing and architecture. The church at the village's centre was once an important fifteenth-century focus of worship with an earlier twelfth century Norman tower.

Continuing south on the A823 brings you to **Auchterarder**, a long Strathearn town with a fairly rich historical past and most of its older buildings hugging the High Street. The town became chief burgh of the important earldom of Strathearn shortly after the turn of the eleventh century. During an early Jacobite rising in 1715 the town was destroyed by the retreating Earl of Mar. The tower in the old churchyard is the only remnant of the town's turbulent past. In rooms above the tourist office, a heritage display illustrates the regions past. The sumptuous Gleneagles Hotel, golf courses and leisure complex sits above a scenic wooded and moorland glen surrounded by the Ochil Hills with Glen Devon to the south. Contrary to its inference, the name, Gleneagles, is not associated with that majestic bird of prey but is Gaelic for 'glen of the church'.

Ardoch Roman Camp, 10 miles (16km) south of Crieff near Braco on the A822, dates back to the second century. This was one of the largest Roman encampments of ancient Britain.

To the west of Crieff about 1 mile (2km) on the A85 is Scotland's oldest Malt Scotch Whisky distillery. Established in 1775 alongside the Shaggie Burn, the **Glenturret Distillery** offers guided tours around the stills. It also has an award winning visitor's heritage centre. The distillery also offers two good restaurants, the Smuggler's and the Pagoda Room, a gift and whisky shop with, of course, a whisky tasting bar.

Comrie's claim to fame might be that it sits directly on the Highland Boundary fault and experiences regular earth tremors of no great consequence. Earthquake House, built in 1874, situated just outside Comrie at the Ross, contains a replica of the first seismometers set up here in the Victorian era. At midnight on Hogmany in Comrie, a unique Flambeaux Procession takes place, a torchlight parade through the streets to drive out the evil spirits for the coming year, followed by the usual Scottish exuberance for this particular holiday period. Just north of Comrie is the Deil's Cauldron which is a grand waterfall carrying the River Lednock down to meet the River Earn. Two miles (3km) south of town on the B827 is the Auchingarrich Wildlife Centre which holds the largest bird collection in Scotland in its 100 acres (40hectares). There are 17 ponds with 100 species of water-fowl and a wild bird hatchery where you can watch newly hatched chicks. Wallabies, Highland cattle and deer occupy the larger enclosures. Afterwards there is the welcoming Pine Lodge restaurant.

At the eastern end of Loch Earn still following the A85, **St Fillans** is frequently regarded as one of Scotland's best kept secrets and another choice stopping place. The village, formerly known as Port of Lochearn, was later called St Fillans after the Celtic missionary from Ireland called Faolan. In the sixth century he established himself on Dunfillan or St Fillan's hill and set about converting the local Picts to Christianity. Here too, are water-sports and sailing although most of the activity is based around Loch Earn Caravan Park on the south side of this end of the loch. A more sedate site is the St Fillan's Caravan Site at the old railway station.

Following the shoreline to Lochearnhead then north to Killin on the A85, both villages part of Perthshire but now governed by Central Region, it is possible to return to Perth along the shores of Loch Tay on the A827. **Ben Lawers** is Tayside's highest mountain at 3,984ft (1,215m) and famous for its alpine plants growing on southerly facing slopes. To find them may not be easy but a visit to the Ben Lawers Visitor's Centre run by the National Trust for Scotland will help to understand this rare and special environment. Ben Lawers has been a National Nature Reserve since 1975.

Glen Lyon can be entered continuing past the Ben Lawers Visitor Centre on the minor road heading north, an interesting drive over some high moorland. It is the longest of the Scottish Glens and was Campbell country before the Clearances but now it caters mainly for sheep. Set back a few miles from Loch Tay at its eastern end is the village of **Fortingall**. The row of cottages are particularly enchanting, most of them still thatched. Near the church at the east end of the village is the Fortingall Yew. This undistinguished piece of vegetation, now split and sagging like a badly tended and overgrown bush, is perhaps the oldest living thing in Europe. At around 3,000 years old it was in existence during the era of the Roman Empire and the birth of Christ. Another surprising aspect of Fortingall is the myth that Pontious Pilot was born here. It is said that his father was a Roman envoy sent by Caesar Augustus to help quell the warlike activities of the Picts and he had a child with a local woman, perhaps one of the Menzies Clan. The father returned to Rome with his son. Later in life, Pontious returned to retire and die here in Fortingall. The legend has been further substantiated by the discovery earlier this century, of a large stone slab near the village bearing the initials P.P.

Kenmore is one of Perthshire's activity centres. Situated on the east end of Loch Tay there is a host of water-sport activities such as water-skiing, jet skiing, sailing, and further down the river, white-water rafting. It is also one of Scotland's premier salmon fishing sites.

There is a good camping site on the banks of the river for touring caravans and tents or for renting holiday caravans. The farm steading also offers accommodation in cottages or, for hikers, in a communal bothy. There is an excellent bistro on site along with a boules pit, a 9 hole golf course and, in the bistro in the evening, regular musical entertainment. On the opposite side of the loch is Croft-na-Caber Activity Centre where, along with trying jet skis and dinghies, you can visit a fascinating, educational development where a replica Crannog or Bronze Age defensive loch-dwelling has been built. These habitats, the replica being 50ft (15m) in diameter and thatched with examples of tools and domestic utensils inside, were popular in this area from the Bronze Age until around 300 years ago. There were 18 crannogs in Loch Tay alone. The onshore interpretive centre shows artifacts, timbers and other underwater discoveries as well as video and slide presentations.

From Kenmore you can take the steep back road climbing across Glen Quaich to Amulree (10 miles/16km). Once you have negotiated the steepest part of the road stop and look back over the valley of Loch Tay and Kenmore. The prospect is exceptional and this is a fine spot for a pastoral picnic with views. The narrow road then twists over moorland and past lochan. Isolated as it is, this area was once a favourite hunting ground for Scottish Kings. **Amulree** was an important junction of the old drove roads where the cattle drovers broke their long journeys. There is a hotel in Amulree, established in 1714, where Bonnie Prince Charlie rested. Following the old drove road, the A822 descends from Amulree towards Crieff. It passes through the 'Sma Glen', a colourful valley surrounding the River Almond. In the late summer the hills, rising steeply on either side of the glen, come alive with blossoming purple heather. You can also see salmon leaping at various points on the river at this time of the year. The best place is the Buchanty Spout in Glen Almond on the B8063.

Returning north on the A826, **Aberfeldy** has been a popular touring centre for the past two centuries. The Birks are worth visiting and only require a short stroll from a car park on the A826 or a slightly longer walk from the town following the Moness Burn. The cool glades and waterfalls surrounding this small glen gave inspiration to the Bard and many after him. The town is busy throughout the summer but there is still the air of a rural village with little 'tourist' pressure evident on the area. There are a fair amount of amenities such as cafés, restaurants, shops and accommodation but it is scaled down compared to other tourist parts. Aberfeldy Water Mill, driven by the Moness Burn which runs through the town centre, is a restored and working mill which still produces its

Scone

Scone Palace just north of Perth is a site of great historical significance. Here, at Moot Hill, just in front of the present-day palace, Scotland's Kings from Robert the Bruce to James VI came to be crowned. The tiny chapel you see today is perched on a small mound known as Moot Hill. The earls and chieftains allied to the king were charged to bring soil from their land in their boots and swear fealty to the Lord High Ardh while standing on their own 'land'. Having taken the oath, they emptied out the contents and formed Moot or Boot Hill.

The ancient Abbey of Scone, which stood nearby the present palace, was another victim of the followers of John Knox and nothing remains of this site. Scone is also known to have been the centre of the Scoto — Pictish Kingdom. Kenneth MacAlpin, King of Scots, established the ceremonial enthronement of the Scottish Kings on the Stone of Destiny here. The famous stone was brought to Scone in the ninth century for this purpose and such was the Stone's importance that it was removed to Westminster Abbey in London by Edward I following his victory over the Scots in 1296. It has been part of the Coronation Chair ever since although it was temporarily removed by Scots Nationalists in the 1950's and supposedly recovered but rumours have circulated that it was hidden in a church in Dundee and a false stone put in its place.

Scone Palace, originally a sixteenth century castellated mansion, enlarged and embellished in 1803, is richly furnished in neo-Gothic style with some superb pieces of French furniture, ivory and porcelain. It is still a family home and is open from Easter until October for the public. There are good facilities in and surrounding the house making it worth a prolonged stop.

own stone-ground oatmeal. In the late summer, look out for the Kenmore to Aberfeldy Raft Race where various teams from local companies and organizations paddle their way down the tumbling Tay rapids to scoop the prize or otherwise. There are other 'sights' to be seen before the race in Kenmore where there is a contest between the crews to see who comes up with the zaniest attire.

Wades Bridge, a short stroll from the town centre, was designed by William Adam in 1733 and built by General Wade to carry troops north over the River Tay to suppress the warring Highlanders. It is perhaps the finest example of Wade's designs and a vital link in the network of roads that he created. Nearby is the Black Watch Monument and cairn, an imposing statue of a kilted soldier commemorating the formation of that

Regiment in 1739. Crossing the bridge, **Castle Menzies**, 1 mile (2km) west of the town on the B846, is a sixteenth-century tower-house, home of the Clan Menzies. Their history and mementos are displayed in a small museum which is open from Easter until October. Although under restoration by the Menzies Clan Society following years of serious neglect, the Z-plan fortified residence has splendid plaster-work ceilings and also a single, green satin, eighteenth-century lady's shoe found behind one of the walls, all making it worthy of a visit. This road carries on to Tummel Bridge.

Aberfeldy Distillery on the east side of Aberfeldy was founded in 1898 by the Dewar family and has a free visitor's reception and shop. St Mary's Church is a few more miles east on the A827 — take the signposted farm road past Pitcairn Farm to the top of the hill. Inside is one of the best examples of seventeenth-century painted, wooden ceilings containing pastoral scenes from the local Stewart landowners period as well as biblical and heraldic designs that remain quite clear. Grandtully on the A827 between Aberfeldy and Ballinluig is known for its white water rapids and attracts canoeists from all over the country. The rapids are said to be the fastest, natural white-water in the UK and it is a thrilling sight to watch the experts career through the narrow gates whilst negotiating fierce currents and eddies.

Returning to the notorious A9, a road that should always be treated with care, you find the Victorian Spa town of **Pitlochry**, the touring mecca of Perthshire. There are plenty of hotels, restaurants, cafés, gift shops and woollen mills to while away the day. Since the coming of the railway in 1863 it has been a fashionable holiday or retirement spot and the town retains a Victorian air of dignified repose. Queen Victoria favoured the spot with its longer-than-unusual hours of sunshine and lack of rain.

One of the main attractions in the town is the Pitlochry Dam which created Loch Faskally, an acceptable example of a man-made loch. There are nine hydro stations in the Tummel Valley and the Exhibition and Visitor Centre on the west side of the dam shows how hydro electricity works and how it benefits the country and the environment. Next to the Visitor Centre is a fish ladder with an intriguing observation chamber. Here it is possible to watch the migrating salmon take a rest before tackling the next rung on the ladder. This helps the spawning fish to return to their egg-laying grounds further up the river. Rowing boats are available on Loch Faskally from a pier just beyond the Green Hotel.

Blair Atholl Distillery on the south side of the town offers guided tours around one of the best known distilleries with a free dram available at the end. There is an excellent whisky gift shop as well as a coffee shop.

Hidden away in woods 3 miles (5km) east of the town is Edradour Distillery. Founded in 1825 by a group of farmers, this is one of the most delightful little distilleries in Scotland.

Pitlochry is a good place for easy walks either north towards Killiecrankie or south along the river and across the bridge to the Pitlochry Festival Theatre. Its lively summer programme runs eight plays in 6 days. The tent-like interior of the foyer reflects the old marquee from which the theatre started in 1951. Just 1 mile (2km) or so south of Pitlochry is the Dunfallandy Stone, an eighth-century Pictish Sculptured slab. Just ⊓ outside Pitlochry on the A924 going east is the interesting village of **Moulin**. For exercise that will be rewarded, a path just behind the Moulin Hotel will take you up an easy ascent to the top of Craigower Hill where you can enjoy a magnificent view of Strath Tummel to the west. The church in the village was rebuilt in 1874 on a site which was used for Christian worship for many centuries. The ruins of the thirteenth-century Castle Dubh is also in the village. Legend has it that in 1500 the men of the castle contacted the plague and, in an effort to contain the disease, the stronghold was battered down by cannon with the soldiers inside. There now stands a mournful cairn for the men of the garrison.

A glimpse to your left as you travel north on the A9 past Pitlochry reveals a deep wooded gorge, the scene of one of the most significant battles in Scottish history. The Jacobite uprising in the late seventeenth and early eighteenth centuries was an attempt by the supporters of the Stewart dynasty to prevent the Hanoverian succession. In 1689 the first shots of this long and bloody struggle were fired at the Pass of Killiecrankie. The National Trust for Scotland centre at **Killiecrankie** tells the story of the battle and the natural history of the area. It also provides guides and ranger services. A much visited spot is the 'Soldier's leap' where a government troop, Duncan MacBean, successfully leaped 18ft (5m) to escape the Highlanders. The centre is open from March to October and there is a Trust shop and snack bar. There is an excellent circular walk through varied woodland from the Visitor's Centre to Pitlochry with options that take in the Pass of Killiecrankie, River Garry, Loch Fascallay, Pitlochry Dam and Clunie Power Station.

Following the B8090 west out of Pitlochry turn left at Garry Bridge. There is a car park at the far end of the bridge and it is worth stopping to walk back and enjoy the views. Looking out from either side of the bridge there are fine vistas over the Pass of Killiecrankie with the rounded bulk of Beinn a' Ghlo in the distance and the Rivers Garry and Tummel to the south. From here the road twists and dips for a few miles but it makes for an interesting drive through ever more beautiful countryside. The **Queen's View**, car park and Visitor Centre appear on the left after a sharp bend. The spectacular vista that looks up the length of Loch Tummel was brought to acclaim following Queen Victoria's visit in 1866 but it bore the same title well before this. The loch has been enlarged with hydro electric schemes that operate throughout these lochs and rivers. The new Visitor Centre illustrates the activities taking place in Loch Tummel Forest including its wildlife and conservation efforts.

South of Loch Rannoch and visible from Queen's View is the cone-shape of one of Perthshire's most distinctive mountains, the Schiehallion at 3,547ft (1,082m), otherwise known as the Fairy Mountain of the Caledonians and a place of worship for the Picts. This is a popular hike for those that are suitably equipped. A car park about 6 miles (10km) south

Blair Castle

Blair Castle is one of the most popular visitor attractions in Scotland. It began as a tower in 1269 then went on to become the centre of the Atholl Dukedom held successively by the Stewart and Murray families. It was occupied by Cromwellian troops in 1652 and transformed into its present appearance in the nineteenth century. The entrance to the castle is often graced by the presence of the castle piper, welcoming visitors as they enter the halls. Inside is a diverse collection of weapons, furniture and china from many different eras in the castle's history. The Tapestry Room contains a noteworthy four-poster bed topped with ostrich feathers. The Old Scots Room is a fascinating representation of a typical Victorian estate worker's cottage, furnished with a box bed, a child's cradle and spinning wheel. There are deer and Highland cattle in the surrounding fields. Inside the castle, next to the gift shop, is a self-service licensed restaurant.

Amongst Blair Castle's most famous visitors are: Mary Queen of Scots, Bonnie Prince Charlie, Robert Burns and Queen Victoria. Today, it is the home of the present Duke of Atholl who is the only individual in Britain to retain his own private army. The eighty strong Atholl Highlanders are the sole survivors of the ancient clan system where the king relied on his chiefs to bring forth men and build the king's forces.

The village of Dunkeld on the banks of the river Tay

of Tummel Bridge marks the beginning of the walk which is quite steep at first but eases as you scale the magnificent broad back of this mountain. In 1774, the Schiehallion was used for early experiments to judge the weight of the Earth, not very successfully, but in the process one of the scientific members, Charles Hutton, invented Contour Lines as an aid in surveying the mountain. It is possible to scale and descend Schiehallion in around 5 hours but good hill walking boots are essential to cope with the fields of shale near the top.

Following the B8090 from Queen's View brings you to Tummel Bridge, Kinloch Rannoch and Rannoch Station. The road stays close to the loch sides and offers the best views of Schiehallion's coned configuration. To the south you can see the remains of a native pine forest, the Black Wood of Rannoch.

Returning to the A9, the village of **Blair Atholl** is one of the last Perthshire outposts before going north through the Grampians at the Drumochter Pass. It is popular for holidays, hill-walking, hunting and fishing. Blair Atholl Mill in the village centre is a rebuilt corn mill where you can follow the various stages of the process. The Atholl Country Collection in the old school house gives a good insight into this area's past. The museum exhibits tools and implements made by blacksmiths and wheelwrights from several periods of the region's antiquity.

About 4 miles (6km) north of Blair Atholl are the Falls of Bruar. Its circular route takes in several water-falls and deep pools which have cut through to expose solid granite. Before the walk is the House of Bruar, a

✳ new visitor centre which incorporates a Wild Flower Garden Centre, Scottish Food Hall, Tartan and Tweed Hall, Cashmere Room, Countrywear Shop, a restaurant and gift shop so there is something for everyone. This is the northern gate of Perthshire and beyond is the Glen Garry and the Drumochter Pass into the Highland Region.

Returning south on the A9 towards Perth, the Hermitage, 2 miles (3km) west of Dunkeld, is an agreeable nature trail through part of Craigvinian Forest to a water fall and pool on the River Braan. The pool, called the Black Pool, is crossed by an ancient bridge leading to further forest walks. Above the falls is an eighteenth-century folly recently refurbished which allows an impressive view of the cascading river and surrounding woodland. Access to the falls and folly is available by car for the disabled.

Dunkeld is another focal point in the historic and scenic fabric of Perthshire. Historically, it was the centre of Scottish ecclesiastical life in the ninth century. The first monks establishing themselves here in AD729 were St Columba's driven from Iona by Viking warriors. The ancient Cathedral, set in spacious parkland leading down to the River Tay, was refounded in the early twelfth century. Today, the choir has been restored and is used as the parish church. The great north-west tower and the nave date from the fifteenth century and have been under restoration for several years. At the back of the Cathedral you will find a huge larch tree known as the 'parent larch'. It may be the first grown in Scotland, planted in 1737 and has, no doubt, many off-spring decorating forests, parks and gardens around the country.

Dunkeld Little Houses date from the rebuilding of the town following the Battle of Dunkeld in 1689 when the Jacobite army was trapped in their lodgings and the Cameronians set the houses alight. Only the cathedral and three houses survived. The National Trust for Scotland own and restored most of the early eighteenth-century houses in Cathedral Street and the High Street. The Ell Shop, also Trust owned, is named after a hand weaver's measure that was embedded in the wall. Across the square from the Ell Shop is the military Museum of the Scottish Horse Regiment. Two miles (3km) north-east of Dunkeld is the Loch of Lowes, a nature reserve where a family of Ospreys have returned to nest for several years. These birds and many other species that frequent the Loch can be seen from a specially constructed hide and wildlife exhibition at the Visitor Centre.

The adjoining village of **Birnam** lies just across the bridge from Dunkeld. Birnam is probably best known for its Shakespearian associations where, in the play *Macbeth*, the moving of Birnam Wood to Dunsinane, 12 miles (19km) to the south-east, heralded the death of Macbeth.

✳ Between Dunkeld and Perth is the Perthshire Visitor Centre, just off the A9 and incorporating a multi-media exhibition that contrasts Shakespeare's character of Macbeth with the real eleventh-century Scottish King.

Additional Information

Places of Interest

Aberfeldy
Aberfeldy Distillery
A827 on the east side of Aberfeldy
☎ 01887 820330
Open: Easter to October, Monday to
Friday 10am-4pm.

Castle Menzies
Off B846 near Weem just west of
Aberfeldy
☎ 01887 820982
Open: April to October, Monday to
Saturday, 11am-5pm. Sunday 2-5pm.

St Mary's Church
Near Grandtully at Pitcairn Farm off
A827, 3 miles (5km) of Aberfeldy
Historic Scotland ☎ 0131 244 3101
Open: At all times.

Alyth
Alyth Folk Museum
Off the A94 north of Meigle
☎ 01738 632488
Open: May to September, Tuesday to
Saturday, 1-5pm.

Arbroath
Arbroath Abbey
Historic Scotland ☎ 0131 244 3101
Open: April to September, Monday to
Saturday, 9.30am-7pm. Sunday, 2-7pm.
October to March, Monday to Saturday,
9.30am-4pm. Sunday, 2-4pm.

Arbroath Signal Tower Museum
Lady Lawn
☎ 01241 875598
Open: All year, Monday to Friday, 2-5pm.
Saturday, 10.30am-1pm and 2-5pm. July
& August open Sundays 2-5pm.

Kerr's Miniature Railway
Running along seafront
☎ 01241 879249
Open: April to September, Saturday &
Sunday, 2-5pm. July and 1st half of
August, daily, 2-5pm.

St Vigeans Museum
Near Arbroath
Historic Scotland ☎ 0131 244 3101
Open: April to September, Monday to
Saturday, 9.30am-6pm. Sundays, 2-6pm.

Blair Atholl
Blair Castle
6 miles (10km) north of Pitlochry in
Blair Atholl off the A9
☎ 01796 481207
Open: Daily, April to October, 10am-
5pm. Sundays, 2-5pm.

Brechin
Brechin Museum
In the Library in St Ninians Square
Open: All year, Monday, Tuesday
Wednesday and Friday, 9.30am-6pm.

Brechin Round Tower
Viewed from the Churchyard
Historic Scotland ☎ 0131 244 3101
Open: April to September, Monday to
Saturday, 9.30am-7pm. Sunday,
2-7pm. October to March, Monday to
Saturday, 9.30am-4pm. Sunday,
2-4pm.

Comrie
Auchingarrich Wildlife Centre
2 miles (3km) south of Comrie on B827
☎ 01764 679469
Open: Daily, 10am to dusk.

Coupar Angus
Meiklour Beech Hedge
On the A93 16 miles (26km) north-east
of Perth
Open: At all times.

Crieff
Crieff Visitor Centre
South of Crieff on the A822 towards
Muthill
☎ 01764 654014
Open: All year daily, 9am till late.

Drummond Castle Gardens
2 miles (3km) south of Crieff off A822
☎ 01764 681257
Open: May to October daily 2-6pm.
November to April, closed.

Glenturret Distillery
From Crieff, take the A85 west for 1
mile (2km) and turn right at crossroads
☎ 01764 652424
Open: March to December.

Innerpeffray Library
B8062, 4 miles (6km) south-east of Crieff
☎ 01764 652819
Open: All year, Monday to Saturday,
10am-12.45pm & 2-4.45pm. Sundays,
2-4pm.

St Bean's Church
At Fowlis Wester off A85, 5 miles (8km)
north-east of Crieff
Stuart of Strathearn
Muthill Road south of town
☎ 01764 654004
Open: June to September, daily, 9am-
7pm. October to May, 9am-5pm.

Dundee
McManus Art Gallery and Museum
Top of Reform Street in Meadowside
☎ 01382 432020
Open: Monday to Saturday, 10am-5pm.

Barrack Street Museum
Next to the Howff off Ward Road
☎ 01382 432067
Open: Monday to Saturday 10am-5pm.

Broughty Ferry Castle Museum
Next to harbour in Broughty Ferry, 4
miles (6km) east of Dundee
☎ 01382 776121
Open: Monday to Thursday and Saturday 10am-1pm and 2-5pm. Sundays,
July to September only, 2-5pm.

Mills Observatory
Balgay Hill at west end of town
☎ 01382 667138
Open: October to April, Monday to
Friday, 3-10pm. May to September,
10am-5pm, Saturdays 2-5pm.

RRS Discovery & Discovery Point
Next to Olympia Leisure Centre and
opposite railway station
☎ 01382 201245
Open: April, May and September,
Monday to Friday, 1-5pm. Saturday and
Sunday, 11am-5pm. June to August
10am-5pm.

HM Frigate Unicorn
Victoria Dock, east along foreshore
from *Discovery*
☎ 01382 200900
Open: April to mid-October, Monday to
Friday and Sunday, 10am-5pm. Saturday 10am-4pm. Mid-October to March,
daily, 10am-4pm.

Claypotts Castle
Claypotts Roundabout on A92 3 miles
(5km) east of centre.
Historic Scotland ☎ 0131 244 3101
Open: April to September, Monday to
Saturday, 9.30am-5pm. Sunday, 11am-
5pm. October to March, Monday to
Saturday 9.30am-4.20pm. Sunday 12.30-
3.45pm.

Camperdown Wildlife Centre
Off A923 3 miles (5km) north-west of
Dundee centre
☎ 01382 623555
Open: daily all year 10am-4pm.

Shaw's Dundee Sweet Factory
Fulton Road west end of Kingsway
☎ 01382 610369
Open: phone for tour-times

Dunkeld
Dunkeld Cathedral
High Street
Historic Scotland ☎ 0131 244 3101
Open: April to September, Monday to
Saturday, 9.30am-7pm. Sunday,
2-7pm. October to March, Monday to
Saturday, 9.30am-4pm. Sunday,
2-4pm.

Dunkeld Little Houses
High Steet
Open: Houses are privately occupied but
more information is found in the TIC.

Hermitage
Off the A9 2 miles (3km) west of
Dunkeld
☎ 01796 473233
Open: At all times.

Loch of Lowes
Off A923, 2 miles (3km) north-west of
Dunkeld
☎ 01350 727337
Open: April to September for visitor
centre but observation hide is permanently open.

Museum of the Scottish Horse Regiment
Open: Easter to September, 10am-
12noon, 2-5pm. Closed Tuesday &
Wednesday.

Edzell
Edzell Castle & Garden
B966 1 mile (2km) west of Edzell.
Historic Scotland ☎ 0131 244 3101
Open: April to September, Monday to
Saturday, 9.30am-7pm. Sunday, 2-7pm.
Closed October to March.

Glenesk Folk Museum
16 miles (26km) north-west of Brechin
☎ 01356 670236
Open: Easter weekend and every
weekend thereafter until 1 June, then
Monday to Saturday, 2-6pm. Sundays,
1-6pm until end of September.

Forfar
Aberlemno Sculptured Stones
Near Aberlemno on the B9134, 6 miles
(10km) north-east of Forfar
☎ 0131 244 3101
Open: All year.

Meffan Institute (Forfar Museum)
20 West High Street
☎ 0307 464123
Open: Monday to Saturday, 10am-5pm,
all year apart from Christmas and 1st,
2nd January.

Glamis
Angus Folk Museum
In the village of Glamis
☎ 01307 840288
Open: April to Sept daily, 11am-5pm.

Kenmore
Croft Na Caber Activity Centre
South side of Kenmore — east Loch Tay
☎ 01887 830588
Open: All year except Christmas. April
to October 9am-6pm daily. November
to March, 9-5pm.

Kinross
Kinross Museum
High Street, Kinross at the side of town
Open: May to September, Tuesday to
Saturday 1-5pm.

Loch Leven Castle
Kinross, access by boat
Historic Scotland ☎ 0131 244 3101
Open: April to September, Monday to
Saturday, 9.30am-7pm. Sunday, 2-7pm.
Closed in winter.

Vane Farm Nature Reserve
On the south shore of Loch Leven
☎ 01577 862355
Open: April to October, daily, 10am-5pm
and Nov to March, daily 10am-4pm.

Kirriemuir
Barrie's Birthplace
9 Brechin Road, Kirriemuir
☎ 01575 572646

Open: Easter weekend & late April to
September, Monday to Saturday, 11am-
5.30pm, Sunday, 2-5.30pm.

Glamis Castle
Village of Glamis off A94, 5 miles (8km)
south-west of Forfar
☎ 01307 840242
Open: Easter and April to October,
daily, 12noon-5.30pm.

Meigle
Meigle Museum
In the village on A94, 12 miles (19km)
south-west of Forfar
Historic Scotland ☎ 0131 244 3101
Open: April to September, Monday to
Saturday, 9.30am-7pm. Sunday, 2-7pm.
October to March, Monday to Saturday,
9.30am-4pm. Sunday, 2-4pm.

Montrose
House of Dun
On the A935 3 miles (5km) west of
Montrose
☎ 01674 810264
Open: Easter and May to October daily,
11am-5.30pm.

Red Castle
Off the A92 7 miles (11km) south of
Montrose
Open: At all times.

St Cyrus Nature Reserve
From St Cyrus take the A92 S for 1 mile
(2km) to North Esk River and turn left
☎ 01674 830736
Open: April to October, Tuesday to
Sunday, 9am-5pm.

Perth
Perth Leisure Pool
Glasgow Road, Perth
☎ 01738 630535
Open: Daily all year.

Abernethy Round Tower
Abernethy on A913 9 miles (14km)
south-east of Perth
Apply to keyholder for access.

Balhousie Castle & the Black Watch Museum
Off North Inch Park, Perth
☎ 01738 621281
Open: Monday to Friday, 10am-4.30pm.
Winter 10am-3.30pm. Sundays & public
holidays, 2-4.30pm.

Bell's Cherrybank Gardens
In Perth off Glasgow Road
☎ 01738 627330
Open: Daily May to October, 11am-5pm.

Branklyn Gardens
East side of Perth on Dundee Road, Perth
☎ 01738 625535
Open: Daily, March to October, 9.30am-dusk.

Caithness Glass
Inveralmond Industrial Estate on north side of Perth off A9
☎ 01738 637373
Open: All year, April to October, Monday to Saturday, 9am-5pm, Sunday, 1-5pm.

Fair Maid's House
North Port, Perth
☎ 01738 625976
Open: Daily, 10am-5pm except Sunday.

Huntingtower Castle
Off the A85, 3 miles (5km) west of Perth
Historic Scotland ☎ 0131 244 3101
Open: April to September, Monday to Saturday, 9.30am-7pm. Sunday, 2-7pm. October to March, Monday to Saturday, 9.30am-4pm. Sunday, 2-4pm.

Perth Art Gallery & Museum
George Street on east side of town.
☎ 01738 632488
Open: All year, Monday to Saturday, 10am-5pm.

St John's Kirk
St John's Street, Perth
☎ 01738 626159

Scone Palace
Off the A93, 2 miles (3km) north of Perth
☎ 01738 652300
Open: Easter to October, Monday to Saturday, 9.30am-5pm. Sundays, 1.30am-5pm, July & August, 10am-5pm.

Pitlochry
Blair Atholl Distillery and Visitor Centre
On the south entrance to Pitlochry
☎ 01796 472234
Open: All year, Monday to Saturday, 9.30am-5pm. Sundays, Easter to October, 12-5pm.

Edradour Distillery
2 miles (3km) east of Pitlochry
☎ 01796 472095
Open: Daily, March to October, 9.30am-5pm.

Pass of Killiecrankie
Off the A9 3 miles (5km) north of Pitlochry
☎ 01796 473233
Open: April to October, daily, 10am-5pm. June to August, 9.30am-6pm.

Pitlochry Festival Theatre
West side of town over the River Tummel
☎ 01796 472680
Open: 28 April to 7 October. Coffee shop open 10am to after performance. Matenee performances on Wednesday & Saturday at 2pm. Evening performances from around 8pm. Monday to Saturday.

Pitlochry Power Station & Dam
Accessible from town or off A9 by-pass
☎ 01882 634251
Open: Late March to late October, 9.30am-5.30pm.

Queen's View
Loch Tummel, on B8019 8 miles (13km) north-west of Pitlochry
☎ 01796 473123
Open: At all times.

Other Useful Information

Emergencies
Ambulance, Police & Firebrigade ☎ 999
Dundee Airport
☎ 01382 643242

Rail
Dundee Station
☎ 01382 28046
Perth Station
☎ 01738 37117
Weathercall for this Area
☎ 01898 500423

Cinemas, Theatres & Galleries
Perth
Perth Repertory Theatre
High Street in town centre
☎ 01738 621031

Murray St Perth
Playhouse
☎ 01738 623126

Dundee
Seagate Gallery
36-40 Seagate
Open: 10am-5.30pm Monday-Friday
10am-5pm Saturday.

Dundee Rep Theatre
Tay Square
☎ 01382 223530

The Steps Film Theatre
Central Library
Contemporary films.
The Stack Leisure Park

Odeon Cinema Complex
☎ 01382 400855

Seagate
Cannon Cinema
☎ 01382 225247

Tourist Information Offices

Dundee
4 City Square ☎ 01382 434664

Carnoustie
The Library, High Street ☎ 01241 852258

Arbroath
Market Place ☎ 01241 872609

Forfar
40 East High Street ☎ 01307 467876

Brechin
St Ninians Place ☎ 01356 623050

Montrose
Bridge Street ☎ 01674 672000

Aberfeldy
The Square ☎ 01887 820276

Auchterarder
90 High Street ☎ 01764 663450

Blairgowrie
26 Wellmeadow ☎ 01250 872960

Crieff
High Street ☎ 01764 652578

Dunkeld
The Cross ☎ 01350 727688

Kinross
Kinross Service Area, Junction 6, (M90)
☎ 01577 863680

Perth
45 High Street ☎ 01738 638353

Inveralmond
A9 Perth By-pass ☎ 01738 638481

Pitlochry
22 Atholl Road ☎ 01796 472215

Accommodation

Auchterarder
Auchterarder House ***
☎ 01764 663646

Aberfeldy
Farleyer House **
☎ 01887 820332

Blairgowrie
Kinloch House **
☎ 01250 884237

Crieff
Crieff Hydro **
☎ 01764 655555

Dundee
The Old Mansion House, Auchterhouse **
☎ 01382 320366

Stakis Earl Grey **
Riverside
☎ 01382 229271

Dunkeld
Dunkeld House **
☎ 01350 727771

Glen Clova
Clova Hotel *
☎ 01575 550222

Kinross
Green Hotel **
☎ 01577 863467

Pitlochry
Burnside Apartments *
☎ 01796 472203

Campsites

Aberfeldy Caravan Park
☎ 01887 820662

Taymouth Holiday Centre
☎ 01887 830226

Twentyshilling Wood
Comrie
☎ 01764 670411

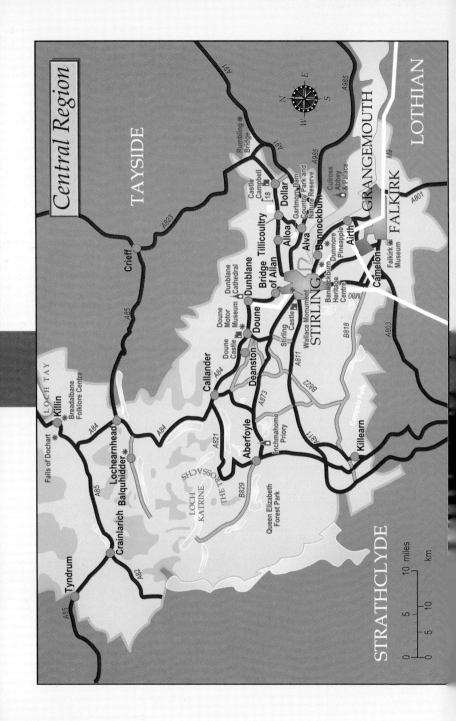

Central Region

TAYSIDE
STRATHCLYDE
LOTHIAN
GRANGEMOUTH
FALKIRK

Tyndrum
Crianlarich
Balquhidder
Lochearnhead
Killin
Falls of Dochart
Breadalbane Folklore Centre
LOCH TAY
Crieff
Callander
THE TROSSACHS
LOCH KATRINE
Aberfoyle
Inchmahome Priory
Queen Elizabeth Forest Park
Killearn
Campsie Fells
Deanston
Doune
Doune Castle
Doune Motor Museum
Dunblane
Dunblane Cathedral
Bridge of Allan
Tillicoultry
Alloa
Alva
Dollar
Castle Campbell 18
Rumbling Bridge
Gartmorn Dam Country Park and Nature Reserve
Bannockburn
Airth
Cambus
Camelon
Stirling
Stirling Castle
Wallace Monument
Bannockburn Heritage Centre
Dunmore Pineapple
Falkirk Museum
Cutross Abbey & Palace

10 miles
5
0
km
10
5
0

N S E W

110

Central Region

6

From Kinross and Tayside the A91 or alternatively the A977 enters Central Region. At this eastern end two intriguing names appear on local signposts, the 'Rumbling Bridge' and the 'Yetts o' Muckhart'. 'Yetts' means gates and applies to this entrance to the 'Hillfoots' area, a long string of medium-sized elevations known as the Ochils.

The **Rumbling Bridge** is signposted on the A823 south of the Yetts o' Muckhart or only a few yards north off the alternate A91. The road passes unhindered over this nineteenth-century bridge belieing the mighty work of nature below. There is an official Gorge Car Park next to the Rumbling Bridge Nursing Home otherwise parking on or near the road is rather dangerous. From the Ice Age and subsequent 10,000 years fast flowing water has carved a deep, dark gorge in the basalt rock creating an impressive cleft with fern-fringed cascades and deep, dark pools. There are paths and wooden stairs leading to well-constructed viewpoints. A deep pot called the Devil's Mill is where the crashing of the water onto boulders makes an eerie reverberation much like the sound of an old working textile mill. To the chagrin of the staunch church-goers of the area it refused to stop even on a Sunday hence its name.

The area between the Yetts o' Muckhart and the east side of Stirling is the Clackmannan District or the 'Wee County'. This quiet backwater was once alive with the sounds of industry when the 'Hillfoots' were a thriving manufacturing base for the textile trade of the eighteenth and nineteenth centuries. The lush slopes of the Ochils supplied grazing for sheep, in turn supplying the fabric while rivers pouring off the hills became a source of power for the mills that sprang up in the area. By the mid-1800's they had created a busy woollen and tartan manufacturing trade rivalling that of the Scottish Borders.

Because of its reputation as a seat of learning, the town fathers of Dollar discouraged the development of the mill industries which allowed the town to take on a more genteel aire, still palpable today. It is best known for its nineteenth-century academy, made possible by John McNabb, a local lad who made a fortune in shipping in London and returned to share his wealth with his home community. Dollar Golf Club is set at the back of town and appears to have no golf course attached to it unless you look above the clubhouse to see the 18th green and 1st tee which gives an indication how hilly this course can be.

The road to the right of the river leads to **Dollar Glen** and Castle Campbell. The glen is a wild, tangled ravine that the waters of the River Devon have deepened through thousands of years. There are three options on how to approach the glen and castle. One is to leave your car in the village and walk up East Bankside and on through the glen taking around 3 to 4 hours round trip including a stop at the castle for refreshments. Alternatively, you can drive to a car park half-way up that still offers a good walk through the glen or up the steep road leading to the castle. Either way is most scenic. Finally, you can drive to a small car park higher up and avoiding the glen altogether. If you are averse to walking at all, there are still some steep hills to be negotiated to the castle. The walk through the glen covers some very rough paths so adequate footwear is necessary. It has been made safer and more accessible with the introduction of stout wooden bridges built by the men of the 75th Engineer Regiment.

At the head of the glen, surveying all below it, is **Castle Campbell**. The castle dates back to the fifteenth century though an earlier fortress did exist on this site before it. The Campbells of Argyll changed its name from Castle Gloom in 1489 when it was passed to them through marriage. The Campbell family were staunch Presbyterians and invited John Knox here to preach on the knoll now known as Knox's Pulpit. From the castle roof there are excellent views over the village of Dollar to the Forth Valley and beyond. Behind the Castle is the King's Seat, a very popular hill-walking area.

The next town to the west is **Tillicoultry**, the largest of the 'Hillfoot' communities and, at one time, supporting eighteen textile mills. Its Clock Mill Heritage Centre is at the heart of the Mill Heritage Trail. The story of weaving and woollens is illustrated here with displays of equipment,

preceding page; Stirling Castle overlooks the wide plain of the Firth of Forth

audio-visual programmes and workshops. This former mill building, dating from 1624, also houses the local tourist information centre.

Carrying on west towards Stirling and behind the town of **Alva**, there is the romantically named Silver Glen where indications of the silver mines that operated here dating from the seventeenth century are still evident. There is also a complex system of water channels and weirs on the lower slopes of the hill that were once used to power the textile mills of Alva. From here it is relatively easy to scale the Ochils highest peak, Ben Cleuch at 2,363ft (721m), a hike well rewarded with views over much of Central Scotland.

Closer to the north banks of the River Forth, **Alloa** does not present itself much as a tourist stop having a long tradition as an industrial town with coal mining, textiles production and glass-making but there are several key points that may bear further investigation. The Erskines of Mar, the hereditary keepers of the royal castle of Stirling and one of Scotland's most influential families made their home here and their four-teenth-century tower, recently restored can be visited. **Gartmorn Dam Country Park and Nature Reserve** is found near Sauchie. The dam and reservoir were originally created as a source of power for the many textile mills in the area. There is a visitor centre where rangers commence guided walks of the park. Alloa is still dependant on water for its brewing industry as it is still one of the largest brewing centres in Scotland.

If you wish to explore the southern banks of the Forth, which, although now fairly dedicated to the petro-chemical industry, has several gems worth seeing, then take the A907 from Alloa towards the Kincardine Bridge.

Falkirk is another example of an older centre that whole-heartedly gave itself over to industrialisation in the eighteenth and nineteenth centuries and is now trying to find a way back to creating a more pleasant environment for both residents and visitors. It has a busy, rather unat-tractive shopping area in its centre with sections of defunct factories on the outskirts. There is however, a wealth of history going back to Roman times when the Antonine Wall, the north-west extent of the Roman Empire, was constructed in AD142 across Scotland's narrow waist to try and curb the war-minded Picts. Having little effect, the Centurions finally abandoned the area and all lands northward leaving the Picts to fight it out amongst themselves and later be passified by Christian influences. At Rough Castle, 5 miles (8km) west of Falkirk, you see some of the best remaining examples of the wall. The Roman road, used to supply the wall garrisons can be seen nearby at Seabegs Wood.

At the Falkirk Museum, 15 Orchard Street, Falkirk's archaeology and military history are explained in depth.

If you are driving along the A905 north of Falkirk, turning off on the B9124 near Airth, you will be surprised to see one of the most exotic pieces of architecture Scotland has to offer. A stone pineapple built in 1761, stands 45ft (14m) high at the side of the road. No one knows who built this folly or the surrounding buildings which were centrally-heated and used to grow real pineapples. The 'Dunmore Pineapple' is run by the National Trust for Scotland and the out-houses can be rented as self-catering holiday homes.

An interesting debate arose a few years ago when an American Professor reported that the stone lying at Meagle was Queen Guinevere's burial stone and that the Arthurian legend took place in Lowland Scotland and not the West Country of Cornwall as is more popularly believed although other areas such as Wales and Essex make a similar claim. The village of **Camelon** on the western outskirts of Falkirk seems too obvious a prop to add to the speculation but it was noted that this could have been the site of that legendary castle or at least the meeting place of Arthur's Round Table. Today, the village offers the ubiquitous swimming complex complete with wave machines and chutes with no sign of an Excaliber or round table.

South-west of Stirling lie the Campsie Fells, a group of low-lying hills that separate the pastoral Forth Valley from the populated areas around Glasgow. This is a secret area of spruce little villages each vying to put on the best floral displays. Its out-of-the-wayness has preserved its character as if caught in amber. Most of the cottages were once mill-workers homes as this area was also instrumental in textile production. The village of **Fintry** takes the prize when it comes to floral flamboyance. Named the Best Kept Small Village in Scotland several times in the past few years one wonders at the almost fanatical zeal that must be required to turn even the pavements into blossoming walk-ways. Further west are Killearn and Drymen, two equally enticing spots with a 100ft (30m) obelisk found in front of the church manse in **Killearn**, commemorating George Buchanon (1506-1582) who was the tutor to King James I/VI.

Returning to Stirling via the A811 turn south-west to **Bannockburn**. Above the Bannockburn Heritage Centre, the Saltire flag proudly flies perhaps more so here than in other places. Here, in 1314, lead by their unstoppable leader, Robert the Bruce, the Scots gave their 'Auld Enemy' a sound thrashing and, as they sing in Scotland's alternative national anthem, *Flower of Scotland* sent them homeward to think again.

The craggy crown of Stirling Castle and the massive rock on which it stands can be appreciated from any angle of approach. As a symbol, it represents a measuring rod of Scotland's history. Over the past 400 years there have been seven major battles fought over these lands mainly in the cause of Scottish independence. There is no doubt that it is the hugely advantageous position that made Stirling Castle so important. The River Forth collects from numerous other waters and meanders back and forth to form a wide alluvial plain. Before the eighteenth century this was impassable marshland with the only decent north-south route crossing through the town. Stirling was also the first point on the river that could be bridged further compounding its position as the 'Key to Scotland'.

The city of **Stirling** is now effectively two towns in one. There is the Castle and Old Town set on and around the outcrop of basaltic rock while

Now the reservoir for the city of Glasgow, Loch Katrine is one of Scotland's loveliest lochs

Rob Roys' grave in the village of Balquidder

the rest of this fairly typical twentieth-century Scottish conurbation stretches south and east.

The Old Town is still well preserved not only with the magnificent castle but a splendid medieval church, the Holy Rude, as well as merchant's dwellings, the Guild Hall, the Tolbooth and a broad market place. The aristocratic Argyle's Lodging built in 1632 is one of Scotland's finest surviving Renaissance mansions and all of this is easily explorable in a half-day.

There is a tourist information centre and a Stirling Castle Visitor Centre which can equip you with some insight into the castle's history. It was the Stuart kings who embellished the castle and held court here in the fifteenth and sixteenth centuries and it was in the Chapel Royal where Mary Queen of Scots was crowned at the age of 9 months. Outside in Broad Street or throughout the Old Town, the local tourist board have lead initiatives to bring the area's history alive by organising various events. There is a good transport link to see most of Stirling on the Castle Shuttle or the open top Heritage Bus Tour which both leave from the railway station and town centre.

A visit to the Wallace Monument is a constant climb but it is well worth the effort. First you scale the 220ft (67m) high Abbey Craig hill on the otherwise flat Carse of Forth, supposedly the position from which Wallace watched his men defeat the English at the Battle of Stirling Bridge in 1297. The monument sits like some kind of Victorian rocket ship about to take off. Above the door is a bronze statue of William Wallace and inside is his double-handed claymore which gives you some idea of the stature of its owner. William Wallace was the father of Scottish patriotism when the concept of a nation was almost nonexistent amongst the Scots, the Norse, the Anglo-Saxon and Norman factions. Wallace came from an average background — a young man in his twenties with the burning idea of one nation of Scotland at a time when the country was cruelly subservient to its English overlords.

There are some 249 steps to reach the top of the monument. The Hall of Scottish Heroes, two flights up, is a rather clinical collection of white marble busts featuring such 'champions' as John Knox, David Livingstone and Adam Smith. Further on is a parapet just below the cap of the monument from where you can enjoy excellent views of Stirling Castle and the Forth Valley with the Trossachs away in the northern distance. It is possible to drive to the monument if you are unable to walk the half mile up the hill but most park in the facilities at the bottom.

Bridge of Allan, north-east of Stirling, is an elegant residential area established as a Victorian Spa town when the healing qualities of its water was discovered. Now, there is the University of Stirling on its western end, one of Scotland's newer universities until colleges and polytechnics recently acquired university status. The wooded grounds of the university are worth seeing for their landscaping and views over to Wallace's Monument. There is a par 3 golf course for the students while Bridge of

Allan Golf Club, turn up the hill at the bridge crossing the River Allan, is a fairly hilly 9 hole course with stupendous panoramas of the Ochils and Forth Valley.

Dunblane is a pleasant little residential town only a few minutes drive from Stirling, built around and in close proximity to its cathedral, a rare occurrence in Scotland most cathedrals and communities kept separate. Once on the main route between Perth and Stirling it is now by-passed, a quiet and compact little town with narrow streets and walks along the Allan Water. Dunblane Cathedral was originally built in AD600 by St Blane of Bute. The present cathedral was built in the thirteenth century although it fell foul of the Reformation and was partly destroyed. After lying in ruin for nearly 300 years it was restored in 1892 to its present exceptional condition. There are still parts of the old Celtic church found in its red sandstone walls. The interior is well worth exploring for both its stained glass and modern wood carving.

Three miles (5km) along the A820 is **Doune**, once the pistol making capital of the country. It produced beautifully crafted weapons which are now museum pieces. Its coat of arms has pistols incorporated. Doune is an attractive little village on the banks of the River Teith and nestles in a vale with attractive wooded hills to the north. In the seventeenth century it was also a thriving sheep and cattle market with ramshackle stalls selling ale and broth to the locals and drovers. Doune Castle, built in the fourteenth century, is one of the best preserved medieval fortifications in Scotland. It was established by Robert Stewart, first Duke of Albany, who was one of the most powerful and unscrupulous men in medieval Scottish history. Doune Motor Museum contains a collection of vintage cars, some in working order and including such makes as Hispano Suiza, Bentley, Jaguar, Rolls Royce and Aston Martin. A number of events take place throughout the summer including car and radio-controlled aeroplane rallies.

From March to September **Callander**, the capital of the Trossachs on the A84, 8 miles (13km) from Doune is choked with cars and pedestrians. It is, however, a suitable base and starting point for a tour of the Trossachs with good accommodation and restaurants. The Trossachs and Rob Roy Visitor Centre is situated in a converted church in the middle of town. Rob Roy MacGregor (1671-1734), a Highland rapscallion, made a nuisance of himself to the local gentry and passed on the booty to his less affluent clansmen. Cattle rustling and smuggling were his main forte before disappearing behind waterfalls or hidden caves when the heat was on. Noted for his exceptionally long arms, his antics might have passed unnoticed was it not for Sir Walter Scott's novel.

There are low-level walks around the town such as a stroll up to Bracklinn Falls on the River Keltie, an easy round-trip of 2 miles (3km) past the golf course east of town. Flanked by the River Teith and overshadowed by Ben Ledi, the town was also known to millions in the 60's as the 'Tannochbrae' of *Dr Finlay's Casebook*, filmed in Auchtermuchty in Fife.

The Falls of
Dochart, Killin

One great way of exploring the Trossachs is by jumping on the Trossachs Trundler, a genuine 1950's country bus, conductor and all, that takes you on a round-trip tour of some of the area's beauty spots. You can hop off anywhere for a cup of tea or a hike and catch the next Trundler a couple of hours later. The Trundler provides a summer service between Aberfoyle and Callander calling at the steamer pier at Loch Katrine where it is timed to link with the sailings of the *Sir Walter Scott*. Loch Katrine was raised 17ft (5m) and became the reservoir for the Greater Glasgow area.

Aberfoyle is the other Trossachs town, nestled between the Highland grandeur of the Menteith Hills and Ben Lomond. The town of Aberfoyle is much more relaxed than Callander. There is a marvellous 18 hole golf course and, next door, one of the best restaurants in the area, the Braeval Old Mill, which is so popular booking ahead is advised (☎ 01877 382711).

Rob Roy's Cave, one of his hiding-places from the government soldiers, is a pleasant drive away on the Loch Lomond road to Inversnaid.

Carrying on along the A81 from Aberfoyle heading east is the Port of Menteith which looks over Scotland's only lake, the Lake of Menteith, a simple misnomer made by a Dutch surveyor. On one of the islands stands **Inchmahome Priory**, reached by a small ferry boat, much as did the young Mary Queen of Scots, in 1547. Following the Scots defeat to the English at the Battle of Pinkie, 4-year-old Mary was hidden here for 3 weeks before she was spirited off to France to prevent her marriage to the sickly son of Henry VIII. The priory is in ruin with some parts still quite well preserved along with well-tended lawns.

Striking north again on the A84 past the long roadside stretch of Loch Lubnaig, **Balquidder** is a tiny village on the way to Loch Viol, just off the A84. Its significance is supported by the graves of Rob Roy, his wife Helen and their two sons placed outside the old ruined church. This was Rob Roy's home territory though his adventures ranged well south into the Stirling area. He died in his bed at the age of 63 having evaded the hangman's gibbet.

Lochearnhead is the next stop, an attractive and busy village with plenty of activity. There is boating, board-sailing, Canadian canoeing and a water-skiing centre making the water at this end of Loch Earn almost boil on a good day. There are also gift shops and restaurants. The A85 runs along Loch Earn's north shore into Tayside. Loch Earn is a long stretch of water surrounded by the high peaks of Ben Vorlich 3,231ft (985m) to the south and Ben More 3852ft (1175m) to the west. The loch is 6 miles (10km) long running from Lochearnhead in the west and St Fillan's to the east.

The road to Killin climbs Glen Ogle, a weary struggle for cyclists who are rewarded at the other side with a free-wheel of around 4 miles (6km) into the village. **Killin**, on the A827, is a comely little place with an almost alpine appeal, the towering hulk of Ben Lawers above it. The River Dochart runs through the village and its falls are a popular spot for photography or just sitting on the rocks. The Old Bridge provides a crossing over the river at this point and is set on two islets which form the burial ground for the Clan MacNab. Most of the clan emigrated to Canada during the Clearances but in their time they were an aggressive lot constantly at war with their neighbours. This and many other tales are told in the Breadalbane Folklore Centre overlooking the Falls of Dochart. The life and legends of this area, known as the High Country of Scotland is evinced with audio-visual displays with the ghost of St Fillan doing some of the narration. The Tourist Information Centre is on the ground floor. Killin Golf Course is situated on the east of the village and is said to have the most scenic closing hole in Britain. Fishing is also available on Loch Tay and the Rivers Dochart and Lochay. Permits, at a reasonable cost, are available from the newsagent's shop in the village as well as some hotels.

Returning west to explore the northern border of Central Region, **Crainlarich**, a meeting point of railway and road networks, is also the isolated half-way point on the West Highland Way and a good base for hill-walking especially around Ben More. Another famous cross-roads in the north-west corner of this region is **Tyndrum**. Here, the A82 carries on north to Glencoe and Fort William while the A85 branches off for Oban and Inverary. Its status as a holiday town has rapidly grown with an increase in facilities for tourists although it has always been popular with hill-walkers. But for many years, local people have known that the real wealth lies in the hills. Gold prospectors have proved that there are millions of pounds of the precious metal beneath the surface and tunnelling has recently started in earnest.

Additional Information

Places of Interest

Aberfoyle
Inchmaholme Priory
On island in Lake of Menteith, A81 4 miles (6km) east of Aberfoyle. Access by boat from lakeside.
Historic Scotland ☎ 0131 244 3101
Open: April to September, Monday to Saturday, 9.30am-7pm. Sunday, 2-7pm. Closed October to March.

Queen Elizabeth Forest Park Visitor Centre
Off the A821, 1 mile (2km) north of Aberfoyle
Open: Mid-March to mid-October, daily, 10am-6pm.

Sir Walter Scott
Trossachs Pier, east of Loch Katrine, 9 miles (14km) west of Callander
☎ 0141 355 5333
Open: Sailings early May to late September at various times.

Rob Roy and Trossachs Visitor Centre
Anncaster Square in centre of town
☎ 01877 330342
Open: March to May and October to November, 10am-5pm. June to September, 10am-6pm. July and August, 9.30am-7.30pm. December and February, Saturday and Sunday, 10am-4.30pm.

Rob Roy's Grave
West end of Balquhidder Churchyard off A84 14 miles (23km) west of Callander
Open: At all times.

Dollar

Castle Campbell
In Dollar Glen, 1 mile (2km) north of the village of Dollar
Historic Scotland ☎ 0131 244 3101
Open: April to September, Monday to Saturday, 9.30am-7pm. Sunday, 2-7pm. October to March, Monday to Saturday except Thursday and Friday, 9.30am-4pm. Sunday, 2-4pm.

Rumbling Bridge
A823 near Dollar
Open: At all times.

Doune

Doune Castle
Off A84 8 miles (13km) north-west of Stirling
Historic Scotland ☎ 0131 244 3101
Open: April to September, Monday to Saturday, 9.30am-7pm. Sunday, 2-7pm. October to March, Monday to Saturday, 9.30am-4pm. Sunday, 2-4pm.

Doune Motor Museum
On A84 north of Doune
☎ 01786 841203
Open: April to October, daily, 10am-5pm.

Scotland's Safari Park
Between Stirling and Doune on the A84 at Blair Drummond
☎ 01786 841456
Open: May to September, daily from 10am.

Dunblane

Dean House
Cathedral Square
☎ 01786 824254
Open: Easter weekend, June to September, Monday to Saturday 10.30am-12.30pm, 2.30-4.30pm.

Dunblane Cathedral
In Dunblane
Historic Scotland ☎ 0131 244 3101
Open: April to September, Monday to Saturday, 9.30am-7pm. Sunday, 2-7pm. October to March, Monday to Saturday, 9.30am-4pm. Sunday, 2-4pm.

Falkirk

Dunmore Pinapple
North of Airth between Falkirk and Stirling
☎ 01738 631296
Open: Only available for viewing from outside.

Falkirk Museum
15 Orchard Street
☎ 01324 624911
Open: All year, Monday to Saturday, 10am-12.30pm & 1.30-5pm.

Rough Castle
B816 6 miles (10km) west of Falkirk
Historic Scotland ☎ 0131 244 3101
Open: At all times.

Killin

Ben Lawers
Off A827 14 miles (22km) west of Aberfeldy
☎ 01567 820397
Open: Visitor Centre, April to September daily 10am-5pm.

Breadalbine Folklore Centre
By the Falls of Dochart ☎ 01567 820254
Open: March, June, September and October, 10am-5pm daily. July & August, 9am-6pm daily. November, December & February, 10am-4pm, weekends only. Closed January.

Stirling

Bannockburn Heritage Centre
Off the M80, 2 miles (3km) south of Stirling
☎ 01786 812664
Open: April to October, daily 10am-6pm.

Stirling Castle
Central to town
Historic Scotland ☎ 0131 244 3101
Open: April to September, Monday to Saturday, 9.30am-5.15pm, Sunday,10.30am-4.45pm. October to March, Monday to Saturday, 9.30am-4.20pm. Sunday, 12.30-3.35pm.

Wallace Monument
Off A997 2 miles (3km) north-east of Stirling
☎ 01786 472140
Open: February, March & October, 10am-4pm, Closed Wednesdays and Thursdays, April, May & September, daily, 10am-5pm. June, July & August, daily, 10am-6pm.

Tillicoultry

Clock Mill Heritage Centre
Upper Mill Street, Tillicoultry
☎ 01259 752176
Open: April to October, daily, 10am-5pm.

Other Useful Information

Weathercall for this area
☎ 01898 500423

Emergencies
Ambulance, Police & Firebrigade ☎ 999

Rail
Stirling Station 01786 464754

Tourist Information Offices

Aberfoyle
Main Street
☎ 01877 382352

Alva
Mill Trail Visitor Centre
☎ 01259 752176

Callander
Ancaster Square
☎ 01877 30342

Falkirk
2-4 Glebe Street
☎ 01324 20244

Killin
Main Street
☎ 01567 820254

Kincardine Bridge
Pine'n'Oak
☎ 01324 831422

Pirnhall Motorway Service Area
Near Stirling (Junction 9 on the M9)
☎ 01786 814111

Royal Burgh of Stirling
Entrance to Stirling Castle
☎ 01786 479901

Stirling
Dumbarton Road
☎ 01786 475019

Tillicoultry
Clock Mill
☎ 01259 752176

Tyndrum
Main Street
☎ 01838 400246

Accommodation

Alloa
Gean House ***
☎ 01259 219275

Callendar
The Roman Camp **
☎ 01877 30003

Brook Linn Country House *
☎ 01877 330103

Dollar
Castle Campbell Hotel **
☎ 01259 742519

Dunblane
Cromlix House **
☎ 01786 822125

Drymen By Loch Lomond
Buchanan Arms Hotel **
☎ 01360 60588

Near Stirling
Blairlogie House Hotel **
☎ 01259 761441

Port of Menteith
Lake Hotel **
☎ 01877 385258

Stirling
Stirling Highland ***
☎ 01786 475444

Campus Accommodation

Stirling University
☎ 01786 467140

Youth Hostels
Stirling
St John Street
☎ 01786 473442

Campsites
Stirling
East of town
☎ 01786 474947

Aberdeen and the Grampian Region

7

The Grampian area is one of the largest regions in Scotland comprising of the former counties of Aberdeen, Banff, Kincardine and Moray. It is acknowledged for its quantity and quality of castles as well as whisky distilleries but there are many more natural delights found around the coast or varied interior stretching over to Strathspey. The main route from the south to Aberdeen is the A90. The A94, as shown on older maps still in circulation has been re-designated as the A90 to coincide with the upgrading on the main section from Dundee to Aberdeen. This is the fastest means of covering the distance from the south to Aberdeen but the coastal route, the A92, is more scenic and less busy. Travelling north from Tayside, you enter the region called the Howe of the Mearns noted for its ochre-red soil and productive agricultural activity. 'Howe' in old Scots means a flat area surrounded by hills. The Howe of the Mearns is really an extension of the fertile Vale of Strathmore stretching north-east from Coupar Angus in Tayside to Stonehaven on the coast.

Long sweeps of sandy beach characterise the coast from Montrose to the village of **St Cyrus** after which the shore line rises into ragged, red granite cliffs with small fishing communities clinging to tiny coves. St Cyrus occupies the headland above the beach and is chiefly distinguished for its nature reserve favoured by the many unusual wild flowers that grow on the south facing hills and dunes. Springing from the

Grampian Mountains, the River North Esk empties into the North Sea at St Cyrus Bay and otters can be seen around the mouth of the river. Seals are other regular off-shore visitors. A peculiar method of salmon fishing is employed here using vertical nets hung on stakes and stretched out into the sea.

Johnshaven and **Gourdon** are grey little fishing villages to the east of the A92 approached by steep roads that lead down to the shore. Further up the A92 is the larger village of **Inverbervie**, referred to as 'Bervie' by the locals. Its only historic claim to fame is that David II and his 16 year-old French wife were beached here after being chased by the English. The king bestowed a Royal Charter on the town for his safe deliverance but, unbelievably, the town somehow lost it and they had to apply for a replacement. The 'Bervie' fish and chip shop is one of the best in this area.

Carry on along the B967 west from Inverbervie to the village of **Arbuthnott**. This area, from Inverbervie to Stonehaven and inland to Arbuthnott and Drumlithie is effectively drawn in a trilogy called the *Scot's Quair* written earlier this century by Lewis Grassic Gibbon. His books, especially *Sunset Song*, contain some of the best prose ever written about rural Scotland. Gibbon's real name was James Leslie Mitchell and his tombstone stands at Arbuthnott Church, referred to as the 'Kirk of Kinraddie' in *Sunset Song*. An excellent museum, the Grassic Gibbon Centre has recently been opened in Arbuthnott. There is a good café and gift shop.

Continuing inland on the B967 which joins with the B966 the entrance to the village of **Fettercairn** is remarkable. A triumphant, red sandstone Victorian Arch forms a gateway. The arch was built in 1861 to commemorate the visit of the royal party of Queen Victoria and Prince Albert. Besides this arch, Fettercairn comprises of little more than a square with several roads leading off. The creamy white buildings lying to the west is Fettercairn Distillery, Scotland's second oldest whisky distillers established in 1824. Old Fettercairn is a pure single malt, well worth sampling while you watch the video presentation which also contains good information of the farming communities of the Mearns and the history of the village.

The northern route out of Fettercairn, the B974, leads to a large Victorian mansion called **Fasque**, the home of one of the best known of Britain's Prime Ministers, William E. Gladstone. The house was built in 1809.

Continuing up the same road past the Clatterin' Bridge, a rushing burn that passes beneath an old wooden bridge, a steep climb leads to Cairn o' Mount. A car park, vantage point at the top gives spectacular views of the Howe of the Mearns to the south and east while a barren, eerie moorland exists to the north. This road continues towards Banchory and Royal Deeside or take the B966 north-west from Fettercairn towards Stonehaven. Before entering Stonehaven, a diversion to **Dunnottar**

Castle, a mile or two south on the A92, is essential. There is a small car park off the road and a short walk leads down towards the cliffs and castle. Sheep inhabit the grassy headland before you reach the castle promontory and add to the photogenic appeal if you can persuade one to stay in the frame. Ruined buildings appear above the grassy knoll but it is on reaching the edge of the steep bank that you fully appreciate the magnificence of this fortified promontory. A wide chasm divides the castle rock from the mainland, an advantageous approach that would be easy to defend. Wild, rock-infested seas surround the other three sides creating a virtually impregnable fortress.

The site has a long history dating back to the Picts who built a fort here followed by early Christians who erected a chapel. Dunnottar has seen many attempts to overpower it including that of William Wallace in 1297, when he tried to burn out an English garrison. The castle's bloodiest tale was when 167 Covenanters including 40 women were imprisoned and tortured for their allegiance to their cause. During the Cromwellian period the crown, sceptre and sword of the Scottish Regalia or crown jewels were dispatched to Dunnottar Castle from Edinburgh Castle to avoid destruction. When Cromwell's men had Dunnottar surrounded with the purpose of finding the Regalia, two local women escaped with them hidden in their clothing and later buried the precious jewels at nearby Kinneff Church. There they lay under the flagstones of the church for 8 years until returned to Edinburgh Castle to be sealed away and almost forgotten about for a further 111 years. More recently Dunnottar Castle was taken over for Zeffirelli's film production of *Hamlet* starring Mel Gibson.

Following the coast road around a wide headland, the fishing town of **Stonehaven** appears below. From this vantage point you can enjoy the best view of the town but parking is limited and precarious. Stonehaven is a popular holiday resort with a good leisure centre, caravan parks, open air swimming pool, boating ponds, windsurfing and golf. Stonehaven's central Allardice Street and adjoining square have a variety of small gift shops as well as the tourist information centre, closed for lunch from 1.15-2pm. Access to the curving pebble and sand beach is east off Allardice Street. The oldest part of the town surrounds the harbour where the Tolbooth Museum, Stonehaven's oldest building and once the storehouse for Dunnottar Castle is found. It contains an interesting collection of local artifacts and fishing memorabilia.

The Marine Hotel on the harbour front is probably the most popular bar serving a variety of ales and reasonable pub meals. Every New Year's Eve, Stonehaven celebrates 'Swinging the Fireballs' ceremony which goes back to Pagan times when fireballs were swung through the streets to ward off evil spirits. Just off the A90 is Muchalls Castle, better described as a 'guest castle' where B&B can be enjoyed in a genuine fortified dwelling. Directions and bookings can be obtained at Stonehaven Tourist Information Centre. The 18 hole golf course on the north side of Stonehaven occupies a spectacular setting along the cliffs.

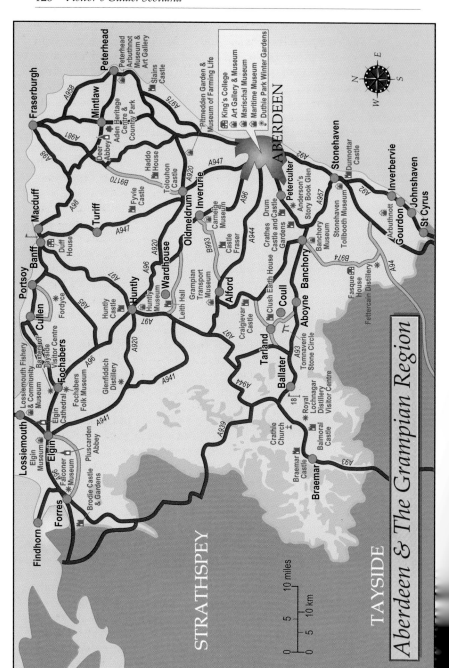

Aberdeen & The Grampian Region

The outlying villages to Aberdeen such as Portlethen and Hillside are now surrounded by retail parks and industrial warehouses along with modern housing developments to cater for the employees of the north-east's yet profitable, if not now booming, oil industry. As you drive into **Aberdeen's** suburbs the outline of the grey 'Granite City' comes into view. The River Dee once formed the city's southern defences and the Bridge of Dee, the first bridge over the Dee, completed in 1527 and widened in 1840, still carries traffic over the river to Holburn Street which connects with the Aberdeen's principal thoroughfare, Union Street. Alternately, carry on east towards the harbour and join Union Street at its eastern end. Either route affords the opportunity to appreciate the unique building material and architecture that characterize this city.

At one time there were around 100 quarries in and around Aberdeen. Now there are only two and granite for Aberdeen's newer buildings has occasionally been imported from Cornwall. The hard, glistening stone became Aberdeen's trademark to the world and two families of architects were greatly responsible for the city's clean-cut appearance. Archibald Simpson designed many of the civic buildings along with John Smith who, around 1804, designed many of the more classical structures near the town centre. His work so impressed Prince Albert that he was commissioned to design the royal castle at Balmoral.

Aberdeen has, over the past 20 years, been dubbed the 'Houston of the North' due to the tremendous boom in oil production in the North Sea. Fortunately for Scotland's third largest city, it was well placed to serve this new industry and has gained from it in many ways. Unemployment in Aberdeen stands at only 4 per cent. Some say Aberdeen's rugged northern spirit has been taken over by an avaricious, commercial attitude but the essence of Aberdeen is probably, like its tough granite buildings, quite robust and should withstand this modern onslaught.

The 'Flower of Scotland' is another more recent epithet given to the city perhaps to try and soften the image of hard granite and hard working oil men. There are explosions of colour along the streets and in its many parks with 11 million daffodils blooming throughout the city in the spring. Aberdeen has won the Britain in Bloom contest so many times that it has been barred from the competition. A true Aberdeen accent, referred to as 'the Doric' can be as hard to follow as any foreign tongue, even for other Scots.

Aberdeen Harbour is a fascinating place to wander at most times but early on a weekday morning provides the spectacle that takes place around the fish market where the catch is auctioned. The fishing fleet now is much reduced with only around twenty trawlers leaving room for the oil supply vessels. It is the most modern, medium-sized harbour in Europe with three main docks. The Maritime Museum, otherwise known as the Provost Ross's House, is situated on the old cobbled street of Shiprow, once the only route into town from the docks. This is the third oldest building in Aberdeen, constructed in 1593 when there was little more than a couple of square miles of town surrounding the harbour.

The history of Aberdeen and its strong fishing connections are presented within this substantial old building. Models of boats from every era including detailed constructions of the oil rigs that presently work in the North Sea are on view. Aberdeen is linked to Lerwick in Shetland as well as Orkney, the Faro Islands and now Norway by P&O's ferries sailing regularly from the harbour.

On the northern shore of the River Dee at its mouth stands the enclosed, conservation village of **Footdee**, pronounced locally as 'Fitee'. Built in the early 1800's when the original fishing village was demolished to make way for harbour extensions, it is still a very close-knit community. All the houses face inward onto two squares to ward off the worst of the north-east winds. A number 14 bus from Union Street bound for 'Sea Beach' will take you there otherwise drive towards the beach and turn right until you meet the harbour. From the outer harbour walls a group of bottle-nose dolphins frequent the river mouth and are often seen. Along Beach Esplanade there are various diversions such as Codona's Amusement Centre and the Beach Ballroom as well as cafés and ice-cream parlours. The beach comprises of clean, fine sand and the sustained breakers provide sport for the largest windsurfing club in Great Britain.

As the capital of the Grampian area, so renowned for castles, it is surprising that Aberdeen no longer has one of its own. In the early 1300's it was burned to avoid occupation by the garrisons of Edward I. The castle lay just beyond the foot of Union Street, the busy main thoroughfare linking the older part of the city to its westward expansion. Planned over 200 years ago Union Street's construction nearly made the city bankrupt and it is worth observing more closely the bridges and buildings that span this once very uneven terrain. Now Union Street is the main shopping precinct with the enclosed Bon Accord and St Nicholas Centres housing most popular shops.

The east end of Union Street and its adjoining streets are marked with several of the best examples of Aberdeen's architecture. Provost Skene's House, near the shopping centres, is a restored domestic building dating from 1545 and now museum of civic life with furnished period rooms and a painted chapel. Around the corner on Broad Street stands the neo-Gothic Marischal College, the second largest granite building in the world. It houses Marischal Museum, a remarkable display of items collected by the University's graduates from around the world as well as tracing the history of north-east Scotland from prehistoric times. Founded in 1593 as a Protestant University, although the present-day buildings date from the nineteenth century, Marischal is regarded as the finest achievements in granite masonry. The building is in need of a clean-up to emphasise its fine, filigreed spires but it is never-the-less, most impressive. There is some current rumour that it might be bought over and converted in to a hotel.

Schoolhill is an appealing side-street just beyond the St Nicholas Centre with interesting arty shops and the Aberdeen Art Gallery and Museum in its purpose built building of 1884. It has a good collection of paintings, sculpture, silver, glass and hosts a variety of temporary exhibits. The house of James Dun is across the road. He was the master of Aberdeen Grammar School in 1769 and his home now houses modern art exhibitions along with audio-visual presentations and information of the town's history. Further up and into Rosemount Viaduct is the gracious, solitary shape of His Majesty's Theatre, a delightful Georgian building and the city's main concert hall with seating for 1,500. At the west end of Union Street where it joins Holburn Street and off to the left near the cinemas, you will find the Sratosphere, an imaginative science and technology encounter with plenty of hands on experiments for kids of any age.

As a spin off from the oil industry and its wealth there are plenty good restaurants in Aberdeen. One of the best at the west end of Union Street is the 'Courtyard of the Lane' in Alford Street. The lower Martha's Vineyard Bistro is a lighter, more simple menu while the Courtyard upstairs is more serious. Accommodation in Aberdeen tends to cater for business visitors and is generally expensive through the working week but very good deals can be found at weekends.

From the centre of town, it is around a 15 minute bus ride to Old Aberdeen using a number 20 or any bus going north on Kings Street. If you are driving follow Kings Street to St Machar Drive on the left and the Chanonry, the narrow lane leading to the heart of Old Aberdeen, is on the right. This is the most historic part of town that was, in fact an independent burgh from 1489 until 1891 and it still maintains its own Town House. It also retains its air of independence with narrow, cobbled streets and well preserved seventeenth- and eighteenth-century architecture, quite dissimilar from that of the more modern city. King's College and its chapel are the main focus of the area founded by the Bishop William Elphinstone in 1495. The chapel is diminutive but most impressive with the original carved stalls lining the chancel and nave and an intricately carved rood screen. The stained glass windows are by Douglas Strachan. Adjacent is the King's College Visitor Centre which presents a multimedia display of the university's history over 500 years and has a restaurant and excellent gift shop.

Following the cobbled Chanonry north to St Machar's Cathedral, this structure was founded in AD580 by Machar, a follower of St Columba as a centre for their northern propagation of Christianity. The present cathedral's foundation dates from 1130 although it was considerably larger than the twin-spired west front left today. The central tower collapsed in 1688. Inside is a splendid heraldic ceiling of the sixteenth century with nineteenth- and twentieth-century stained glass. St Machars sits on the edge of Seaton Park with its riverside and woodland walks. The Brig o' Balgownie spans the River Don much as it has since 1329 when it was the main crossing of the river. The poet, Lord Byron who stayed in this area for periods, often crossed it and stared into its 'pool of bewitchment'.

Anderson Drive is the main circular route around Aberdeen and this leads on to the A93 which passes through Cults, Peterculter and Maryculter and the beginning of Royal Deeside. Grampian Highlands and Aberdeen Tourist Board have devised several theme trails to help tourists pursue certain interests and Royal Deeside neatly combines two of these, the Castle Trail and the Victorian Heritage Trail. It was Queen Victoria, once again, who popularised this part of Grampian much to the surprise of other royalty and aristocracy who were more in favour of warmer climes with less rainfall. But Queen Victoria and Albert were deeply taken with the rugged, refreshing terrain and the purposeful pace of life. The royal presence persists to this day helping to bring this bountiful stretch of the River Dee the fame it enjoys as well as preserving its natural beauty and the orderliness of its Victorian villages.

The first post on this part of the Castle Trail is **Drum Castle** just beyond the suburb / village of Peterculter. Built in the thirteenth century, it combines a medieval keep and a Jacobean mansion house with a Victorian extension. The old keep, dating from 1290, is one of the three oldest towers in Scotland. Set in the Forest of Drum with some splendid oak and pine trees the castle originally was a royal hunting seat of Robert the Bruce who then bequeathed it to his Standard Bearer, William de Irvine for his services at the Battle of Bannockburn. It remained in that family for twenty-four generations until it was passed to the National Trust for Scotland in 1976. The interior of the seventeenth-century mansion is mainly Victorian with its library extending into the middle level of the old tower which is otherwise uninhabited. There is a pleasant arboretum and walled garden of historic roses in which to stroll.

Only 4 miles (6km) down the A93 is **Crathes Castle** with its rather special gardens. The castle you see today has seen many changes since the original 16th century granite tower house but is still a fine example of a Scottish tower house that reflects the power of the family who lived in it for over 350 years. The Burnetts of Leys were also supporters of Robert the Bruce who gave them the land along with the Horn of Leys, a symbol of their position that still hangs on the wall of the main hall. Made of ivory, banded in gilt and set with semi-precious stones, this is also the central symbol on their coat of arms. The interior of the castle displays items from a wide period starting from the first laird to the present family. Painted ceilings in the upper rooms such as the room of the Nine Nobles are a fascinating decorative style featuring great heroes of the past such as Julius Caesar, King David and King Arthur. The Long Gallery runs the width of the castle with a ceiling of Scandinavian Oak.

There is a legend of the ghost of the Green Lady, still reported to be haunting the castle, in particular the Green Lady's Room where she has been seen with a small baby in her arms. The skeleton of a baby was discovered beneath the floor-boards during the nineteenth century and a story is handed down that a young woman under the laird's protection mysteriously disappeared after becoming pregnant by one of the servants. The delightful gardens are as much a part of Crathes as the castle. Crathes Gardens are a creation of the twentieth century when Lady Cybil Burnett designed them with eight separate interlocking enclosures each with a theme such as the Colour Garden or the Camel Garden. The splendid yew hedges date from 1702 suggesting the previous existence of

Crathes Castle in Deeside is the royal place of worship during the family's Scottish holidays

Braemar Castle, Royal Deeside

a formal garden. Crathes is set in a large estate with 7 miles (11km) of forest walks to choose from.

The A93 leads you ever deeper into a promising landscape of Silver Birches, Scots Pines and heather-clad hills. The respectable holiday town of **Banchory** hosts buildings with a gorgeous pink tinge to their granite. The River Dee is a main attraction both visually and for the salmon and trout fishing it offers although salmon beats on this stretch of the Dee are notoriously expensive. Trout fishing is much more affordable on the River Feugh. At the Bridge of Feugh just south of town, there is a rocky channel where salmon boldly leap to reach their spawning grounds. Banchory Golf Club is sandwiched between the town and the river, a demanding little course in sumptuous surroundings. Banchory Museum tells the history of the area and the tourist office, a cabin in the main car-park, can help find accommodation.

If you have resisted visiting Deeside's castles until now there is one you should not miss. Climb the A980 out of Banchory towards a lonely, fairy tale fortress that overlooks the rolling Grampian hills and valleys. As one of the most captivating castles in Scotland, **Craigievar** is ever busy, so much so that the National Trust for Scotland have taken to omitting it from their leaflets.

Craigievar's sandy, pink facing and ornamental battlements remain relatively unchanged since they were first built in the sixteenth century. A local entrepreneur, William Forbes, better known as 'Danzig Willie' who had made his fortune trading with Scandinavia and the Baltic, decided to leave his mark in the time honoured manner and built himself a castle. Started in 1626, his edifice took shape and turned out to be the crowning accomplishment of local masons. It has its defensive features, the small, single entrance, no windows at ground level and battlements around the top although these were ornamental. Otherwise it is a traditional Scottish tower house in its original form that has stood the rigours of civil war and a Victorian trend to embellish such buildings.

Inside you find a welcoming and intimate Scottish retreat with genuine 'lived-in' appeal. Its heart is the great hall with a splendid moulded ceiling of great intricacy that extends down the walls above the fireplace. There is no electric light even yet in the castle and the white plaster-workboard along the walls and ceilings helped to lighten the wood panelled rooms. There are short walks through the wooded grounds with some very productive chestnut trees bearing copious 'conkers' in the autumn.

Returning to the main Deeside route via the B9119 you pass through the village of **Tarland** with its Culsh Earth House, a well preserved souterrain and a stone circle at **Tomnaverie**. South is the community of **Aboyne**, well known for its traditional Highland Gathering held every year in September and a fairly good, though quiet, central base from which to explore Deeside.

Ballater, 11 miles (18km) west of Aboyne, was the end of the line for the royal train before that railway closed. The coming of the railway to

Deeside in 1867 increased its popularity and Queen Victoria travelled regularly by royal train from Windsor to Ballater. Ballater Station was rebuilt to incorporate a 'Royal Waiting Room' but today the station is taken over by a wool shop, café and the royal waiting room is now council offices. Ballater first became established in the nineteenth century when an old woman discovered the healing powers of a bog at the foot of Pannanich Hill. Now it is visited for its close location to Balmoral Castle which is only about 8 miles (13km) to the west. In town there are signs of 'royal appointment' above many of the shops and the Royals do drop in occasionally during their yearly summer vacation. There is a Victoria Week held every year in early August and its highlight is the Highland Games.

Despite the clamour to soak a piece of 'Balmorality' there are many other things to do in this area. Ballater golf course is one of the most charming, the surrounding hills protecting it from bad weather and creating a micro-climate for the course and town. Forty miles (64km) away in Aberdeen it can be chucking it down while Ballater is bone dry. Making Treks is a shop opposite Ballater Station organising anything from pigeon shooting to quad-bikes and gliding trips. Ballater is also a great place to dine. Per head of population there are more good eating houses than anywhere else in Britain. The Glen Lui Hotel has a fine restaurant but the meals in the Bistro, at bar prices are as good as the restaurant and you get a lot more on your plate. The Green Inn on Golf Road is a well-classed establishment with a good chef while more upmarket are the Daroch Laird and Balgonie Hotels.

Balmoral Castle and its grounds are open to the public through the months of May, June and July, Monday to Saturday, 10am-5pm, unless members of the Royal family are in residence although this is usually confined to the month of August. This was the sanctuary of Queen Victoria and Prince Albert who had it built on the site of an older castle, commenced in 1853 and completed by 1855. The original castle had been leased by the royals on the advice of the Queen's physician and they instantly fell in love with the area. Unfortunately it was Prince Albert whose health failed and he died at the age of 40 with typhoid fever. He only enjoyed seven summers at their beloved castle and hide-away.

Balmoral has been the much-loved Highland home of succeeding monarchs ever since. A visit to the castle can be a bit of a let-down with only the ballroom and grounds open to the public along with a refreshment room and gift shop although there is pony-trekking and pony-cart rides available. But Balmoral is surrounded by some extraordinary countryside, well preserved due to the royal patronage. The fragment of primeval forest at Ballochbue, for instance, would have been felled if not for the intervention of Queen Victoria when she bought it in 1878. The Balmoral Estate fronts the south side of the River Dee for 12 miles (19km) and stretches back over to Lochnagar. For rugged grandeur there is little to beat Lochnagar and the 6,350 acres (2,540 hectare) Glen Muick (pronounced Mick) and Lochnagar Wildlife Reserve accessed from Ballater via the Bridge of Muick. This was Queen Victoria's favourite part of the estate and she built the 'Glas alt Shiel', later known as the Widow's House. John Brown, the son of a Crathes small farmer began at Balmoral as a stable lad, became a gillie and then a great favourite of the Queen and Prince Albert.

Royal Lochnagar Distillery on the south side of the Dee behind the Balmoral Estate was established by John Begg in 1845 and Queen Victoria was invited to visit in 1848. The royal party sampled the dram and duly placed a royal Warrant of Appointment as supplier to Queen on his produce. There is a free guided tour and complimentary dram. Crathie Church stands across the River Dee near the entrance to the Balmoral Estate. This lonely little kirk perched on a knoll above the road was opened by Queen Victoria in 1895. It then cost £6,000 which was raised by private donations. The Royal Family attend services in the kirk when staying at Balmoral.

Braemar, despite its proximity to Balmoral has a life of its own and is a delightful little village to stroll around. At its eastern entrance is Braemar Castle, a seventeenth century turreted outpost. In town the Invercauld Arms Hotel stands on the spot where the Earl of Mar raised the Jacobite standard in 1715 and there is a plaque inside. The Clunie Water clatters through the village and under a road bridge that offers splendid views from both sides. The most important event in the area is the Braemar Royal Highland Gathering held on the first Saturday in September with upwards of 50,000 people in attendance. It is a well run affair despite the numbers with traditional events and the eventual arrival of the royal party.

Twelve miles (19km) beyond Braemar is the **Linn of Dee** a famous beauty spot where the River Dee is forced through a narrow chasm in the rocks then under a bridge although the drive along is perhaps even more splendid. There are many fine walks and mountain bike trails up to the White Bridge and Mar Lodge. The road goes no further west so from Braemar it is possible to return to the south via Glen Shee, Blairgowrie and Perth or Dundee or strike north via Tomintoul, one of the highest villages in the Highlands at 1,150ft (351m) above sea level, to Grantown on Spey, a particularly dramatic drive.

The area to the north of Royal Deeside and Aberdeen is a great, broad shoulder land renowned for its malt whisky distilleries, castles and big skies. There are eight malt whisky distilleries and one cooperage in the Grampian Highlands connected by the Malt Whisky Trail, approximately 70 miles (113km) long but once you have visited one or two distillers you have probably gathered all there is to know about the malt whisky process. The best to see are Glen Fiddich, 14 miles (23km) from Huntly and 53 miles (85km) from Aberdeen near Dufftown with Glen Grant to the north and Glen Livet to the southwest.

Grampian Highlands has over seventy castles with the best of them presented on the Castle Trail. **Castle Fraser** stands between Alford and Aberdeen on the A944, a most imposing structure of the late sixteenth

The popular Glenfiddich Whisky stand at the Braemar Gathering

century. One of the grandest of the 'Castles of Mar' it has two distance aspects, the rear overlooked by the car park seems almost French in style while the front is more in keeping with traditional Scottish fortified houses. Interior furnishings are not bountiful but the Great Hall gathers the most impressive together. Continue north-west to see the Grampian Transport Museum at **Alford**. This is a diverse display showing basically anything that moved from a 1902 dog cart to an Art Deco Belgian dance organ that takes up most of one wall.

Inverurie's history is represented at the Carnegie Museum in the Town Hall which specialises in archaeology and Great North of Scotland Railway memorabilia. The area surrounding Inverurie is noted for Pictish relics, details of which can be found at the museum or tourist information centre, also in the Town Hall. **Leith Hall**, some 6 miles (10km) south of Huntly on the A97 or the B9002 from Inverurie is on the castle trail although it is more of a mansion with the earliest part of the house dating from 1650. This was a turreted tower and subsequent additions through the ages have resulted in a square courtyard surrounded by a divergence of buildings. Bonnie Prince Charlie presented Andrew Hay, the Laird, with a writing case on the eve of the Battle of Culloden and this is displayed along with the only pardon given to a Jacobite following that same battle.

Huntly is an important meeting place of roads and a market centre for Strathbogie area of Grampian. The Gordon family built Huntly Castle as their stronghold in the seventeenth century although it is pretty much a high ruin now set in parkland with Huntly Golf Club at its edge. In the castle basement medieval graffiti covers the walls. Huntly Museum is found in the library on Main Street and gives an overall impression of the area's history.

Carrying on up the A97 the scenery becomes more dramatic. The town of Keith is noted for its unusual ornamental Catholic church built in 1830 with a donation from King Charles X of France who sought refuge in Scotland following his exile. The Auld Brig built in 1609 is the oldest bridge still standing in Moray, and one of the oldest in Scotland. The Strathisla Distillery in Keith is the most northerly on the Whisky Trail.

Fochabers is the next town 8 miles (13km) north-west on the River Spey and a final staging post on the Speyside Way walking route. Fochabers Folk Museum has a large collection of horse-drawn vehicles and a reconstructed village shop along with a multitude of early domestic items. Most visitors stop at the Baxter's Visitor Centre on the north edge of town, impossible to miss and a masterpiece of modern marketing for the humble can of soup. The history of the family who still own and run the company is intriguing with George Baxter, a gardener at Gordon Castle in the 1870's opening a grocer's shop in Fochabers that sold his wife's preserves. From this modest start a world-wide business in quality, canned products has grown and kept pace with modern demands. There is an introductory video before a tour of the factory, a Victorian kitchen and old shop along with a gift shop to purchase the stock.

Elgin is 9 miles (14km) west of Fochabers and the main centre for this region of Moray. On the banks of the River Lossie it is a lively little town set in good order with some interesting ancient buildings, plenty of shopping and several places worth seeing. In July it holds its Highland Games and, in September, a famous Fiddlers Rally. Elgin Museum in the High Street is particularly well laid out and won the Museum of the Year award in 1990. Nearby Elgin Cathedral was founded in 1224 creating a centre almost as important as St Andrews and Dunfermline. This building which, like all Scottish cathedrals, bore the wrath of King Edward I and later in 1650, the wanton vandalism of Cromwell's troops. Restoration began in 1825 and still continues today. A solitary Pictish stone slab stands in the middle of the ruin. Moray Motor Museum is in Bridge Street with a collection of ancient but gleaming means of transport including a 1914 Renault and a 1929 Rolls Royce Phantom.

Directly north of Elgin towards the coast is **Lossiemouth**, a popular holiday resort with extensive sandy beaches either side of the town. Sea angling is popular and it has one of the best 18 hole golf courses in an area renowned for good links layouts. Golfers have reported bouncing balls off Royal Air Force fighters as they land at the nearby airfield. Lossiemouth is the birthplace of James Ramsay MacDonald, the UK's first Labour Prime Minister, born here in 1866. Lossiemouth Fishery and Community Museum is found in Pitgaveny Street with scale models of fishing vessels and a reconstruction of James Ramsay MacDonald's study with some of the original furnishings.

South-west of Elgin on minor roads near the Black Burn is **Pluscarden Abbey**, a priory founded by King Alexander II in 1230 for a French order of monks. It was given to a Benedictine community in 1948 when restoration began and continues. Pluscarden was elevated to the status of Abbey in 1974.

Forres is a well ordered little town prominent for its topiary adorned gardens in Grant Park. It has been an established settlement for at least 2,000 years as it appears on maps of that time. Forres was once popular as a spa town but that has been replaced with its reputation for beautiful gardens. Overlooking the town is Nelson's Tower erected in 1806 and recently refurbished, celebrating Nelson's victory at Trafalgar. The Falconer Museum in Tolbooth Street was founded in 1870 to display the town's history with changing temporary exhibitions throughout the year and a dedication to one of Scotland's best loved folk singers, the late Roy Williamson of the Corries.

On the north-eastern side of town stands Sueno's Stone, a 23ft (7m) glass encased Pictish stone, age unknown though probably not less than 1,000 years old. It is thought to commemorate a victory over Norse invaders. In Victoria Road is the Witches Stone also dating from Pictish times and marking the resting place of 1 of 3 barrels in which three witches were rolled down the Cluny Hill.

Heading towards the coast on the B9011 is the sailing village of **Findhorn** set along the mouth of the river of the same name. This area is probably best known for the Findhorn Foundation, renowned in the 1970's for producing gigantic vegetables. It is still an international spiritual community, founded in 1962 by Peter and Eileen Caddy and Dorothy MacLean. Their vision of a better society, which started from a caravan site and has expanded into a 'New Age' and much respected centre for personal advancement, attracts aspirants from around the globe. Most areas are open to visitors and there are presentations on the work and aims of the community as well as a fascinating bookshop.

Brodie Castle is 3 miles (5km) west of Forres, the home of the Brodie family since 1160 and now controlled by the National Trust for Scotland. It contains a notable collection of furniture and paintings with its gardens noted for their daffodil displays in spring. There is an excellent gift shop and restaurant by the side of the A96 leading to woodland walks and the castle.

Another route north from Aberdeen provides several castles and other places of interest worth visiting as a day trip. The A947 runs from Aberdeen to MacDuff on the Moray coast. **Oldmeldrum** is 18 miles (29km) out of Aberdeen and just east is **Pitmedden Garden** and Museum of Farm Life. Alternatively you can follow the B999 which branches off the A92 north of Bridge of Don. The gardens were commenced in 1675 by Alexander Seton, formerly Lord Pitmedden before his title was removed for his opposition to King James VII's Catholicism. The geometric, box hedge-enclosed, split-level gardens each have an elaborate and colourful design copied from gardens in Holyrood Palace in the 1640's. The National Trust for Scotland took over and restored the gardens to their original state in 1952. Forty thousand plants are needed every year to form the design traced out by 3 miles (5km) of boxwood hedge. At the entrance is the Museum of Farming Life with the tools once used by the estate workers. A mile or so north and west of Pitmedden following a simple track is **Tolquhon Castle**, a medieval remnant now ruined but once the pride of the Forbes family. There is an art gallery and gift shop along the track.

Haddo House is 4 miles (6km) north on the B999 and was commenced in 1732 by William Adam, father of the famous Adam brothers, preferred architect of the period. Many an important visitor has arrived at the foot of the sweeping steps of Haddo House and royal visitors today such as Prince Edward still use it for overnight stays when in the area. The avenue leading from the house to the deer park was planted to commemorate Queen Victoria's visit and it is a Scott's Mile long which is 200 yards longer than the English mile. There is a tea room with homemade baking. The chapel, built in 1881, was a later edition and houses a particularly fine pipe organ built by Father Henry Willis, one of the most famous organ builders of his day and worth closer inspection. There is a new theatre added to the side of the house for productions of operas and concerts.

Pitmedden Gardens near Oldmeldrum were commenced in 1675

Portsoy Harbour looks over the Moray Firth

⚲   Six miles (10km) north of Haddo near the A947 is **Fyvie Castle**, one of the most spectacular castles in Scotland. The castle dates from the thirteenth century and has been owned by various families through its existence. The five soaring towers represent each of the ruling dynasties of Fyvie lairds. Its imposing ochre façade has been described as 'the crowning glory of Scottish Baronial architecture', much spruced up by Alexander Forbes-Leith who made his fortune in the American steel industry of the late nineteenth century and bought the estate in 1889. The interior was largely his responsibility also, adorning it with treasures from around the world. There are twelve works by Sir Henry Raeburn, a Gainsborough portrait and other works by Romney, Opie and Pompeo Batoni including his portrait of Colonel William Gordon. The elegant dining room is often used for high-brow entertainment such as classical music recitals and pipers sometimes play outside. A few miles further north is the town of **Turriff** once a Pictish capital with the annual Turriff Show held in August.

The final main route north from Aberdeen is the A92 becoming the A952 to follow the coast and is part of the Coastal Trail leading to Peterhead, Fraserburgh and the host of coastal villages along the Moray Coast. Just out of town is two of Aberdeen's finest golf courses, Royal **⚐** Aberdeen and Murcar adjoining one another over a swelling range of dune-land. One of the most distinctive is Cruden Bay golf course, some 25 **⚲** miles (40km) north of Aberdeen. Jutting out on a headland is Slains Castle, the inspiration for Bram Stoker's *Dracula*. It is from Cruden Bay that the vampire waded ashore to give his blood-lusting attention to Lucy. Bram Stoker frequented this area on holiday and finally retired in the nearby village of Whinnyfold.

⚲   **Peterhead** is a further 5 miles (8km), the wide sweep of a bay heralding the outskirts of town, famous for its harbour, fish-market and prison. This is the busiest white-fish port in Europe and the harbour is worth a glance although there is nothing picturesque about it. The Ugie Salmon Fishings in Golf Road is the oldest working fish house in Scotland, smoking **⚑** salmon and trout by traditional methods. Also in town is the Arbuthnott Museum and Art Gallery which gives information about fishing and whaling as well as displaying a collection of Arctic artifacts from the collector Adam Arbuthnott. Fish suppers are good here.

♣   Travel west on the A950 to Aden Heritage Centre and Country Park near **Mintlaw**. Its centre-piece is Home Farm, an early nineteenth-century steading which has been reconstructed and evokes the sights, **⚑** sounds and smells of farm life of that era. Also nearby is Deer Abbey, an enclosed ruin that was founded in 1218 by William Cowyn, Earl of Buchan for a Cistercian Order.

Fraserburgh, like Peterhead has made its wealth from the fishing industry and judging by the standard of the homes and cars in town, it has done well from the 'silver darlings'. During the herring boom days of the late 1800's over 1,000 sailed fishing boats would cram the harbour to off-load their catch. Fraserburgh today is not a noted holiday destination but for those that decide to visit or stay it is very friendly and likeable with several good restaurants such as Findlay's Bar and Uptown Restaurant (☎ 01346 519547) located in the modern suburbs. There are long stretches of beach where the North Sea meets the Moray Firth and these are known for their cleanliness. There are two good golf courses nearby with Fraserburgh and Inverallochy both difficult links layouts and, of course, there is also sea angling.

The coastline improves further west following the B9031 with charming little cottages and villages such as **Pennan** where some scenes from *Local Hero* were filmed. For those seeking an undiscovered retreat this area is ideal. Striding west into the Banff and Buchan District, **MacDuff** is a quaint little town with a bright outlook across the Moray Firth. This former spa town is still active in the fishing and boat building industry and construction of small yachts or boats can be seen in the local yards. The Seaway Net Company supplies nets to the trawlers in Fraserburgh and Peterhead as well as other parts of the country and you can look in on the process. Moray Firth Leisure nearby organises fishing trips with equipment.

Across the seven arched bridge is the town of **Banff**, a mecca for golfers with Duff House Royal and Royal Tarlair golf courses being the most noted. Duff House, is a Georgian Baroque home of some architectural distinction that has been put to use as a hotel, prisoner of war camp and hospital. It has recently been refurbished and opened as a country house art gallery containing tapestries, paintings and some furniture. There is also a coffee shop and souvenir shop.

Further on along this pleasant coast, its hinterland rich in agriculture, is the fishing town of **Portsoy** built around a seventeenth-century harbour which is its central attraction. Many of the old buildings around the harbour and town square are also worth noting. Portsoy Marble Workshop is set on the west side of the harbour and sells products made from local Portsoy marble which was once sent to Versailles. This ranges from brooches and rings to paperweights. Inland a mile or two from the A98 is the village of **Fordyce** with its ancient castle and pleasantly cultivated lanes.

The village of **Cullen** back on the coast was begun in 1817 as a purpose-built community and, soon after, its small harbour was busy with herring fishing boats. The village specialised in the export of smoked haddock and 'Cullen Skink' became a fish soup recipe that has since caught on. The town is distinguished by the series of impressive railway viaducts which divide the older Seatown from the more agrarian upper town. The viaducts were built because the Countess of Seafield would not allow the railway line to cross the grounds of Cullen House. Nearby, taking a detour on the A942 along the coast are the villages on the edge of the Spey Bay where the river enters the Moray Firth. Portknockie, Findochty and Buckie are distinctive communities, once given over to fishing but increasingly sprucing themselves up for the tourist trade. The A98 continues west to Fochabers described earlier in this chapter.

Additional Information

Places of Interest

Aberdeen
Aberdeen Art Gallery and Museum
Schoolhill
☎ 01224 646333
Open: All year, Monday to Saturday,
10am to 5pm, Thursday, 10am to 8pm,
Sunday 2-5pm.

James Dunn's House
Schoolhill
☎ 01224 646333
Open: All year, Monday to Saturday,
10am to 5pm.

Duthie Park and Winter Gardens
Polmuir Road off Riverside Drive
☎ 01224 583155
Open: All year 10am to dusk.

Aberdeen Fish Market
Off Market Street
☎ 01224 897744

His Majesty's Theatre
Rosemount Viaduct near City Centre
☎ 01224 641122

King's College
High Street
Open: All year, weekdays, 8am to 5pm,
Saturday, 8am to 12pm.

Marischal College Museum
Broad Street
☎ 01224 480241 ext 243
Open: Monday to Friday, 10am to 5pm,
Sunday, 2-5pm.

Maritime Museum
Provost Ross's House, Shiprow
☎ 01224 585788
Open: All year, Monday to Saturday,
10am to 5pm.

Provost Skene's House
Guest Row off Broad Street
☎ 01224 641086
Open: All year, Monday to Saturday,
10am to 5pm.

St Machar's Cathedral
Chanonry
☎ 01224 485988
Open: All year, 9am to 5pm

Stratosphere
Justice Mill Land off Union Street
☎ 01224 213232
Open: All year, Monday to Saturday,
10am to 4pm, Sunday, 1.30-5pm. Closed
on Tuesdays.

Anderson's Storybook Glen
Maryculter South-West of Aberdeen
☎ 01224 732941
Open: March to October, 10am to 6pm,
November to February, Saturday and
Sunday, 11am to 4pm.

Castle Fraser
3 miles South of Kemnay of the A944
☎ 01330 833463
Open: Daily, May to September, 2-6pm.
Gardens open all year.

Craigievar Castle
On A980 6 miles South of Alford
☎ 01339 883635
Open: May to September, 11am to 6pm
during summer months.

Drum Castle
Off A93 10 miles West of Aberdeen
☎ 013308 204
Open: Aporil to September, 2-6pm,
October, Saturday and Sunday, 2-6pm.

Alford
Grampian Transport Museum
Alford, 25 miles W of Aberdeen on A944
☎ 01975 562292
Open: April to September, daily,
10.30am to 5pm.

Arbuthnott
Grassic Gibbon Centre
☎ 01561 361668
Open: April to October, daily, 10am-
4.30pm.

Aviemore
Cairngorm Chairlift
Off the A951 from Aviemore
☎ 01479 861261

Cairngorm Reindeer Centre
Reindeer House near Loch Morlich on
the A951
☎ 01479 861228
Open: All year, daily and subject to
weather.

Ballater

Balmoral Castle
On the A93 W of Ballater
☎ 01339 742334
Open: May, June, July, Daily except
Sunday, 10am to 5pm.

Crathie Church
8 miles W of Ballater
☎ 01339 784208
Open: April to October, daily, 9.30am to
5.30pm. Sunday 2-5pm.

Royal Lochnagar Distillery Visitor Centre
Off A93 at Crathie near Ballater
☎ 01339 742273
Open: Easter to October, Monday to
Saturday, 10am to 5pm. Sunday, 11am
to 4pm. November to Easter, Monday to
Friday, 10am to 5pm.

Banchory

Banchory Museum
Bridge Street
☎ 01779 477778
Open: Easter to 31 May and October,
weekends & Public Holidays, 11.00am-
1pm & 2-5pm. June to September, daily,
10am-1pm & 2-5.30pm.

Crathes Castle and Gardens
3 miles East of Banchory
☎ 01330 844525
Open: April to October, daily, 11am to
6pm.

Banff

Duff House
Near Golf Course in Banff
☎ 01261 818900
Open: All year except Tuesdays and
Christmas and New Year. Monday to
Saturday 10am-5pm, Sunday 2-5pm.
October to March, Monday to Sunday
2-5pm.

Braemar

Glenshee Cairlift
7 miles South of Braemar
☎ 01330 83 320
Open: Daily, 9am to 5pm.

Dufftown

Glenfiddich Distillery
N of Dufftown on A941
☎ 01340 820373
Open: All year, weekdays, 9.30am to
4.30pm. Also Easter to mid-October,
Saturday, 9.30am to 4.30pm, Sundays
12-4.30pm.

Elgin

Elgin Cathedral
North College Street, E of centre
Historic Scotland ☎ 0131 244 3101
Open: April to September, Monday to
Saturday, 9.30am, to 7pm. Sunday,
2-7pm. October to March, Monday to
Saturday, 9.30am to 4pm. Sunday,
2-4pm.

Elgin Museum
1 High Street
☎ 01343 543675
Open: Easter to October, Monday,
Tuesday, Thursday, Friday. 10am-5pm,
Saturday 11am-4pm. Sunday 2-5pm.

Moray Motor Museum
Bridge Street, Bishopmill
☎ 01343 544933
Open: Easter to October, daily, 11am-5pm.

Pluscarden Abbey
From the B9010 at Elgin follow unclassified road to abbey, 6 miles SW of Elgin.
☎ 01343 890257
Open: All year daily, 5am to 8.30pm.

Ellon

*Pitmeddon Gardens and Museum of
    Farming Life*
Outskirts of village on the A920, 14
miles North of Aberdeen
☎ 01651 842352
Open: May to September, daily, 10am to
6pm.

Fettercairn

Fasque House
1 mile N of Fettercairn of the B974
☎ 01561 340201
Open: May to September, daily, except
Fridays, 1.30-5.30pm.

Fettercairn Distillery
1 mile W of village
☎ 01561 340205
Open: Monday to Friday, 10am to 4pm.

Fochabers

Baxter's Visitor Centre
1 mile W of Fochabers
☎ 01343 820393
Open: March to December, Monday to
Friday, 10am to 4.30pm.

Fochabers Folk Museum
In village
☎ 01343 820362
Open: All year daily, 9,30am to 1pm,
2-5pm.

Forres
Brodie Castle & Gardens
Off the A96 5 miles west of Forres
☎ 01309 641371
Open: Easter and April to September,
Monday to Saturday, 11am to 6pm,
Sundays, 2-6pm.

Dallas Dhu Distillery
Off the A940 2 miles S of Forres
Historic Scotland ☎ 0131 244 3101
Open: April to September, Monday to
Saturday, 9.30am, to 7pm. Sunday,
2-7pm. October to March, Monday to
Saturday, 9.30am to 4pm. Sunday,
2-4pm.

Falconer Museum
Tolbooth Street, Forres, 12 miles West of
Elgin
☎ 0309 701
Opening times vary

Findhorn Foundation
B9011 from Forres
☎ 0309 30311
Open: All year Monday to Saturday
9am to 5pm. Sunday, 2-5pm.

Grantown on Spey
Glenfarclas Distillery
Off the A95, 17 miles West of Keith and
the same from Grantown on Spey
☎ 01807 500234
Open: All year Monday to Friday, 9am to
4.30, and in June to September, Saturdays,
10am to 4pm and Sundays, 1-4pm.

Glenlivet Distillery Visitor Centre
Off the B9008, 10 miles North of
Tomintoul
☎ 01542 886294
Open: Easter to the end of October,
Monday to Saturday, 10am to 4pm.

Huntly
Huntly Castle
Castle Street
Historic Scotland ☎ 0131 244 3101
Open: April to September, Monday to
Saturday, 9.30am, to 7pm. Sunday,
2-7pm. October to March, Monday to
Saturday, 9.30am to 4pm. Sunday,
2-4pm.

Huntly Museum
In the library in main square
☎ 01779 477778
Open: All year, Tuesday to Saturday,
10am to 12pm and 2-4pm

Leith Hall
7 miles from Huntly on the B9002
☎ 01464 831216
Open: May to September, daily, 2-6pm.
October, Weekends, 2-6pm.

Haddo House
Off the B999 4 miles N of Pittmendon
☎ 01651 851440
Open: April to October, daily, 2-6pm.

Inverurie
Carnegie Museum
Town Hall, Market Place
☎ 01779 477778
Open: All year, Monday, Tuesday,
Thursday, Friday, 10am-5pm. Saturday,
10am-1pm & 2-4pm.

Lossiemouth
Lossiemouth Fishery Community Museum
Pitgaveny Street
☎ 01343 813772
Open: Easter to end of September,
Monday to Saturday, 10am-5pm.

Peterhead
Aden Country Park
A950 between Old Deer and Mintlaw
☎ 01771 622857
Open: All year, May to September,
11am to 5pm, October to April, weekends only12-5pm.

Arbuthnott Museum and Art Gallery
St Peter's Street
☎ 01779 477778
Open: All year daily except Sunday,
10am to 12pm, 2-5pm.

Slain's Castle
Off the A975, 7 miles S of Peterhead
☎ 01779 471904
Open: At all times

Royal Deeside
Braemar Castle
Off the A93 on east side of Braemar
☎ 01339 741219
Open: Daily, May to October, 10am to
6pm.

Stonehaven
Dunnottar Castle
Off A92 South of Stonehaven
☎ 01569 762173
Open: All year, Monday to Saturday,
9am to 6pm. Sundays 2-5pm.

Kineff Old Church
E of A92 off unclassified road, 2 miles
North of Inverbervie

Stonehaven Tolbooth Museum
Quayside at Stonehaven harbour
☎ 01779 477778
Open: June to September, daily except
Tuesdays, 2-5pm, plus Monday, Thursday, Friday and Saturday, 10am to 12pm.

Tarland
Culsh Earth House
On B9199, 2 miles (3km) north-east of
Tarland
Open: No fixed hours. Flash light
required to see inside.

Tomintoul
Lecht Ski Centre
Strathdon, off the A939, 7 miles South-East of Tomintoul
☎ 01975 651440
Open: During ski season only.

Turriff
Fyvie Castle
A947 8 miles South-East of Turriff
☎ 01651 891266
Open: Daily, May to September

North East Falconry Centre
Cairnie by Huntly with displays and cafe.
☎ 01466 760328
Open 1000-1800

Glenfiddich Distillery
Dufftown-free guided tours
☎ 01340 820373
Open: 9.30am to 4.30pm.

Glenfarclas Distillery
Ballindalloch, Near Aberlour on A95
☎ 01807 500257
Open: Daily, 9.30am to 4.30pm

Russell Gurney Weavers, Country workshop
Brae Croft, Muiresk, Turriff.
☎ 01888 63544
Open: Monday to Saturday, 9.30am to
5.30pm.

Dallas Dhu Distillery
☎ 01309 676548
Open: 9.30am to 6pm

*Buckie Maritime Museum and Peter Anson
Gallery*
Town House West, Cluny Place.
☎ 01542 32121.
Open: All year, Monday to Friday, 10am
to 8pm, Saturdays, 10am to 12pm. free.

Other Useful Information

Weathercall for this area
☎ 01898 500424
Skicall
☎ 01898 500440
Aberdeen Airport
☎ 01224 722331
Car Hire at Aberdeen Airport
Avis ☎ 01224 722331,
Budget ☎ 01224 725067
Europcar ☎ 01224 725080
Hertz ☎ 01224 722373
Aberdeen Railway Station
☎ 01224 594222

P&O Scottish Ferries
☎ 01224 572615
Open Top City Circular Tour
From June to late August
Tickets on board. Starts at 9.30am then
every 90 mins.

Emergencies
Ambulance, Police & Firebrigade ☎ 999

Cinemas, Theatres & Galleries

Aberdeen Arts Centre & Gallery
King Street. Open all year Mon-Sat 10-
5pm. theatre and concert venue.
☎ 01224 635208

Aberdeen Art Gallery
Permanent collection of Impressionist,
Victorian and 20th century paintings.

Aberdeen Music Hall
Concert, entertainment and conference
venue with free entry to some exhibits.
☎ 01224 632080

Tourist Information

Aberdeen
St Nicholas House
Broad Street
AB9 1DE ☎ 01224 632727

Aboyne
Ballater Road ☎ 01339 886060

Alford
Railway Museum ☎ 01975 562052

Ballater
Station Square ☎ 01330 822000

Banff
Collie Lodge ☎ 01261 812419

Braemar
The Mews ☎ 01339 741600

Buckie
Cluny Square ☎ 01542 834853

Crathie
Car Park ☎ 01339 742414

Cullen
Seafield Street ☎ 01542 840757

Dufftown
Clock Tower, Square ☎ 01340 820501

Elgin
High Street ☎ 01343 542666

Ellon
Market Street ☎ 01358 720730

Forres
Falconer Museum ☎ 01309 672938

Fraserburgh
Saltoun Square ☎ 01346 518315

Huntly
The Square ☎ 01466 792255

Inverurie
Town Hall ☎ 01467 620600

Keith
Church Road ☎ 01542 882634

Lossiemouth
Station Park ☎ 01343 814804

Peterhead
Broad Street ☎ 01779 471904

Tomintoul
The Square ☎ 01807 580285

Turriff
High Street ☎ 01888 563001

Accommodation

Aberdeen
Caledonian Thistle Hotel **
☎ 01224 640233

The Brentwood Hotel **
☎ 01224 595440

South-west Aberdeen
Ardoe House **
☎ 01224 867355

Banchory
Invery House **
☎ 01330 24782

Braemar
Cranford Guest House *
☎ 01339 741675

Buckie
The Old Monastery **
☎ 01542 832660

Elgin
Royal Hotel *
☎ 01343 548811

Fordyce
Academy House B&B *
☎ 01261 842743

Huntly
Castle Hotel *
☎ 01466 792696

Near Stonehaven
Muchalls Castle ☎ 01475 568685
☎ 01569 731170

Westhill, Near Aberdeen
The Westhill Hotel **
☎ 01224 740388

Campsites

Aberdeen
Hazelhead Caravan Park
☎ 01224 321268
Banchory Lodge
☎ 01330 822246
Findhorn Sands Caravan Park
☎ 01309 690324

Youth Hostels
King George VI Memorial Hostel
8 Queens Road, Aberdeen
☎ 01224 646988

Orkney and Shetland

8

During television weather reports or in many maps the islands off the north coast of mainland Scotland are often presented in a box. Orkney occasionally makes it to its true position but Shetland inevitably gets pulled down from its high latitude and placed somewhere closer to the mainland. The cartographer's problem speaks volumes about the connection between these wild, wind-swept archipelagos and the United Kingdom that now governs them. Physically the islands of Orkney and Shetland are closer to Bergen in Norway than Aberdeen and traditionally their links with the Norse countries have been as intimate. They are like stepping stones with the Faroe Islands and Iceland towards the north-west and Norway due east as well as being at the confluence of the North Sea and the Atlantic Ocean with the Norwegian Sea directly north.

They area often considered rather bleak places best suited for ornithologists and fishermen and they do get their share of strong winds and rain but both Shetland and Orkney enjoy moderate summers similar to the rest of Scotland. Their economy through the ages has been linked to their strategic position for trade and the fertile countryside of Orkney is said to be some of the best in Britain while more rugged Shetland has benefited greatly from the oil found off its shores.

Orkney's fertile soil must have attracted settlers throughout the ages and there is a greater concentration of prehistoric remains here than any where else in Britain especially in Orkney although Shetland is also covered in brochs and of the late Stone Age. It is worthwhile taking time to learn a little of the islands long and multi-faceted history before you visit the sites.

Also, be prepared for the cosmopolitan air in both Shetland and Orkney. Besides the fact that there are tourists from all around the world there is a noticeable influx of oil personnel and fishermen from Russia in Shetland and many English immigrants who have found their dream cottage in some Orkney village and established it as their home.

THE ORKNEY ISLANDS

There are a variety of ways to reach the islands of Orkney but perhaps the most interesting, if you are travelling by car or back-packing, is to take the mail-boat ferry, the *St Ola*, sailing from the mainland port of Scrabster near Thurso to Stromness on the west Mainland or the main island of Orkney taking nearly 2 hours. The islands of Orkney, clearly visible from John o' Groats or Dunnet Head on the mainland appear like giant chunks of chocolate topped with a green icing as the ferry nears them. Further inland are medium-sized, rounded mountains reminding you that this was once, many thousands of years ago, part of the Scottish mainland. From the ferry, with binoculars, grey seals can be spotted basking on coastal rocks while the air is full of sea birds. The Old Man of Hoy, a 450ft (137m) rock stack off the southern island of Hoy comes into view.

The St Ola slips noiselessly past Point of Ness to dock at the North Pier in **Stromness** and bands of eager back-packers abandon the outer decks to spill onto the dock. The scale of the large ferry transporting around 400 people and 100 cars to the tiny, grey town seems disproportionate. Having been enthralled by the views from Dunnet Head on the mainland, across the Pentland Firth and passed the great sandstone pillar of the Old Man of Hoy, the ferry passengers are usually beguiled by the size of Stromness. Grey-lagged cottages line the waterfront with their gable-ends sea-ward to conserve heat and stave off draughts.

For an hour or so the narrow flagstone-paved street, just wide enough for one car, rings with accents from around the world as arrangements are made for accommodation, transport and food then it subsides back to a serene harbour community, little changed in a hundred years. Stromness is Orkney's second main town and once a principal sea-fairing outpost supplying ships bound for the Atlantic and North America. Vessels belonging to the Hudson's Bay Company regularly stopped here for supplies and to hire local men to work in Nor' Wast up until the early

preceding page; Though there were originally 60, the Ring of Brogar in Orkney comprises of 36 stones

1900's. Whaling provided another good source of commerce with ships sailing for Greenland and back and then there was the herring boom of the late 1800's. The town remains a fishing port today with a colourful mixture of trawlers and several lobster and crab boats.

Stromness Natural History Museum has stood since 1858 exhibiting the highlights of Stromness's history and natural surroundings with presentations on indigenous birds, fossils, shells, and butterflies. There are also exhibitions on the Hudson Bay Company, whaling, fishing, and the scuttling of the German fleet at Scapa Flow. Nearby, the Pier Arts Centre on Victoria Street houses contemporary art exhibitions as well as a permanent display of works of the St Ives School. There are other areas worth exploring by foot if you stay in the area and the Tourist Office on the quayside will give details although do not call there when the ferry has just landed as it gets very busy. There is a very respectable 18 hole golf course at the south end of town with most of the fairways open to the stiff south-west winds. If you follow the beach or cross the hill near the golf course there are good walks past the course and on toward the Point of Ness.

Orkney's 'mainland' as it is referred to, is the largest island on which three-quarters of the 22,000 population live. The archipelago had 70 islands altogether. Known as Orkney and not 'the Orkneys', there are only 20 of these islands are populated. **Kirkwall**, 17 miles (27km) east of Stromness, is the main town of Orkney and a good base for accommodation which combines modern amenities and yet still retains plenty of the essential colour and culture of the islands. The narrow shopping area of Albert Street, although thronging with locals and visitors on foot, is still used by cars so be prepared to make way for slow-moving vehicles.

Vikings of the late eighth to thirteenth century played a major role in the islands development using their ocean-going sailing ships or long boats to transport men of arms, livestock, goods and emigrants across the North Sea and beyond. The existing Pictish culture was soon absorbed and political control of Orkney and much of the far north and west of Scotland was achieved by the ninth century bringing advancements in metal-work, farming, shipbuilding and joinery.

Kirkwall's centre holds one of the most impressive symbols of the north's Norse past. The rich, red sandstone edifice of the twelfth- century St Magnus Cathedral dominates its surroundings and comes as a surprise to many visitors who did not expect its grandeur. The impressive stature of this building gives a sense of the vast power of the Viking jarls or earls who commanded these lands. Commenced in 1137 by Earl Rognvald in honour of his uncle, Earl Magnus Erlendson, the story behind his canonisation is perhaps owed more to political intrigue than to his religious piety. As part of the Viking territories, the islands were governed by the two cousins, Hakon Paulson and Magnus. It was the more popular Magnus's refusal to fight over the islands and his turning to prayer in the face of his cousin's treachery and murderous greed that elevated the Earl to the position of a saint. The bones of St Magnus and his nephew, St

Rognvald, discovered in 1919, are buried in the north and south choir pillars of the cathedral. The cleft in the scull found in the south arcade correspond to the mortal wound delivered to St Magnus by Hakon's cook, the only man who would consent do the deed.

The Romanesque features of the cathedral are similar to that of Durham Cathedral in England's north-east mainly due to the role of Durham stone masons in its construction. Not as large as Durham, St Magnus

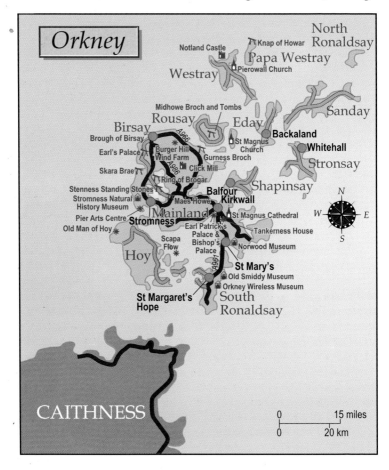

Cathedral makes up in its solitary grandeur. The interior appears larger due to the great height of the nave and choir. An interesting interior embellishment is the many seventeenth-century grave slabs that line the gallery walls. The bell tower was added to the main twelfth-century building in the early fourteenth century. Fortunately, the ravages of the Reformation that destroyed most of the Scottish mainland's religious buildings did little to effect the cathedral. The building is not owned by any one religious body but belongs by Royal Charter of 1486 to the people of Kirkwall.

Albert Street in Kirkwall, Orkney

To the west of St Magnus Cathedral on the other side of the street are the ruins of the twelfth-century Bishop's Palace. Originally built in the time of King Haakon Hakonsson of Norway who came here following defeat at the Battle of Largs in 1263 and died that winter from his wounds. The palace fell into ruin in the fourteenth century but was rebuilt by Bishop Reid in the mid-sixteenth century. A more graceful ruin, the Earl's Palace lies, once again, across the road to the south, a tribute to one of Orkney's darker figures, the Earl Patrick Stewart or Black Pate.

Opposite the cathedral in Albert Street is Tankerness House, Orkney's main museum. This former sixteenth-century merchant's house presents a broad overview of Orkney's past from prehistoric to present times. Many facets of Orcadian life have been brought together including examples of the Orkney straw chair, an intriguing devise intended to keep drafts off the occupants by a close-knit straw plaiting forming a large cowl. There are several old houses nearby including the Orkney Library which is one of the oldest public libraries in Scotland dating back to 1683 and its Orkney Room contains detailed information on the history of the islands. There are some interesting shops in Broad Street and Albert Street, Kirkwall's main shopping parades. There is an Ortak jewellery shop in Albert Street selling beautiful Scottish jewellery but if you wish to see it made the factory sits just outside town in the Hatston Industrial

Estate and welcomes visitors. In Holm Road on the south side of town heading towards the airport is Highland Park Distillery, the most northern Scotch whisky distillers in the world where tours are held and drams are offered.

Kirkwall's harbour is still busy but relaxing to stroll around and watch the variety of vessels berthed there. Sheltered between two wide peninsulas, Kirkwall and its harbour were natural sites for early settlement and this area was probably the first to be developed. Formerly the harbour frontage was a line of defence for the small community and the present Shore Street and Harbour Street were then called the Ramparts.

You are bound to hear about one of Kirkwall's more unusual traditions on your explorations, the 'Ba'Game'. The 'Ba' Game is a tradition played out every Christmas and New Year's Day by the young men of the town where two teams, the Uppies and the Donnies, originally referring to which part of town you came from but now more connected with family or peer group allegiance, struggle to place the ball in the other teams goal, either the harbour or the corner of Main Street. The game can go on for hours with massive 'scrums' stuck in one of the narrow lanes. To explore the rest of Orkney's mainland there are several options. To the south and east of Kirkwall is several spurs of land. East Mainland encompasses the areas of Holm, pronounced 'Ham', St Andrews and Deerness. On the A960 is Kirkwall's airport, Grimsetter. There are minor roads allowing access to the coast on the St Andrews and Tankerness Peninsula where the remains of World War II gun emplacements can be seen at Rerwick Head. The strategic significance of these islands is borne out by the amount of such sites throughout the islands. On Deerness recent archaeological excavation have revealed the presence of considerable Pictish and Norse remains especially near Skaill. Further on is a natural chasm where a cave has collapsed leaving an arch that causes an unusual sound. There is a RSPB reserve further north at Mull Head.

The East Mainland's roads filter down to the little community of St **Mary's**. In Graemeshall House on the eastern side of the village is a collection of antiques called the Norwood Collection after its founder, Norris Wood who has gathered relics of all sorts since he was a teenager. He is now in his 80's. There are five rooms of assorted paraphernalia from around the world that is well worth seeing.

The Churchill Barriers are a series of man-made causeways linking the mainland to the smaller islands of Burray and South Ronaldsay. On the west side of these islands is a great, natural deep-water inlet called Scapa Flow. Here the Grand Fleet of the British Navy during World War I gathered although constantly aware of the danger of German U-Boats entering the Sound between the two islands. One did but decided not to attack although his periscope was spotted and he was rammed by a British mine-sweeper. Various old ships were sunk between the islands to try and prevent further attacks and some of these can still be seen. At the end of the war this was where the German fleet were brought following their surrender, some seventy-four ships. They stayed for some months waiting on the terms of the Armistice then on 21 June, 1918, Rear Admiral Ludwig von Reuter gave the signal 'Paragraph Eleven' which was the code to scuttle. Some of his fleet still lie on the bottom of Scapa Flow and little could Reuter have realised that he had created, some 70 years later, an underwater theme-park for the thousands of divers that come here each year. Fishing boats in the area have found a new lease of life by taking divers out to dive the wrecks of Scapa Flow.

The story of Scapa Flow does not end there. During World War II a German U-boat succeeded in a daring midnight raid to penetrate the British defences and sink the battleship *Royal Oak*. One of its torpedo propellers can be seen in Stromness Museum. After this the Churchill Barriers were rapidly constructed to block the eastern entrance of Scapa Flow. The labour problem in building the causeways was solved by using Italian prisoners of war taking 4 years to finish the job. It was these men who, on Lamb Holm, the island south of Holm, created the Italian Chapel from scrap metal and two Nissen Huts. It was later called the 'miracle of Camp 60' and some of the men returned recently to refurbish this incredible little shelter of worship.

The next island is **South Ronaldsay** where the village of **St Margaret's Hope** denotes the time in 1290 when 7 year-old Margaret, the Maid of Norway, the daughter of Alexander III of Scotland, died on her way to marry Prince Edward later to become Edward II with the hope that the marriage would unify Scotland and England. The village of St Margaret's Hope is reminiscent in style to Stromness and has the Old Smiddy Museum with artifacts of that trade. There is also the Orkney Wireless Museum at the entrance to the village which houses various communications equipment with special interest in the radar and air defence gear used to protect Scapa Flow. The Creel in St Margaret's Hope is a nice dinner-only restaurant serving delicious seafood.

Near Wind Wick Bay grey seal mothers are often seen with their pups. Nearby is the **Tomb of the Eagles** where an ancient burial cairn was discovered when a farmer saw what looked like a dyke and, taking away a few stones, discovered the burial chamber. In it were some 16,000 bones from around 340 bodies estimated to be around 5,000 years old. A recent interesting study showed that the gene markers from these bones were very similar to Orkney's present native population showing that the Viking influence is not as marked as many believe and that many Orcadians remain closely related genetically to their ancient relatives. There is a summertime only ferry running from Burwick on the south of the island to John o' Groats.

Returning to the Orkney Mainland the area to the west of Kirkwall offers some of the most ancient sites of human habitation in Northern Europe. The first is **Maes Howe**, 10 miles (16km) west of Kirkwall on the A965. From the air Maes Howe must appear like a giant sombrero. The centre lump is a burial cairn and probably the best to be found in Britain. It is reached from the car park at Tormiston Mill by a quarter mile walk following the perimeter of a field. The walls and roof of the entrance passage are made of huge stone slabs some 18ft (5m) in length and 4ft (1m) wide. The central chamber is similarly formed with a precision that defies the weight of its own structure. During the winter solstice a shaft of sunlight shines directly down the single passage, eerily illuminating the interior.

The tomb, probably the burial place for important priests or kings of an era around 2,500BC and was broken and entered by Norseman of the twelfth century and any treasure or artifacts were then removed. In its place they left graffiti, the largest collection of runic characters found in any one place. Their messages, unfortunately, are not always so merito-rious. Whilst there is a notation that indicates the tomb's treasure lies buried north-west of the mound others describe the sexual attributes of certain Norse maidens.

On a well sign-posted right turn found further along the A965 is the **Ring of Brogar** set on a strip of land between Harray and Stenness Lochs. This is a most impressive place especially as the sun sets between the 36 standing stones set out in a great circle. There were 60 stones when the ring was first created around 1560BC. There is wide speculation as to the purpose of such rings from a landing pad for inter-galactic travellers or goal posts for some ancient football game to the more sensible idea of a lunar observatory. There is a worn path around the ring of stones with heather in its centre and an outer ditch. Nearby are the **Stenness Standing Stones** which date from around the third millenium BC. There are only four remaining but the tallest of these stand at 16ft (5m). Evidence of cremation and burial has been found around the site.

Perhaps Orkney's best know treasure is **Skara Brae** located on the west shores of the mainland and overlooking the Bay of Skaill and the Atlantic Ocean. Easily the best preserved of its kind in Europe this late Stone Age village dates back 5,000 years. Ironically it was only inhabited for around 600 years before a severe sandstorm sealed it away. In 1850 a similar storm revealed this time capsule to the world. In all there are six houses and a workshop situated around an adjoining passageway. Much of what we see now, although incredibly intact, excludes the wood and animal hide furnishings that must have accompanied the stone dressers, beds and cupboards that remain. Although the Bay of Skaill was smaller and further away from the site in their time, the inhabitants of Skara Brae made use of the drift wood and whale carcasses that were blown ashore to augment their furniture.

From Skara Brae take the B9057 east to **Click Mill**, 8 miles (13km) on, a vertical-axis water wheel built about 1800. Similar in design to Norse mills of a much earlier era they made a clicking sound when in operation. Five miles (8km) further on and following a road down to the beach is **Gurness**, the best preserved broch or village in Orkney dating from around the first century BC. The site was probably occupied well into Viking times where the defensive tower surrounded by the domestic dwellings was probably frequently used. Looking back to the mainland from Gurness you cannot fail to notice the huge aerogenerator of wind-

The Italian Chapel on South Ronaldsay, Orkney, was built by Italian POW's from two Nissen huts and other scrap metal

The prehistoric village of Skara Brae

mills at **Burger Hill Wind Farm**. This experimental scheme chose this area due to the high average wind speeds that prevail. There is a small, explanatory Visitor Centre and the RSPB Birsay Moors Reserve nearby.

Around the north coast of the Mainland to its western tip is the parish of **Birsay** with its imposing sixteenth-century ruin, the Earl's Palace. Birsay was once an important Viking settlement until the cathedral was constructed in Kirkwall and the Viking seat of power was transferred there. Before the Vikings there was a Pictish and early Christian community settled on the Brough of Birsay, the small island reached by stepping stones at low tide and only passable for around 2 hours each day. There is much evidence of the buildings that stood here, now meer outlines of stone in the rich meadow that surrounds them.

The island of **Hoy** to the south of Mainland is Orkney's second largest island and quite different in topography with elevations such as Ward Hill rising to 1,577ft (481m), Cuilags at 1,420ft (433m) and Knap of Trowieglen at 1,310ft (400m). This makes for good hill walking country although more serious mountaineers make for the Old Man of Hoy to scale its vertical walls. The island is reached by either of the two ferry services, the first from Stromness Harbour to the village of Hoy is passenger and summer only while the roll on-roll off service from Houton on south-west Mainland to Lyness on the east side of Hoy runs all year.

Between Hoy, the south coast of Mainland and South Ronaldsay lies **Scapa Flow**, the scene of so much naval activity during both World Wars and so Hoy and its east coast village of Lyness were much involved. In fact Lyness was the main naval base with over 60,000 personnel living in mainly makeshift wooden huts. It was here that the German Fleet of World War I, what was left of it, was beached and stripped. The Lyness Naval Base was finally closed in 1959 and now an Interpretation Centre remains to try and convey the important role this area played in both World Wars. The area to the south of Lyness is more flat and fertile with the road leading on to South Walls. On the island of South Walls you may be surprised to see a person running around fields flapping their arms. Here they employ a human scarecrow to keep Barnacle Geese off of the crops in late summer and autumn and the system seems to work quite well.

The north of Hoy is more availing to sight-seeing with the route over to Rackwick being the best option. The **Dwarfie Stane** is a cramped rock tomb thought to date from around 3000BC and is sited just south-east of the road. There is a good path but it deteriorates so wear proper boots or waterproofs. At the end of the road is a view of dramatic coastal cliffs and a wide, sand and boulder beach. It is a sheltered area on most days. From here there are good walks inland by Ward Hill or following the coastal footpath to the **Old Man of Hoy** which takes around 3 hours there and back. It is possible to carry on to the awesome 1,140ft (348m) vertical cliffs at St John's Head but this would take considerably longer and bear in mind you get an excellent view of the cliffs and the stack from the Stromness to Scrabster ferry.

Lying north-west of Kirkwall and the Mainland are a spattering of lovely islands collectively called the **Northern Isles**, a more elemental and quite addictive side to Orkney. Almost all their names end in -ay-which was Norse for 'island'. **Shapinsay** is closest to Kirkwall and the most developed, a 25 minute crossing on the ro-ro ferry. The island's system of runrig farming was 'improved' in the 1850's by the Balfour family, originally from Fife who built Balfour Castle around an existing house and occupied it until 1961. Now it is owned by the Zawadzki family who offer tours of their home and gardens followed by a traditional Orkney farmhouse tea served in the servant's hall.

The island of **Rousay** is just 1 mile (2km) north of the Mainland and is reached by the short ferry crossing from Tingwall. It is a perfect escape for those interested in archeology, bird-watching or fishing. A single circular route runs round the island and passes near most of the prehistoric, Pictish, Viking, ornithological and good fishing sites. The best archeological sites are found on the south-west shores of the island and the most impressive is about 5 miles (8km) west of the ferry terminal, **Midhowe**, a communal burial cairn similar in age to Maes Howe and referred to as the 'ship of death'. Nearby Midhowe Broch is the remains of a small, fortified Iron Age village or large family dwelling. Nearer the ferry terminal is **Taversoe Tuick**, a two-story tomb which is quite unusual although another exists like it on Eday. The low-lying islands of Wyre which contains the Cubbie Roo's Castle, a twelfth-century stone building and Egilsay, best know for its' St. Magnus' Cenotaph and church can be visited by asking the ferry staff to drop you there.

If you are waiting in Orkney's main airport at Grimster and hear announcements for flights leaving for London do not get confused. London Airport, in this case, is on the island of **Eday** set in the middle of the North Isles and not Heathrow. The island's central position has made it an exporter of peat to other less-endowed islands and most of the hilly interior is given over to this occupation. The ferry lands at Backaland on the south-east side but most of the interest is further north. It is around a 5 mile (8km) drive on the islands main road to the **Stone of Setter**, a single, lofty, Pictish monolith. The nearby chambered cairn of **Vinquoy** is the best of many found on this island and it is similar to Maes Howe and Midhowe with its large stone block walls and four chambers set into them.

Westray is a spindly long island to the north-west of Eday and the largest of the North Isles with **Peirowall** being its main community. It is a surprisingly prosperous place with cattle farming and fishing being its main occupations although it is noted also for its knitwear. Notland Castle, built in 1560, is about $1/2$ mile (1km) walk from the village, a set of square sections forming a Z-plan that is adorned with some seventy gun loops. Noup Head Cliffs are on the north-west side of the island, a haven for bird-watching that rates as one of the most important breeding sites for sea-birds in Europe. The Pierowall Hotel is the best bet for lunch.

Papa Westray or Papey has an international reputation as having the shortest scheduled airline flight in the world lasting between one and two minutes depending on the wind. This takes place between Westray and the beach of Papa Westray. The north part of this island around North Hill is uninhabited apart from thousands of Arctic Terns and Scuas who will buzz you if you wander to close to their nesting sites and deliver a nasty peck unless you wear some head protection. Underfoot is some interesting vegetation such as Spotted Orchids, Primrose and Dog Violet. The Knap of Howar near the airfield is very similar to Skara Brae on Mainland where a sand-storm covered a farm dwelling of 3500 BC which was consequently uncovered to reveal what is claimed to be the oldest standing house in Europe.

If you land on the island of **Sanday** on a warm summer's day you may think the ferry was blown off course and landed in the Caribbean. Sanday, as its name implies, is surrounded by fine, powdery beaches and is the flattest of the North Isles with the only noticeable rise being the aptly named 'Wart'. Its position on the eastern edge of Orkney's outlying islands has made it a hazard to shipping and scores of ships have been cast to a watery grave off its eastern most point where a lighthouse now stands, constructed in 1807. This is an area worth visiting so to reach it take the route out of Kettletoft and turn right along the Lady Peninsula. En-route there is a worthwhile stop at the Knitters Wool Hall in Lady Village.

On **Els Ness** there is perhaps the best of Sanday's many prehistoric sites, Quoyness Chambered Cairns, again similar to Maes Howe but smaller. There are other neolithic burial mounds throughout this island.

Stronsay is the most eastern island of the archipelago with several lovely, sandy beaches and is also well known for its rich, arable land. Stronsay was a point of convergence for the herring industry through the nineteenth century but it was more famed for the 'Great Kelp Boom' of the early nineteenth century where sea-weed was harvested and sold as potash and soda. Now it has settled back to doing what it does best, farming. The village at **Whitehall** is little more than two rows of cottages with a hotel and a pub but the main attraction of this area is exploring the coast. Bird-watching is always available throughout the Northern Isles so it is useful to bring a pair of compact binoculars. The Vat o' Kirbister on the island's south-east shore is a dramatic opening or 'gloup' spanned by the finest natural arch in Orkney. It gets its name from the peculiar gulping sound made as the sea swells through it.

From the air, the most northerly island in the group, **North Ronaldsay**, lies like a mechanic's rag across the North Ronaldsay Firth, again a fairly featureless rock apart from a slight rise on its north-western spur. This remote island, some 30 miles (48km) north of Kirkwall has a very unique, native breed of sheep that feed mostly on seaweed. This mottled breed has supposedly been on North Ronaldsay since before the Viking period. A dry-stone dyke has stood for over 100 years almost surrounding the island to keep the sheep off the arable land. Kelp has also been important as part of the island's economy as an exportable commodity but now it is farming that sustains North Ronaldsay's aging population. With a lack of other distractions its the wildlife, migratory birds and seals that attract attention here. The best seasons for bird-watching are spring and autumn but there is some activity through most of the year. There is the North Ronaldsay Bird Observatory on Twingness Croft on the south-west side of the island, a wind and solar powered cottage that offers accommodation and board along with insider information on how to make the most of 'twitching'.

SHETLAND

Up-Helly-Aa Festival is held every January in Lerwick

Compared to the wide, pastoral islands of Orkney, Shetland is a long, stringy strip of land that has given way to the sea at the edges to create its craggy outer islands and skerries. Thrust between the North Sea and Atlantic Ocean it offers more rugged and dramatic landscapes than its smoother, southerly neighbour. The terrain is generally quite stark with few bushes and no trees to talk of but there is a radiance, a special quality of light that comes from its northerly position. With the 60 degree line of latitude passing through the South Mainland, Bergen in Norway and Torshavn in the Faroe Isles are as close to Lerwick as Aberdeen and it is the nearest piece of the Britain to the North Pole. Having said that its potentially fierce climate is greatly moderated by the effects of the Gulf

Stream and there is plenty sunshine throughout the summer months. The 'simmer dim' is the term given to the near endless light through the summer and if you are camping it can make it a bit difficult to sleep for the first night or so.

Set at the main sea crossroads between Scotland and Scandinavia, like Orkney, Shetland's heritage was strongly Norse. They were ruled by the Vikings from the eighth to the twelfth century but its path in history differed from then on. The Stewart Earls who drained Orkney's economy left Shetland alone while great fishing nations such as the Dutch sought its harbours to take advantage of the bountiful surrounding waters. There are nearly 100 islands and only 15 of them inhabited. The harsh landscape that forged the hard working community is now balanced by the comforts of modern living and the revenue of a major oil production. The Shetlanders are a warm and fascinating people.

While the Ordcadians became admirable farmers, Shetlanders accepted the consequences of their environment and became noted seafarers and fishermen. Reaching back to their Norse heritage, the men of Shetland exploited deep-sea fishing grounds in the late eighteenth century working mainly for landlords at ridiculously low wages in boats directly evolved from Viking long-ships — yaols. Fishing industry has declined today and is centred in Lerwick and Whalsay.

❊   Shetland's capital, **Lerwick**, lies on the east coast of Mainland, sheltered from the North Sea by the island of Bressay and the Isle of Ness. Being the most northerly town in the British Isles, it is surprising cosmopolitan, an international centre for fishermen, oil workers and holiday-makers from around the globe. The main thoroughfare, the flagstone-paved Commercial Street, fairly throngs with foreigners, some from the Russian, Norwegian or Polish factory ships, 'Klondykers', anchored in Bressay Sound with their crews eager to buy up British goods. This has created a thriving market for local shopkeepers and they offer a surprising range of quality items. The P&O ships, the *St Claire* and the *St Sunniva* land at Lerwick from Aberdeen.

Sitting above Commercial Street and reached by tiny lanes is Fort Charlotte, built by Cromwell during the Dutch wars when English were trying to control fishing rights and the only Cromwellian fort still in reasonable order. The fort was burned by the Dutch in 1673. Shetland Museum on Lower Hillhead presents an appealing display of the history of man in Shetland from prehistory to the present.

You will hear plenty about the Up-Helly-Aa festivities no matter what time of year you visit the islands. This pagan, New Year festival started in its present form, although its roots are no doubt much older, in the late 1880's as a life-renewing festival and the end of Yule. The 'Guisers' are the main participants dressed in fantastic Viking costumes holding aloft their blazing torches and singing at the tops of their voices. A wild time is had by all climaxing in the burning of a mock Viking long-ship but the high spirits carry on through the night. An Up-Helly-Aa exhibition is found in a facility off St Sunniva Street. Lerwick's Up-Helly-Aa takes place on the last Tuesday in January although there are Up-Helly-Aa programs in other communities throughout the islands during January and February. Lerwick's is by far the biggest.

Opposite the town across the Sound of Bressay is the island of **Bressay** reached by a regular roll on roll off ferry service from Lerwick. Behind it facing the North Sea is one of the islands most important bird reserves. The **Island of Noss Nature Reserve** is about 5 miles (8km) east of Lerwick and reachable by inflatable boat. The 600ft (183m) cliffs facing the sea are inhabited by vast colonies of breeding auks, gannets and gulls. The noise can be terrific as it echoes around the fissured rocks. There is also a Shetland Pony stud farm of the island. One of the best places to eat is the Maryfield House Hotel on Bressay, only 3 minutes walk from the ferry terminal so easily reached from Lerwick. The prawn dishes are supreme.

If time is limited the south part of mainland contains the some of the islands most interesting parts. From Lerwick, the well-paved A970 stretches down the 24 miles (39km) to Sumburgh Head and the airport. The South Mainland is a long, thin ridge of flat, peat moorland, edged by lush, herb-rich meadows. There are no elevations higher than 1,000ft (305m) so views of the ocean are possible, at some points, on both sides of the road. No where is further than 3 miles (5km) from the sea in Shetland.

Eleven miles (18km) out of Lerwick on the east side is the village of Sandwick where a thirty passenger boat runs out to the island of **Mousa** and one of Britain's best preserved brochs, the **Broch of Mousa**. The broch sits like a giant bee-hive or a small cooling chimney near the sea-edge on this small island and probably, along with a similar structure on Mainland, guarded the Mousa Sound. It is 45ft (14m) high and some 50ft (15m) in diameter with the walls commencing at 12ft (3m) thick and tapering to around 7ft (2m). This was an easily defensible tower built around 2,000 years ago. The rest of the island is now inhabited only by sheep or ponies although there is evidence of cottages and crofts, long abandoned.

Shetland Croft House Museum is at **Boddam**, 5 miles (8km) south of Sandwick, just off the main road and it houses, in an old Shetlands croft house of the mid-nineteenth century, furniture made from driftwood, bearing in mind Shetland's lack of timber. There are also high-backed Shetland chairs, spinning wheels and domestic baskets woven from heather. There is an old water-mill down the road. Sumburgh International Airport is about 5 miles (8km) south of here on the A970 and it is not unusual to see a white strech-limo driving up from the airport carrying some oil industry executives.

Beyond the airport is **Jarlshof**, one of the most famous archeological sites in Britain representing six to eight distinct periods of human habitation covering 3,000 years from neolithic to Viking times. The popularity of the site through the centuries is attributed to a good anchorage in the adjacent bay, a fresh water nearby and green, pastoral land surrounding the site. The remains are fairly sparse but excellent displays around the site as well as the informative guide book and a small adjacent museum

Shetland

Herma Ness
Burrafirth
Haroldswick
Baltasound
Unst
Gloup
Balta
A968
Muness Castle
Yell
Fetlar
A970
Mid Yell
A968
Esha
Ness
Old Haa of Burravoe
Hillswick
A970
Burravoe
A968
Brae
N
A970
W E
A971 A971
S
Walls
Shetland Museum
Fort Charlotte
Walls
Museum
Scalloway
Lerwick
Scalloway Castle
Scalloway Museum
Island of Noss Nature Reserve
Bressay
A970
St Ninian's
Isle
Broch of Mousa
Boddam
Shetland Croft
Sumburgh
House Museum
Jarlshof
0   15 miles
0   20 km
Ness of Burgi

help to illuminate the various multi-layered periods and their dwelling places. The most interesting of these are the wheel houses of the medieval period. The name Jarlshof was an invention of Sir Walter Scott for his book *The Pirate*, written after his visit in 1814 but at that time he could not have been sure of the Viking connections. The airways near the site are busy with helicopters ferrying crew back and forward from the many oil fields some miles to the east of Shetland. The Sumburgh Hotel is sited next to Jarlshof and provides shelter if the winds are too fierce as well as excellent bar lunches and very reasonably priced accommodation.

About 1 mile (2km) south of Jarlshof, off the coast at the tip of Scatness is the **Ness of Burgi**, a stone-built defensive structure dating back to the Iron Age and resembling the many brochs of this area. To the west around the Bay of Quendale is the ragged headland of Fitful Head where the Lithuanian oil-tanker, *Braer*, ran aground in a howling gale on the 5 January 1993, spilling its cargo of 83,000 tons of crude oil. The disaster was somewhat lessened by the constantly turbulent sea surrounding this coast at that time of year that helped to break up the slicks. The prow of the sunken ship can still be seen.

St Ninian's Isle, a glorious little island off the west coast of Mainland, is linked by a tombolo or hour-glass shaped crescent of shell-sand. On this uninhabited islet are the ruins of a twelfth-century church where a horde of eighth-century Pictish silver treasure was found by Aberdeen University students and this is now on display in the Royal Museum of Scotland in Edinburgh as well as a replica display in Lerwick Museum.

Travelling west from Lerwick for around 6 miles (10km) by a circuitous route brings you to Shetland's second town, **Scalloway**, standing over an attractive bay and looking out to the Atlantic Ocean beyond the nearby island of Trondra. Only 200 years ago Scalloway was the capital of Shetland and its main fishing port but this shifted to Lerwick with increased international fishing activity in the North Sea using the eastern town as its base. Scalloway, though is still responsible for large catches of cod, haddock and whiting and overlooking the harbour is the North Atlantic Fisheries College.

Scalloway Museum in the middle of the village is one of the few focal points but it contains fascinating details on the so called 'Shetland Bus', a World War II clandestine shipping operation that maintained communication with the resistance movement in Nazi occupied Norway. Lunna House, now a guest house in north-east Mainland, was the headquarters of the Norwegian Resistance Movement for part of the war, responsible for organising the ferrying refugees or shipment of secret agents or weapons but then it was transferred to the better provided Scalloway. A book called the *Shetland Bus* by David Howarth tells of the many incidents surrounding these brave affairs.

Scalloway's narrow streets and ancient cottages are dominated by the ruins of Scalloway Castle, a turreted shell that stands on a narrow promontory near the water. The infamous Earl Patrick Stewart was responsible for its construction in 1600 using forced local labour. His and his son's tyrannical behaviour was known throughout Shetland and Orkney until he was executed for his crimes. Knitwear and glass-blowing workshops are found in the village and these offer some of the best examples of such island crafts. Taking the road south of Scalloway there are bridges crossing to the small islands of Trondra, West Burra and East Burra.

Returning north, the A971 branches off the main A970 and, passing Tingwall Airport, leads on to the western spur called West Mainland. This is a bleak but often beautiful prominence that terminates, some 29 miles (47km) away from Lerwick, at its highest point, Sandness Hill at 750ft (229m) before the land slopes into the Atlantic. The road is often diverted by deep-cut voes or fiords and breathtaking coastal scenery that break the monotony of the desolate moorland. **Walls** is the only village of consequence with a small local museum. There are walks available around the shores or near Sandness which offer views of the island of Papa Stour to the north-west. **Papa Stour** is reached by passenger ferry from West Burrafirth which operates 5 days a week during the summer but round trips are only available on Friday and Saturday.

The A970 is the main route north on Mainland and from the Walls road this can be reached by taking the Aith road to Voe, the B9071 which joins the main route some miles north although it is a sometimes tortuous winding, single track route. Easier but less scenic is the shorter single-track route, the B9075 further east, which also avails you to the workshops around Weisdale and Whiteness that produce fine silver, gold and enamel jewellery following intricate Norse, Celtic and original designs.

Heading north-west from here the terrain grows ever wilder with bleak moorland and dramatic voes dappled with simple, white cottages. For those that appreciate such dramatic, lonely landscapes this is the place to come. Shetland sheep are frequent road users so take care and allow them time to amble to the side. The famous Shetland ponies are often seen in nearby fields. Salmon, sheep and pony farming play a major part of the economy in these parts. Despite Shetlands success with oil the landscape in this northern sector remains unspoiled and with the special northern light shimmering off the sea it can be quite enchanting. If the weather is bad it can also be quite depressing.

Staying on the A970, North Mainland is reached by crossing a spit of land where the North Sea almost meets the Atlantic, cut off from each other by a mere 100 yards. Further on, **Hillswick** is the main community sporting Shetland's oldest pub, the Booth but a better bet for refreshment is the more salubrious St Magnus Bay Hotel set in its Norwegian building that was transported first to Glasgow for the Great Exhibition in 1896 then dismantled and brought to Hillswick. The minor B9078 leads on west to Brae Wick where there is a natural arch just off the coast and the road terminates at **Esha Ness** where there are dramatic cliffs beside the old lighthouse. Puffins favour this area and it is possible to sit amongst the wild flowers on the headland and watch them.

The north-east part of Mainland is reached by returning east and taking either of the B roads that continue north. The protected eastern shores of this area have been more populated due to their good harbours and access to fishing grounds. If you have never experienced the Auroa Borealis or Northern Lights you have more chance here than in any other part of Scotland. September and October are the most likely months. Returning south the village of **Brae** is surprisingly developed but this is accounted for by the large number of oil refinery workers based there. The oil refinery at Sullom Voe, the largest in Europe, is well hidden in this secluded inlet.

If you are setting out to explore the islands of Yell and Unst be sure to book your accommodation before hand as it is quite scarce. A drive-on/ drive-off passenger ferry operates from Toft on the north-east Mainland to the island of Yell. With its lack of foliage, **Yell** is a rather startling place with grim, heather moors reaching in every direction to the cliff edges and what habitations there are not fussy where they leave their cast-off cars. It is a bit of an acquired taste but for those that are prepared to explore and ignore some of the less attractive sides of life in these remote places there are wonderful cliff-side walks and ample wildlife especially seals and otters around the bays and coves.

The village of **Mid Yell** is a busy fishing port in the mid-eastern side of the island where a deep voe reaches across and almost joins with a lengthy fjord coming from the west. Most of the notable habitations are on this eastern coast. The A968 goes all the way to the top of the island where, at **Gloup**, there is the Gloup Fishermen's Memorial which marks the tragedy, in 1881, when 58 men were lost in a great storm. The village of **Aywick** just south of Mid Yell is a good place to find high-quality Shetland knitwear. Further south on the island's south-west corner is the **Old Haa** (hall) **of Burravoe**, once the centre of this region's fishing industry and the Old Haa being its oldest building. This former merchant's house now has a museum upstairs which presents the tale of the wrecking of a German sail-ship, the *Bohus*, in 1924 as well as displays on local flora and fauna, old photographs and taped recordings. There is a tea room in the Old Haa.

The A968 continues north through Yell and onto **Unst**, Britain's most northerly, inhabited island and a contrast to its bleak neighbour although there are stretches of joyless moorland that are similar. It is rich in bird-life and hosts a range of alpine-arctic flowers that draw naturalists from around the world. The A968 heads north towards Baltasound but turn right at the B9084 to reach **Muness Castle** on the island's south-west tip. This is Scotland's most northern stronghold built in the late sixteenth century and Shetland ponies often graze nearby to make a charming picture.

Baltasound is the island's main town with the only pub for many miles. This was a fishing centre and evidence of the once great curing sheds can still be seen. The lochs and voes throughout this island provide excellent fishing sport. There is an RAF base on the island which testifies to its strategic position overlooking this conference of the North Sea, Norwegian Sea and the Atlantic. For those that appreciate flora there is a famous botanical site just over a mile north-east of Baltasound at the Keen of Hamar where various montane species such as moss campion, Norwegian sandwort and Shetland mouse-ear thrive.

Travelling north from Baltasound on the A968 you arrive at **Haroldswick** with its carmine-coloured post office and small heritage centre. Taking the B9086 north-west from here leads to a wide voe called **Burrafirth**. From the end of the road there is a path leading to the cliffs at Herma Ness which stand around 600ft (183m) tall and are usually covered with sea birds. The profusion of several varieties such as puffins, gannets, and skuas all vying for a place on the sheer rock-face makes for a tumultuous but thrilling scene.

Returning to Yell, the island of **Fetlar** is reached on the ro-ro ferry from Gutcher and is called the 'garden of Shetland' but then most people have just driven through Yell to get there. For the epicurean it offers little except the sheer joy of unaffected scenery and, of course, wild flowers and birds. There is only one settlement called Houbie, a gathering of cottages and an interesting little Interpretative Centre giving an account of the island's history.

Getting to Fair Isle has to be planned as there are only limited ferry services from Lerwick or Sumburgh operating on certain days. This isolated chunk of land is caught mid-way between Shetland and Orkney and can be seen from the Aberdeen-Lerwick ferry if you are still awake at that time of night and the 'simmer dim' is bright enough.

The island is best known for its knitwear which differs from that of Shetland, more colourful with designs relating to Scandinavia although it is said the use of vivid colour springs from the forced landing of a Spanish ship and its crew in the sixteenth century who encouraged the islanders to brighten up their rather dull patterns.

In human terms **Fair Isle** is one of the most remote of British islands yet its position is perfect for migrating birds of many varieties travelling from the Arctic to Africa and back again. There are also some 750,000 sea birds making it their yearly nesting home. Meanwhile, there are only 70 people resident on the island. The main concentration of this population is around Stonybreck. Besides the bird life there is spectacular cliff scenery.

Additional Information

Places of Interest in Orkney

Birsay
Earl's Palace
Historic Scotland ☎ 0131 244 3101
Open: All times.

Brough of Birsay
North end of Orkney Mainland,
11 miles (18km) north of Stromness.
Open: Tide permitting.

Burger Hill Wind Turbine Site
Orkney mainland
☎ 01856 872073
Open: All year. Visitor Centre open,
April to October, Wednesday, Friday,
Saturday and Sunday, afternoons only.

Dounby
Click Mill
Historic Scotland ☎ 0131 244 3101
Open: April to September, Monday to
Saturday, 9.30am-7pm. Sunday, 2-7pm.
October to March, Monday to Saturday,
9.30am-4pm. Sunday, 2-4pm.

Gurness Broch
Off the A966 at Aikerness, 4 miles
(6km) north-west of Kirkwall
Historic Scotland ☎ 0131 244 3101
Open: April to September, Monday to
Saturday, 9.30am-7pm. Sunday, 2-7pm.
October to March, Monday to Saturday,
9.30am-4pm. Sunday, 2-4pm.

Kirkwall
Highland Park Distillery
☎ 01856 874619
Open: All year, Monday to Friday,
April to October. Tours from 10am-
4pm. Also open Saturdays in June to
August. November to March, Monday
to Friday. Tours at 2pm and 3.30pm.

Ortak Jewellers
Hatston Ind. Est.
Kirkwall
☎ 01856 872224
Open: Regular business hours.

St Magnus Cathedral
Kirkwall centre
Open: May to August, 9am-5pm and
closed Sundays except for services.

Tankerness House
Broad Street
☎ 01856 873191
Open: All year, Monday to Saturday,
10.30am-12.30pm & 1.30-5pm. Also May
to September, Sunday, 2-5pm.

Earl Partick's Palace and Bishop's Palace
Historic Scotland ☎ 0131 244 3101
Open: April to September, Monday to
Saturday, 9.30am-7pm. Sunday, 2-7pm.
October to March, Monday to Saturday,
9.30am-4pm. Sunday, 2-4pm.

Lambholm
Italian Chapel
south of Kirkwall
Open: At all times.

Stromness Natural History Museum
☎ 01856 850025
Open: May to September, daily, 10.30am-
5pm. October to April, Monday to Saturday, 10.30am-12.30pm and 1.30-5pm.

Maes Howe
Off the A965 9 miles (14km) west of
Kirkwall
Historic Scotland ☎ 0131 244 3101
Open: April to September, Monday to
Saturday, 9.30am-7pm. Sunday, 2-7pm.

October to March, Monday to Saturday,
9.30am-4pm. Sunday, 2-4pm.

Ring of Brogar
Between the Lochs of Harray & Stenness,
5 miles (8km) north-east of Stromness
Historic Scotland ☎ 0131 244 3101
Open: At all times.

Notland Castle
Island of Westray
☎ 01857 677480
Open: By arrangement but call at castle.

Outer Islands
Dwarfie Stane
On island of Hoy
Historic Scotland ☎ 0131 244 3101
Open: All times.

Skara Brae
9 miles (14km) north-west of Kirkwall
Historic Scotland ☎ 0131 244 3101
Open: April to September, Monday to
Saturday, 9.30am-7pm. Sunday, 2-7pm.
October to March, Monday to Saturday,
9.30am-4pm. Sunday, 2-4pm.

South Ronaldsay
Orkney Wireless Museum
11 miles (18km) south of Kirkwall
☎ 01856 831462
Open: April to Sept, daily, 10am-7pm.

Stenness Standing Stones
Between the Lochs of Harray & Stenness,
5 miles (8km) north-east of Stromness
Historic Scotland ☎ 0131 244 3101
Open: At all times.

St Margaret's Hope
Old Smiddy Museum
☎ 01856 831567
Open: Varied times. Contact by telephone.

St Mary's
Norwood Collection
Parish of Holm, Mainland Orkney
☎ 01856 781217
Open: May to September, Sunday,
Tuesday, Wednesday, Thursday, 2-5pm
and 6-8pm.

Stromness
Pier Art Centre
Victoria Street, Stromness
☎ 01856 850209
Open: All year, Tuesday to Saturday,
10.30am-12.30pm and 1.30-5pm.

Orkney: Other Useful Information

Airport
Kirkwall Airport
Orkney
☎ 01856 872421
Weathercall for this area ☎ 01898 500426

Emergencies
Ambulance, Police & Firebrigade ☎ 999

Tourist Information Office
Kirkwall
☎ 01856 872856
Orkney Tourist Board
Commercial Street
Kirkwall
☎ 01595 3434

Accommodation in Orkney
Harray
The Mercistar Hotel **   ☎ 01856 771366

Kirkwall
Albert Hotel **   ☎ 01856 6000

Stromness
Ferry Inn *   ☎ 01856 850280

Stromness Hotel **
☎ 01856 850298

Tourist Information Office
Lerwick
Shetland Islands Tourism
Market Cross
☎ 01595 693434

Places of Interest in Shetland

Boddam
Shetland Croft House Museum
Open: Daily except Mondays, May to
September, 10am-1pm and 2-5pm.

Island of Noss Nature Reserve
5 miles (8km) east of Lerwick. Access by
inflatable boat.
☎ 01591 693434
Open: mid-May to end of August.

Jarlshoff
Sumburgh Head, 22 miles (35km) south
of Lerwick
Historic Scotland ☎ 0131 244 3101
Open: April to September, Monday to

Saturday, 9.30am-7pm. Sunday, 2-7pm.
October to March, Monday to Saturday,
9.30am-4pm. Sunday, 2-4pm. Closed
Tuesday & Wednesday afternoon in
winter.

Lerwick
Fort Charlotte
Above Commercial Street
Historic Scotland ☎ 0131 244 3101
Open: April to September, Monday to
Saturday, 9.30am-7pm. Sunday, 2-7pm.
October to March, Monday to Saturday,
9.30am-4pm. Sunday, 2-4pm.

Shetland Museum
Lower Hillhead
☎ 01595 695050
Open: All year, Monday, Wednesday
and Friday, 10am-7pm. Tuesday,
Thursday & Saturday, 10am-5pm.

Up-Helly-Aa Exhibition
Off Sunniva Street in Lerwick
Open: May to September, Tuesday
2-4pm & 7-9pm, Friday, 7-9pm,
Saturday, 2-4pm.

Ness of Burgi
On the coast at the tip of Scatness 1 mile
(2km) south-west of Jarlshoff
Historic Scotland ☎ 0131 244 3101
Open: April to September, Monday to
Saturday, 9.30am-7pm. Sunday, 2-7pm.
October to March, Monday to Saturday,
9.30am-4pm. Sunday, 2-4pm.

Scalloway
Scalloway Museum
Main Street in Scalloway
☎ 01595 880256
Open: May to October, Tuesday,
Wednesday & Thursday, 2-5pm.
Saturday, 9am-1pm & 2-5pm. Sunday,
2-5pm.

Scalloway Castle
6 miles (10km) west of Lerwick
Historic Scotland ☎ 0131 244 3101
Open: April to September, Monday to
Saturday, 9.30am-7pm. Sunday, 2-7pm.
October to March, Monday to Saturday,
9.30am-4pm. Sunday, 2-4pm.

South Mainland
Mousa Broch
On the island of Mousa, accessible by
boat from Sandwick
Historic Scotland ☎ 0131 244 3101

Open: April to September, Monday to Saturday, 9.30am-7pm. Sunday, 2-7pm. October to March, Monday to Saturday, 9.30am-4pm. Sunday, 2-4pm.

Boat to Mousa Broch-the *Solan III* ☎ 01950 431367 Summer months only, weather permitting.

St Ninian's Isle
B9122 off west coast mainland
Open: At all times.

Unst
Muness Castle
South-east of corner of Isle of Unst
Historic Scotland ☎ 0131 244 3101
Open: April to September, Monday to Saturday, 9.30am-7pm. Sunday, 2-7pm. October to March, Monday to Saturday, 9.30am-4pm. Sunday, 2-4pm.

Walls
Walls Museum
Open: mid-May to mid-September, Wednesday, Friday and Sunday, 1-6pm.

Yell
Old Haa of Burravoe
Island of Yell
☎ 01957 722339
Open: April to September, Tuesday to Friday, Saturday and Sunday, 10am-4pm.

Shetland: Other Useful Information
Sumburgh Airport
☎ 01950 60654

British Airways, Scotland
Aberdeen to Sumburgh, Shetland
☎ 01345 222111 4 daily from Aberdeen, 3 on a Saturday and 2 on Sunday.
2 daily from Inverness, 1 on a Saturday. From Glasgow, 2 per day and 1 on a Saturday. From Edinburgh, 1 a day Monday to Friday.

P&O Scottish Ferries
Jamieson's Square, Aberdeen
The ferry St Clair takes 14 hours to cross from Aberdeen to Lerwick. Leaves 6pm and arrives in Lerwick at 8am. Cabins are available. Monday to Friday and not Tuesdays, June to August.
☎ 01224 572615

Loganair
☎ 0141 889 3181 or Sumburgh ☎ 01595 840246
From Edinburgh, 1 flight per day.

Shalder Coaches
Scalloway, Shetland
☎ 01595 880217
Weathercall for this area ☎ 01898 500426

Emergencies
Ambulance, Police & Firebrigade ☎ 999

Accommodation
Brae
Busta House **
☎ 01806 522506

Bressay
Maryfield House *
☎ 01595 820207

Fair Isle
Fair Isle Lodge *
Fair Isle, Shetland
☎ 01595 760258

Island of Unst
Clingera Guest House, Baltasound *
☎ 01957 711579

St Magnus Bay Hotel *
Hillswick
☎ 01806 503371

Lerwick
Keveldsro House Hotel **
Greenfield Place, Lerwick
☎ 01595 692195

Sumburgh
Sumburgh Hotel **
☎ 01950 460201

Campsites in Shetland
Brae
Valleyfield Campsite
☎ 01806 522365

Lerwick
Camping Bods or Barns
Building that used to accommodate fishermen during the fishing season and now offer simple shelter for campers. You will need everything but the tent.
☎ 01595 693434

Lerwick
Clickimin Caravan and Campsite
Lochside, near Lerwick
☎ 01595 694555

Lerwick
Scottish Youth Hostel
☎ 01595 692114

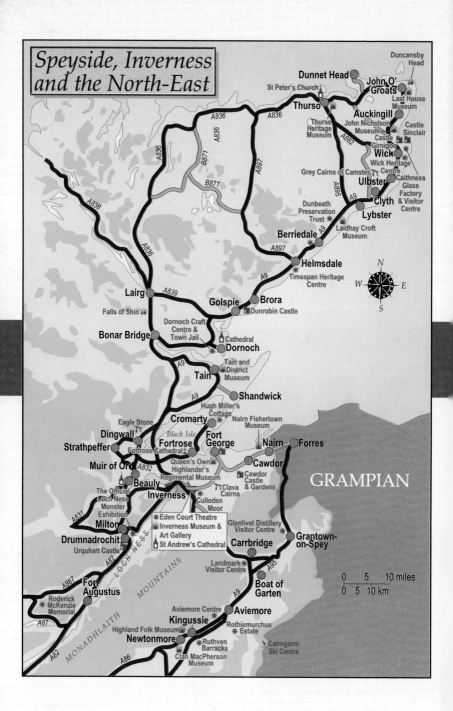

Speyside, Inverness and the North-East

Duncansby Head

Dunnet Head

St Peter's Church

Thurso

A836

A836

A836

B871

A897

B871

Thurso Heritage Museum

John O' Groats

Last House Museum

Auckingill

John Nicholson Museum

Castle Girnigoe

Wick

Castle Sinclair

A882

Caithness Glass Factory & Visitor Centre

Wick Heritage Centre

Grey Cairns of Camster

Ulbster

A9

A895

Clyth

Lybster

A838

A836

Dunbeath Preservation Trust

Laidhay Croft Museum

A9

Berriedale

A897

Helmsdale

Timespan Heritage Centre

Lairg

A839

A9

Falls of Shin

Golspie

Brora

Dunrobin Castle

Bonar Bridge

Dornoch Craft Centre & Town Jail

Cathedral

Dornoch

N

W   E

S

A9

Tain and District Museum

Tain

A9

Shandwick

Hugh Miller's Cottage

Nairn Fishertown Museum

Cromarty

Eagle Stone

Dingwall

Black Isle

Fort George

Nairn

Forres

Strathpeffer

Fortrose

Fortrose Cathedral

Cawdor

Muir of Ord

A832

Queen's Own Highlander's Regimental Museum

Cawdor Castle & Gardens

GRAMPIAN

Beauly

Clava Cairns

The Official Loch Ness Monster Exhibition

Inverness

Culloden Moor

A831

Eden Court Theatre

Inverness Museum & Art Gallery

St Andrew's Cathedral

Milton

Glenlivet Distillery Visitor Centre

Grantown-on-Spey

Drumnadrochit

Urquhart Castle

A82

Carrbridge

A95

Landmark Visitor Centre

0   5   10 miles

0   5   10 km

Fort Augustus

A887

Roderick McKenzie Memorial

A9

Boat of Garten

A87

Aviemore Centre

Aviemore

Kingussie

Rothiemurchus Estate

Highland Folk Museum

Cairngorm Ski Centre

Newtonmore

Ruthven Barracks

Clan MacPherson Museum

A86

MONADHLIATH MOUNTAINS

LOCH NESS

Speyside, Inverness and the North-East

9

The infamous Drumochter Pass was a formidable, natural barrier to the Highlands until General Wade built his military roads in the early eighteenth century. Today, once across this lofty gateway, whether by rail or the main A9 North road, an unrivalled region is entered, rich in history and awe inspiring vistas. The first stop on the A9 is the village of **Dalwhinnie**, the highest Highland village at 1,173ft (358m) above sea level. Dalwhinnie Distillery is the first of many whisky distillers that stand close to the banks of the River Spey and it contains a small visitor centre showing the social history of the village as well as offering visitors a warming dram.

This area's history was most noticeably impacted in July, 1724 with the arrival of General Wade and his squad of road builders. By December of that year he had finished his survey of the central Highlands and reported his plans to 'reduce the Highlands to obedience'. Roads and bridges were built between barracks to facilitate better communication of 'His Majesty's troops' and between 1725 and 1735, 250 miles (402km) of relatively good surfaces were laid. Today, the A9 is the main North Road, a fast-flowing combination of dual and single carriageway that is notorious for thoughtless drivers in a hurry to reach Inverness or Perth to the south. A new scheme of 'speed cameras' is helping to restrain those with a heavy foot but care should always be taken on this route.

Just off the A9 at Ralia, near Newtonmore, is a good rest place with a picnic area and Tourist Information Office. There are viewpoints of the surrounding mountains and, through the summer months, an exhibition reflecting facets of the local community. To best appreciate the serenity and stirring panoramas of Speyside at a much slower pace it is a good idea to come off the A9 here anyway and use the old A9 road. This is Shinty country, a Scots game more ancient than golf and still very popular in this region. It has lead to an unusual incidence of left-handed golfers (40 per cent) using the facilities at Newtonmore Golf Club. These 18 holes adjacent to the River Spey is a regular venue for the Scottish left-handed golf championships.

Newtonmore is MacPherson country and there is a small museum dedicated to the clan. Apart from the peace and quiet there is also a new attraction at the north end of Main Street, Waltzing Waters. You could not fail to see its shimmering frontage, somewhat of an anomaly in this sober little Victorian town. Inside is an elaborate though sometimes comical display of dancing water fountains and coloured light displays presented in a theatre configuration with accompanying Scottish and Classical music. It takes itself, at times, rather too seriously and that is where the humour comes in. There are various displays and a good little café in the upstairs foyer.

A few minutes on is the village of **Kingussie**. The name is derived from the Gaelic meaning 'the Head of the Pinewood'. Before the arrival of the railway in 1890, Kingussie was a centre for weaving and spinning. It, along with Newtonmore, became a popular tourist stop with wealthy English families journeying to the Highlands by train, bringing their household from the south and setting up home for the summer. Shooting and fishing were popular as well as taking the beneficial Highland air. Beautiful Victorian houses built as holiday homes are still evident. One of Kingussie's main attractions is the Highland Folk Museum found just off the main street. Originating on the island of Iona, the museum moved around the Highlands quite a bit before settling in Kingussie in 1935. It has amassed a fascinating collection of items that give an insight into aspects of Highland life. In the Hebridean Black House from Lewis, a replica of the houses used around 200 years ago, there are short legged stools to keep you 'out of the peat reak' as well as an adjacent byre to keep the animals in. There is a farming museum and varying demonstrations of traditional crafts.

The nearby ruins of **Ruthven Barracks** or the 'Red Place' are set on a man-made mound and backed by the Cairngorms. In their time they commanded one of the major crossing sites on the Spey and this is still easily appreciated when you see them towering over the Spey valley. It was built by government militia in 1718 as part of the Highland campaign and used as a staging post for troops and horses. To the followers of the

---

Jacobite cause, however, this was a stain on their land, a symbol of suppression by the House of Hanover. In February, 1746 the Jacobite army took control of the barracks and blew them up to avoid them falling back into English hands. Two and a half months later, following their dire defeat at the battle of Culloden, the tattered remains of Prince Charlie's forces came back to Ruthven expecting to carry on the campaign but received orders to disperse as the young pretender made his escape back to France.'Let every man seek his own safety in the best way that he can' was the word from Charles. The barracks remain roofless and bare, much as they were left in 1746.

The River Spey, meandering through this part of the area, has been a keynote in Scottish and Highland history and amply contributes to the magnificent scenery surrounding it. It commences its 98 mile (158km) journey to the Moray Firth at Loch Spey in the heart of the Monadhliath Mountains passing through the communities of Newtonmore, Kingussie, Aviemore, Boat of Garten, Grantown on Spey, Fochabers and finally entering the sea at Spey Bay.

Behind Kingussie, the **Monadhlaith Mountains**, reaching from the Spey River over to Loch Ness to the west appear quite desolate, littered with peat bogs and glacial debris scattered over a granite base. The Cairngorms, on the other side of the Spey valley are higher and more typical of the Highlands, offering perhaps one of the most magnificent landscapes in Europe. They reach to over 4,000ft (1,219m) but have been more accessible to sportsmen and sightseers than neighbouring ranges throughout the years and have become a major attraction. As well as low level walks through the forest to high mountain climbing for experienced mountaineers there is also shooting, fishing, camping, canoeing and the area's biggest draw, skiing.

About 20 miles (32km) south-east of Inverness and 80 miles (129km) north of Perth at the foothills of the Cairngorms is **Aviemore**. The village is a nodal point on the tourist map for this part of the Highlands, although, in recent years, it has been criticised for its rather tired and disagreeable 60's styled amenities. This problem is currently being addressed and there is no doubt that it will return to the favoured resort it was when first established some 30 years ago. The majority of the concrete blocks you see were devised and built as part of a grand plan to facilitate more tourists and extend the season especially to take advantage of the nearby skiing facilities. The village was originally little more than a few cottages and a couple of hotels but local initiative has created a haven of bistros, bars, amusement arcades and numerous hotels. The Aviemore Centre contains an ice rink, swimming pool, theatre and cinema so there is usually something to do even in the foulest weather. ✳

Outdoor pursuits are found at Glen More which is part of the Cairngorm National Nature Reserve a few miles up the glen past Coylumbridge. On **Loch Morlich** is sailing and windsurfing while the surrounding woods and glens offer walking and more strenuous hiking in the higher hills. There are plenty loch-side parking areas with adjacent course sandy beaches in which to paddle. If you wonder where reindeer go when they are not busy over the Yuletide then visit the Cairngorm Reindeer Centre found near Loch Morlich. The herd was established here in the early 1950's and has grown to 500. The young calves are born in May. The nearby **Rothiemurchus Estate** has done exemplary work in providing an outdoor experience for visitors in this area and there is a host of activities organised only a few minutes from Aviemore. Forest and wildlife walks are organised with rangers through the ancient Caledonian Pinewoods or following the River Spey. Various educational projects are available as well as farm tours, estate tours, clay pigeon shooting and fishing. Their visitor centre is found on the B970 before Coylumbridge, Tel: 01479 810858.

Still on or near the banks of the River Spey is a triangle of holiday villages, Carr Bridge, Boat of Garten and Grantown of Spey a few miles north and east of Aviemore. **Carrbridge** comprises of a few cottages lining the main street but at its south end is the Landmark Visitor Centre. This forested mini-theme park seems to expand every year with new attractions. Besides the nature and tree top trails which are educational but tend to be a romp through the woods for kids, there is a presentation on the forestry industry including a steam powered sawmill and a tree-felling display. There is a good restaurant and shop along with a High-lander multi-vision show and exhibition telling the story of man's struggle to survive in this once remote and infertile area.

In the village itself, it is hard to belief that the thin sliver of a bridge, the original pack horse crossing over the River Dulnain, still stands but local teenagers, despite the dangers, delight in climbing up and diving off into the peaty, swirling depths below. **Grantown-on-Spey** is another Victorian resort, evident as soon as you enter the wide, well designed main street. For a more sombre Highland holiday this is the place to come, away from the flurry of Aviemore. Fishing and golf are the main activities with investigation of the nearby Speyside whisky distilleries an enjoyable diversion. To get onto the Malt Whisky trail follow the A95 east and enter an area rich in distilleries, once the stronghold of the illegal distilling trade. The Glenlivet, one of the most popular Scotch whiskies, dates back to the early 1800's founded by an illicit distiller and smuggler, George Smith. The distillery and centre make visitors most welcome and the displays are educational and samples, on a cold day, most warming. For an award winning plate of fish and chips try Smiffy's licensed restaurant in Grantown's town square.

Boat of Garten might seem an odd name for a Highland village but a small ferry operated here crossing the River Spey until a bridge was built in the late nineteenth century. The 'Boat' is the northern terminus for the Strathspey Steam Railway leaving from Aviemore and taking around half an hour. There is a nostalgic old station and various carriages in disparate states of repair. Loch Garten nearby is the spot where Scotland's rare Ospreys return year after year to raise clutches of chicks, gradually repopulating the Highlands with this beautiful bird of prey.

Ruthven Barracks, near Kingussie, were a government troop staging post

The luxury barge cruise, Loch Ness

❋   The approach to **Inverness** on the A9 is quite dramatic coming down a long decline above the town and heading for the Kessock Bridge. The best turning off the A9 into the town centre is just before the bridge. This is the social, cultural, transport and administration centre of the north Highlands serving a huge area that includes the west and islands as well as the communities to the north. The first written references to Inverness came in the sixth century in Amdamnan's account of the life of St Columba when he describes the saint's visit to King Brude's fortress to convert the northern Picts. Inver means 'mouth', with the town being established near the mouth of the River Ness where it meets the Beauly Firth. There are lovely views looking from the lower bridges up to the town and its red-sandstone castle perched on the southern banks. The original Inverness Castle was the possible scene of the murder of King Duncan by Macbeth and stood in the Crown area to the east of the present Castle Hill.

🏰   The present castle, built between 1834 and 1846 contains the offices of local government and law courts. Just below the castle is the Tourist Information Office in Upper Bridge Street, adjacent to the town's mu-

🏛   seum which contains various items relating to the town's history and that of the Highlands as well as an art gallery.

Most of Inverness's High Street has been pedestrianised so it is easy to amble through an area mostly given over to typical retail shops. There is little of architectural interest. For indoor-shopping there is the modern Eastgate Centre and various supermarkets if you wish to stock up on reasonably priced groceries before venturing further north or west. Inverness caters well to the archetypal tourist who wishes to trace and identify with their Scottish ancestors. Besides the usual tartan shops and woollen mills, at the local library at Farraline Park beside the bus station there is a genieologist-in-residence thorough the summer months who offers an initial free consultation to those that wish to discover their Highland roots. The Clan Tartan Centre at Holm Mills can also work out which tartan you are entitled to wear and for a small fee include this and your clan history on a certificate.

Following Church Street you come to Abertarff House, one of the

🏛   oldest building in Inverness dating from 1592 and containing a wonderful turnpike stairway. It also serves as the Highland regional headquarters for the National Trust for Scotland.

Crossing the river by the Ness Bridge and turning left along the river

❋   along Ness Walk you come to Eden Court, the most northerly theatre in the UK, built in 1976 and named after the Bishop Robert Eden who commissioned the adjacent cathedral a century before. The main hall has 800 seats and the building has a variety of uses as a theatre, conference centre and art gallery. There is a small restaurant. Nearby St Andrew's

⛪   Cathedral, built in 1866 and 1869, has an elaborate interior with a choir screen and rood cross by Robert Lorimer well worth seeing. The font is a copy of Thorwalden's Font in Copenhagen Cathedral.

For a pleasant walk you can follow the banks of the river and on either side and cross the Georgian bridges to Ness Islands which have been turned into attractive public parks. Also worth seeing is the northern end of Telford's Caledonian Canal. Here the Brahan Seer, a sixteenth- or seventeenth-century Highland prophet, predicted the coming of the canal, allowing ships to sail across Scotland. 'Strange as it may seem to you this day, a time will come when full-rigged ships will be seen sailing eastward and westward by the back of Tomnahurich near Inverness'. Tomnahurich is the noticeable lump, otherwise know as the 'Fairy Hill' near to the canal. The Brahan Seer touched on many other facets of Highland life that have since came true. 'That the clans will become so effeminate as to flee from their native country before an army of sheep,' was another poignant premonition.

A popular excursion from Inverness is down the A82 to Loch Ness as far as Drumnadrochit and Castle Urquart. There is only a small stretch of the man-made canal at this end of the loch where it runs parallel with the River Ness. The Caledonian Canal stretches from the Beauly Firth in the north to Loch Eil in the south linking Loch Lochy, Loch Oich, Loch Ness and the small Loch Dochfour. Less than half of its 60 miles (97km) are man-made. The rest is a massive geological fault called the Great Glen which runs diagonally across Scotland, already half full of water when Thomas Telford commenced the canal in 1803. One of the reasons the government employed Telford to institute his plans was to give employment to the hundreds of Highlanders who had poured into the area following the Clearances. The canal was never the industrial success that was hoped for and has been used mainly for fishing or pleasure craft but the feat of digging this trench through some of Scotland's most inhospitable countryside still stands as a momento to the men who made it.

Loch Ness is a spectacular stretch of water to drive alongside albeit the A82 is the main route to the west and can be quite busy. The natural Highland vegetation that lines its banks, birch, alder, rowan and hazel trees now struggle to resist the intense forestry schemes of pine that continue to engulfed wide swathes of the Highlands. It was the construction of this road in the 1930's that sparked off the modern craze for monster spotting when many sightings were claimed by workmen and locals. Perhaps the monster was disturbed by the digging and blasting. The first mention of 'Nessie', as he or she is colloquially known, goes back to St Adamnan's chronicle of St Columba who had to placate the monster following its attack on a fellow monk.

For the chance of a closer encounter with the monster the best bet might be to go underwater. Operating from the Clansman Marina about 6 miles (10km) south of Inverness is the Swatch Loch Ness Submarine where a small submersible dives several times a day to the floor of the loch usually at around 400ft (122m). As it is primarily a scientific project, various daily missions are set to observe things like plankton, fish or sediment. Samples of the sediment taken by the submarine show changes in the atmosphere over the past 10,000 years and incidents such as Chernobyl and the accumulated debris from the Industrial Revolution have all been charted. Visibility is good at lower levels although, because of the peat stain in the

Boats queue to ascend the locks at Fort Augustus

Cawdor Castle, near Nairn

water, it is a bit like diving through a glass of whisky. Places in the submarine are limited so advance reservations are nearly always necessary (☎ 0456 450709).

At **Drumnadrochit**, a third of the way down the loch, the Loch Ness experience congeals into a thickened mass of commercial monster madness. About the best chance visitors have of seeing the elusive Nessie is by standing next to the model in the pond at the 'The Official Loch Ness Monster Exhibition Centre'. Using sight and sound in a multi-media presentation the centre offers the facts about the monster and leaves you to draw your own conclusion. There are shops and craft outlets as well as a restaurant, lounge bar, coffee shop and hotel at Drumnadrochit.

Many visitors to **Urquhart Castle** 2 miles (3km) further along the A82 reserve a portion of their attention for the choppy waters of the loch hoping for a chance-sighting and a fortune-making photograph. It is around this area that most of the sightings have been made. Urquhart Castle was once one of the largest castles in Scotland and it stands on a rocky outcrop that juts out into the loch, part of a series of forts that controlled the Great Glen. Since Pictish times the site has been strategic. It was partly dismantled by the English during the Jacobite rebellion to avoid it becoming a rebel outpost and through the centuries since its decay has continued. The castle is reached by crossing the defensive ditch and enter the crumbled stone walls through a series of arches and tunnels before reaching the outer loch-side walls and tower.

The A82 continues through Invermorist where you can take a diversion through Glen Moriston to see the memorial for Roderick McKenzie, a follower and look-alike of Bonnie Prince Charlie. He was captured and killed by the Redcoats but before he died he cried, 'You have killed your prince' thus delaying the pursuit of the true monarch. **Fort Augustus** is a crossing point of the Caledonian Canal and the main A82. Here, sailors and their craft often gather at the quaysides and adjourn to the bars waiting to pass through the locks the next morning. Following the 1715 Jacobite uprising a garrison was established in the town to quell further trouble and a fort was built and named after George II's son, William Augustus, Duke of Cumberland later to become known throughout the Highlands as 'Butcher Cumberland' following the defeat at Culloden. The fort was dismantled and incorporated into an abbey, now a public school with its church open to visitors. A golf course is found on the edge of town, moved there in 1925 to make way for tree planting. The proviso was that it would have to share the ground with sheep and that remains so today.

It is possible to return to Inverness via the south road of Loch Ness but it is twisting and hilly although very scenic so allow enough time. The plunging **Falls of Foyers** are 10 miles (16km) north of Fort Augustus on this B862 and quite spectacular. The estates of Coignafearn in the heart of the Monadhliath Mountains can be reached from the B851 where a variety of deer, red kites, wild goats and the occasional eagle can sometimes be seen but it is a fair drive through forest and mountainous single track road to this remote glen that surrounds the River Findhorn. It can also be reached via Tomatin on the A9 about 16 miles (26km) south of Inverness.

Four miles (6km) to the east of Inverness following the B9006 is the **battlefield of Culloden**. This could be a rather disappointing excursion as there is only a stretch of boggy, bracken and heather-covered land but thanks to the effort of the National Trust and their excellent Visitor Centre, the incidents leading up to, during and following this tragic battle are given their due credit. On the 16 April 1746 Prince Charles Edward Stuart and his 5,000 kilted supporters faced the 9,000 strong Hanovarian forces under the command of the Duke of Cumberland. Following their march to Derby, well over the English Border, the Jacobite army, exhausted and starving as well as pursued by the largest army ever mustered against the Scots, attempted to surprise their foes at Nairn, some 12 miles (19km) east of Culloden. Their night march and early morning attack failed miserably.

Later at Culloden, facing a battery of cannon and superior muskets with few similar weapons to reply the Highland army were forced to attempt their notorious, blood-curdling charge over boggy ground and through wind-driven sleet. The Highlanders, who were more used to a close fighting technique using their 'targe', a rounded shield and broad swords were held off by the better drilled and armed southern forces. Nearly 1,000 Jacobites fell and those that were wounded were slain where they lay. There were only around fifty Redcoat casualties. This was the last major battle to be fought on British soil. Bonnie Prince Charlie, with a price of £30,000 on his head, remained hidden in the Western Highlands for 5 months before departing on a frigate for France and debauched oblivion. So ended the 'romantic' tale of Bonnie Prince Charlie and the Jacobites. He had arrived in Scotland with only seven men and no money to speak of and raised an army of wild clansmen who could hardly agree with one another yet they would follow him. He virtually walked through Scotland claiming all as he went, succeeded in reaching deep into England and some say he might have been successful if he had continued to London.

The Visitor Centre admirably outlines the reasons for and the results of the battle using historic tableaux, audio presentations and slides. Outside, various plaques identify the clans and their positions as well as their graves. Fenced trails lead around the moor and battle site. The supposed position from where Cumberland commanded his troops is marked by a flat stone. The 'Well of the Dead' is a site where wounded Highlanders were slain as they attempted to take water. A restored, thatched cottage, Old Leanach still stands, the only building to survive the battle and where 300 Highlanders were burnt alive. It was inhabited until the beginning of the twentieth century and is now a folk museum.

The aftermath of Culloden was almost as savage as the battle. Cumberland, now known as the Butcher, had his troops scour the Highlands and Islands for any possible Jacobite supporters, had them imprisoned or put to death, burned cottages and raped the women thereby ensuring no further insurgence. The possession of weapons, wearing of the kilt and tartan, playing of bagpipes and the Gaelic language were all banned although it was hard to enforce the latter. A propaganda campaign finally sealed the Highlander's reputation and everything about the Highlands became regarded as uncouth by everyone south of the Drumochter Pass. Not until Sir Walter Scott's very popular novels often set in the Highlands, the coming of King George IV in 1822 and finally Queen Victoria in the middle of that century did this attitude change in the minds of British people.

Just off the same road as Culloden about 1 mile (2km) further east turning right on the B851 is the **Cairns of Clava**, known as mainland Scotland's Stonehenge. Sheltered in a copse of beech trees are these late neolithic or Bronze Age burial cairns. Standing stones encircle the burial sites with inscriptions carved into some of them. The middle cairn, known as a ring cairn, had its centre open to the heavens while the others remained covered although their roofs have since collapsed.

Continuing along the B9006 for several miles you will arrive at **Cawdor** village and Cawdor Castle, best pronounced 'Cawdir' and one of the most romantic and commodious castles in Scotland. Still lived in by the Cawdor family, it maintains an air of pleasant domesticity making it more of a home than an ancient, chilly keep. The main tower is 600 years old with several quixotic additions that flourish around it. This is the Cawdor of Shakespeare's *Macbeth* where the character becomes Thane of Cawdor thus fulfilling the witches' prophecy, encouraging him to murder Duncan to become king. One of its most pleasant aspects is the walled garden, not so stately and formal as some but more congenial for its simple arrangements. Be sure to obtain a copy of the castle guide book which humorously helps to make a visit more interesting, especially how the castle was founded.

Nairn is primarily a holiday town on the shores of the Moray Firth, supposed to be known for its milder weather but in Scotland that is a rather nebulous assertion. It is also known as the 'Brighton of the North' and again, apart from being next to the sea, there is little resemblance. It has an old fashioned, courteous air and was planned well in Victorian times. There is a long, sandy beach and an over-abundance of accommodation. Not an overly exciting place, it is perhaps best known for its two golf courses, particularly Nairn West which is visited by golfers from around the world. Nairn Fishertown Museum in the Laing Hall in King's Street has interpretive displays about the old fishertown of Nairn with a good collection of photographs from the steam drifter era. There are model boats and exhibits on the domestic and social life of the area.

Returning to Inverness, a diversion on the B9092 north-west to **Fort George** is essential. Built on a strategic headland that juts into the Moray Firth less than a mile across the water from the Black Isle, this Hanovarian stronghold, named for George II was the final nail in the Jacobite coffin. Erected to replace the castle at Inverness that was blown up by the Jacobites in 1746, its construction commenced in 1748, 2 years after the

Battle of Culloden. When it was finished in 1769 there was no longer any trace of hostility from the Highlanders. Kept as a military barracks, which it still is, it is a large fortress essentially in its original condition and fascinating because of this. Many generations of Highland soldiers have been trained within these walls and the Regimental Museum of the Queen's Own Highlanders reflects their exploits with its collection of arms, colours, uniforms and medals connected with every major campaign fought by the British Army over the past two centuries. The chapel's stained glass windows include an image of the bagpipes but the most impressive aspect of the place has to be its vigourous military architecture, perhaps the most impressive of its kind in Europe.

Inland and north from Inverness takes you over the **Kessock Bridge** built in 1982 to replace the ferry that operated here for many centuries. The bridge lands on the **Black Isle**, not entirely an island but a large peninsula protruding into the North Sea and bound by the Moray and Cromarty Firths. The Black Isle consists of gently sloping and very green farmland edged by beaches with several curious little fishing villages intermittently spaced.

It is a short drive along the A832 to **Fortrose** where small boat sailing is popular and the Fortrose and Rosemarkie golf course lies out on a peninsula stretching out into the firth like a wizened old finger. At the end of this Chanonry Point is the memorial stone to the Brahan Seer and frequent visits of the most northerly pod of dolphins can sometimes be seen. They range from here to Aberdeen Harbour. Fortrose Cathedral stands in the village, another great church founded by David I.

The village of **Cromarty** on the north-east tip of the isle is where most visitors stop to enjoy the pebble beach and visit the home of Hugh Miller. Run by the National Trust for Scotland, the cottage contains writings, geological specimens and personal memorabilia surrounding this famous geologist, naturalist and writer. A nice walk or drive on the small road north-east of the village leads to the Sutors of Cromarty with wide views across to the Moray Coast and north to Easter Ross and the Tain Peninsula. The route continues along the north side of the Black Isle to rejoin the A9. The Cromarty Firth is dotted with old or renovated oil rigs being serviced at Invergordon on the north shore.

The area inland from the Black Isle is popular holiday country again stemming back to the Victorian trend for the Highlands. **Dingwall** is a main centre with plenty shops and supermarkets to stock up for more remote adventures. Macbeth was born here. The Town House is worth stopping for the local museum, mostly dedicated to a local soldier made good, General Sir Hector MacDonald. The village of **Strathpeffer** is due east of Dingwall, a popular spa town in the 1800's and remaining a quiet resort with plenty of hotels. Walking is a popular and none to exerting pastime with the Eagle Stone, a Pictish symbol stone found just east of the village being one of the most repeated. It was predicted by the Brahan Seer that if the stone fell from its perch three times then ships would tie up to it. It has already toppled twice and the Cromarty Firth flooded up to

Dingwall's county buildings. Perhaps the clairvoyant foresaw some result of global warming. Today, the stone is firmly cemented to its base.

Further south are the villages of Conon Bridge, Muir of Ord and Beauly. The Black Isle Show is held just outside Muir of Ord in August of each year. **Beauly** is a genteel little place with the ruins of a thirteenth-century priory and a world famous and long established wool and tweed shop, Campbell's. It is also an established centre for salmon and brown trout fishing. Beats of the River Beauly are quite expensive for salmon but much less expensive brown trout fishing is available around Beauly itself. Permits can be had from Beauly Angling Club. Beauly Music Festival is held late in September and features a variety of bands from around Britain. The Priory Restaurant and hotel is a little expensive but worth the extra.

There are interesting excursions away from Beauly into some of Scotland's most spectacular glens. Following the B831 south-west, **Glen Affric** is one of the most untamed, wide chunks of Highland country. The hills are the highest in Scotland north of the Great Glen. It is quite remote and you are as likely to see a red deer as a fellow human being here. **Glencannich** lies north just above Loch Affric where a Hydro Electric dam has turned two lochs into one, the biggest in Scotland at 9 miles (14km) long.

The Tain Peninsula forms the boundary of Easter Ross with two routes crossing it, the A836 heading directly north to Bonar Bridge or the more travelled A9 across the new Dornoch Bridge and all points north. With Glenmorangie Distillery on its doorstep producing the best selling malt whisky in Scotland, the market town of **Tain** has an air of noble antiquity as well as malted barley. The Tain and District Museum in Castle Brae just off the High Street forms a good introduction to the town's past as well as being the Clan Ross Centre. The Tolbooth is the most distinctive piece of architecture, a sixteenth-century tower with an equally ancient bell. Tain golf course, laid out near the Whiteness Sands and overlooking the Firth to Dornoch, has the markings of a true links course and was designed by Tom Morris.

The rest of the Tain Peninsula is rather bleak with the countenance of heavy oil associated industry marring the southern shores. The community of **Shandwick** is known for its caves and a cross slab standing 9ft (3m) tall in a field above the village, erected in memory of three Norse princes who were shipwrecked near here. The villages of Hilton and Shandwick are not so attractive with modern holiday bungalows and jets constantly roaring overhead from Lossiemouth on the opposite side of the Firth.

The new Dornoch Bridge has saved much motoring time by cutting off an 18 mile (29km) trip along the Dornoch Firth via Bonar Bridge and back along the other side. Now the A9 slices across the Firth but there are good reasons to continue along the old A9 towards Bonar Bridge unless you are in a hurry to travel north. Just before the bridge of Bonar Bridge where salmon neters are often seen hauling out their empty nets, there is a turning to **Strath Carron** and Croick Church, some 10 miles (16km) up the glen. Here, in the spring of 1845 the families who had been evicted from their crofts in Glencalvie sought shelter in makeshift lean-to's and scratched messages on the church windows that can still be read. 'Glencalvie people was here, May 24th 1845' reads one while another states 'this place needs cleaning'.

Bonar Bridge is a gateway to a relatively undiscovered interior of this part of the Highlands. Following the A836 north, Carbisdale Castle Youth Hostel at Invershin is a particularly well-appointed convenience for back-packers exploring this part of the country where accents from most parts of Europe mingle. Nearby are the **Falls of Shin**, a well known tourist stop with a large coach park, gift shop and restaurant often with a young lady piper who appears as soon as a well-laden coach pulls in. The falls, reached by a series of stairways are a major obstacle for migrating salmon that recklessly hurl themselves into the tubular torrent.

Five miles (8km) on, either following the minor road or back-tracking to the slightly better A836 is the village of **Lairg**. While this is no metropolis it is a welcome outpost of civilisation for those that have just taken the A836 north to Tongue or the A838 along Loch Shin to Laxford Bridge and the north-west. They step out of their cars looking like they have just come off a roller-coaster. The railway line north stops here at Lairg and it is a popular holiday retreat with fishing, boating and walking in the hills behind the town. From Lairg it is a pleasant drive back to the coast at Loch Fleet where you pick up the A9 north or turn south to explore Dornoch.

First time visitors to the Edwardian town of **Dornoch** may come expecting something more rugged and isolated in this northern zone but are pleasantly surprised to find an elegant, rather refined community in a setting that would be equally fitting in Somerset or the Cotswolds. At its centre is the compact but engaging form of Dornoch Cathedral, its friendly cruciform shape surrounded by an island of grass and trees. The town became a bishopric in 1224 and the cathedral dates from then but, as is usual, the Victorians chose to embellish the exterior and, to all accounts, made a mess of it. In 1924, to celebrate the cathedral's 700 years, the fabric was restored to its former glory and it is now one of the most welcoming of Scottish religious buildings.

Opposite the Tourist Information Office in the town square is Dornoch Craft Centre and Town Jail, a rather curious but effective combination. Open daily except in winter, the restored jail gives an impression of conditions in a nineteenth-century prison although most of the inmates were probably guilty of too much libation rather than any serious crime. The craft shop is a little Spartan with a few odd woollen ties along with some books and tins of short bread. There is a coffee shop.

Golf was played in this area at least as far back as 1616 when the Earl of Sutherland was recorded to have ordered golf clubs and balls to take up the game that was becoming so popular further south. This makes Royal Dornoch the third oldest golfing community in Scotland and it is definitely one of the most rewarding. The course would be an Open venue if its situation was more immediate to the modern world and its transport links. Thankfully, for those that love to play carefree golf on one of the world's finest courses, Royal Dornoch Golf Course remains out of reach of the masses.

From the top of Benn Bhraggie above the little holiday town of **Golspie** there is a tall statue to the Duke of Sutherland standing on top of a 70ft (21m) plinth. It is amazing that it has not been pulled down for the despair this one man caused. George Greville Levenson-Gower was the second Marquess of Stafford and the third Earl Gower as well as the first Duke of Sutherland. A Londoner, he came from a coal mine-owning family and married into the Sutherlands who owned most of the land in this area. When he inherited his father's estates in England he became the wealthiest landowner in Great Britain. In 1814 with the help of his commissioner, James Loch and factor Patrick Sellar, he set about 'improving' his Sutherland estate mainly by removing the native inhabitants to make way for sheep. Five thousand men, women and children, a third of the population of Sutherland were compelled to emigrate mainly to Canada or try and eek out a living from the impoverished coastal land they were confined to. The ultimate irony was that the remaining tenantry were asked to donate money for the building and erection of his statue that is so visible above Golspie.

The 'Clearance' theme is strong in this area so it is as well to know the background. The idea of land 'improving' caught on throughout the Highlands and crofters of once well-populated glens and hills were forcefully evicted to make way for sheep or sporting estates. Clan chiefs who had for centuries been charged with the welfare of their people began to see themselves as land-owners which was never truly the case. Never the less the Clearances took place and many families had to move south to work in mills and factories or migrated to the USA, Canada, New Zealand and Australia. The lairds quickly moved in sheep or arranged sporting holidays for their English friends in peaceful Highland glens so conveniently cleared of their peasant tenants. The effects of this, like the Battle of Culloden, was to deeply demoralise the Highland psyche and it has taken at least a century to recover.

A mile or so beyond Golspie stands **Dunrobin Castle**, the most northerly of Scotland's great houses and the seat of the Sutherlands. From the entrance, which is at the rear of the castle, Dunrobin does not appear over-impressive but from its seaward aspect it stands like a sprawling Bavarian palace above immaculately manicured gardens. This is an excellent example of Victorian over-exuberance trying to take the idea of Highland romanticism to the extreme. Originally, the site was occupied by an ancient broch which was replaced by a thirteenth-century structure. Inside is a dusty, dark hodge-podge of items, some quite magnificent such as the two Canaletto paintings.

Brora is the next stage on this long north road, an uninspiring stop if the sun does not shine but known for the electric fences that keep the cows off its golf course greens. Further on the coastline becomes more rugged and

The Last House Museum, John O'Groats

Duncansby Head is a less touristy location near John O'Groats

the village of **Helmsdale** is set on a craggy headland with its harbour squeezed in a cleft between the rocks. Helmsdale is grey and not much to look at but stop and investigate as there are a few things to discover. The most obvious attraction is the Timespan Heritage Centre which reaches ✳ back into the dim and distant past to consider the stone circles and cairns that are quite frequent in these parts. There is a very good section explaining the Highland Clearances as well as the Kildonan gold rush. A few miles up the A897 on the Kildonan or Suisgill Burns you will see campers and day-trippers up to their knees in gold fever. There are still specks of golf to be had in the burns and gold panning equipment can be hired from the Strath Ullie shop in the town. When you have come back with a tiny golden sliver looking lost in its glass collection tube go into the 'La Mirage' tea room to examine it. The authoress, Barbara Cartland has a holiday home near Helmsdale and the owner of the café, Nancy Sinclair, is a devout fan.

Further on the A9 is another unusual stop, the Kingspark Llama Farm near **Berriedale**. Brian and Mary Gough started this fascinating farm ✳ 5 years ago as a caravan site and B&B which has developed into a miniature menagerie. Beside the herd of llamas, other animals include pigmy goats, peacocks, raccoons, golden pheasants and wallabies. The llamas can be taken on walks where they carry the back-packs containing lunch. This, including the picnic, can take around 4 hours. Further on a fifteenth-century castle is just visible from the road. This is part of the **Dunbeath Estate**, now owned by a Californian millionaire, Ray Stanton Avery of sticky label fame, who has done much to restore the estate and the villages within it. The castle is not open to the public but a Heritage Centre gives information on the Author Neil Gunn who was born here as ✳ well as local history and wildlife.

The road is quite desolate between Helmsdale and Wick so you cannot fail to see the **Laidhay Croft Museum** off to the right, a popular stopping 🏠 place for coach parties. Inside the reconstructed croft is an emporium of memories for senior travellers, old biscuit tins, newspaper cuttings from the wars and ancient pedal sewing machines.

There is a nice little tea room opposite as well as an out-house containing rusting farming equipment. Further on in an old parish church looking over the turbulent North Sea is the Clan Gunn Museum and Heritage 🏠 Centre.

The fishing port of **Lybster** is the next town. Turn off the A9 into the broad main street. There is really nothing here apart from the picturesque harbour but that is part of the charm. The Portland Arms Hotel is a pleasant stop for food. At **Clyth** a couple of miles on is a minor turning ᴨ north to the Grey Cairns of Camster a collection of burial mounds from around 2500BC. Nearby, a ¹/₄ mile off A9 near Kyleburn is the Hill o' Many Stanes, a desolate group of early Bronze Age stones, some 200 in all spread over a heather crest. From the second millenium BC their average height is only 18 inches, laid out in a fan-shape. Their purpose is unknown.

The last stop before Wick is the fishing village of **Ulbster.** There is little to see in the village but drive through to the cliffs which are forbidding and on a bad day the wind can blow sea water straight up them. There is a narrow stairway leading down to the tiny, rock strewn harbour with 365 steps to descend. Now overgrown, it can be very slippery. It is hard to believe that fishermen would bring their boats right in to the churning cove to unload the fish and the village women would carry the catch back up the steps.

Wick, pronounced Week by the locals who are referred to as Weekers became a royal burgh in 1140. Before that it had been primarily a Viking settlement from which it took its name of Vik, actually after the burn that runs through it. The busy little town that we see now only properly developed in the nineteenth century when Thomas Telford was asked by the British Fisheries Society to design a model village for them at Pultneytown. This was to help meet the demand from the herring fishing industry as Wick was becoming the busiest herring port in Europe. This is the background the established this stalwart little community, the largest in the north-east after Inverness. The Wick Heritage Centre near the harbour tells the story in detail especially the fishing element, with a superb collection of models, fishing equipment and photographs. It is run by the Wick Society who take a great pride in their museum. There is also a small museum within the Carnegie Library, open during library opening times, which contains a history of the areas fishing and farming communities.

One of the best eateries is the Lamplighter Restaurant which has excellent food especially the sweets. If you stay in the B&B or drop in for breakfast you might find it a bit too much as they serve a full Scottish spread along with American style pancakes.

On the outskirts of town, on the 'Groats Road' as a native would point out, is **Caithness Glass Factory and Visitor Centre**. This spacious facility, lovely and warm on a cold or wet day, offers a chance to see the famous glass-ware being molded and blown and the opportunity to buy it in their gift shop restaurant. The road north out of Wick on the 'Groats' Road, still the A9 whereas the A882 carries north-west directly to Thurso, sets out over an old red sandstone plateau past Wick Airport, a wide flat north-eastern corner of mainland Scotland edged by abrupt cliffs.

Sinclairs Bay is off to the east with Sinclair and Girnigoe Castles, two ruins accessible by foot overlooking the bay. Ackergill Castle has a commanding view over to Duncansbay Head up the coast. This is a private castle that can be hired by groups and there is a small golf course just along the bay. Sinclairs Bay is believed to be one of the earliest inhabited places in Scotland with evidence of middle Stone Age man living here in large numbers. This is best explained in the John Nicholson Museum near **Auckingill** at the north end of the bay which unfolds the archaeology of the area as explored by this nineteenth-century antiquarian who spent his life studying local history.

For those that have trekked or cycled or pushed a pram all the way from Land's End in Cornwall, Britain's supposed most south-westerly point to here, **John O' Groats**, accepted as the most north-eastern point, on a day whipping with wind-driven rain or sleet, they must seriously wonder if it was worth it. John O' Groats is really nothing more than a tacky tourist attraction with little to recommend apart from saying that you have been there. In fact, like its southern counterpart it is not the mainland's extreme but nearby Dunnet Head is. The harbour and the Last House Museum are worth seeing, the latter a tiny, old cottage that contains a vivid pictorial display of the naval activities around this area and Orkney during both World Wars. There is a hotel along with rather tacky tourist gift shops selling sea-shells and coconuts that have little to do with Scotland. Of course, you can have your picture taken at the famous John O' Groats signpost.

For a more natural encounter take the minor road to **Duncansby Head**, some 2 miles (3km) east of 'Groats'. Its impressive rock stacks can be seen after a short walk from the lighthouse parking area or by boat which leaves from John o' Groats harbour. The cliff faces are like high-rise apartments for the myriad of sea-birds nesting on them in the spring and early summer. Their constant squeals echoing of the rocky canyon is quite overwhelming. Guillemots and shags are most common with some puffins burrowing into the grassy edges. There is a good walk out over the headland with the path skirting the cliff edge but it is fenced and fairly safe.

The A9 terminates at John O' Groats. **Dunnet Head** on the other side of John O' Groats taking the A836 then the B855 is Scotland's true northernmost point. From the lighthouse on a windy day you need only sit in your car to watch the incredible aerial displays performed by sea birds catching the up-draughts from the cliffs. A climb up the grassy rise behind the lighthouse affords some fabulous views along the coast with its precipitous rocks. Orkney is clearly seen to the north.

The town of **Thurso** is 20 miles (32km) west of John O' Groats following the A836. It is a well ordered and airy little place with a wide central square, the main shopping areas and hotels leading off it. This was a chief trading port between Scotland and Scandinavia in the Middle Ages exporting beef and fish. Thurso Heritage Museum in the High Street contains the 'Ulbster Stone' a Pictish relic of some note and exhibits gathered by the naturalist Robert Dick. There is also a reconstruction of a croft house kitchen. Near the harbour is Thurso's other tourist attraction, St Peter's Church, a twelfth- or thirteenth-century construction that was restored in seventeenth century.

Thurso's current claim to fame is the excellent surf it offers off local beaches. In September and October international surfing championships bring enthusiasts from around the world but windsurfing is popular through the summer months. The Pentland Arms Hotel is said to be the best food in town although this can be rather average with vegetables fresh from the freezer. Try the Bower Inn midway between Thurso and Wick in Castletown or the Upper Deck in Scrabster. Most visitors pass through Thurso to catch the ferry from Scrabster, a short distance north of town to Stromness in Orkney. There are special days out through the summer where you catch the St Ola and, 2 hours later connect with a bus in Stromness for a tour of Orkney's mainland before returning to Scrabster in the evening. Check with the tourist office for more details.

Thurso's economy was considerably boosted by the construction of Dounreay Fast Reactor Power Station some 8 miles (13km) along the A836. The facility is no longer open for tours by the public. A few miles on is the humpy, single-track route, the A897 leading south to Helmsdale through an area known as the Flow Country. This is a flat, peat bog morass with large numbers of limestone lochs that offer excellent trout fishing. It is also the home to waders and divers. It may not be much to look at from the road but if you know what you are after the Flow Country does have a lot to offer. The A836 carries on towards Bettyhill and the north-west corner of mainland Scotland.

Additional Information

Places of Interest

Auckingill
John Nicholson Museum
☎ 01955 603761
Open: June to Septmeber.

Aviemore
Aviemore Centre
Off the A9, 32 miles (52km) south of Inverness
☎ 01355 247177
Open: All year, daily from 10am.

Glenmore Forest Park
7 miles (11km) east of Aviemore, off the B9152
☎ 05404 223
Open: All year.

Boat of Garten
Loch Garten Nature Reserve
Off the B970, 8 miles (13km) north-east of Aviemore
☎ 01479 831694
Open: If Ospreys are present, daily, mid-April to August, 10am-8pm.

Rothiemurchus Estate Visitor Centre
1 mile (2km) east from Aviemore
☎ 01479 810858
Open: All year, 9am-5pm.

Strathspey Railway
Aviemore to Boat of Garten
☎ 01479 810725
Open: Phone station for current times.

Carrbridge
Landmark Visitor Centre
Carrbridge, 6 miles (10km) north of Aviemore on old A9
☎ 01479 841613
Open: All year.

Cawdor Castle and Gardens
Village of Cawdor on the B9090, 5 miles (8km) south-west of Nairn
☎ 01667 404615
Open: May to September, 10am-5pm.

Clava Cairns
Near Culloden off the B9006
Historic Scotland ☎ 0131 244 3101
Open: April to September, Monday to Saturday, 9.30am-7pm. Sunday, 2-7pm. October to March, Monday to Saturday, 9.30am-4pm. Sunday, 2-4pm.

Cromarty
Hugh Miller's Cottage
On the Black Isle, 22 miles (35km)
north-east of Inverness
☎ 01381 600245
Open: April to September, Monday to
Saturday, 10am-12noon & 1-5pm.
Sundays, 2-5pm.

Culloden Moor
Off the B9006 between Inverness and
Nairn
☎ 01463 790607
Visitor Centre open all year daily:
Summer 9am-6.30pm, 9.30am-5.30pm
the rest of year.

Nairn Fishertown Museum
Laing Hall, King's Street
☎ 01667 453331
Open: May to September, Monday to
Saturday, 2.30-4.30pm. Monday,
Wednesday & Friday, 6.30-8.30pm.

Dingwall
The Town House
High Street
☎ 01349 865366
Open: May to September, Monday to
Saturday, 10am-5pm.

Dornoch
Dornoch Cathedral
In Dornoch
☎ 01862 810325
Open: All year, 9am to dusk.

Dornoch Craft Centre and Town Jail
Town centre
☎ 01862 810555
Open: Monday to Saturday 9.30am-5pm,
Sunday 12noon-5pm except winter.

Drumnadrochit
Urquhart Castle
2 miles (3km) south-east of
Drumnadrochit on west shore of
Loch Ness
Historic Scotland ☎ 0131 244 3101
Open: April to September, Monday to
Saturday, 9.30am-5.15pm.
Sunday,10.30am-4.45pm. October to
March, Monday to Saturday, 9.30am-
4.20pm. Sunday, 12.30-3.35pm.

Official Loch Ness Monster Exhibition Centre
Loch Ness
☎ 01456 450573
Open: daily, 9am-9.30pm. Off season
times vary.

Dunbeath
Dunbeath Heritage Centre
The Old School
☎ 01593 731233
Open: Easter to September.

Dunrobin Castle
North side of Golspie on A9
☎ 01408 633177
Open: May, Monday to Thursday,
10.30am-12.30pm, June to
September,Monday to Saturday,
10.30am-5.30pm. Sundays, 1-5.30pm.

Fortrose
Fortrose Cathedral
On Black Isle
Historic Scotland ☎ 0131 244 3101
Open: April to September, Monday to
Saturday, 9.30am-7pm. Sunday, 2-7pm.
October to March, Monday to Saturday,
9.30am-4pm. Sunday, 2-4pm.

Helmsdale
Timespan Heritage Centre
Bridgend, Helmsdale
☎ 01431 821327
Open: Easter to mid-October, Monday
to Saturday, 10am-5pm, Sundays, 2-
5pm (6pm in July and August).

Inverness
Inverness Museum and Art Gallery
Castle Wynd, near centre
☎ 01463 237114
Open: Monday to Saturday, 9am-5pm,
July and August, Sunday 2-5pm.

Eden Court Theatre
Bishop Road
☎ 01463 239841

St Andrews Cathedral
☎ 01463 233535
Open: Daily at 8am.

John O'Groats
Last House Museum
☎ 01955 611250
Open: January to December.

Kingussie
Highland Folk Museum
Off the A9 at Kingussie, 12 miles (19km)
south of Aviemore
☎ 01540 661307
Open: All year, April to October,
Monday to Saturday, 10am-6pm.
Sundays, 2-6pm. November to March,
Monday to Friday, 10am-3pm.

Ruthven Barracks
B970 just south of Kingussie
Historic Scotland ☎ 0131 244 3101
Open: At all times.

Laidhay
Near Dunbeath
Laidhay Croft Museum
☎ 01593 731325

Latheron
Clan Gunn Museum and Heritage Centre
Old Church
☎ 01593 721325
Open: June to September, Monday to
Saturday.

Nairn
*Fort George and Queen's Own Highlanders
    Regimental Museum*
Near Ardesier off the A96 north
between Inverness & Nairn
☎ 01463 224380
Open: April to September, Monday to
Saturday, 10am-6pm, Sunday, 2-6pm.
October to March, Monday to Friday,
2-4pm.

Newtonmore
Clan MacPherson Museum
In Newtonmore off A9
☎ 05403 332
Open: May to September, Monday to
Saturday, 10am-5.30pm. Sunday 2.30-
5.30pm, November to March 2-4pm.

Tain
Tain and District Museum
Next to the Tolbooth Tower off High
Street
☎ 01862 893054
Open: Easter to end of September,
10am-4.30pm.

Thurso
Thurso Heritage Museum
Situated in the Town Hall
☎ 01847 892459
Open: June to September, Monday to
Saturday, 10am-1pm & 2-5pm.

Wick
Caithness Glass Factory & Visitor Centre
Wick on north side of town
☎ 01955 602286
Open: All year, April to October,
Monday to Saturday, 9am-5pm, Sun-
day, 1-5pm.

Wick Heritage Centre
Bank Row
☎ 01955 603385
Open: June to September, Monday to
Saturday, 10am-12.30pm, 2-5pm.

Other Useful Information

Inverness Railway Station
☎ 01463 238924
Inverness Airport
☎ 01667 462280
Wick Airport
☎ 01955 602215
Mountain Call East Highlands
☎ 01898 500 442
Skicall
☎ 01898 500440
Weathercall for this area
☎ 01898 500424

Tourist Information Offices

Aviemore
Grampian Road
☎ 01479 810363

Carrbridge
Main Street
☎ 01479 841630

Daviot Wood
A9 by Inverness
☎ 01463 772203

Dornoch
The Square
☎ 01862 810400

Fort Augustus
Car Park
☎ 01320 366367

Grantown on Spey
High Street
☎ 01479 872773

Helmsdale
Coupar Park
☎ 01431 821640

Inverness
Castle Wynd
☎ 01463 234353

John O' Groats
County Road
☎ 01955 611373

Kingussie
King Street
☎ 01540 661297

Ralia
A9 North by Newtonmore
☎ 01540 673253

Thurso
Riverside
☎ 01847 62371

Wick
Whitechapeel Road
☎ 01955 602596

Accommodation

Beauly
*Dower House * * ***
☎ 01463 870090

Grantown on Spey (near)
*Auchendean Lodge **
☎ 01479 851347

Inverness
*Culloden House * * ***
☎ 01463 790461

Inverness
*Mrs Lee **
☎ 01463 237254

Lairg
*Sutherland Arms * ***
☎ 01549 402291

Nairn
*Clifton House * * ***
☎ 01667 53119

Thurso
*Mrs Tuck B&B **
☎ 01847 894511

Wick
*Wellington Guest House **
☎ 01955 603287

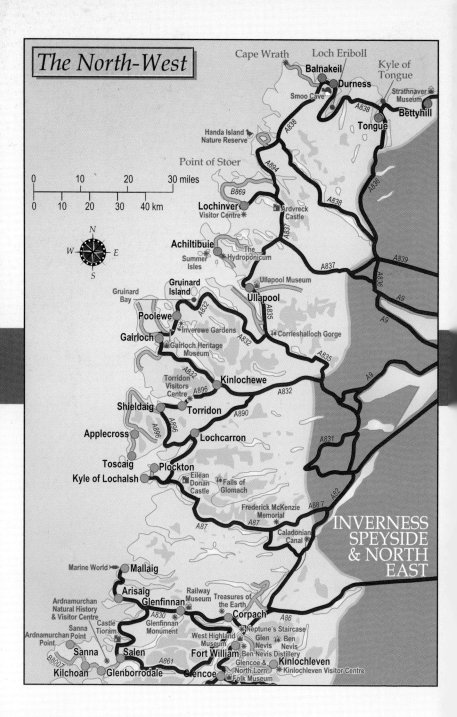

The North-West

Cape Wrath
Loch Eriboll
Balnakeil
Durness
Kyle of Tongue
Smoo Cave
Strathnaver Museum
A838
Bettyhill
Handa Island Nature Reserve
A838
Tongue
A894
A836
Point of Stoer
B869
A838
A839
Lochinver
Visitor Centre
Ardvreck Castle
A837
A836
A837
Achiltibuie
The Hydroponicum
Summer Isles
A9
Ullapool Museum
Gruinard Island
A835
A9
Gairloch Bay
Poolewe
A832
Ullapool
Inverewe Gardens
Corrieshalloch Gorge
Gairloch
A832
Gairloch Heritage Museum
A835
A832
A9
Torridon Visitors Centre
Kinlochewe
A896
A832
Shieldaig
Torridon
A890
A896
A896
Lochcarron
A831
Applecross
A896
Toscaig
Plockton
Kyle of Lochalsh
Eilean Donan Castle
Falls of Glomach
A82
Frederick McKenzie Memorial
A887
Caledonian Canal
A87
A87
INVERNESS SPEYSIDE & NORTH EAST

Marine World
Mallaig
Arisaig
Railway Museum
Treasures of the Earth
Ardnamurchan Natural History & Visitor Centre
Glenfinnan
A830
Corpach
A86
Castle Tioram
Glenfinnan Monument
Neptune's Staircase
Sanna Point
Ardnamurchan Point
West Highland Museum
Glen Nevis
Ben Nevis
Sanna
Salen
Ben Nevis Distillery
Kinlochleven
B8007
A861
Glencoe & North Lorn
Kinlochleven Visitor Centre
Kilchoan
Glenborrodale
Fort William
Glencoe & North Lorn Folk Museum
Glencoe

N
W   E
S

0   10   20   30 miles
0   10   20   30   40 km

The North-West

10

The roads in the north-west region of Sutherland are often single to tracked and quite winding with passing places every few hundred yards so it is advisable to allow more time than usual to cover distances.

The Strathnaver Museum in **Bettyhill** commemorates the drastic effects of the Highland Clearances of Caithness and Sutherland.

The Invernaver National Nature Reserve between the mouths of the Rivers Borgie and Naver on the west side of Bettyhill is one of the most important botanical sites in Scotland with a wide variety of lime and acid loving species such as crowberry, mountain avens, moss campion and bearberry.

The village of **Tongue** largely exists on a hairpin bend as the road descends to the Kyle of Tongue with only a few cottages, a couple of hotels and a garage. The garage occasionally runs out of certain types of fuel so stock up wherever you can. Atop the hill behind town is Castle Varrich, a former Norse stronghold now in ruins. A walk down to Scullomie Pier approximately 3 miles (5km) east of Tongue leads to one of the points where crofters were put on boats during the Clearances. A lonely pile of rocks forming a desolate harbour is all that remains.

The **Kyle of Tongue** is a sea loch below the village and crossed by a two to lane causeway. There are stopping places along the causeway that provide good views of Ben Loyal behind the village. From here the road improves towards Durness but soon reduces again to a single track around **Loch Eriboll**. Dramatic outlooks over the deep channel of Loch Eriboll can be enjoyed from several stopping places. At the cessation of World War II, German U to Boats sailed up Loch Eriboll to offer their surrender.

There are fish farms sheltering near the bays and coves along this coastline and a recent and novel method of warding off salmon destroying seals has been devised. A life-sized fibre-glass killer whale called Wally was put in the water near the fish tanks and this has proved 100 per cent effective. The seals who took at least 200 fish per week now take none.

If the weather holds **Durness** and this north to west corner are one of the most special places in Scotland. If it rains, visitors crowd into Durness's steamy cafés to sit for hours waiting on a break in the weather. Smoo Cave is a useful excursion on such a day, reached by descending a long wooden staircase to the beach where a limestone cavern is entered, as big as an airplane hanger. The inner caves are accessible by rubber raft for a small charge to observe the dramatic 80ft (24m) waterfall in the rear cavern called Allt Smoo.

Another diversion near town is **Balnakeil Craft Village**, formerly a MOD Early Warning Station and now taken over by a group of craft to workers and turned into a kind of alternative holiday camp with its own hotel and various shops selling candles, paintings, woodwork and pottery. The hotel, whilst rather spartan, has a homey feel and is renowned for good vegetarian food. But Durness is best enjoyed for its wild, open headlands and long, broad beaches. From early spring until June colonies of puffins can be seen around Faraid Head. Ask the ranger in the Durness Tourist Information outpost for directions to the colony that he recommends. The walks along the headlands are generally safe but care should be taken with small children near the steep grassy slopes. On Wednesdays, the RAF carry out bombing raids on a tiny island 2 miles (3km) north of the mainland using live ammunition. The 9 hole golf course at Durness, set behind the ancient Balnakeil Church, is the most northern course on the Scottish mainland.

The trip to Cape Wrath is very weather dependant with a short ferry crossing from the Keoldale slipway, 1 mile (2km) or so south of Durness. The small ferry boat links up with a minibus to cover the remaining 10 miles (16km) to the Cape. From the lighthouse, on a clear day, you can see the Orkneys as well as the Outer Hebrides and several varieties of sea birds so take binoculars. It is possible to walk to beautiful Sandwood Bay from Cape Wrath but it is a fair hike and in some places rather tedious. It is much easier to approach it from Kinlochbervie off the A838 where you can drive to Balchrick then walk the remaining 4 or 5 miles (6 or 8km) staying near to the coast. Further south beyond Laxford Bridge is a turning for **Tarbert** where there is a site of 'special scientific interest' on the island of Handa. A boat runs from Tarbert to the island where you can take a 3 hour walk following paths along the sandstone cliffs to observe more than 100,000 nesting sea birds including puffin, fulmar, shag and guillemot. It is a good idea to bring a flask and sandwiches as there are no facilities on the island.

At **Kylestrom** there are hotels and a boat service that runs from Unapool across the loch to Eas a' Chaul Aulinn, Britain's highest waterfall dropping 658ft (201m). En-route you may see deer, seals and if particularly lucky, a golden eagle so, once again, pack binoculars. From Newton, basically the next group of houses south, you can continue on the main A894 for a smooth run into Lochinver or follow the more spectacular route around the coast, the B689. The Old Man of Stoer, a famous sea stack can be reached from the Stoer Lighthouse but stick to the coast or you will end up wading through boggy land.

East beyond the meeting point of the A894 and the A837 stands **Ardvreck Castle**, a ruin perched precariously on a spit of the north shore of Loch Assynt. It can be a soggy, cow to pat infested walk from the road over to the castle and the remaining slabs of sandstone do not appear very safe.

The village of **Lochinver** straddles the River Inver where it pours into Loch Inver. The main deviation from car to touring is boat trips to view colonies of cormorants, shags and seals perched or preening on the many little islands off the coast. In the right season you may see a whale or two. Boat trips can be chartered formally or simply by knocking on the door of one of the owners such as Ewen Sharp who owns the Lunga Boat, a converted lifeboat. If it is a nice evening and he is not doing anything else, he will take you out. From the loch you can best appreciate the magnificent setting of the village with the bowler to hat shaped Suilven peaking over lower hills at 2,399ft (732m).

There is a visitor centre in the village that describes the lives of the people and the land of Assynt Parish. Lochinver Village Hall puts on a 'Summer Cinema'. Following the road round the north side of the loch leads to Baddidarroch and the factory of Highland Stoneware Pottery where some of the finest tableware is turned out and hand to painted before your eyes.

For nourishment the Lochinver Larder and Riverside Bistro is surprisingly refined with excellent wholefood and fish dishes as well as sweets that compliment this heavenly setting. The harbour area is less cultivated, and the nearby hotel serves freshly-caught fish.

Continue west and south of Lochinver for a spectacular drive with views of Suilven and Canisp with Stac Pollaidh in the distance at 2,009ft (613m). Beyond, if you care to drive this far, is the **Summer Isles** and the village of **Achiltibuie**, worth a visit for the hydroponicum, where bananas, figs and lemons are cultivated in a soil free environment. Achiltibuie also boasts one of the areas finest hotels, the Summer Isles, especially renowned for its cuisine.

The northern coast has many wide and secluded beaches

The fishing and holiday village of Lochinver

The distinctive form of Stac Pollaidh

On the north shore of Loch Broom stands the still important fishing village of **Ullapool**. Now Russian factory ships or 'Klondykers' congest the sheltered loch. Sea fishing and boat trips to the Summer Isles are popular from here and ferries to Stornoway on the Outer Hebridean island of Lewis leave regularly. The local museum has gathered evidence of life in Wester Ross over the centuries. **Corrieshalloch Gorge**, 12 miles (19km) south to east of Ullapool on the A835 near Braemore is a dramatic ravine, 1 mile (2km) long and 200ft (61m) deep is a backdrop for the Falls of Measach which drop 150ft (46m). There is a suspension bridge from which to get a safe and spectacular view.

The A835 continues back towards Dingwall and Inverness but it is possible to branch west on the A832 past Little Loch Broom to the spectacular Gruinard Bay. **Gruinard Island** was infected with anthrax during World War II but it is now decontaminated and returned to its former owner. Following the A832, the popular **Inverewe Gardens** just outside the village of **Poolewe** is a northern outpost for touring coach parties. There are some 2,500 species including palm trees, Himalayan lilies and giant forget to me to nots from the South Pacific all growing at the same latitude as Siberia. The reason for this profusion, besides the care taken by the National Trust for Scotland who now run the gardens, is the warm waters of the Gulf Stream that bathe so much of Scotland's west coast.

The holiday village of **Gairloch** is only about 7 miles (11km) away. Unaffected by the Clearances, Gairloch held on to west Highland life until the tourist invasion. The Gairloch Heritage Museum gives a good insight into the times before holiday homes. The road through the village leads to Big Sand, an excellent camp to site if you like dramatic views over to the Torridon range and miles of smooth beach. Gairloch Golf Club is the best 18 hole course found this far north on the mainland.

The road down to Kinlochewe is blessedly straight and fast compared to those further north with views over one of Scotland's prettiest stretches of water, Loch Maree. At the village of **Kinlochewe** it is time for more single track roads unless you wish to opt out and return to Inverness missing some of the most dramatic of the north-west's panoramas. The drive along to **Torridon** gets better and more impressive as it enters the 26,000 acre (10,400 hectare) Torridon Estate run by the National Trust for Scotland. In the village there is a Visitor Centre that introduces this fascinating landscape with its three great mountains, Liathach, Beinn Eighe and Beinn Alligin. Torridon is of particular interest to geologists as Torridonian sandstones, at 750 million years old, is the oldest in Scotland. This is also a paradise for wildlife with otters, pine martins, wild cat and wild goats being plentiful but quite elusive. Look out for ancient pines known as Grannie Pines on the slopes of Beinn Eighe, once part of the ancient Caledonian Forest. Some are over 350 years old.

The peaceful village of **Shieldaig** forms a crescent around the head of Loch Shieldaig, an ideal outlook for holiday cottages or the camp to site perched above the village. From Shieldaig there is a winding, minor road that circumvents Applecross Forest to the village of Applecross past fish farms and tiny lochside hamlets. There is a rough stretch of grassland and beach to the north of the village of **Applecross**, ideal for a picnic if the midges are not too fierce. A religious centre was established here in AD673 when a monastery was built by the Irish monk, Maelrubha, almost as important as Iona and later ruined by Vikings. It is possible to continue south past the village to a dead to end at Toscaig Pier where fishing for mackerel is quite productive. From Applecross the infamous Bealach na Bo Pass or Pass of the Cattle is a low gear climb with hair to pin bends to the summit at Meall Gorm, some 2,328ft (710m) up with incredible views looking back over to the islands of Rassay, Rona and Skye.

The descent overlooks Loch Kishorn and finally arrives at the holiday town of **Lochcarron** on the shores of the loch of that same name. There is not much here but views, two local hotels, one of which has varying menus such as Italian or Indian evenings and Lochcarron Golf Course at

the end of the village which is a fun, 9 holer. Strome Castle, or what is left ♖
of it, stands on a spur overlooking the mouth of the loch near where a
ferry used to run.

On the opposite side is **Stromeferry** (no ferry) as the sign points out,
reached by following the high A890 overlooking Loch Carron from the
south. Just beyond Stromeferry is a turning for the scenic route to
Plockton and Kyle of Lochalsh. In spring this road is dense with wild
rhododendron bushes in full bloom. **Plockton**, sometimes referred to as
the 'Jewel of the Highlands' is many people's favourite west coast village
with its trim little cottages lining the shores of Loch Carron and multi to
coloured yachts bobbing in the sheltered bay. Pine trees stand next to
palms. With such an attractive environment it can be quite busy and
makes good use of this with craft shops, cafés and gift shops. There is ⚓
sailing, canoeing and windsurfing on the loch with equipment for hire
from Leisure Marine who also run hour long boat trips to look for seals.

The main road into **Kyle of Lochalsh** used to be backed up for miles
with traffic waiting to board the ferry for the Isle of Skye. With the new
bridge whisking vehicles over the channel in seconds, Kyle is now less of
a bottle to neck. Despite this transitory feel there are plenty shops and a
few good walks with views that take in the smaller islands along with the
darker background of Skye. There is the Kyle Golf Course with its 'hon-   ⚑
esty box' and 9 holes now slightly overshadowed by the new bridge but
a nice, little par 3 test.

Returning south via the A87, some 8 miles (13km) from Kyle is the most
dramatic and photographed castle in the country, **Eilean Donan**. The   ♖
castle was built in 1230 on a rocky outcrop, the stronghold of the
MacKenzies. The interior, only two rooms and a shop accessible, is no
match for its outer aspect and spectacular location. There is a view point
above the castle reached by driving up the minor road towards Keppoch.
From this point, the best light for photographs is obtained in the morning.

Further on, at Morvich is access to the **Falls of Glomach**. The National   🔆
Trust for Scotland has an audio to visual presentation nearby that gives
details of the Kintail estate and all that goes on there. There are many
walks but the most spectacular lead to a 370ft (113m) waterfall, the Falls
of Glomach. The A87 is a splendid drive through Glen Shiel passing the
Five Sisters of Kintail, passed Loch Cluanie and on to Loch Garry. There
is a parking area that overlooks Loch Garry and with the evening sun
descending, the 'map of Scotland' can be discerned in the outline of the
loch. At Spean Bridge further on there is a junction that divides east to
Dalwhinnie and the A9 or south to west for Fort William which is 10 miles
(16km) away.

Fort William, once a military outpost, is now a mixture of light industry, service facilities, transport and tourism. It is surrounded by some of
Scotland's most attractive places and so is a worthwhile base for explor-   ✳
ing this part of the Highlands. With B&B's and hotels lining most streets
and several good pub to restaurants, Fort William looks after the droves
of climbers, skiers and sight to seers that descend upon every year.

The main street is lined with stores to serve your every outdoor need from crampons to croutons. For really foul days, and Fort William does get more than its fair share, there is a small cinema in Cameron Square (☎ 0397 705095) behind the very well stocked Tourist Information Office. Fort William is an important rail link and summer steam trains run on the West Highland Line to Mallaig through some spectacular scenery that you would not see from the road. The West Highland Museum in Cameron Square is another wet weather retreat but one you should take in anyway if you have been lucky weather to wise.

The road up Glen Nevis is popular, usually dotted with Continental hitch to hikers thumbing a lift back to the camp to site or youth hostel a mile or so into the glen. This is the area where most ascents of Britain's highest mountain, **Ben Nevis** at 4,406ft (1,345m), commence. Hundreds climb the Ben everyday through the summer. Unfortunately, because it seems easy, many visitors set out with only running shoes or worse. This is fine on the ascent but coming back down from such a long hike is usually hard for seasoned and well equipped walkers. The summit is usually covered in snow all year round.

A herd of Highland cattle wander freely through the upper reaches of Glen Nevis often standing in the burn to cool down or to munch the greener grass on the other side. The valley road terminates in a wonderful, mountainous corral lined with silver birch and rowan trees. There is a waterfall, Steall, a short distance on up the ravine from where it is possible to walk through to Corrour Station on Rannoch Moor, some 16 miles (26km) on.

Fort William is also the southern gateway to the Caledonian Canal at **Banavie** where Neptune's Staircase climbs from sea level to 80ft (24m), through eleven hydraulically operated locks. This stretch of the canal enters Loch Lochy 8 miles (13km) to the north-east and carries on through Loch Ness to Inverness.

North-east out of town is the Nevis Range at **Torlundy** where enclosed gondola cars take skiers or summer sight to seers to the summit of Aonach Mor mountain at 4,006ft (1,221m). The cable car takes 12 minutes to reach 2,300ft (701m) where there is the Snow Goose Restaurant, a fine sheltered view point with tea and scones at hand.

Back in Fort William, the best eating house with lovely views across the loch is the Crannog Seafood Restaurant on the Town Pier (☎ 0397 705589). They serve succulent seafood from their own fishing boat but book ahead if you do not wish to wait. Nearby is Seal Island Cruises which spends $1^1/_2$ hours sailing Loch Linne. The Crofter Pub, 7 to 11 High Street, serves good food in a nice setting and at a fair price. You may be enticed into McTavish's Kitchen in the High Street which advertizes its Scottish show held nightly.

The Road to the Isles, the A830 west of Fort William through Corpach leads to the Glenfinnan Monument at the head of Loch Shiel. En to route you pass the Treasures of the Earth exhibition in **Corpach** where uncut gemstones crystals and exotic minerals are on display. There is an am-

Neptune's Staircase, Banavie, Fort William

Seal Island Cruises

ethyst geode weighing over 200lbs while the exhibition also incorporates Dinosaur World which has a display of dinosaur fossils. There is a gift shop.

✳   The best view of the **Glenfinnan Monument** and loch is gained by climbing the small hill behind the National Trust for Scotland's Visitor Centre. The monument was erected in 1815 to commemorate Bonnie Prince Charlie's raising of the standard on the 19 August 1745. Behind the hill is the Glenfinnan Viaduct carrying the West Highland Line from Fort William to Mallaig. There is a small station at Glenfinnan where the train stops that is also a railway enthusiasts museum where the building and restoration of the West Highland Line is displayed in photographs along with ancient tickets other railway paraphernalia.

Beyond the wild glens of Moidart where Jacobite legends abound, the road opens to the Sound of Arisaig with spectacular vistas over to the islands of Eigg and Muck with the Cuillins of Skye in the distance. Loch nan Uamh is a wide sea to loch just past the settlement of Arnipol where, on 25 July1745, the French ship *Du Teillay* landed Prince Charles Edward Stuart and his seven companions to commence the Jacobite uprising.

The small settlement of **Arisaig** is a refuge for sailors at the head of Loch Nan Call and boat trips leave early to explore the smaller islands and wildlife haunts. The Old Library Lodge and Restaurant in Arisaig (☎ 0687 450651) is Egon Ronay recommended and includes good vegetarian meals.

A few miles further on is the **Sands of Morar** set on a beautiful estuary with expansive bands of gleaming white sand evident at low tide. The Falls of Morar pour into the estuary from the shortest river in the UK coming down from Loch Morar which is over 1,000ft (305m) deep and one of Europe's deepest hollows. There is a superb walk along the northern shore and the best view of Loch Morar is experienced by climbing Carn a' Ghobhair (1,794ft / 547m). From here you can also see the entire length of Loch Nevis to the north and the range of mountains at its head.

Mallaig, at the end of the Road to the Isles is a rather disappointing conclusion to such a lovely drive but it is a hard working, supply town to the Outer Isles and a major fishing port, one of the top white fish and prawn ports on the west coast of Britain. The Queen sends a tender from the HMS *Britannia* to Mallaig on her yearly Scottish holiday for a supply of Mallaig kippers which are indeed succulent. The steam trains or other services from Fort William terminate here and the ferry service departs for Armadale on Skye. There is plenty of accommodation but generally it is a rather bleak place. There is, however, an excellent exhibition near the harbour called Mallaig Marine World. There are conger eels, lobsters, and a 'Maternity Unit' where younger specimens are reared. There are also sea cruises available, weather permitting to Eigg, Loch Nevis and Skye.

South of the Road to the Isles and west of Fort William is one of the most untamed areas left in Northern Europe, the **Ardnamurchan Peninsula**. More of an island thrusting out into the Atlantic, it has largely resisted the onslaught of modern man and remains a refuge for creatures and plant to life less suited to our presence. The easiest approach is from Fort William, crossing Loch Linne at the Corran Ferry and winding ever further into this fertile landscape. Alternatively, follow the A861 through Moidart from the Road to the Isles. Taking a turn to the sparse community of Cul Doirlinn near Acharacle, the grim silhouette of **Castle Tioram** comes into view. Situated on a small island it is accessible unless the tide is high but water to proof boots are advised. Otters can sometimes be seen playing in the channel of water adjacent to the castle.

Salen on the banks of Loch Sunart belies the ruggedness of the peninsula beyond with its ice to cream signs and yachty setting. Once on the twisting, rolling B8007 that leads out to the far Point of Ardnamurchan, you notice a certain gleam in other driver's eyes, probably ornithologists returning from an enthralling field trip. With a little diligence, seals, red deer, sea otters and Golden Eagles can be spotted. Inland are largely inaccessible rolling hills and secluded lochans. At **Glenborrodale** is the Ardnamurchan Natural History and Visitor Centre which gives detailed information on the peninsula's geological past and its present range of wildlife and flora. There is a dramatic 13 minute audio to visual presentation with photography by Michael MacGregor, the local game stalker and postcard producer. There is also a shop selling locally produced craft to ware as well as a good café.

The ruins of **Mingarry Castle** are set near the village of Kilchoan where, in 1588, the crew of a Spanish galleon of the Armada that had sailed into Tobermory Bay on Mull along with MacLean of Duart and his men attacked Mingarry unsuccessfully. When the Spanish returned their ship had been blown up and its wreck still lies in Tobermory Bay along with its treasure trove. **Kilchoan** is the terminus for the small ferry to Tobermory on Mull. There is a guest house here, 'Meall mo Chridhe' or 'Little Hill of my Heart' (☎ 09723 238) that is furnished to a high standard and offers excellent fresh local produce in its farm shop. Evening meals can be booked if you are not staying.

Ardnamurchan Lighthouse is the most westerly point on the British mainland. The facility is closed to the public but it is possible to explore the rocks and watch the occasional ship thrust through the Sea of the Hebrides towards Stornoway on Lewis. Sanna Bay with its wide sands is nearby for a walk from Portuairk or you can drive back towards Kilchoan and drive to the village of Sanna.

Returning to the Fort William area via the Corran Ferry the A82 winds past North Ballachulish and crosses the mouth of Loch Leven towards the village of **Glencoe**. Ballachulish is an ideal place to rent a cottage or spend a few days in hotel accommodation with fine walks along a lochside that is surrounded by some of Scotland's most dramatic scenery. The Isles of Glencoe Hotel in Ballachulish also offers good leisure facilities as well as a pleasant restaurant. The village of Glencoe is a popular stopping place and holiday centre with a 'heather thatched' museum and memorial to the massacre that took place further up the glen. From the village the B863 carries on around Loch Leven to **Kinlochleven**, one of the first industrial towns in the Highlands where Scottish and Irish itinerant workers in the 1900's were paid 6 pence an hour constructing the Blackwater Dam. Many died in the snow trying to make their way back to lodgings from the pub. The dam was part of a larger project to establish an aluminium smelter here in 1904. The full story is told in the Kinlochleven Visitor Centre. The West Highland Way passes through Kinlochleven.

The National Trust for Scotland have created a visitor centre at the foot of the glen but perhaps no greater intimation of that terrible event can be gained than by standing and looking back down upon Glencoe itself, the

Glencoe, 'Glen of Weeping'

'Glen of Weeping'. The true Gaelic translation means 'Glen of the Dog' but this is never quite so moving.

Beyond the A82 passes the White Corrie Ski Lift at Glencoe. The glen has seen skiing here since 1917 when Ladies Scottish Climbing Club started using the slopes for skiing around the Black Rock Cottage base. Then there is the massive cone of the Buachaille Etive Mor to the right before the road runs over a bleak moorland plain and progresses into Strathclyde.

Additional Information

Places of Interest

Achiltibuie
Hydroponicum
In Achiltibuie
☎ 01854 622201
Open: April to October, daily. Tours at 10am & 12noon, 2pm, & 5pm.

Ardvreck Castle
A837 11 miles (18km) north-east of Lochinver
Open: At all times.

Bettyhill
Strathnaver Museum
A836 near Bettyhill
☎ 06412 330
Open: Monday to Saturday, 2-5pm.

Castle Tioram
On islet on Loch Moidart, approached by an unclassified road of the A861, 6 miles (10km) north-west of Salen
Open: at all times.

Corpach
Treasures of the Earth
Near Fort William
☎ 01397 772283
Open: Daily, summer, 9.30am-7pm and winter, 10am-5pm. Closed in January.

Durness
Balnakeil Craft Village
☎ 01971 511277
Open: 9am-5pm daily most of the year.

Smoo Cave
A838 in Durness
☎ 01971 511259
Open: At all reasonable times.

Eilean Donan Castle
Off A87, 9 miles (14km) east of Kyle of Lochalsh
☎ 01599 555202
Open: Easter to September daily, 10am-6pm.

Fort William
West Highland Museum
Cameron Square
Open: Monday to Saturday, 9am-5pm. July & August, Sundays, 2-5pm.

Ben Nevis Distillery
Open: Saturday, 10am-4pm, Monday to Friday, 9am-5pm except July to August, 9am-7.30pm.

Caledonian Canal
From Inverness to Fort William
☎ 0141 332 6936 or ☎ 01463 233140
Open: At all times.

Glenfinnan Monument
Off the A830 18 miles (29km) west of Fort William
☎ 01397 722250
Open: April, May, September, October, daily, 10am-1pm and 2-5.30pm. June to September, 9.30am-6.30pm.

Gairloch
Gairloch Heritage Museum
A832
☎ 01445 741243
Open: Easter to end of September, 10am-5pm, Monday to Saturday.

Glenborrodale
*Ardnamurchan Natural History and
    Visitor Centre*
☎ 01972 500254
Open: April to October, Monday to
Saturday, 10.30am-5.30pm, Sunday
12noon-5.30pm.

Glencoe
Glencoe Visitor Centre
A82, 3 miles (5km) of Glencoe Cross
☎ 01855 811307
Open: April, May, September, October,
daily 10am-5.30pm. June to September,
9.30am-6.30pm.

Glencoe and North Lorn Folk Museum
In Glencoe village off the A82
Open: May to September, Monday to
Saturday, 10am-5.30pm.

Glencoe Chairlift
Off the A82 by Kings House
☎ 01855 851226
Open: January to April, Thursday-
Monday inclusive of Easter. June to
September daily, 10am-5pm.

Glenfinnan
Glenfinnan Railway Museum
Road to the Isles
☎ 01397 722295
Open: Daily, Easter to October and by
appointment.

Handa Island Nature Reserve
3 miles (5km) north of Scourie; access
by boat from Tarbert
☎ 0131 557 3136
Open: April to mid-September, Monday
to Saturday, 10am-5pm.

Inverewe
Inverewe Gardens
☎ 01445 781200
Open: April to October, daily 9.30am-
9pm, November to March, daily
9.30am-5pm. Visitor Centre and shop
open April to October, 9.30am-5.30pm.

Kinlochleven
Kinlochleven Visitor Centre
01855 831233
Open: Daily, June to October, 10am-
4pm and October to June, Monday to
Friday, 9am-12pm and 2-5pm.

Lochinver
Lochinver Visitor Centre
Open: End of March to October.

Mallaig
Marine World
At the harbour
Open: Daily, 9am-7pm.

Torridon
Torridon Range
Off the A896, 9 miles (14km) south-west
of Kinlochewe
☎ 01445 791221
Open: At all times.

Torridon Visitor Centre
☎ 01445 791221
Countryside centre
Open: 28 April to 1 October, Monday to
Saturday, 10am-5pm, Sunday 2-5pm.
The Estate, Deer Park and Deer Museum
is unstaffed and open all year, daily.

Ullapool
Corrieshalloch Gorge
A835 at Braemore
☎ 01463 232084
Open: All times.

Ullapool Museum
7/8 Argyll Street
Open: Late March to early November,
Monday to Friday, 10am-5pm and June
to September, 10am-9pm.

Other Useful Information

Weathercall for this area
☎ 0898 500425
Emergencies
Ambulance, Police & Firebrigade ☎ 999
Fort William Railway Station
☎ 01397 703791
Skicall
☎ 01898 500440
Mountain Call West Highlands
☎ 01898 500441
Watt's Walks
☎ 01397 704340
Several graded walks throughout the
West Highlands.

Accommodation

Achiltibuie
The Summer Isles Hotel*
☎ 01854 622282

Arisaig
Arisaig House* * *
☎ 01687 450622

Fort William
'Crolinnhe' B&B*
☎ 010397 702709

The Moorings Hotel* *
☎ 010397 772797

Crolinnhe Deluxe B&B*
Grange Road
☎ 010397 702709

Near Fort William
Ballachulish **
The Isles of Glencoe Hotel
☎ 01855 581602

Lochinver
Mrs Garner B&B*
Veyatie
☎ 01571 844424

Corpach
Fort William
Mr and Mrs Moreland B&B*
☎ 01397 772309

Sheildaig
Tigh to an to Eilean*
☎ 01520 755251

Tongue
Diane Sallis Croft B&B*
☎ 0184 755 234

Ullapool
The Ceilidh Place* *
☎ 01854 612103

Tourist Information Offices

Ballachulish
☎ 01855 811296

Bettyhill
Clachan
☎ 01641 2342

Dornoch (Sutherland)
The Square
☎ 0862 810400

Durness
Sango
☎ 0971 511259

Fort William
Cameron Square
☎ 01397 703781

Glenshiel
☎ 01599 511164

Kilchoan
☎ 01972 510222

Kyle of Lochalsh
☎ 01599 534276

Lochcarron
☎ 01520 722357

Mallaig

☎ 01687 462170

Spean Bridge
☎ 01397 712576

Strontian
☎ 01967 402131

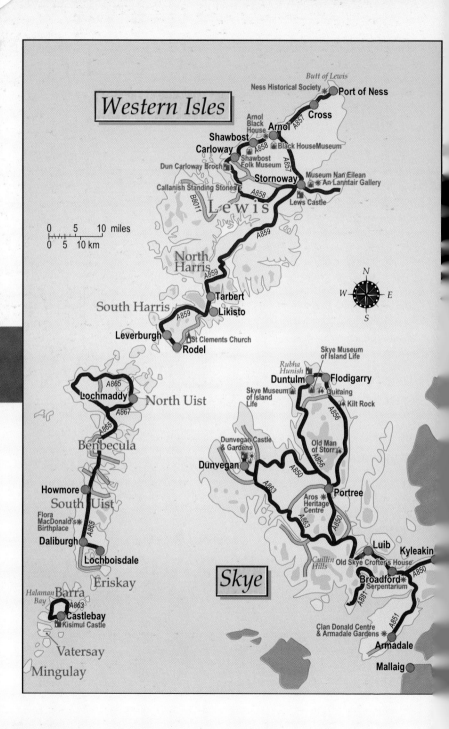

Western Isles

Butt of Lewis

Ness Historical Society • **Port of Ness**

Cross
A857

Arnol
Black
House **Arnol**

Shawbost
A858 Black HouseMuseum
Carloway
Shawbost
Folk Museum
Dun Carloway Broch
A858
Stornoway Museum Nan Eilean
Callanish Standing Stones ✱ An Lanntair Gallery

Lewis Castle

Lewis

B8011

A859

North
Harris

A859

South Harris
A859 **Tarbert**
Likisto

Leverburgh
St Clements Church
Rodel

Skye Museum
of Island Life
Rubha
Hunish
Duntulm **Flodigarry**
Quiraing
Skye Museum
of Island
Life Kilt Rock

A865 A856
Lochmaddy *North Uist*
A867

A865
Dunvegan Castle
& Gardens Old Man
of Storr
Benbecula
Dunvegan A850
A856
A863

Howmore
South Uist Aros ✱ **Portree**
Heritage
Flora Centre
MacDonald's ✱ A863
Birthplace A865 A850
Daliburgh
Luib
Lochboisdale **Kyleakin**
Cuillin Old Skye Crofters House
Eriskay *Hills* A850
Skye **Broadford** ✱
Serpentarium
Halaman *Barra* A881 A851
Bay A863
Castlebay
Kisimul Castle Clan Donald Centre
& Armadale Gardens ✱
Vatersay **Armadale**
Mingulay
Mallaig

N
W   E
S

0   5   10 miles
0   5   10 km

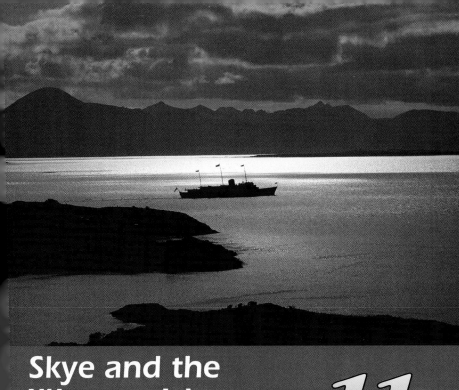

Skye and the Western Isles

11

There is no doubt, as you look around Portree or Dunvegan that, despite its unpredictable weather, tourism is Skye's main industry. From Kyle of Lochalsh there are two main access points to the island using the ferry from Kyle or via the new road bridge which sweeps from a western tip of the mainland to a point just outside Kyleakin. Further south, taking the famous 'Road to the Isles' from Fort William to Mallaig, you can cross to Skye by ferry to Armadale and land on the southern spur of the island.

The railway reached Kyle of Lochalsh in 1897 and since then the journey to and 'over the sea to Skye' has been a relatively easy one. The new road bridge, opened in autumn 1995, from Kyle of Lochalsh via the tiny island of Eilean Ban, is the biggest, balanced cantilever bridge in the world at 820ft (250m). The Gaelic name for Skye means 'Island of Mist' which most visitors will find apt at some time during a stay. Often several weather conditions will occur in one day so it is best to be prepared for what ever the elements decide.

In years gone by travellers came to know **Kyleakin**, the first village immediately on reaching the island's easternmost peninsula, by simply driving through it on their way to better known places or by queuing for long periods waiting to board the ferry back to the mainland. There is a twelfth-century castle visible from the road on a rocky knoll by the water's edge at the entrance to the harbour that can be reached by walking along the beach or clambering over the rocky peninsula.

A round-about marks the land-fall for Skye Bridge traffic. There is an excellent little restaurant just beyond called the Crofters Kitchen with a gift shop and licensed bar. Eight miles (13km) on along the A850 is **Broadford**, the island's second largest community. At the north end of Broadford there is an unusual attraction at the Old Mill, a stone croft-type building signposted as the Serpentarium. Inside is a collection of snakes, lizards and frogs including the uniquely marked Poison Arrow frog from the owner's private collection. He keeps a further 200 snakes at home.

If you take a left on the A881 travelling south-west you will come upon the villages of Torrin and Elgol. The reason for this diversion along a single track road to appreciate one of the best views of the **Cuillin Hills**. From the beach at Elgol, looking over Loch Scavaig, the great ragged dimensions of these sturdy peaks can be clearly surveyed. There is a small boat that crosses to Loch Coruisk at the foot of the range at least twice a day through the season. As long as the weather is reasonable, the trip is very impressive. It can be cold and wet even in the height of summer.

Returning to the A850, 7 miles (11km) north-west of Broadford, near **Luib**, you come upon a traditional thatched cottage which is furnished in a turn of the century style that was indigenous to the Highlands and Islands of that time. The Old Skye Crofters House also contains some interesting newspaper clippings, dating from the mid 1800's, when the government attempted to clear the island's small-holders and make way for sheep and hunting sports. The 1886 Crofting Act gave legal tenure and some rights to the local crofters.

Many visitors choose to approach Skye from the more southern mainland port of Mallaig, crossing the Sound of Sleat to Armadale. The A851 then carries north to Broadford. There is a good knitwear and gift shop on the Armadale Pier called Ragamuffin selling hand knits, original cotton clothes, pottery and jewellery. Only half a mile from the pier at **Armadale** is the Clan Donald Centre, its building adjoining the ruins of Armadale Castle. As well as an opportunity to trace your family roots and learn about the old clan system, the centre gives an excellent introduction to Skye and the Western Islands. Armadale Castle was built in 1815. It is surrounded by 40 acres (16hectares) of mature gardens from which there are fine views over the Sound of Sleat.

Portree is the island's commercial and administrative centre. It was originally known as Kiltaragleann (the church at the foot of the glen) but gained its present title of Portree or Port Righ, meaning the King's Harbour, when James V landed in 1540 to try and unite the bickering clans of the MacLeods and the MacDonalds and also to enlist them to his cause. The most interesting part of Portree is its harbour. People tend to hang out there enjoying the boats or taking a walk up to the Lump, a headland overlooking the bay where they can admire the little cliff-side gardens or take advantage of the best photo-spot of the harbour. This was the site of the local gallows where condemned prisoners were ushered from the jail house, now the tourist office, to meet their fate.

The Royal Hotel above the harbour is said to contain the room where Bonnie Prince Charlie bid his farewell to Flora MacDonald following his defeat at the Battle of Culloden in 1746.

On the Sligachan Road you find Skye's Heritage Centre. This is one of the newest and best of such exhibitions of Highland and Island life with a dramatic and convincing narrative delivered on multi-lingual headsets and based around Skye's history. There is also a very good restaurant and gift shop.

On the north side of town is the Skye Woolen Mill and Coffee shop. The Totternish Peninsula stretches above Portree for about 25 miles (40km) to Rubha Hunish and is one of the island's largest and most remote sections. **The Old Man of Storr** stands like a giant's bowling pin, perched on the side of the hill. It stands 160ft (49m) tall and is part of a landslip that has created several unusual stacks in this area. It is possible to hike to the base of the Old Man up Storr but scaling the stack itself is left only to those with plenty experience. Towards the shoreline below the Old Man of Storr, an incredible haul of silver broaches, bracelets and other jewellery as well as tenth-century coins was uncovered in 1891. This could have been a Norse treasure trove, and can now be seen as part of the Royal Antiquities Museum of Scotland in Edinburgh.

The A855 and A856 form a long 49 mile (79km) loop from Portree and back again via Uig and the western side of the Totternish peninsula. There are expansive views all along this road to the Applecross peninsula backed by the ranges of Torridon with the islands of Rona and Raasay in the foreground. At **Flodigarry** beyond the village of Staffin is the home of Flora MacDonald during her married life from 1751 to 1759. There is a minor road from Quiraing Lodge near Staffa leading to the **Quiraing**, an eyrie set of pinnacles and table top formations that are best experienced on foot. At **Duntulm** on the western side of the peninsula stands the wreck of Duntulm Castle, once a MacDonald stronghold from where they attempted to control the Hebridean clans during the sixteenth century. A few miles south is the community of **Kilmuir** and just before it is a cemetery where Flora MacDonald lies buried.

The Skye Museum of Island Life is nearby, a group of thatched cottages with farming implements and memorabilia. The spot where Bonnie Prince Charlie was hidden is near Monkstadt House just above the ferry port of Uig. From Borve it is possible to drive back into Portree or turn west towards Skeabost and Dunvegan. The Skeabost Hotel on the River Snizort has a challenging little 9 hole golf course, also offers fishing and is a good place to stop for lunch.

From the car park of **Dunvegan Castle**, the first impression is of a gray-green medieval tower block sitting on top of a craggy rock. The earliest

The Gaelic Language

You will notice that nearly all the road signs on the Western Isles are in Gaelic. This ancient Celtic language has held on throughout the islands and has in fact enjoyed a resurgence over the past few years with more support in schools as well as television programmes being made or adapted for Gaelic speakers.

The language probably stems from early Indo-European roots and travelled with the Celts through France, Ireland, Wales and onto the western side of Scotland. The early fourth century Celtic tribe of Scotti from Ireland who established their kingdom 'Dalriada' on the Kintyre Peninsula probably brought with them the precursor to the language. Although there are many similarities, the Scottish version has developed separately from its southern relatives. Most Gaelic speakers on the islands slip easily from English to their local tongue. Usually when an English speaker is in their midst, islanders give them the courtesy of speaking that language.

*Dunvegan Castle,
Isle of Skye*

part of Dunvegan Castle dates back to the ninthth century and the present structure has some fourteenth-century sections although there have been much additions and alterations. Access into the cast in those days could only be gained from the seaward side. From here the warships of the MacLeod's sailed to control the Western Isles similar to their Viking predecessors. The castle remains the seat of Macleod of Macleod and has been continuously inhabited for some 750 years.

There is a small jetty near the castle's southern flank where boat cruises set off to see seals on the little islands of Loch Dunvegan. It is possible to walk out on the rocks and get a better overall impression of Dunvegan's secure position and there are also several acres of castle gardens to explore. From Dunvegan a minor road lead across the Durinish Peninsula to the western shores of the island on the Little Minch with views over to North and South Uist on the Western Isles. The A863 the carries on towards Sligachan and Sconser where you can turn north to Portree or south to the ferry or bridge at Kyleakin.

THE WESTERN ISLES

The real beauty of these wild outer-lands is in their natural form. Man's interaction has done little to disturb this and it is, no doubt, the remoteness from modern civilisation that has helped to preserve some of the most essential elements of the place. If you are walking or even driving the grey skies and barren landscapes still enter your sight and soul. Some may find this disconcerting but others relish it and most feel curiously uplifted having visited such a wild and forbidding place.

Getting to the Western Isles may seem like an arduous task. You can take ferries from Ullapool on the north-west mainland or from Uig on Skye, not easy places to reach in themselves or from Oban to South Uist and Barra. Regular airline services also leave from Glasgow flying into Stornoway, Benbecula and Barra. In essence, it is a pure place with little evidence, apart from Stornoway, of modern pressures to spoil it. Urban congestion, if you could call it that, only takes place in Stornoway on a Saturday night and noise pollution consists of the howl of the wind. The scenery throughout this island string is simple, essentially sea, sky and low-lying, bare-boned rocks with ample scatterings of fine, sandy beaches.

Stornoway is the main town on the east coast of **Lewis** and the centre of Hebridean life with some 8,000 of the Western Isles population living in and around the town. Still a fishing centre whose heart is its harbour, that industry now exists as a mere echo of the activity that took place here a hundred years ago. A thousand fishing boats and coastal steamers used to fill Stornoway harbour throughout the nineteenth-century landing their catch and preparing to return to the bountiful Atlantic. Following World War I, Lord Leverhulme of the Lever Brother's empire decided to develop some of the facilities on the islands with the hope of making them the capital of a huge fishing industry. He actually bought the island of Lewis but a recession and collapse in the herring market put an abrupt end to his plans.

The regular ferry from Ullapool causes a stir around Stornoway with the arrival of tourists as well as cargoes of mainland wool for Harris Tweed weavers, timber for an almost tree-less land and various manufactured goods. The town of Stornoway can be rather grey and unappealing if the weather is similar but on a warm summer's day it has a pleasant mainland market-town air, a fine place to sit and watch island life go by. There are plenty amenities such as hotels, bars or grocers but bear in mind that everything including filling stations close on Sunday to observe the Sabbath. Hotel restaurants are kept open for meals but this is about all. Some B&B landlady's prefer you to book ahead on Saturday for a Sunday stay. They even padlock the swings in children's parks. The same situation exists throughout Lewis, Harris and North Uist, the domain of the Free Presbyterian Church while the more predominantly Catholic islands of South Uist and Barra are more moderate regarding opening times.

The town is crowned by Lews Castle which is surrounded by the pleasant, wooded grounds of Ladylever Park with advantageous views over the harbour. Next to the park is a good 18 hole golf course and the town is a good sea-angling centre. Just off the main square in the town hall there is an art gallery, 'An Lanntair' which displays local and national exhibitions and hosts various musical events while the Museum 'Nan Eilean' is in Francis Street.

From the Butt of Lewis these islands, only twelve of them are populated, run along a 130 mile (209km) vertebral column lying 30 to 50 miles (48 to 80km) off the Scottish mainland. The northern most land masses of Lewis and Harris are joined by a narrow isthmus although, despite their close proximity, each has its own unique topography and character. Lewis is largely rolling moorland with low-lying hills, hundreds of sparkling little lochans and a rugged coastline while Harris is more mountainous.

It is worth seeking out a bi-lingual map such as the *Western Isles Leisure Map* from one of the outlets in Stornoway before you depart as all the road signs are in Gaelic. Following the A857 out of town and travelling north-west the interior of Lewis looks bare, a peat moor where the only sign of human activity is in the dark, loamy channels cut everywhere to extract peat fuel, the islands main source of heat. If it is May or June the men will be cutting peat which costs no more than the labour of cutting, stacking it and later in the summer, collecting it.

The A857 continues up the north-west coast to the **Butt of Lewis**, a rocky headland some 30 miles (48km) from Stornoway, worth the trip to see thousands of seabirds that congragate around the lighthouse and cliffs. The village of **Ness** and its surrounding area are surprisingly well-populated and the Harbour View Tea Room is worth a re-fueling stop. Following the road south again leads on to the A858 and the small community of **Arnol** where the Arnol Black House Museum shows the lifestyle of crofters not so long ago. This house was built in the 1870's and inhabited until the mid 60's which is a fairly chilling thought if you are used to all the comforts of a modern home. There was no chimney and so the interior rafters and much else caught the soot from the fire. These long dwellings were common throughout the Hebrides, built without mortar or bricks and usually thatched but without eaves. At **Bragar**, the next group of houses on the main road stands a massive whalebone archway with the harpoon used to kill the poor beast hanging from its centre.

Shawbost is the next community and has a small museum which illustrates the old way of life for islanders. This was brought together by school shildren of the area some years ago and a few of the items are the worse for wear. **Carloway**, a bit further down the A850 is another taste of life before the twentieth century reached Lewis. Carloway Broch, found on a minor turning a mile or so beyond the village and a slight hike over a track is a 2,000-year-old, circular, drystone, fortified tower and probably one of the best preserved brochs of its kind in Scotland. The sea-ward wall stands around 30ft (9m) high.

There are many brochs along Scotland's coasts but apart from Mousa Broch in Shetland, few are in such good order. These were probably built to protect natives from sea-borne raiders, possibly Roman slave-traders.

Located close to A858 beyond the village of Callanish along the B8012 is the 5,000-year-old standing stones of **Callanish**, a circle and avenue of megaliths almost as famous as Stonehenge in England. Its cruciform shape was probably formed over many centuries from 3000BC to 1500BC. Nineteen monoliths lead north from a circle with more fanning east and west. The fact that the avenue of stones to the north completes a Celtic cross is rather baffling as it was constructed at least 1,500 years before Christ.

To drive to **North Harris** from Callanish is a distance of around 50 miles (80km) as you have to back-track to Stornoway then follow the A859 south. This leads through the area known as the 'Lochs' due to the multitude of small lochans and deep, penetrating sea lochs. The bare peaks of North Harris appear, a stark contrast to moors and bogs of its larger northern neighbour. The highest peak is An Clisham at 2,621ft (799m), clearly seen from the road. The most elevated areas are found on the east side of Harris with more fertile land on the west. These rocks were old, long before the glaciers of the Ice Age scraped them clean of soil, a part of a North Atlantic that was once part of Greenland until the Atlantic drove in between them.

The mountains of Harris trap the township of **Tarbert** in its narrow isthmus reached by descending down into this ferry port. There are many good walks around this area and these can be detailed from the tourist office in Tarbert. Here you will also find out where to see the world famous Harris Tweed being woven. The nineteenth century brought the sporting gentry to the Hebrides and they adopted the local, hand woven tweed originally made by the women of the islands to cloth their families. The success of the cloth is borne out with nearly every croft having its weaving shed. The colours of the Hebridean landscape are said to be woven into the tweed. To see the techniques used in their original form a good stop is Clo Mor in the village of **Likisto**, some 4 miles (6km) south of Tarbert following the A859 then branching left at the sign-post to the village.

The single track road winds over to the west coast of the island and offers glimpses of the superb stretches of sparkling beaches that the Western Isles are famous for.

Leverburgh is past on the south-west corner where Lord Leverhulme turned his attention after the failure of his enterprise in Stornoway. He spent a fortune building new harbours and buildings but died soon afterwards. A passenger ferry crosses from here to North Uist and Bernaray. The island of Beranary lies off the north coast of North Uist, a favourite destination of Prince Charles. It is the only populated island in the Sound of Harris.

Continuing east from Leverburgh you enter **Rodel** on the southern tip of Harris. St Clements Church in Rodel is one of the finest in the west of Scotland and contains the magnificent sculptured tomb of Alisdair Crotach Macleod, a chief of the clan and the eighth chief of Dunvegan.. The Sound of Harris separates Lewis and Harris from North Uist to the south which is reached either by the passenger ferry at Leverburgh or by car ferry from Tarbert or Uig on the Isle of Skye both of which land at Lochmaddy.

Lochmaddy is a pleasant little town, the main centre for **North Uist** and a good place to establish a base if you wish to tour this area. There are banking, provisions and accommodation facilities. There is a useful circular route following the A867 and it is advisable to explore the side roads that lead down to trout filled lochans mainly on the rolling east side and broad silver beaches mainly found on the west of the island. There is also agreeable farming country on the west but it is the great expanses of white sand beaches that are the islands best feature. The remote island of St Kilda lies 41 miles (66km) WNW of Griminish Point which is on the north-west corner of North Uist and the remote island's nearest substantial landfall.

North Uist connects by a long causeway and bridge with Benbecula via Griomasaigh or Grimsay. **Benbecula** is where Bonnie Prince Charlie and Flora McDonald met and then departed 'over the sea to Skye'. Apart from that piece of romance it is a rather water-sodden, spongey spot apart from its west coast which holds a fertile strip and along with the ubiquitous west coast beaches. There is an airport and army base on the north-west corner which swells the population and economy significantly but recent government cut-backs have threatened this. The main road cuts straight through Benbecula covering its 4 mile (6km) length then joins another causeway on the the island of **South Uist**.

Both the Uists as well as many spots on Benbecula are ideal angling terrain with hundreds of erratically shaped lochans. Sea trout, brown trout and salmon can be caught. Fishing is particularly popular on the machar lochs of South Uist for beautiful, wild, brown trout and in the

Tarbert Pier, Harris

Crofting

Apart from the main centre of Stornoway, there is today less reliance on modern amenities whereas the two essential elements to the place, the sea and the soil 'still play a key role in islanders' lives. Crofting has had to be and remains an important element in the islands economy.

Crofting is a social way of life and a few households are usually grouped in long rows gathered above the more fertile strips of land that surround the bays. The phenomena of crofting brought together all the available resources in an attempt to be self-sufficient. The thin soil found near the coasts is gathered in long narrow strips called 'lazy-beds' and fertilised often with seaweed brought up from the shore. A few sheep, chickens, perhaps some cows and a boat are the other necessary ingredients. Peat is the basic resource for fuel and is cut from the boggy hinterland in the spring and left to dry through the summer in stacks.

shallow sea for salmon, sea trout and mackerel. A variety of shell fish are collected and eaten by the locals including cockles that can be gathered when the tide is out on either side of the causeway.

Your entry into the long island of South Uist is marked, about 5 miles (8km) after the causeway, by a 125ft (38m) Statue of Our Lady of the Isles, perhaps to remind visitors that they have left the land of the 'Wee Free' Kirk and are now on Catholic soil. The A865 is the back-bone communication route through South Uist travelling around 20 miles (32km) from north to south. Off of this there are numerous side-roads leading west to the most wonderful stretches of beach. The village of **Howmore** is worth stopping at, very pretty in itself, but offers a good trek over to a breathtaking part of the western coast. The next turning after Howmore leads to a minor coastal route but it is easy to lose your way. Close inspection of a good map is recommended. A stone cairn marks the birthplace of Flora MacDonald in 1722 just off the main road at Milton.

The main base for a stay on this island might be **Lochboisdale** but, in spite of its facilities such as a bank, shop and harbour, it is not an inviting place. Better still to seek out B&B in one of the cottages around the south end or the hotel at Daliburgh although pre-booking is always advised especially in the summer months.

Off the south end of South Uist you can see the island of Eriskay amongst the splendid view that graces this coastline, where the SS *Politician* went down in 1941 with her cargo of 24,000 cases of whisky bound for Jamaica from Liverpool. This inspired Compton Mackenzie to write his novel, *Whisky Galore* where the islanders made brave attempts to 'rescue' the cargo much as happened in reality. A car ferry runs from Ludag on South Uist to the island of Eriskay although it is not really necessary to have a vehicle on this tiny island as most of it can be better appreciated on foot. This was the first landing place of Bonnie Prince Charlie on Scottish soil on 23 July 1745.

Barra and Vatersey form the southern tip of the Hebridean Island chain. Again, a single track road provides the main link for the tiny island community of **Barra** although the airport is situated on a spur to the north of the island. Here the daily Loganair service from Glasgow, Benbecula and Stornoway lands on a long strip of white shell sand timed to catch low tide. Near here at Eoligarry is the arrival and departure point for the passenger ferry to South Uist.

The approach by ferry from Oban, Mallaig or Lochboisdale to Barra is quite delightful with the striking Kisimul Castle standing out on an islet in the Sound of Vatersay. Its main tower dates from around 1120 and it is completely surrounded by water. The castle was completely ruined by fire in the late eighteenth century until the forty-fifth chief of the MacNeil clan, an architect, returned in the 1960's from his adopted home in America and restored it to its present admirable condition. **Castlebay**, Barra's main town, stands out on the rocky eastern coast, a gem of a little port with well-ordered cottages and shops. Above is the rise of 1,260ft (384m) of Heavel, the highest in Barra and upon its slopes stands the statue of the Blessed Virgin and Child.

Barra is an ideal escape for walkers who can circumnavigate the island in a day. Thousands of species of wild flower can be found and Barra is carpeted with primroses in springtime. Halaman Bay on the west coast is one of Barra's most bountiful. The popular Gaelic festival, 'Feis Barraigh' is held on the island every year in the first fortnight in July.

The nearby island of **Vatersay** can now be reached by a causeway from Barra. Again, it offers lovely beaches and invigorating coastal walks.

A string of tiny, flatter islets form the tails of the Outer Hebrides. The island of **Mingulay** at the southern end of the Western Isles is like a scene from *Robinson Crusoe*. It is often referred to as Bird Island as it was evacuated by people at the turn of the twentieth century and given over to populations of seabirds that inhabit the cliffs. When there was a community here they made a harvest of the birds, climbing up from boats onto the treacherously sheer walls to catch them on their nests.

One hundred years ago there were 150 people living here. The only substantial house left standing is the priest's house but it was never really occupied as around the same time that it was completed the people decided to leave the island in 1908. Tiree, with beaches facing every direction, is a haven for wind surfers.

Additional Information

Places of Interest on the Isle of Skye

Armadale
Clan Donald Centre and Armadale Gardens
At Armadale on the A851 just outside the village on the island of Skye
☎ 01471 844305
Open: April to Oct, daily 9.30am-5.30pm.

Broadford
Serpentarium
Old Mill
☎ 01471 822209 or 01471 822533
Open: Easter to October, Monday to Saturday, 10am-5pm. July and August daily.

Dunvegan Castle and Gardens
☎ 01470 521101
Open: March to October, 10am-5.30pm. Castle only closed on Sundays.

Luib
Old Skye Crofter's House
7 miles (11km) north-west of Broadford
☎ 01470 521296
Open: Daily, 10am-6pm.

Kilmuir
Skye Museum of Island Life
Off the A855, 20 miles (32km) north-west of Portree, near Uig
☎ 01470 552213
Open: Easter to October, 9.30am-5.30pm, Monday to Saturday.

Portree
Aros Heritage Centre
South side of Portree
☎ 01478 613649
Open: May to October, daily, 9am-9pm, November to April, 10am-6pm. Closed Sundays through winter until Easter.

Isle of Skye: Other Useful Information

Emergencies
Ambulance, Police & Firebrigade ☎ 999

Accommodation
Portree
Portree Hotel*
☎ 01478 612511

Cuillin Hills Hotel**
☎ 01478 612003

Broadford
Ptarmigan*
☎ 01471 822744

Sleat
Duisdale Hotel**
☎ 01471 833202

Tourist Information Offices
Broadford
☎ 01471 822361
Open: April to October.

Portree
Meall House
☎ 01478 612137

Places of Interest on the Western Isles

Arnol
Black House Museum
☎ 01851 71501
Open: April to September, 9.30am-7pm.
October to March, 9.30am-4pm and
closed on a Sunday.

Barra
Kisimul Castle
Castlebay
Boat required for access — call for date
and times.
☎ 01871 810336

Callanish Standing Stones
Off the A858 12 miles (19km) west of
Stornoway on the Western Isles
Historic Scotland ☎ 0131 244 3101
Visitor Centre: (☎ 01871 703625)

Shawboast
Folk Museum
☎ 01851 710213

Stornoway
Lews Castle
☎ 01851 703311
Open: Castle not open to public.
Grounds open all year and Lews Castle
College has display of local crafts.

Museum 'Nan Eilean'
Francis Street
☎ 01851 703773

Western Isles: Other Useful Information

Accommodation
Ness
Gaison Farm Guest House *
☎ 01851 850492

Stornoway
Seaforth Hotel **
☎ 01851 702704

Callanish
Mrs Morrison B&B *
☎ 01851 621392

Lochs
Handa Guest House *
☎ 01851 830334

Barra
Castlebay Hotel *
☎ 01871 810223

Self catering Apartment *
Mrs Sheila MacIntosh
☎ 01871 810580

North Uist
Burnside Croft *
☎ 01876 840235

Harris
Ardvourlie Castle Guest House *
☎ 01859 502307

South Uist
Orassay Inn *
☎ 01870 610296

Benbecula
Inchyra Guest House *
☎ 01870 602176

Emergencies
Ambulance, Police & Firebrigade ☎ 999

Airport
Stornoway Airport
☎ 01851 702256
Loganair fly inter-island between
Bennbecula and Stornoway.
British Airways
☎ 0141 889 1311

Caledonian MacBrayne Ferries
☎ 0141 889 4050
Scalpay Car Ferry
☎ 01859 540266
Eriskay Ferry to South Uist & Barra
☎ 01878 720233
Sound of Harris Ferry Services
☎ 01876 540230

Weathercall for this area
☎ 01898 500421

Tourist Information Offices
Stornoway
26 Cromwell Street ☎ 01851 703088

Tarbert
Isle of Harris ☎ 01859 502011

Lochboisdale
Isle of South Uist ☎ 01878 700286

Lochmaddy
Isle of North Uist ☎ 01876 500321

Strathclyde

12

Strathclyde is a large area covering the sea-cracked western coast of Scotland from the foot of the Great Glen, south to Grivan in Ayrshire and a huge diverse section to the interior. There are several distinctive areas and each is best explored as a single entity. The region north and west of Glasgow covers the west side of Loch Lomond, Argyll and the southern islands or Inner Hebrides.

Although relatively close to the urban blanket that surrounds Glasgow there are parts of Strathclyde that are quite isolated. If you intend to stay in places like Iona, Coll or Tiree, your trip should be planned in advance and include pre-booking of ferries where possible and possibly accommodation. Other areas like Oban or Inverary are the opposite, very popular and quite crowded through the summer so it is a good idea to book ahead here also and save time trying to find a room.

Loch Linne drives itself into the heart of the Highlands through the district of Lorn and starts the great channel created both by nature and man that stretches all the way to Inverness. From the bridge at Ballachulish it is an agreeable drive on the A828 to a similar structure at Connel just north of Oban. Coming from the north at the crest of a hill just before the tiny community of Portnacroish you happen upon one of the most dramatic stages for a Scottish castle. **Castle Stalker** was first built in the thirteenth century by the McDougalls of Lorn and later rebuilt in the mid-sixteenth century as a tower for the Stewarts of Appin. Recently restored, it is only accessible by rowing boat and is in private ownership but visits can be arranged by ☎ 01631 73234 (April to August). Carry on to the foot of the hill and turn right where a track takes you to the beach edge and good picture spots.

Port Appin is a ferry point for the 15 minute 'foot passenger only' crossing to the island of Lismore seen out on the loch. Many visitors prefer to sail from Oban using the car ferry to Achnacroish. **Lismore** is a stretching, fertile strip of an island still supporting 300 people but was once more heavily populated. It carries several ancient relics in the form of three castles.

Back on the mainland, on the shores of Loch Crenan is the Oban Sea Life Centre which displays locally captured sea creatures. There is a restaurant and gift shop as well as a wide selection of marine life, some of which can be handled.

The cantilever bridge at Connel stands above the mouth of Loch Etive, a winding sea loch that penetrates deep into the Grampian Mountains. Here the **Falls of Lara**, as they are called, create a churning fight between incoming and outgoing tides at this narrow entrance to the sea. This is also the road junction for either Oban or Inverary, the two nodal points for touring this area. Taking the A85 towards Oban, the resolute shape of **Dunstaffnage Castle** comes into view on the right over a yachted inlet. Built on a ponderous rock foundation, the thirteenth-century stronghold was the home of the MacDougalls until it was captured by the Robert the Bruce in 1309 then taken over by the Campbells. It is still owned by the Duke of Argyll. Flora MacDonald was imprisoned here in 1746 before a brief sentence in London.

The major ferry port of **Oban** started life as a fishing village until its importance grew as a farming, ferry and shipbuilding centre. The arrival of steam-ships and the railway in the later half of the nineteenth century made it a key staging post to the islands such as Mull, Colonsay, Coll, Tiree and the Outer Hebrides. It is now, by far, the largest port and gateway on the west coast serving the Hebridean Isles.

The town is a solid, Victorian, holiday mecca with coach-loads of visitors arriving daily to commandeer larger hotels and storm the multitude of gift shops and cafés waiting for them along George Street on the front. The most imposing structure in the town is the slightly absurd 'Craig's Folly' set directly above the town centre and harbour. Like a miniature Colosseum of Rome, it stands out like a sore thumb amidst more sober Victorian bungalows. Banker, John McCraig, intended to create work for unemployed masons and labourers but local chatter of the time put it down more to a personal memorial to a rather vain man. Nevertheless, the views over the harbour and the activities of the fishing and ferry boats are excellent from this point.

preceding page; Castle Stalker sits on the tiny island in Loch Linnhe

There are good quality fish-mongers set up in small huts around the harbour. If the weather turns foul, and it can quite readily, there is the ✳ World in Miniature exhibition on the northern arm of the harbour containing some sixty scaled down models of sitting rooms and their furniture from around Britain. By the railway station is the 'Oban Experience Centre', a shopping and gift arcade with the Caithness Glassworks being the best place to get warmed up on a cold summer's day whilst watching the molten glass being transformed. Oban Distillery is just off George ✳ Street and conducts tours offering more body-warming activity. If you like getting wet then head for the Atlantis Leisure centre on Dalriach Road just north-east of George Street.

Oban has hotels and B&B's of every size. There are a few good eating places, one of the most popular and economical being the Studio Restaurant on Craigard Road, ideal for the seafood and steak lover. For a more elegant culinary outing go to the Manor House on Gallanach Road heading for the Kerrera ferry. Just north-west of town on the road to Ganavan is **Dunollie Castle**. This present tower-house was probably built in the 🏰 fifteenth century as a seat of the MacDougalls.

There is an excellent, highly scenic excursion south of town to the islands of Seil, Easdale and Luing, collectively known as the Slate Islands as they once produced over 9 million slates annually in the mid-nineteenth century. Follow the A816 to the B844 then cross via the Clachan Bridge, known as the only bridge to cross the Atlantic. The village of **Ellanbeich** is also locally known as **Easdale**, which is the name for the island opposite. An unusual art gallery and visitor centre exists in Ellanbeich run by C.J. Taylor who paints most of the exhibits himself. A small ferry from Ellanbeich runs on demand to **Easdale Island** through the winter, push the fog-horn button on the small wooden shed on the jetty. Otherwise, through summer months it runs regularly. Near the Easdale Jetty there is a folk museum which focuses pictorially on the slate quarry industry that was once so prolific here. The quarries, now full of 🏛 sea water, can be dangerous cliffs so take care of small children. The sea can be quite dramatic dashing against the cliffs with its blue-green spray.

The island of **Luing** is reached by the small Cuan Ferry crossing the channel of the same name from the southern tip of Seil Island. The Cuan Ferry regular through the summer, and on demand at other times. The island is quite scenic but not very commercialised. The population here was shifted during the Clearances to make way for cattle which are still known for their quality beef.

Back in Oban, the ferry for Mull leaves Oban six times a day during the summer and takes 50 minutes. If you intend to take your car it is best to make a vehicle reservation. Mull is the second largest of the Inner Hebridean islands. 'Isle of the Cool High Bends' is the translation from Gaelic.

Mull suffered similar deprivations to other Highland areas during the ✳ Clearances and potato famine which led to a rapid decline in its mainly crofting and fishing population. In recent years this trend has been reversed with a noticeable influx of settlers from the south. Its terrain

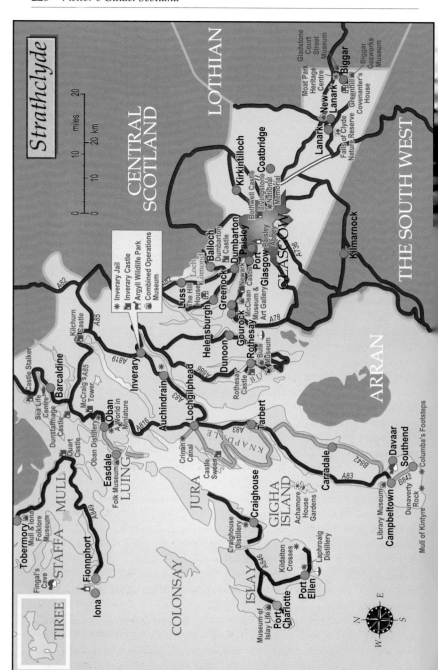

Strathclyde

consists of a mix of mountains, moorlands, forest and craggy cliffs with the occasional stretch of white, sparkling beach.

Duart Castle is seen from the ferry during the approach to the harbour, set on its outstanding location of Lady's Rock and accessible just south of the small village of Craignure. It was built as a simple fortification by the Lord of the Isles in the thirteenth century but transformed through the centuries into a classic residence of the Highland chieftain.

The road south and west to Fionnphort (pronounced 'Finnafort'), the A849, is uneventful through forestry land and moors apart from the last stretch along Loch Scridian with impressive views of Ben More to the north. **Fionnphort** is little more than a parking place for those that take the 'passenger only' ferry service the 1 mile (2km) across the Sound of Iona. There is a prohibition on driving on the roads on Iona. The only visitor's vehicles allowed over are those specifically adapted for a disabled person and not just a registered disabled vehicle. For an application you must phone Strathclyde Roads Department in Oban (☎ 0631 62125 well in advance of your trip). A wheel-chair, if required, is available at Cal Mac ticket office in Fionnphort. On the island side it is an ideal, $^1/_2$ mile (1km) walk to the abbey.

Iona was the site chosen by St Columba to establish his Celtic church in AD563. The Irish saint landed here and began converting the heathen Picts to Christianity throughout Scotland. Through the following centuries no less than forty-eight Scottish kings were buried here, as was John Smith, the leader of the British Labour Party, following his sudden death in 1994.

The narrow road leads past the thirteenth-century Nunnery of St Mary constructed of lovely pink granite. The present abbey was constructed in 1938 by the Presbyterian Socialist, George Macleod who established a new community on the island to rebuild and revitalise the holy site. For the many Christians who come here now there is special significance but some feel the essence of the place is missing, driven away by the slightly commercial enterprise they encounter. For the more eclectic, the beautiful natural bays and pure white sands of the west side of Iona hold more spiritual substance most notably 'The Bay at the Back of the Ocean' or Camus Cul an Taibh' in Gaelic. The island is only 3 miles by 1 mile (5km by 2km) and worth exploring further.

Returning to Mull and the north B8035 route to Tobermory following the west coast, Ben More, the islands highest peak at 3,169ft (966m) dominates the panorama. The village of **Calgary** on the north shore with its lovely white beaches breaking the craggy coastline gave its name to the Canadian city. The island of **Staffa** is 6 miles (10km) north-east of Iona and a short boat ride from this western side of Mull, a small and uninhabited rock famous for its basaltic formations and unusual caves. Fingal's Cave is the best known, made famous by Mendelsshon in his *Hebrides* overture. To reach Staffa there are boats leaving from Dervaig on Mull.

To reach the town of **Tobermory** it is possible, as well as taking this scenic drive, to sail the ferry from Oban which takes nearly 2 hours. This is the capital of Mull and its most scenic inhabited corner. Though not of great consequence, Tobermory was a fishing village, its harbour being one of the most sheltered in the Hebrides. Today most of the activity around the harbour is of leisure yachts and cruisers coming in to take supplies make use of the ports fine hostelries.

In 1588, following the destruction of the Spanish Armada, a galleon, possibly named the *Florencia*, pulled into Tobermory Bay and there are now many stories surrounding the event. One goes that Spanish soldiers were lent to MacLean of Duart to help him attack Mingarrie Castle, carrying on a feud with Maclean of Coll. It became know that the Armada's treasure of gold coins was on board and while the ship's company was depleted a raider stole aboard and fired the ship's magazine. With 350 men still on board she blew up in the Bay near Calve Island, some 80 yards off shore and sank to 11 fathoms.

Many attempts have been made to rescue the treasure but only a few pieces have been released from the muddy depths. **The Mull and Iona Folklore Museum** on the front tells more about the galleon and treasure seekers from around the world still speculate but the wreck is protected from divers.

Tobermory is one of the best places to enjoy a traditional 'ceilidh' if you can stand the pace. The Mishnish pub is one of the most lively. The whirling and 'heuching' goes on until closing time then there might be similar fun found in the village hall until the early hours. Explore the Upper Town of Tobermory, the more residential and elegant part from which there are superb views over the Sound of Mull.

Other islands served by the ferries from Oban are Coll and Tiree. The island of **Tiree** is known for holding championship windsurfing events as it has become one of the world's top wave sailing venues.

Returning to the mainland the A85 route east surpasses one of Scotland's longest lochs. **Kilchurn Castle** lies at the north end of the 23 mile long, Loch Awe. A stronghold of the Campbells of Glenorchy for 300 years it now stands broken but yet magnificent with the ranges of Ben Lui behind it and almost surrounded by the shallow waters of the loch.

Just beyond Loch Awe there are signs for Inverary. **Inverary** would be a pleasant place if it was not so popular. Inverary is Campbell country on the north-west side of Loch Fyne on the A83. On the harbour is Inverary Jail with its Court Room, squalid cells and life sized models depicting the lot of the in-mates of the time, mending nets, feeding children or being tried for insurance fraud. This establishment functioned until the 1930's. There are many pieces of notable architecture in and around the village especially the two bridges, the Garron Bridge at the head of the loch and the Garden Bridge nearby.

Set apart from the town with its mock Gothic towers peaking above the trees, Inverary Castle is still the seat of the Duke of Argyll. The most impressive display inside is the Arms Room where eighteenth-century weaponry of every type reaches for the ceilings. This was supplied to the Campbells to help suppress the Jacobite insurrection. Inverary was an important training centre during the World War II and a Combined Operations Museum found in the grounds illustrates this period of the castle and community's history. A woodland walk to the summit of Duniquaich gives a wide panorama of the castle, town and loch.

Following the shores of Loch Fyne on the A83 the Argyl Wildlife Park is signposted with its wild cats, wild boar and tame roe deer. A little further on is the old West Highland township of **Auchindrain** appears. The twenty or so thatched cottages have been well restored to present Highland life of the past before the time of Clearances and planned villages such as Inverary. All the old utensils, farm gear and domestic furnishings are gathered in the buildings and a visitor's centre and tea room completes the encounter.

The mid-Argyll market town of **Lochgilphead** marks the start of a tour of the Kintrye Peninsula. This is a hub for the smaller communities nearby with provisions such as the only bank and supermarket for some distance. From Loch Crinan on the west side of the peninsula to Lochgilphead the **Crinan Canal** cuts through. Built at the end of the eighteenth century it remains as an engineering monument and much used by yachts or the sporadic puffer plying the passage from the Clyde to north-west Scotland. Nine miles (14km) long and with fifteen locks, the canal was complete in 1809.

The A83 continues along the mouth of Loch Fyne to Tarbert before crossing to the western side of Kintyre. To the west is the more diminutive lump of Knapdale, a quiet, less trampled corner. There is a circular worth taking, the B8024. It is a delicate environment with admirable views over to Jura and Islay but its main focus is usually Loch Sween with its **Castle Sween** to the north.

The fishing village of **Tarbert** appears idyllic as the road descends into town. This is the terminal end of the deep West Loch Tarbert and each morning small fishing trawlers head out to the seas surrounding the Inner Hebrides. If not for the thin stretch of land inhabited by Tarbert, Kintyre would be an island. There is a rubble reduced castle above the town called Bruce's Castle but the best way to employ your time here is to walk out by the loch and enjoy the peace. The Columba Hotel is one of the cosiest with mesmerising views over the loch. This serves also some of the best bar meals in town.

Just south of Tarbert on the A83 is the ferry terminal of **Kennacraig** which serves the Inner Hebridean islands of Islay, pronounced 'Isla', and Jura. It is a two hour crossing to Port Ellen on **Islay**, some 25 miles by 20 miles (40km by 32km) and the most southern of the Inner Hebrides. In medieval times this was the power base for the Lords of the Isles who ruled Scotland's western seaboard and conducted a fairly independent existence from the rest of Scotland. For today's visitor the southern shores of the island around **Port Ellen** could offer all they might need with three world famous whisky distillers and a unique 18 hole golf course. It is possible to fly to Islay from Campbeltown on Kintyre or from Glasgow Airport with the airport being minutes away from the Machrie Hotel and Golf Course.

Islay Whiskies are at the top of the malt whisky tasting tree but they are usually aspired to after sampling the milder Lowland then Highland malts, thus educating the palate. The strong, peaty, smoky flavour of Islay whisky comes about with the peat burning process and the sea air in which they are stored giving them a tinge of iodine. Bowmore, Lagavulin, Laphroig and Bunnahabhainn are produced here and each distiller offers tours and samples of their produce. There are a total of eight distilleries on the island.

Near Port Ellen is the island's most important artifact, the **Kildalton Cross**, crafted more than 1,200 years ago, inscribed with early Christian symbols and one of the best examples not unlike the one found in Iona's cathedral. **Bowmore**, further north on the A846 was the capital of the island. It is another distillery town with its whisky production established in 1779. Overlooking Loch Indaal is a 200-year- old round church which was designed to do away with corners in which evil spirits could hide. Around the bay is **Port Charlotte** with its Museum of Islay Life set in a converted church and winner of several awards. There are examples of craft working tools, a maritime section and information of the standing stones and burial cairns of the area.

Islay is popular with bird-watchers especially around the sandy bay at Craigens. Fishing for trout and salmon is excellent in the many rivers and lochs and there is easy accessibility to sea angling. Islay's importance as a medieval centre was focused around Finlaggan Castle, a seat of the MacDonalds and now a mossy ruin just off the road before Port Askaig.

From Port Askaig there is a short ferry hop to the neighbouring island of Jura. **Jura** is not developed with only one 24 mile (39km) long, single track road and very few people. The majority of the island is only accessible by foot. This may be why Eric Blair otherwise known as George Orwell chose it as an escape to write his novel *1984*. Towards the headland is the Gulf of Corryvreckan where an infamous whirlpool occurs at certain tides capable of swallowing whole boats.

Deer are abundant on Jura making it popular with stalkers who track the beasts around the Paps of Jura, two breast shaped rises that dominate the skyline. Bird watching and gentler walks are the other main activities on Jura. There is the Craighouse Distillery producing Jura malt whisky in the island's main centre of **Craighouse** where there is also a hotel and general store come post office, a tea-room and hairdresser.

Returning to the mainland there is the ferry terminal for Gigha at Tayinloan. Washed by the Gulf Stream, fertile **Gigha** is the tiny island between Kintyre and Islay best known for its cheese. Arminish is the main centre. The island has changed hands several times since its original laird sold it. One buyer was Sir James Horlick of hot-drinks fame who established the marvellous garden at Achamore House.

Taking the roller-coaster road the B8001 brings you to the desolate little landing for the Claonaig to Lochranza ferry on the island of Arran. If there is nobody else there, wait around and eventually more cars or the ferry will arrive.

The Isle of Iona is indented by glorious white sand beaches

Iona Abbey grounds

There is a choice of traversing the Kintyre peninsula, either by the main A83 which is fast and relatively scenic or the tortuous B842 following the east coast, much more demanding and more rewarding with leafy twists and wide views over to the mountainous side of Arran. You eventually reach the village of **Carradale** which has a delightful little harbour and a testing 9 hole golf course. There are walks through Carradale Forest and out to Carradale Point. Carradale Hotel ✈☎ 05833 223) with the golf course adjacent, offers golf breaks where you stay at hotel and play free golf as well as a leisure club, 2 squash courts, sauna and solarium with occasional, large screen film shows. Carradale House Gardens are walled gardens dating from about 1870.

Campbeltown is the central municipality for the area, a former herring fishing port and once hub of an assiduous whisky production recalling the song *O' Campbeltown Loch, I wish ye were whisky* . Only two whisky distilleries are now left in the area, but at one time there were a total of thirty-four such businesses in and around town.

A fourteenth-century cross graces the only round-a-bout in town in front of the harbour and Tourist Information Office. There is a small museum in the local library with some parochial information. Campbeltown Creamery on Witchburn Road produces and sells 'Truckle' which is a mature cheddar wrapped in wax and worth taking away.

Perhaps the most popular attraction in this area is a cave on **Davaar Island** which lies off Kildalloig Point east of town. Before heading out check with the tourist office the times of the safe walking tide. A shingle spit connects the island with the mainland and here, in a cave, a painting appeared in the late 1800's of the crucifixion, lit only by a shaft of light from above. It was not until 1934 that the artist owned up, a local man called Archibald MacKinnon.

Continuing south on the B842 leads through the Mull of Kintyre, another area made famous in song when Paul McCartney of *The Beatles* retreated here. The coastal town of **Southend** is set south of some of Kintyre's best scenery but the village does little to augment the natural scene. **Dunaverty Rock** was the site for Dunaverty Castle, now no longer in existence.

The return drive from Mull of Kintyre and Campbeltown along the A83 to Inverary or Oban can seem tedious as you are forced to back-tract along the A83. Alternatives back to Scotland's central belt exist, for example by taking the minor B842 from Campbeltown to Claonaig, a windy and lumpy road but with great views of the west side of the island of Arran. During the summer months a ferry crosses from Claonaig to Lochranza on the north tip of Arran from where you can drive down to Brodick on the island's east side and take another short ferry crossing to Ardrossan on the mainland, some 30 miles (48km) south-west of Glasgow. This method is rather more expensive with the cost of the ferries but it avoids a long drive and gives you the chance to see the beautiful island of Arran.

There are several areas quite close to Glasgow that make ideal day trips from the 'Empire's Second City'. The M8 swoops over the Kingston Bridge towards Glasgow Airport passed the communities of Paisley and Renfrew. **Paisley** has several historic connections not least of which is the creation a fashion for fantastic patterned shirts that were the rage around the world in the late 1960's.

Paisley's town centre is graced with several imposing buildings set amongst the more typical lowland town merchandisers. For contrast to the rather oppressive exterior of Paisley Abbey traverse through the High Street to find Thomas Coates Memorial Church, a rather more opulent example of Victorian design.

The M8 bifurcates at Erskine Bridge leading to Dumbarton and Helensburgh while the west route follows the Clyde. **Port Glasgow** was a small fishing village until the late seventeenth century when it was purchased by the town of Glasgow to become their main port. Newark Castle, overlooking the Clyde, stands out amidst the flotsam of the docks. This turreted fifteenth-century construction is in remarkably good condition for its 400 years, once a tower house for the Maxwell family and now open to visitors.

Further on is **Greenock**, another beneficiary of the Clyde's industrial hey-day. In Cathcart Square the main focus is the 245ft (75m) Victorian tower which now houses the Tourist Information Office. In Union Street is the McLean Museum and Art Gallery which contains some of the work of James Watt, the celebrated eighteenth-century industrialist and inventor of the steam engine, who was born in Greenock. **Gourock** just down the coast is a rather tired seaside resort but with still some character and marvellous views over the Clyde to the Cowal Peninsula.

The ferry to **Dunoon** sails form Gourock taking only a few minutes to cross this narrow part of the Clyde to reach this popular holiday resort. The Tourist Office is on Alexander Parade which is useful for finding accommodation although you should not find any difficulties here. Behind the town, the Cowal Peninsula is formed by Loch Fynne and Loch Long and offers a variety of landscapes from the peaks of Argyll Forest Park in the north to the more temperate environs of the south-west.

The **Isle of Bute** stands below the Cowal Peninsula. Its main attraction is the seaside town of **Rothesay** which, like Dunoon, has attracted Scots for decades. There are moves to bring it into the 90's and make use of its Winter Gardens, the Promenade, the pier and the many guest houses. Rothesay Castle sits above the bay.

There is a small display of the area heritage at Bute Museum in Stewart Street. The island of Bute is a mildly contoured domain that is popular with retirees and those keen on growing a garden that reaps the benefits of the Gulf Stream. The A844 follows a figure of eight tour of the island that finishes back at the short ferry crossing onto Cowal or you can catch the frequent ferries back to Wemyss Bay where the mainland ferry terminal is sited. From Wymess Bay the A78 carries on south into Ayrshire or back into Glasgow.

The Clyde Valley follows the A724 passing through Rutherglen and then joins the A72. **Bothwell Castle** is worth detouring for, once one of the finest red-sandstone castles in this part of the land. It stands high above a loop in the Clyde, a mighty stronghold during the English attacks in the early fourteenth century. The nearby village of Blantyre was the birthplace of the explorer and missionary, David Livingstone in 1813.

Following the River Clyde towards its source the effects of Glasgow and its industrial endeavours are finally left behind revealing an area of deep valleys and gentle rises. The area is sometimes referred to as the 'Greenhouse Glen' with quaint little cottages and their attenuated gardens.

Lanark is an old market town with the world's oldest bell cast in 1130 but otherwise it is now rather bleak. The double-laned main street now choked with traffic, is overlooked by a statue of William Wallace who lived in Lanark for a time and struck the first blow for Scottish Independence here after the English had murdered his wife. The Lanark Golf Club is frequently awarded for its challenging heathland course and comfortable new clubhouse.

Following Braxfield Road you approach the village of **New Lanark** only 1 mile (2km) from the centre of the old town and the view is quite stunning although so easily missed if you were simply driving though Lanark. With misty sprays rising above the village, this was one of the first communities to bring together industrialism with social development. Founded by rich industrialist David Dale and his partner Richard Arkwright to yoke the power of the Falls of Clyde for their cotton mills in 1785. It was Dale's son-in-law, Robert Owen that had the vision to create a model community when he became manager of the estate. He called his experiment the 'village of unity' and in 1798 he created the country's first infant school, adult education facilities, and a series of reforms that concerned the welfare of the workers as well as the profitability of the mills.

The 'Annie McLeod Experience' is a tour through the social history of life in the village as seen through the eyes of a mill girl of the era. The path skirting the river leads to the Falls of Clyde Nature Reserve with spectacular falls plunging 90ft (27m) in three stages. En-route is Wallace's Tower or Corra Castle perched on pinnacle above Corra Linn.

The most south-westerly town in the Strathclyde region is **Biggar**, 13 miles (21km) on from Lanark on the A72 and a main stopping point on the A702 from Edinburgh to the south-west. The River Clyde flows nearby, a much junior version of the waterway some 50 miles (80 km) north-west. The main route carries traffic through the centre of this ancient market town of some character.

Biggar has no less than four museums. The Moat Park Heritage Centre just off the High Street in a converted church is exceptionally well put together and gives the annals of the Upper Clyde and Tweed Valleys along with a fascinating display of table covers and other embroidery. The Gladstone Court Street Museum on North Back Road is a recreation

The village of Tobermory on the Island of Mull

The pictorial village of Luss on the banks of Loch Lomond is overlooked by Ben Lomond

of a Victorian Street complete with cobblers, a dressmakers, a chemists and even an early telephone exchange. On Burns Braes is the Greenhill Covenanters House which might help clarify this confusing period in Scottish history.

Near the War Memorial is the Biggar Gasworks built in 1839 and closed in 1973, an unusual museum that might stir memories for those that remember gas mantles and the smell of coal gas works which this is the sole surviving example.

The area north of Glasgow is immediately ringed by residential areas then open agricultural land before coming to an outer ring of towns. These are closely associated with the city but just out of reach of the urban sprawl and so are more countrified than metropolitan. From the northeast of Glasgow these start with **Coatbridge** which now has a tourist centre recently grafted in with an amazing ice-rink and swimming centre called the Time Capsule. Coatbridge was a key element in the Scottish industrial scene providing much of the steel for the thousands of ships that were built on the Clyde as well as for the Forth Bridge.

Travelling westwards in Kirkintilloch and Bishopbriggs with the Campsie Fells, a long string of medium-sized hills protecting this area from the north. The Stables pub and restaurant sits on the banks of the canal between Bishopbriggs and Kirkintilloch and is quite entertaining to sit out on a decent day. **Kirkintilloch** is another town that has been treated badly by modern planners. There are some lovely terraced cottages at the west end of the High Street but from there on there is a gradual deterioration until tasteless video stores and off-licence outlets prevail.

Further west is the Glasgow suburb of Bearsden and nearby Milngavie, pronounced 'Mulguy'. The main route north from here is the A809 passing through the Kilpatrich Hills with the Campsie Fells to the east. Drymen is the next village and acts as a gateway to the Trossachs area.

The A82 travels the north banks of the Clyde, a dual carriageway leading to Dumbarton, Alexandria and Loch Lomond. **Dumbarton** is a rather ugly development of the 60's and 70's despite it having a castle that can trace its origins back to Roman times. To reach it take Victoria Street from the town. Its situation is ideal surrounded on three sides by water with views up and down the Clyde.

Helensburgh developed to serve the needs of Glasgow's better off holiday-makers and became a port of call for those going 'doon the watter'. In fact the trend was actively promoted by the town's bathing master, Henry Bell, who invented one of the first steam boats to help transport visitors to his town. John Logie Baird was born here, the inventor of television as was the architect and designer, Charles Rennie MacKintosh. He was commissioned to design Hill House which can still be visited on Upper Colquhoun Street.

Being the largest stretch of fresh water in Britain at 23 miles (37km) long and 5 miles (8km) wide at its widest point and so close to Glasgow **Loch**

Lomond draws the throngs from the Glasgow area to enjoy its water-sports and scenery. In all, some 2 million visitors now put considerable pressure on the area.

Balloch is just beyond Alexandria on the loch's southern tip and is the starting point for many cruises that are one of the best ways of seeing the loch with its spectacular views such as Ben Lomond on the east side. Apart from this there are several decent restaurants to serve its swollen summer population. Duck Bay is popular with a hotel and marina while Cameron House, next door is a more upmarket establishment that has excellent leisure facilities complete with two swimming pools with flumes, gymnasium, squash courts and its own 9 hole golf course appropriately called the 'Wee Demon'. The food in the hotel's Georgian Room is epicurean but expensive. For more frugal tastes there is a very good youth hostel situated in an old house, built in 1866 that resembles a castle though technically it is not, in the areas referred to as Arden on the opposite side of the road from Cameron House.

The ultra-exclusive Loch Lomond Golf Course is a few miles further up the A82 and has one of the best settings for the game in this part of the country but entry is to members only. Slightly further north is the village of **Luss** famous as the stage for the Scottish soap-opera, *Take the High Road*. Luss's narrow streets can be over-run with tourists at the height of the season. Nevertheless it is worth a visit and there is ample designated car parking areas. The A82 carries on from here towards Crainlarich and Central Region.

Additional Information

Places of Interest

Ardnamurchan
Castle Tioram
Set on an islet in Loch Moidart, north of
A861 and down a rough track.
Open: All year.

Barcaldine
Sea Life Centre
On A828, 11 miles (18km) north of Oban

☎ 01631 72529
Open: March to November, daily.

Biggar
Moat Park Heritage Centre
☎ 01899 221050
Open: Monday to Saturday, 10am to
5pm, Sunday, 2-5pm. Off season call at
the office at rear.

Biggar Gasworks Museum
Gasworks Road near the War Memorial
in Biggar
☎ 0131 225 7534
Open: May to September, Monday to
Thursday, 2-5pm, closed Fridays.

Gladstone Court Street Museum
A702 North Back Road Biggar
☎ 01899 21050
Open: Easter to October daily, 10am-
12.30pm, 2-5pm. Sundays, 2-5pm.

Greenhill Covenanters House
On the 702 in Biggar, 26 miles (42km)
from Edinburgh
☎ 01899 21050
Open: Easter then mid-May to mid-
October, daily, 2-5pm.

Blantyre
Livingstone National Memorial
At Blantyre on the A724
☎ 01698 823140
Open: All year, daily, 10-6pm. Sunday,
2-6pm.

Bowmore
Bowmore Distillery
On the island of Islay
☎ 01466 711441
Open: All year, Monday to Friday,
Tours at 10.30am-2.30pm.

Bowmore Round Church
☎ 01496 810447
Open: Daily, 9am to dusk.

Campbeltown
Library Museum
Hall Street
☎ 01496 552367

Coatbridge
Summerlee Heritage Trust
West Canal Street
☎ 01236 431261
Open: Daily, 10am to 5pm

The Time Capsule
Buchanan St, Monklands
☎ 01236 441444
Open: Daily, 10am-10pm.

Dunstaffnage Castle and Chapel
4 miles (6km) north of Oban on A85
Historic Scotland ☎ 0131 244 3101
Open: April to September, Monday to
Saturday, 9.30am-7pm. Sunday, 2-7pm.
October to March, Monday to Saturday,
9.30am-4pm. Sunday, 2-4pm.

McCraigs Tower
Above town of Oban
☎ 01631 63122
Open: At all times.

Oban Distillery
Stafford Street
☎ 01631 64262
Open: All year, January to December,
Monday to Friday, 9.30am-4.30pm plus
Saturdays Easter to October.

Easdale
Near Oban
Easdale Folk Museum
Open: 9am to 4.30pm.

Ganavan
Dunollie Castle Near Oban
Open: All reasonable times.

Greenock
MacLean Museum and Art Gallery
Greenock ☎ 01475 723741
Open: All year, Monday to Saturday,
10am-12noon & 1-5pm.

Helensburgh
Hill House
Upper Colquhoun Street
☎ 01436 673900
Open: April to December, daily 1-5pm.

Inverary
Inverary Castle and Gardens
Just outside Inverary
☎ 01499 302421
Open: April to October, daily 9.30am to
6pm. November to March, daily, 10am-
5pm.

Combined Operations Museum
Within Inverary Castle
☎ 01499 302203
Open: April to October, Monday to
Saturday, 10am-1pm, 2pm-6pm. Closed
Fridays.

Inverary Jail
Centre of Inverary
☎ 01499 302381
Open: All year, 9.30am-6pm.

Argyle Wildlife Park
2 miles (3km) through Inverary on the
Campbeltown Road.
☎ 01499 302264
Open: Daily, 9.30am-6pm.

Island of Jura
Craighouse Distillery
☎ 01496 820240
Tours by appointment only.

Island of Mull
Duart Castle
Off A849 east of Mull
☎ 01680 812309
Open: May to September, daily
10.30am-6pm.

Isle of Rhum
Kinloch Castle
Access from boat from Mallaig
☎ 01687 462026
Open: March to October as a hotel and
hostel.

Kintyre
Achamore House Gardens
Island of Gigha
☎ 01583 505254
Open: All year, 10am until dusk.

Lanark
New Lanark World Heritage Centre
1 mile (2km) south of Lanark
☎ 01555 661345
Open: 11am-5pm, daily.

Falls of Clyde Nature Reserve
☎ 01555 665262
Open: Visitor Centre, Easter to October,
Monday to Thursday, 11am-5pm,
Friday, 11am-4pm. Saturday & Sunday,
1-5pm. Mid-October to Easter, weekends only and closed in January.

Loch Lomond
Ben Lomond
B837 11 miles (18km) beyond Drymen.
☎ 0141 552 8391

Lochgilphead
Castle Sween
East shore of Loch Sween and 15 miles
south-west of Lochgilphead
Historic Scotland ☎ 0131 244 3101
Open: April to September, Monday to
Saturday, 9.30am-7pm. Sunday, 2-7pm.
October to March, Monday to Saturday,
9.30am-4pm. Sunday, 2-4pm.

Crinan Canal
Crinan near Lochgilphead
☎ 01546 603210

Loch Awe
Kilchurn Castle
☎ 01786 450000
Open: April to September, Monday to
Saturday, 9.30am-6.30pm, Sunday, 2-
6.30pm.

Oban
World in Miniature
North Pier
☎ 01631 566300
Open: Monday to Saturday, 10am-5pm.
Sunday, 2-5pm.

Paisley
Coats Observatory
Oakshaw Street, Paisley
☎ 0141 889 2013
Open: Monday, Tuesday and Thursday,
2-8pm, Wednesday, Friday and Saturday, 10am-5pm.

Paisley Abbey
In town centre, 7 miles (11km) west of Glasgow
☎ 0141 889 7654
Open: All year out with hours of worship, Monday to Saturday, 10am-3.30pm.

Paisley Museum and Art Gallery
High Street in centre of town
☎ 0141 889 3151
Open: All year, Monday to Saturday, 10am-5pm.

Penicuik
Edinburgh Crystal Visitor Centre
Eastfield, Penicuick, 10 miles (16km) south of Edinburgh
☎ 01968 675128
Open: All year, Tours Monday to Friday, 9am-3.30pm.

Port Appin
Castle Stalker
Island off-shore from A828 25 miles (40km) north of Oban
☎ 01883 622768
Open: By appointment.

Port Askaig
Bunahabain Distillery
Island of Islay
☎ 01496 840646
Open: All year, April to October, Monday to Friday, 10am-4pm. Saturday and Sunday.

Port Charlotte
Museum of Islay Life
☎ 01496 850358
Open: daily.

Port Ellen
Laphroaig Distillery
Isle of Islay
☎ 01496 302418
Open: All year but phone for tour times.

Port Glasgow
Newark Castle
See from A8 to north on east side of town
Historic Scotland ☎ 0131 244 3101
Open: April to September, Monday to Saturday, 9.30am-7pm. Sunday, 2-7pm. October to March, Monday to Saturday, 9.30am-4pm. Sunday, 2-4pm.

Rothesay
Rothesay Castle
Historic Scotland ☎ 0131 244 3101
Open: April to September, Monday to Saturday, 9.30am-7pm. Sunday, 2-7pm. October to March, closed Thursday morning and Fridays.

Bute Museum
Stewart Street, Rothesay
☎ 01700 2248
Open: All year, April to September, Monday to Saturday, 10.30am-4.30pm. Sundays June to September 2.30pm-4.30pm. October to March, Tuesday to Saturday, 2.30-4.30pm.

Rothesay Castle
Open: April to September, Monday to Saturday, 9.30am-6pm and Sundays, 2-6pm.

St Kilda
110 miles (177km) west of Scottish Mainland
Access by NTS organised trips.
☎ 0131 226 5922

Tarbert
Skipness Castle & Chapel
B8001, 10 miles (16km) south of Tarbert
Historic Scotland ☎ 0131 244 3101
Open: April to September, Monday to Saturday, 9.30am-7pm. Sunday, 2-7pm. October to March, Monday to Saturday, 9.30am-4pm. Sunday, 2-4pm.

Tobermory
Mull and Iona Folklore Museum
Isle of Mull
Open: May to September, Monday to Friday, 10.30am-4.30pm.

Staffa Island
For boat rides from Mull telephone Richard and Judy Fairbairns.
☎ 01688 400223

Uddingston
Bothwell Castle
Near Uddingston on A74 7 miles (11km) south-east of Glasgow
Historic Scotland ☎ 0131 244 3101
Open: April to September, Monday to Saturday, 9.30am-7pm. Sunday, 2-7pm. Closed through the winter.

Useful Information

Emergencies
Ambulance, Police & Firebrigade ☎ 999

Ferry Services
Caledonian MacBrayne
☎ 01475 634531

Airport
Campbeltown, Macrihanish
☎ 01586 552571

Rail
Oban Station
☎ 01631 630833

Weathercall
☎ 01898 500421

Tourist Information Centres

Abington
Welcome Break Service Area
Junction 13, M74
☎ 018642 436

Campbeltown
The Pier
☎ 01586 552056

Craignure
Isle of Mull
☎ 01680 812377

Drymen
Library
☎ 01360 660068

Dumbarton
Milton A82
☎ 01389 742306

Dunoon
7 Alexandra Parade
☎ 01369 703785

Inverary
☎ 01499 302063

Hamilton
M74 Northbound Services
☎ 01698 285590

Islay
The Square, Bowmore
☎ 01496 810254

Inverary
Front Street
☎ 01499 302063

Lanark
Horsemarket
☎ 01555 661661

Lochgilphead
Lochnell Street
☎ 01546 602344

Motherwell
The Library
☎ 01698 276676

Oban
Argyll Square
☎ 01631 563122

Paisley
Town Hall
☎ 0141 889 0711

Rothesay
15 Victoria Street
☎ 01700 502151

Strathaven
Town Mill Arts Centre
☎ 01357 29650

Tarbert (Argyll)
Harbour Street
☎ 01880 820429

Tarbert (Loch Lomond)
Main Street
☎ 01301 702260

Tobermory
Isle of Mull
☎ 01688 302182

Accommodation

Biggar
Mrs M Stott B&B *
Lindsaylands
☎ 01899 20033

East Kilbride
West Point Hotel **
☎ 01355 236300

Hamilton
Avonbridge Hotel *
Carlisle Road
☎ 01698 420525

Isle of Iona
St Columba Hotel *
☎ 01681 700304

Island of Isla
Bridgend Hotel *
☎ 01496 810212

Jura Hotel *
Craighouse, Jura
☎ 01496 820243

Lanark
Clydesdale Hotel *
15 Bloomgate
☎ 01555 663455

Loch Lomond
Cameron House Hotel * *
☎ 01389 755565

Arden Youth Hostel
☎ 01389 850226

Strathaven
Strathaven Hotel **
Hamilton Road
☎ 01357 21778

Tarbert
The Columba Hotel *
☎ 01880 820808

Glasgow

13

For decades Glasgow was widely associated with hard drinking, pub brawling, massive unemployment and lawless, decaying housing estates such as Easterhouse and the Gorbals. This impression, albeit it rather restricted, remained predominant in many outsiders' minds.

Social problems have been endemic in this city, in large part due to the demise of the once great steel and ship-building industries that ruled the banks of the Clyde and which faltered in the Depression of the 1930's and gradually faded away between the 1950's and 70's. These industries relied on tough, hard working characters, plate-metal workers, welders and riveters who turned out the world's finest locomotives and ocean liners. Drinking was always the shipyard workers favourite hobby and it must have been a terrible knock to their pride as well as their pay-packet to see these great enterprises go.

Following this and years of stagnation, Glasgow began to shake itself and accept that shipbuilding and its associated industries were gone for good and new directions had to be found. In the early 1980's the Glasgow's Miles Better campaign started. People throughout Scotland and those who knew the city around the world looked at the campaign with incredulity but soon it gained momentum and support. By 1988 the Glasgow Garden Festival had brought hundreds of visitors to the town and the transformation was complete when the city became the 'European City of Culture' in 1990. Now 1999 marks another milestone when the city becomes 'City of Architecture and Design'.

Glasgow's history stems back to the sixth century when an ecclesiastical community was established by St Mungo next to a small tributary of the Clyde. His church was built on the site of the present Glasgow Cathedral. From this origin, the town of 'Glas Cau', meaning 'dear, green place', took hold and gradually spread over the many hills that surround the River Clyde. Following the Treaty of the Union in 1707, trade with the New World increased and Glasgow became one of the main European ports handling mainly tobacco and sugar. The Industrial Revolution brought activity such as textile and chemical production but with coal abundant in the seams of Lanarkshire to fuel ironworks the city took to a wide range of heavy industries, ship and locomotive building being the most conspicuous. The Clyde, formerly a shallow river, was dredged in the late 1700's Glasgow became the world's leading shipbuilding centre.

In the 1840's Glasgow's population dramatically increased when thousands fleeing Ireland's potato famine were joined by deposed Highlanders to descend on the city and provide cheap labour. Expensive new areas such as the Gorbals on the south side of the river were quickly taken over to house working class families. These quickly fell into decay and Glasgow's urban problems grew as quickly as its industries. Today, there are 740,000 people living in the city, Scotland's largest conurbation.

To best discover Glasgow, 2 or 3 days are required. Car parking is laborious although there are new parking facilities such as the St Enoch Centre in town that have made it easier. A good reference point for starting a tour of the central and eastern side is Glasgow's Queen Street Station and George Square lying at the heart of the city. **George Square**, a spacious concrete piazza dotted with trees and flower beds and surrounded by wide, Chicago-style streets, was also the heart of Victorian Glasgow. At its centre is the 80ft (24m) high column and statue to Sir Walter Scott who, in truth, had little to do with the town. The column had been intended for a statue of George III but his failure to preserve the American Colonies and Glasgow's lucrative tobacco trade saw the favoured plinth given to someone else. Sir Walter, besides hundreds of pigeons, is surrounded by statues of Queen Victoria, Robert Burns and James Watt.

The **Glasgow City Chambers** form the eastern end of George's Square, a magnificent Italian Renaissance citadel opened by Queen Victoria in 1888. Guided tours of the interior take place on weekdays at 10.30am and 2.30pm or by arrangement. The inner halls and staircases abound with purple and red Italian marble, mosaics, tinted glass windows and splendidly carved mahogany.

---

preceding page; The People's Palace in Green Park

From George Square it is a 10 minute walk or a short bus ride along George Street and left into Castle Street to Glasgow Cathedral. Before you cross to the Cathedral **Provand's Lordship**, the oldest house in Glasgow, dating from 1471, sits on the corner of MacLeod Street and Castle Street. It is now a museum but performed many functions through its long existence commencing as a refuge for the poor then becoming a home for higher clergy. A small group of concerned locals saved it from demolition in the early twentieth-century and it now houses, amongst other things, a rather out of place candy store. More in keeping is an exhibition illustrating the life of its original roomer's, the down-and-outs, prostitutes and match-sellers of sixteenth century Glasgow.

The area surrounding the cathedral is the oldest part of Glasgow from which the first village sprung. The site of **Glasgow Cathedral** was sanctified by St Ninian as a burial ground in AD397 and later a church was built by St Mungo. Dominating the skyline today is a sooty-black and rather intimidating Gothic structure, the cathedral itself. So great was its early reputation that pilgrims made their way here in medieval times. Traces of the original stone building can be seen dating from 1136, the time of King David I. The present building was constructed over a lengthy period until final completion in the late fifteenth century. Its fate at the hands of Scotland's sixteenth-century religious reformers did not look secure and so James Beaton, the last Catholic Archbishop, removed its treasures to France where they were subsequently lost during the French Revolution.

Next to the Cathedral and looking almost as foreboding, is the early twentieth-century **Glasgow Royal Infirmary**. To complete this setting for a Gothic horror film is the Western **Necropolis**, situated behind the Cathedral. On a hill sternly overlooked by the statue of sixteenth-century reformer, John Knox, the shadowy catacombs house the remains of wealthy nineteenth-century merchants and industrialists.

A brighter area to the front of the Cathedral has been revitalised surrounding the new **St Mungo Museum of Religious Life and Art** which brings together information and iconography of many of the world's religions. Salvador Dali's *Christ of St. John of the Cross* has been moved here from Kelvingrove Art Gallery. Scottish religion and life is generally examined but there are no artifacts before 1800 due to the destructive nature of the Reformation. Outside the museum is a Zen Buddhist Garden.

Following Castle Street south into the High Street and **Glasgow Cross**, a seven storey, Victorian rocket-ship appears to obstruct the road. This is **Tolbooth Steeple** and was the centre of the medieval community. Across the road is the entrance to the Tron Theatre, scene of many local productions and occasional concerts and a popular watering hole which was founded by the Glasgow Theatre Club in 1979.

A short distance on towards the river brings you to **Glasgow Green**. This wide swath of grassland is said to the be the oldest public park in Britain. It was originally common grazing land for the medieval burgh and Freemen of Glasgow maintain the right to graze their animals. It has

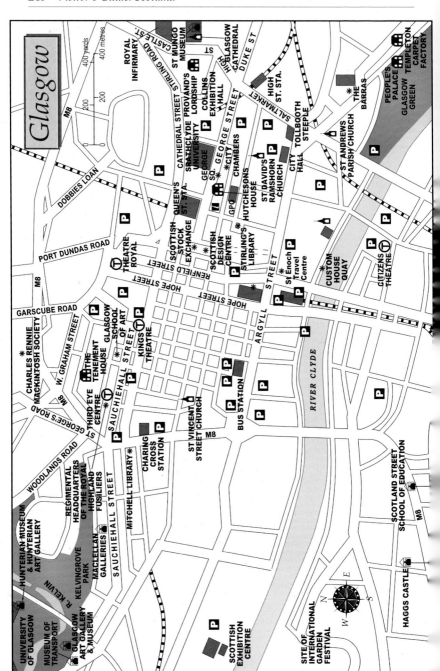

Glasgow street busker

Glasgow Art Gallery & Museum, Kelvinside

Princess Square shopping centre

Templeton's Carpet Factory, opposite Green Park

been a focal point for political and religious meetings for many centuries. Both Nelson and Queen Victoria encaptured in stone, look down upon proceedings. James Watt is said to have hit upon the idea of a separate condensing cylinder for a steam engine whilst strolling here and a boulder marks the spot. At the parks centre is the **People's Palace**, really two structures, a huge glasshouse affair called the Winter Garden containing a wonderful plant collection and cafe that feels 'outdoor' even on a cool, rainy afternoon. A square, brick building holds an unusual museum with exhibits covering much of Glasgow's history.

Templeton's Carpet Factory, now Templeton Business Centre stands out like a brick-red totem pole, a replica of the Doge's Palace in Venice. The fanciful exterior of the building gives some indication what Glasgow's Victorian industrialists thought of themselves.

A taxi or bus will take you back into the centre of town. It is alternatively a fairly pleasant walk along the north bank of the Clyde. Near the Scottish Exhibition and Conference Centre, you see the black frame of the Finiston Crane once used for loading locomotives onto ships. You are now more likely to see a yacht sailing down the Clyde than any working vessel. The docks and warehouses have been replaced with swanky hotels and trendy town-houses.

Glasgow's centre, to the north of the river, is well provided with quality shops. Many are of the High Street variety, but there are plenty of independent stores of good character. There are several book shops such as Smith's or Waterstone's in St Vincent Street and Buchanon Street which sell several books on the local area or the Glasgow dialect known as the 'Patter'. Three of the best shopping street are partly pedestrianized, Buchanon, Argyll and Sauchihall. Buchanon Street is established as the up-market shopping area while the glass enclosed St Enoch's Centre at the bottom of Buchanon Street offers the majority of well-known High Street outlets. There is also a fast-food court and ice-rink here. Princes Square's stores, again in Buchanon Street, are more individualistic with prices to suit along with pleasant, balcony cafés and restaurants on the upper level. There is often a lunch-time concert taking place on the lower lever. The nearby Argyle Arcade is a dated but inviting shopping mall specializing in jewellery.

The Greater Glasgow Tourist Board is located near the south-west corner of George Square on St Vincent Street. They provide a host of booklets not only on Glasgow but most parts of Scotland. Eating out is easy in the town centre with a host of good bars, cafés and restaurants with generally a very high standard of service and food. Cappuccino side-walk bars are now found at various points, lending a continental air. At the weekend, a unique market called the 'Barras' takes place on at the east-end just beyond Glasgow Cross, between Gallowgate and London Road. For collectors of recent memorabilia and bargain hunters, the Barras are a stimulating experience.

Public transport around Glasgow is not easy for first timers. There is the circular subway euphemistically called the 'Clockwork Orange' or the deregulated bus network with several colours of buses sometimes heading for the same destination. **St Enoch Travel Centre** housed in a fantastic, neo-Gothic outhouse at the bottom of Buchanon Street provides maps, timetables and helpful travel information. The *Visitor's Transport Guide* is the best, free map of the city and west end. The easiest way to cover distances is to use a taxi.

Should you wish to avail yourself to Glasgow's night-life (and it is recommended), up-to-date entertainment listings are found in the daily *Glasgow Herald* or the *Glasgow Evening News*. There is also an entertainments guide publication, the *List*, available from the Tourist Information Office or newsagents.

North of the city centre on Buchanon Street is the **Royal Concert Hall**, a modern building staging important events regularly. The lobby houses temporary art exhibitions. Guided tours of the hall and the backstage area are available for a small cost.

Almost opposite the Willow Tearoom at 270 Sauchiehall Street are the **MacLellan Galleries** hosting several major travelling exhibitions a year. The halls were restored following a major fire in 1985. A wide spectrum of events from around globe are held here from local themes to, for example, major exhibitions on the American Indian.

Scotland's cities, in a bid to provide more housing in over-populated urban areas, developed streets of tenement blocks or flats, building up the way instead of out. These became standard accommodation for working class families throughout Scotland and are still very much in evidence today despite moves throughout the 1960's to demolish them — it was found that the sturdy tenement accommodation was superior in many ways to the multi-storey concrete blocks they tried to replace them with.

The **Tenement House** at 145 Buccleuch Street in the Garnet Hill area was the home of Agnes Toward who lived there with her mother from 1911 until she was hospitalized in 1965. Agnes threw little away and her house was a trove of items used in the first half of the nineteenth century. The house was discovered by an actress, Anna Davidson, who bought it to preserve this time-capsule and finally sold it to the National Trust for Scotland. Inside, the original gas lighting has been reinstated and the kitchen has a coal fuelled range with the coal bunker standing near by. Agnes and her mother cared little for modern appliances.

The **Third Eye Centre** is a Grecian looking building at 350 Sauchiehall Street and Scotland's largest and liveliest contemporary arts centre, perhaps the main focus of the arts scene in the country. Opened in 1975, the emphasis is on modern art as well as a small theatre for plays, music, films and poetry readings. There is also a shop and café/bar. There are around thirty exhibitions per year including those on international tour.

Following Sauchiehall Street west leads to **Kelvingrove Park**. This was the wealthy end of town in the 1800's, where merchant's estates were set apart from the grime of the city. The River Kelvin cuts through this green oasis and several notable buildings overlook it. Kelvingrove Park is handy for a game of bowls, flying kites or just sitting around watching

Charles Rennie Mackintosh
(1868-1928)

Charles Rennie MackIntosh was one of the most adventurous architects of the turn of the century. Despite his working-class family's indifference, MackIntosh managed to find a place at the Glasgow School of Art to study architecture which he quickly developed his style which rolled together elements of Gothic and Art Nouveau with Scottish Baronial. His first important commission was the design of the furniture and decor of a tea-room in Buchanon Street for a local business woman, Kate Cranston. Although no longer in existence, a similar commission for the same woman still exists at the Willow Tea Rooms at 217 Sauchiehall Street. During the summer months it tends to be very busy, and is open from 9.30am until 5pm.

There are several other examples of his work in this area, most notably the Glasgow School of Art where at the age of 28 he was asked to submit plans for new premises. His 'modern' approach was not always appreciated by the more stoic element in the city, and there was outcry when the building was finally completed.

The Glasgow School of Art in Renfrew Street is a short walk from Queen's Cross Church. Francis Newbery, the principal of the college, encouraged the board to accept their former student's designs and the Glasgow School of Art was built in two stages between 1897 and 1909. This is the best example, both inside and out, of MackIntosh's work. The exterior oriel windows stretch the length of four floors allowing considerable north light into studios. There is a mock Baronial east wing and a softer western half. Tours led by staff or students are available four times a day during the summer and twice a day in the winter. The interior is actually more fascinating than the outside with the usual MackIntosh touches, high backed chairs and other unusual furniture. The Library is best appreciated looking down from the Furniture Gallery.

Only over the past 50 years the work of Charles Rennie MackIntosh has been more locally appreciated and since Glasgow's 1990 'Year of Culture' which catapulted his style onto everything to do with the city, has it gained wide popularity to the point that his elongated lettering style, furniture design and relish for purple glass embellishments have become omniscient. Besides Glasgow there are other architectural examples of his work in Helensburgh and Comrie.

others. There massive Stewart Fountain commemorates the Waterworks Act of 1855 when water was supplied to the city from Loch Katrine in the Trossachs and improved the health of thousands of Glaswegians. The steep stairway on the east side of the park leads to some of the most elegant Victorian houses in the Park Circus area.

Glasgow Art Gallery and Museum was built to hold the International Exhibition of 1901. The rear of the building faces the road which was a major blunder by the architect who flung himself of the building when it was finished. It now houses one of the finest municipal collections of paintings in Britain.

The Glasgow School or 'Glasgow Boys' as they liked to be known, were active in the late nineteenth century, breaking new ground with a fresh approach and their paintings are well represented in the Art Gallery. Scottish Colourists such as Peplo, Cadell and Fergusson are on displays along with world famous paintings such as Rembrandt's *Man in Armour* or Whistler's portrait of Thomas Carlyle. The ground floor displays an impressive internationally renowned collection or arms and armour including Scottish weaponry. The museum side includes important displays in the fields of natural history and archaeology.

Directly opposite the museum and art gallery in Kelvin Hall is the **Museum of Transport**. The huge space inside offers a rare glimpse of Glasgow's transport systems through the decades. The world's oldest pedal cycle is suspended above squadrons of bikes, bubble cars and other fadish modes of transport. The Clyde Room is said to house the most comprehensive ship model collection in the world gathered from the builders and owners of the full-sized vessels. The 'test tank' hull models of the *QE1* and *QE2* are on display. On the ground floor there is a reconstruction of a 1930's street complete with butcher's, baker's, an underground terminal and cinema which does show old footage of transport related themes pertaining to Glasgow. Outside this is a modern Super X simulator that mimics the more brisk methods of transport such as down-hill skiing or white-water rafting.

At the other side of Kelvingrove Park are the Gothic towers and turrets of the **University of Glasgow**. It can be entered by crossing the bridge to the left of Kelvin Hall and following the path leading up to the buildings or the front entrance is on University Avenue. Founded in 1451 it was one of the three Scottish universities, St Andrews and Aberdeen being the others, established around this time. It occupied several sites before it settled on Gilmorehill overlooking Kelvingrove Park in 1870.

The front gates are fascinating. They 'grow' in five stages showing the expansion of learning. The most notable graduates of the university as illustrated on the gate include Lister, James Watt and Adam Smith, the economist and moral philosopher. Its mock Gothic centre-piece is surrounded by a variety of important buildings such as the Bute Hall and the Hunterian Museum. The **Hunterian Museum**, Scotland's first public museum dating back to 1807, is in the University's main building and contains important geological and archeological displays.

The **Hunterian Art Gallery** is in Hillhead Street and contains Hunter's small but comprehensive collection of paintings, prints, and sculpture. The outstanding collection by James Abbot MacNeil Whistler is bettered only in Washington D.C.'s Freer Gallery. Prints by Hockney Picasso and Durer can also be seen. A side gallery has been used to reconstruct the interior designs of **Charles Rennie Mackintosh's home** at 6 Florentine Terrace where he lived from 1906 to 1914.

The Hillhead area is popular with students and the pubs and restaurants are quite lively. There are several guest houses and B&B's in the area while larger hotels are more generally found on nearby Great Western Road. The **Glasgow Botanic Gardens** to the west are frequented on any sunny day by hordes of locals but visitors tend to head for the **Kibble Palace**, originally known as the Crystal Palace, the magnificent domed glasshouses at the parks centre.

Byers Road is the busiest thoroughfare in this part of town with plenty shops and pubs. The Ubiquitous Chip is one of the better known eateries just off Byres Road in Ashton Lane with its cobbled courtyard restaurant on the ground level and a labyrinth of bars above. The food can be pricey but is always of high quality.

Personal transport is the best way to explore the south side of Glasgow as its attractions are well spread. The baronial **Haggs Castle** is yet another free museum located on St Andrews Drive on the eastern approaches to the Burrell. Built in 1585 and restored in the nineteenth century, it opened in 1976 as a period museum for children, centring around educational activities. Nearby is the **Museum of Education at Scotland** Street School following a similar theme. The classrooms have been reconstructed to cover different periods from the Victorian Age to the 1960's.

Continuing south-west along the B769 or route signposted to Kilmarnock on the A77, the **Burrell Collection** is set in the spacious grounds of **Pollock Country Park** to the right and is free. Opened in 1983 there are many who reckon it was as much an instrument in Glasgow's change of fortune as the 'Glasgow's Miles Better' campaign. The timing of its appearance on Glasgow's cultural scene certainly could not have been better for putting the city into the minds of the art, media and business worlds.

Sir William Burrell was a wealthy Glasgow shipping magnate who, using the fortune amassed from the astute timing of the sale of his fleet, spent his life travelling the world in search of works of art and antiquities that he liked.

The Burrell is now one of the most popular galleries in Britain. Chinese ceramics, Persian carpets, medieval European furniture and stained glass along with modern painting and sculpture make it one of the most diverse collections of artifacts found anywhere in the world. Ancient Mesopotamia and Egypt are also well represented. **Pollock House** is in the same grounds as the Burrell, built in 1750 and housing one of the finest collections of Spanish paintings in this country. There are woodland areas and a pleasant river in front of the house.

Additional Information

Places of Interest in Glasgow

Botanic Gardens
Off Great Western Road (A82)
☎ 0141 334 2422
Open: Gardens open daily, 7am to dusk.
Kibble Palace open 10am-4.45pm.

Burrell Collection
Pollockshaws Road, the A736 on the
south side of town.
☎ 0141 649 7151
Open: All year, weekdays, 10am-5pm.
Wednesdays, 10am-10pm. Sundays
12noon-6pm.

Glasgow Cathedral
East end of Cathedral Street east of city
centre
Historic Scotland ☎ 0131 244 3101
Open: April to September, Monday to
Saturday, 9.30am-7pm. Sunday, 2-7pm.
October to March, Monday to Saturday,
9.30am-4pm. Sunday, 2-4pm.

Glasgow City Chambers
George Square in city centre
☎ 0141 227 4017
Open: Monday to Friday with guided
tours at 10.30am-2.30pm or by arrangement.

Glasgow School of Art
167 Renfrew Street
☎ 0141 332 9797
Open: Tours available throughout
summer.

Glasgow Zoo
6 miles (10km) south-east of city centre
on M74
☎ 0141 771 1185
Open: Daily, 10am-6pm.

Haggs Castle
St Andrews Drive
☎ 0141 427 2725
Open: All year, Monday to Saturday,
10am-5pm. Sunday, 12noon-6pm.

Hunterian Art Gallery
Hillhead Street in Glasgow University
☎ 0141 330 5431
Open: All year, Monday to Saturday,
9.30am-5pm and Sunday, 2-5pm

Hunterian Museum
Glasgow University
☎ 0141 330 4221
Open: All year, 9.30am-5pm and
Saturday, 9.30am-1pm.

Museum of Transport
Kelvin Hall
☎ 0141 357 3929
Open: Weekdays, 10am-5pm, Saturdays,
10am-10pm. Sunday, 12noon-6pm.

Necropolis
Behind Glasgow Cathedral
☎ 0141 649 0331
Open: All reasonable times.

People's Palace
Glasgow Green
☎ 0141 554 0223
Open: Weekdays, 10am-5pm, Saturdays
10am-10pm. Sunday, 12-6pm.

Pollock House
Pollockshaws Road, the A736 on the
south side of town.
☎ 0141 632 0274
Open: Weekdays, 10am-5pm, Saturdays,
10am-10pm. Sunday, 12noon-6pm.

Provand's Lordship
Castle Street, opposite the Cathedral
☎ 0141 552 8819
Open: Monday to Saturday, 10am-7pm,
Sundays, 12noon-6pm.

**Scotland Street School and Museum of
    Education**
225 Scotland Street
☎ 0141 429 1202
Open: 10am-5pm, Monday to Saturday
& 2-5pm on Sunday.

Tenement House
145 Buccleuch Street, Garnet Hill
☎ 0141 333 0183
Open: April to October, daily, 12noon-
5pm. November to April, Saturday and
Sunday, 2-4pm.

Glasgow Galleries, Theatres & Cinemas

Glasgow Art Gallery and Museum
Kelvingrove Park
☎ 0141 221 9600
Open: All year, weekdays 10am-5pm,
Saturday, 10am-10pm. Sunday, 12noon-
6pm.

Glasgow Royal Concert Hall
☎ 0141 332 3123

Citizens Theatre (Rep)
Gorbals Street
☎ 041 429 0022

ABC Cinema (Five screens)
Sauchiehall Street
☎ 0141 332 9513

Theatre Royal
Hope Street
☎ 0141 331 1234

Kings Theatre
Bath Street
☎ 0141 227 5511

MacLellan Galleries
Sauchiehall Street
☎ 0141 331 1854
Open: Monday to Saturday, 10am-5pm.
Thursdays, 10am-10pm. Sunday 12-6pm.

Third Eye Centre
346-354 Sauchiehall Street
☎ 0141 332 7521
Open: Tuesday to Saturday, 10am-
5.30pm. Sunday, 2-5pm.

Useful Information

Airport
Glasgow International Airport
☎ 0141 887 1111

Car Hire - Glasgow Airport
Avis ☎ 0141 887 2261
Eurodollar ☎ 0141 887 7915
Europcar ☎ 0141 887 0414
Hertz ☎ 0141 887 2451
Other companies can be contacted by
direct telephone lines in the airport.

Rail
Glasgow Queen Street and Central Station
☎ 0141 204 2844

Weathercall
☎ 01898 500421

Emergencies
Ambulance, Police & Firebrigade ☎ 999

Accommodation

One Devonshire Gardens ***
Off Great Western Road
☎ 0141 339 2001

The Town House Hotel ***
West George Street
☎ 0141 332 3320

Babbity Bowser **
16 Blackfriars Street
☎ 0141 552 5055

The George Hotel *
235 Buchanan Street
☎ 0141 332 6622

Kirklee Hotel **
11 Kensington Gate
☎ 0141 334 5555

Hostels
SYHA Hostel
7 Park Terrace
☎ 0141 332 3004

Baird Hall, Strathclyde University
460 Sauchiehall Street
☎ 0141 332 6415

For more information on Universities
summer accommodation phone
Stathclyde University (☎ 0141 555 4148)
or Glasgow University (☎ 0141 339 8481)

Camping
Strathclyde Park, Closest to Glasgow.
16 miles (26km) south-east of centre
near Motherwell on M74 getting off at
Junction 6.
☎ 01698 266155

Tourist Information Offices

Glasgow Centre
35 St Vincent Place
☎ 0141 204 4400

Glasgow Airport
International Arrivals
☎ 0141 848 4440

The *South-West*

14

The south-west corner of Scotland includes the town of Largs at the north of Ayrshire, the island of Arran and through Dumfries and Galloway to Gretna Green near the English border. The southern part of this area must be one of the most undiscovered of Scotland's many sections.

Golf is popular throughout the area with strings of verdant links courses especially along Ayrshire's coast. The island of Arran along with Dumfries and Galloway offer more secluded courses that are ideal for holiday golfing. Ayrshire and Dumfries and Galloway are well established fishing areas. Ayrshire has over 80 miles (129km) of coastline, some twenty lochs and reservoirs and many miles of fast flowing rivers. Most places along the coast have some off-shore fishing facilities. Most inland waters are controlled by local clubs and associations to whom you apply for a permit. Listings of these are found in the local Tourist Information Offices.

AYRSHIRE

Largs is one of the most pleasant of the many resorts that sit on the banks of the Firth of Clyde. It retains the air of a traditional family holiday retreat with a bright and airy prospect overlooking the Clyde to the islands of Bute and the Great Cumbrae. The last sea-going paddle steamer in the world, the *Waverley*, stops at Largs on its summer day trips up and down the Clyde where it also stops at Ayr and Millport on Great Cumbrae. The ship has a self-service restaurant, buffet, bar and gift shop.

Skelmorlie Aisle is found in the burial ground of a former parish church in Largs, once the Old Kirk of Largs. This unusual building was converted into a mausoleum for the family of Sir Robert Montgomery in 1636. The church has long since been demolished but inside the remaining structure is a boarded, barrel-vaulted and finely painted ceiling adorned with signs of the Zodiac as well as the imaginary coats of arms of the tribes of Israel and various biblical figures.

About 1 mile (2km) south of the town on Bowen Crag is the Pencil Monument, commemorating the Battle of Largs of 1263. In late August and early September, the Largs Viking Festival attracts a large number of visitors including those from Scandinavia.

The little, lumpy island of **Great Cumbrae** is ideal for a day trip and it only takes a few minutes to cross the strait. For those that do not take their car on the roll-on, roll-off ferry, a bus service links the Cumbrae terminal with the main community of **Millport**. Cycle hire is available at Mapes of Millport in Guildford Street who also stock fishing tackle. On the western side are views of the Island of Bute while to the south across the Tan is the tiny island of Little Cumbrae. The highest point is the Gladestain at 417ft (127m), an easy climb and well worth it for the panorama.

Following the A78 south the entrance to **Kelburn Country Centre** is just beyond the busy marina south of Largs on the left near Fairlie. The estate surrounds a thirteenth-century castle, still the home of the Boyle family, Earls of Glasgow for three centuries and resident here for several more. It is a farrago of diversions for most age groups, natural woodland walks with dramatic waterfalls, secret gardens, wild flowers and leafy gorges, at certain times of the year over-run with golden pheasants. For the motivated there is a Commando Assault course. There is also a congenial café, a craft work-shop and a farmyard with petting centre.

The short run from Kelburn to the next major town of **Ardrossan** offers pleasant views from the coast road over to the island of Arran. There is a spacious, links golf course at West Kilbride as well as a small museum containing a collection of Ayrshire lace and embroidery.

The ferry terminal in Ardrossan is well sign-posted. Fill up with fuel before crossing. There are filling stations on the island in the main communities but they are more expensive. Bear in mind there is also a summer ferry service from Lochranza on the north side of Arran to Claonaig on the Kintyre peninsula so it is possible to continue on to a tour of the Kintyre area from Arran.

Arran is the most southerly of the Scottish islands. The Highland Boundary Fault passes from Stonehaven to Helensburgh dividing Scotland into the Highlands and the Lowlands and continues through Arran effectively slicing it in half. The ball-of-wool shaped land-mass is only 56

preceding page; If the weather is right, Troon's beach front is very popular miles (90km) around the edges so it is easy to circumnavigate by car during a day-visit.

Brodick is Arran's largest population centre. Its wide beach extends around Brodick Bay. Its location at the mid-point of the east coast of the island makes it a good base as well as starting point for further exploration. There are a few gift shops and a Tourist Information Office situated near the pier but otherwise the place is not particularly inspiring. The town's main tourist attraction is **Brodick Castle** overlooking Brodick Bay. The earliest portions of this kidney-coloured, sandstone pile date back to the fourteenth century although a Viking fort previously stood on the site.

Returning to the town of Brodick, the Isle of Arran Heritage Museum is on the left just before entering the town, an eighteenth-century croft farm. The interior displays give an insight into the islander's way of life for several centuries with artifacts set in an old smiddy and stable block. The nearby cottage contains a variety of items from around World War I.

South of Brodick, the neighbouring hamlet of **Lamlash** is only 3 miles (5km) away. As you descend the hill into Lamlash you can appreciate the splendid view across Lamlash Golf Course and Bay to the Holy Island. It was in this sheltered bay that King Hakon returned after his woeful defeat at Largs. The Holy Island has been purchased as a Buddhist retreat and is not open to the public. There is not a lot to do apart from sea-angling or strolling unless some folk entertainment is arranged in one of the several welcoming pubs such as Andy's Place. **Whiting Bay**, the southernmost of Arran's three main east coast villages appeals to keen fishermen but make note that there is no fishing on Sundays. It is also a popular holiday village with cottages and hotel rooms for rent. Facilities are plentiful but it lacks the repose of other Arran locations. **Kildonan**, on the southern tip, is a little more rustic. There is the ruined medieval Kildonan Castle standing out on a craggy spit, sandy beaches, views of the tiny island of Pladda with its lighthouse and the Christmas pudding shape of Ailsa Craig on the horizon. Colonies of seals inhabit the more remote rocky shoreline. The villages of Lagg, Sliddery, and Corrie Cravie on the south-western side are noted for their tropical vegetation due to the warming effects of the Gulf Stream. The Lagg Hotel in Kilmory has one of the best restaurants on the island and is also very comfortable to stay in.

The village of **Blackwaterfoot** is less a resort and more a genuine Hebridean fishing village. Two miles (3km) north of the village past the unusual 12 hole golf course is **King's Cave** where Robert the Bruce supposedly watched the spider who inspired him for future battles against the English. It is possible to take the String Road, the B880 directly back to Brodick from Blackwaterfoot but the circular tour continues following the coast road north. On the desolate **Machrie Moor** and around the abandoned steadings of Moss Farm just north of Blackwaterfoot is a remarkable collection of stone circles and cairns from the neolithic and Bronze Ages.

The omnipresent peak of Goat Fell looms larger as you near the island's zenith following the coastal route overlooking the Kilbrannan Sound to the Mull of Kintyre. Entrance to the village of **Lochranza** is heralded by a

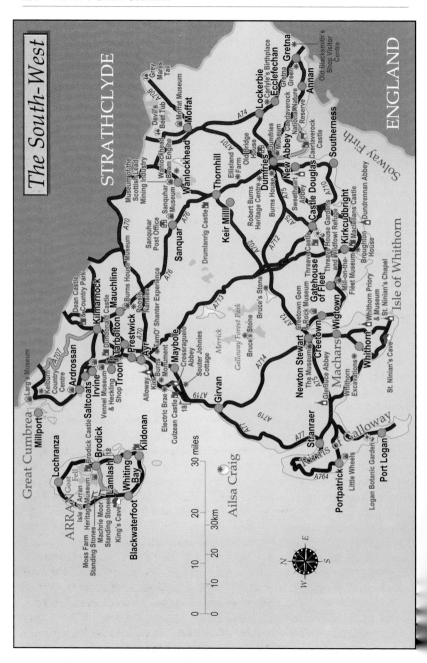

string of colourful cottages called the 'twelve apostles' perhaps best appreciated from the ferry which sails between here and Cloanig on Kintyre during the summer. Set out near the tidal flats is the ruin of Lochranza Castle made famous by Sir Walter Scott in *The Lord of the Isles*. From the route descending back south to Brodick, sweeping slopes are appreciated and dominated by Goat Fell, the islands highest mountain. This is good walking country and it is possible to scale Goat Fell in a day with the right equipment and map which takes approximately 5 hours from the car park at Cladach or Corrie. Sannox Bay is a scattering of houses on the eastern shore with a spectacular 9 hole golf course while the village of Corrie is a photographer or artists delight, a band of adorable cottages overlooking the pebble beach and a tiny inlet harbour.

Returning by ferry to the mainland via Ardrossan then winding south on the A78, this is the gateway to 'Burns Country' where the 'poet of the people' spent most of his life.

Irvine is sometimes referred to as a 'new town', most of it built in the post-war era although there are vestiges of the original maritime community surrounding the harbour area. It was once the main port serving the early industrial endeavours of Glasgow and goods were transported to and from here by cart. In the centre of town, the restored Glasgow Vennel is a cobbled area where there is a museum of local antiquities and a thatched Heckling Shop.

On the inner ring road that leads down to Irvine Harbour, the Magnum Centre stands like a giant aeroplane hanger and from the outside it is difficult to guess exactly what it is. This leisure facility contains an ice-rink, a bowling alley, a theatre, cinema and swimming pool complex. Nearby, the Scottish Maritime Museum gives some indication of the town's past as well as a glimpse of seafaring life on the Clyde. A collection of old vessels moored outside the dock-side museum helps to bring the era to life. The world's oldest clipper ship, the *Carrick*, is on display along with an old steam 'puffer', a lifeboat and others. An intriguing tenement building has been reconstructed next door to illustrate life in an Edwardian ship-workers home.

Kilmarnock, some miles inland from Irvine is more industrial in its background with less tourist facilities but associations with Burns are quite strong. Its most famous product is Johnnie Walker Whisky which is exported world-wide. Tours of the distillery and bottling plant are available through the summer months. The Dick Institute in Street houses the town's museum, library and art gallery. Dean Castle is an impressive fourteenth-century stronghold with dungeon and battlements set in a 200 acre (80 hectare) country park. Ancestral home of the Boyd family, it boasts its own museum housing medieval arms and armour, early European musical instruments and a display of Burns manuscripts. The recently refurbished Burns Monument and statue can be seen in Kay Park, again at the side of town.

Returning to the coast on the A78, a short distance north of Troon is the broken walls of **Dundonald Castle** known as the 'Cradle of the Stewarts' first occupied by the Fitzalans, Lord High Stewarts from whom the Stewart line descended. **Troon** has its origins as a seaport chiefly exporting coal from the once many Ayrshire mines to the heavy industrial cities of England. The town was served by Scotland's first passenger railway which ran from Kilmarnock and that line is still open. Now it is renowned as a golf mecca with the Open Championship regularly returning to Royal Troon Golf Course.

Prestwick Airport was Scotland's main international terminal until Glasgow and Edinburgh's facilities were developed. Now it is mainly used for freight or if fog besets the other airports. **Prestwick** town is one of Scotland's oldest burghs dating from around 1165. It became associated with Robert the Bruce when he gave his name to the town's well. Legend has it that he struck the ground with his lance at this point and water gushed forth to quench his thirst.

Tarbolton is a dejected little village off the A719 slightly northwest of Prestwick but here was the venue for Burns and his cronie's 'Batchelor's Club', a literary and debating society that they formed in 1780. The National Trust for Scotland now runs it with a display of period furnishings within two rooms. Further west the town of **Mauchline** played a major part in Burns' life and on the outskirts of town there is the National Burns Memorial Tower, opened in 1896. A small Tourist Information Office is found on the ground floor and an interpretation centre on the first and second floors. In the centre of town Poosie Nansie's Tavern, was the inspiration for his cantata, *The Jolly Beggars*, and is still very much a working pub. Across the street in Mauchline Kirkyard lie the graves of four of Burns' children. Round the corner and just off the main street is the Burns House Museum where his mistress, soon to become his wife, Jean Armour lived.

Ayr is the most popular of Ayrshire's seaside towns and the county's largest community. It was an important seaport and trading centre through the centuries then became a popular resort for middle class Victorians. Today, it is a busy and prosperous shopping hub serving a wide, surrounding area with its main thoroughfare recently upgraded. Its beach has remained popular for decades. Ayr Race Course is the most prestigious in Scotland and it is worth being aware that it can be difficult to find local accommodation if there is a major racing event.

Belleisle Park is just south of Ayr with colourful gardens, an animal petting centre and aviary as well as two excellent, municipal golf courses. Touring golf professionals visiting nearby Turnberry are often found on the Belleisle course, such is its reputation. Continuing south the outlying village of Alloway is the centre of Burnsland, the place of his birth on the 25 January 1759 and closely associated with some of his most famous poetry. His cottage birthplace stands on Alloway Monument Road, a thatched 'auld clay biggin' built by his father, well signposted and easy to find. This was Robert's home until 1766 when the family moved to Mount Oliphant, a 70 acre (28 hectare) farm near Alloway. The adjacent cottage to Burn's birthplace houses a museum and gift shop with collections or original manuscripts prepared for the Kilmarnock Edition of his poems as well as many other mementos of the poet's life and insights into his work.

Only a few hundred yards down the road is the ancient Alloway Kirk where Burns' father, William Burnes lies buried, his grave standing opposite the churchyard entrance.

The thirteenth-century Brig o' Doon has little to do with the movie of that name but spans the River Doon with a single arch and is only yards from the ghoulish Alloway kirkyard. Between these two is the Burns Monument and Gardens, a landscaped grove overlooking the Doon River with a Grecian style monument dedicated to the poet and splendid views from its top. One of Burns' most famous poems has been brought to life at the 'The Tam O' Shanter Experience' only a few yards from Alloway Kirk. Presented in a 120 seater auditorium the audience is transported back to the 18th century. An audio-visual tells the story of Robert. A restaurant overlooks the centre's gardens.

To continue south there is the choice of following the coast on the A719 or taking the faster A77 route to Girvan and Stranraer but this misses some of this region's best attractions. Wonderwest World, formerly Butlin's Holiday Camp may not be one of them but boasts Wonder Splash Water World with its blue lagoon and rushing flumes.

Nine miles (14km) from Ayr, **Maybole** is the district of Carrick's capital, passed through on route to Turnberry or Stranraer. It has a long High Street characterised by a distinctive and ancient clock tower which stands close to the spot, rumour has it, where Robert Burns' parents first met. **Crossraguel Abbey** is passed on the main road south of Maybole. Much ravished by the passage of time and stone robbers, this was a small Cluniac monastery founded in the early thirteenth century by Duncan, Earl of Carrick and was closely connected with Paisley Abbey. Further on, the **Electric Brae** overlooking Culzean Bay is an optical illusion that makes a vehicle appear to be rolling downhill when it is, in fact, going up. This was first noticed when horses pulling wagons appeared to be out of breath after apparently descending the hill. It is found on the A719, 9 miles (14km) south of Ayr.

Culzean Castle, pronounced 'Culain', is one of the most dramatic and elegant of Robert Adam's eighteenth-century creations and one of Ayrshire's most popular attractions. Its sensational clifftop setting can be appreciated by walking down to the rocky shore when the tide is out. Built between 1772 and 1792 around an ancient tower of the Kennedy family, its sumptuous interior matches the exquisite gardens that face it.

Kirkoswald is a village straddling the main A77 route south to Stranraer. Souter Johnnie's Cottage sits unassumingly on the corner, the home of the village cobbler or soutar made famous as Tam's drinking partner in the poem, *Tam O' Shanter*. The A77 is the main route linking Ayr and the rest of central and northern Scotland to the ferry ports of Stranraer and Cairnryan to Northern Ireland. During the summer months it can be hectic with lorries, cars and caravans.

Girvan is the last major town in Ayrshire, a traditional family resort made popular following the war years. It was once a major landing site for herring. Clustered around its harbour, it offers various seaside diversions such as sea-angling or excursions to **Ailsa Craig**, the 114ft (35m) high granite rock with a 2 mile (3km) circumference that lies 10 miles

The Caledonian MacBrae ferry landing at Brodick, Arran

Lamlash Beach with the Holy Island, Arran

Threave Castle near Castle Douglas

Stranraer to Lorne ferry passes into the Irish Sea

(16km) off the coast and is now a bird sanctuary. Also known as Paddy's Milestone, it lies midway between Glasgow and Belfast and was once famous for its fine, red granite used to make curling stones.

DUMFRIES AND GALLOWAY

The area stretching from Scotland's south-western tip to the border with England is perhaps the most undiscovered in all the country. Now known as Dumfries and Galloway region, it remained autonomous up until the eleventh century, more affiliated with the Vikings than the Scots. Then it was gradually integrated into a unified Scotland by the fifteenth century. To look at, it is a soft, green, placid area but this belies the violent motifs of Dumfries and Galloway's history. Galloway as it was known then, was a stronghold for the Covenanters who resisted the influence of Episcopalian dogma and paid the price.

The Gaelic translation of Galloway means 'Land of the Stranger' but it certainly is a friendly place that makes visitors feel welcome. Fishing, farming and tourism make up the bulk of the local economy but it is set apart from the main tourist routes. There are no motorways crossing it apart from the M74 going north and south on its eastern perimeter. Outlined between the Firth of Clyde and the Solway Firth, the main access routes are the A77 from Glasgow, the A75 roughly following the Solway Firth from Gretna to Stranraer and the A76 dropping down from Kilmarnock to Dumfries.

Stranraer is a nodal point in the area mainly because of its connections across the sea to Ireland. Stranraer's economy, once based on its role as a market centre has increasingly turned to the ferry traffic that constantly pours in and out of town. B&B's and small hotels line the foreshore at Harbour Street and Market Street and the town centre has a few eating places geared to that passing trade. There is little else to recommend but it is a good accommodation base if you wish to explore this area.

The long, rocky-shored annex of land adhering to Galloway to the west is known as the Rhins or Rinns or Rhinns. There are plenty short tours available around this near-island but most people head first along the A77 from Stranraer to the harbour town of **Portpartick**. This is a quintessential holiday retreat with charming streets and cottages and a tranquil harbour backed by small cliffs. This, as opposed to Stranraer, was once the main port for travellers, goods and livestock to and from Northern Ireland, only 22 miles (35km) away but it lost out to the more sheltered facilities at Stranraer when sails were replaced by steam engines.

Portpatrick's centre is a place to leave the car and wander amongst craft shops and cafés and enjoy the refreshing air that blows off the Irish Sea. There is a fascinating museum called Little Wheels where model enthusiasts of all kinds can gather and relive childhood memories. It is from Portpatrick that the Southern Upland Way commences its trail across Scotland's borderlands.

A round-trip tour of the Rhinns to the Mull of Galloway covers some 50 miles (80 km) from Stranraer. The main attraction of this largely dairy herd inhabited and gorse bush encrusted area is its coast with secluded stretches of sand and pleasant little harbour villages such as **Port Logan**. Here you find Logan Botanic Gardens, an annex of Edinburgh's Royal Botanic Gardens with sub-tropical plants such as tree ferns and cabbage palms flourishing outdoors in the mild 'Gulf Stream' climate.

Returning to the main route emanating from Stranraer, 3 miles (5km) east of there on the A75 is Castle Kennedy, best known for its gardens that are set out on a thin strip of land between the Black Loch and the White Loch. The best time to visit here is in late spring when thirty-seven varieties of rhododendrons and azaleas are in their prime.

Glenluce Abbey just off the A75 travelling east is the remains of a twelfth-century abbey and well worth stopping for with its magnificent fifteenth-century Chapter House. A thirteenth-century wizard, Michael Scott, supposedly saved the Glenluce community when he enticed 'the plague' into the church vault and left it there until it starved to death. The recently opened Pilgrim's Way traces the medieval route used by religious travellers commencing at Glenluce Abbey and winding through the Machars to the important religious site at Whithorn.

The A75 cuts directly across this area called the Machars to Newton Stewart. The Machars is rather flat with the two main towns of Whithorn and Wigtown being its best enticements. **Whithorn** is the true birthplace of Christianity in Scotland. St Ninian, a fourth-century bishop, perhaps a local man who had gone to Rome to become consecrated, landed here in AD397, building a church called Candida Casa or the White House and set about converting the Southern Picts and Britons. A priory was built on the site of the first church and the site became a special place for pilgrims for many centuries up until the time of the Reformation. The history of the original church, the priory and Christianity in Britain is well documented in a small museum nearby. The Whithorn Dig is currently being carried on around the site of the early church to further reveal the area's important ecclesiastical connections and guided tours around this are essential to grasp the full archeological significance.

A short excursion to the **Isle of Whithorn**, 3 miles (5km) further southeast, is worthwhile and well sign-posted from Whithorn. There is a small chapel dedicated to St Ninian and it was here that pilgrims would have landed crossing the Solway Firth from England or from further abroad. St Ninian's Cave, some 3 miles (5km) from Whithorn on the west side of the Machars and a walk to the shore from the car park at Kidsdale Farm, is an intriguing place where St Ninian is supposed to have sought repose. There are several crosses carved into the rock inside the cave.

Wigtown, 11 miles (18km) north of Whithorn on the A746, is an unsophisticated little holiday town. From the hill on which the town is built you can see Bladnoch Bay and the stone pillar that marks the spot where two martyrs, Margaret McLachland and Margaret Wilson were tied to stakes and drowned as the tide rose around them. Their crime was attending the illegal Covenanter's prayer meetings and opposing Episcopalians.

Returning to the A75 the typical Galloway town of **Newton Stewart** sits on the banks of the River Cree. The local museum is located in St John's Church on York Road and contains information on the district's history. Game fishing is popular in this area and permits can be obtained from the Creebridge House Hotel near the old bridge.

The best access point into Galloway Forest Park is via the A714 north of Newton Stewart to Glen Trool Village then following the minor road to Glen Trool Lodge. **Galloway Forest Park** comprises of some 190,000 acres (76,000 hectares) of hills, lochs, moorland and forest that are a haven for wildlife. The Merrick at 2,766ft (844m) is the highest peak in the south of Scotland. It is worth the steady, fairly demanding hike to enjoy the views over Glen Trool. Start at the car park at Bruce's Stone.

The route to New Galloway is called the Queen's Way and this passes through some of the Galloway Forest Park where the Forestry Commission have mapped out various walking trails near to the road.

The A75 branches south and east towards Gatehouse of Fleet and Kirkcudbright with Castle Douglas further east. At **Creetown**, some 6 miles (10km) south of Newton Stewart, is the Gem Rock Museum, a cavern of over 10,000 specimens of gem stones, crystals and minerals from around the world. The village of **Gatehouse of Fleet**, a further 12 miles (19km) along the coast of Wigtown Bay, is a good example of late eighteenth-century town planning spurred on by the rise of a cotton industry that was developed by James Murray. This industrial boom lasted for nearly 100 years before other towns took over and Gatehouse slipped back into obscurity. The Mill-on-the-Fleet Museum gives credit to the towns hey-day.

Kirkcudbright, pronounced 'Kircoobrie' is a delightful centre for fishing and agriculture as well as tourism. MacLellan's Castle is in the centre of town, a fine model of Scottish fortified architecture. The town has been an enclave for artists and still draws landscape painters to its inspiring, thalassic environment.

The southern loop of the A711 to Dalbeattie and Castle Douglas is graced by **Dundrennan Abbey**, a ruin of a sizeable Cistercian Abbey founded in 1142. In 1568, Mary Queen of Scots spent her last night in Scotland here before she sailed for London and execution. **Threave Gardens and Wild Fowl Refuge**, just west of Castle Douglas, is set in 60 acres (24 hectares) and is the training grounds of the National Trust for Scotland's horticulturalists. There is a walled garden and greenhouses surrounded by various peat, rock and woodland garden projects. The Wildlife Refuge on the marshy banks of the River Dee is equipped with observation points from which to observe several species of duck and geese.

Threave Castle, a short distance away, is reached by a path of around a half mile's walk from a farmyard car park. Visitors wishing to cross the water to the castle have to ring a bell to summon the boatman.

Castle Douglas is another planned village of the eighteenth century, laid out by William Douglas, a local lad who made good in West Indies trading. His ambitions included transforming Castle Douglas into a prosperous centre for commerce and industry along with a canal system serving this part of Galloway both of which never came to full fruition.

The A710 and A711 meeting at Dalbeattie form a final lobe on the Solway Firth's north coast that makes a good day's tour from the nearby centre of Dumfries. Passing through the Dalbeattie Forest to the hamlets of Kippford and Colvend, the route offers some breathtaking views over the village of Sandyhills to the wide Mersehead Sands. The village of **Southerness**, set on a point, is popular as a holiday and caravanning centre and has probably the best golf course in the south-west. There are magnificent beach-side walks here stretching for miles in either direction.

Eight miles (13km) from Dumfries in the tiny village of New Abbey is 'Dulce Cor' or **Sweetheart Abbey**, one of the most elegant medieval buildings of this area and the last Cistercian foundation in Scotland. **New Abbey** village is itself, very gracious with delightful cottages lining the main road and an endearing village centre that gets congested with any more than four parked cars. There is ample parking next to the abbey from which to explore the village and the abbey ruins. Also nearby is Shambellie House with its museum of costume, an elegant country house that displays period costume, accessories, furniture and paintings.

The central community of Dumfries and Galloway is **Dumfries**, a red-sandstoned town of sturdy character bestriding the River Nith. Known as the 'Queen of the South' it became established as a seaport and trading centre from the Middle Ages. Being close to the English Border, it was regularly invaded and flattened especially during the fifteenth and six-teenth centuries. Despite this it has remained important as the focus of this area's agricultural prosperity.

Caerlaverock Castle near Dumfries

Burns House, where he spent the last 3 years of his life before his death in 1796 is found in what is now called Burns Street, near the southern end of the High Street. Stop at the Globe Inn on the way, one of Burns favourite taverns and still retaining great character. Burns House is now a small museum full of correspondence and manuscripts relating to the poet. An upstairs bedroom-study where he worked contains his writing desk and, on a window pane, the etching of his signature perhaps carved there in a moment of absorbed contemplation. The box-bed is original and is where he died. The Burns Mausoleum in the grounds of nearby St Michael's Church is where the bard is buried along with Jeam Armor, his wife and several of their children.

Near the centre of town where the High Street meets Buccleuch Street is a statue of Burns. Friars Vennel leading from the High Street to the ancient Devorguilla Bridge is one of Scotland's oldest streets. Across the River Nith on the Devorguilla Bridge is the Old Bridge House Museum containing furniture and everyday articles from households of the area. The Robert Burns Heritage Centre sited in an old mill slightly further down river explores the years that Burns spent in this area. Dumfries Museum sits nearby on the side of a hill. Overlooking the town and river Dumfries Museum contains local collections on geology and social history. There is a working Camera Obscura on the upper floor of this eighteenth-century windmill, one of the three found in Scotland.

The A75 now by-passes Dumfries on its northern side. Heading north from town following signs for Kilmarnock, **Ellisland Farm** is found on the A76, the Kilmarnock Road about 8 miles (13km) on the right. Burns leased this poor piece of farming land in June, 1788. It was here at Ellisland that he wrote *Tam O' Shanter*. Today, the farm is run by a friendly couple who allow visitors to see a room filled with artifacts of the poet's life and guide you to a walk along the Nith River where Burns frequented to seek inspiration.

Further north on the A76 is the area known as Nithsdale excellent for fishing and further into the Lowther Hills, for its stark scenery. The village of **Thornhill** straddles the A76 and there is an tenth-century Anglican cross seen at the Nith Bridge to the west of the town. The smithy at **Keir Mill** was where the world's first pedal cycle was constructed. Further inland along the B729, **Maxweltown House**, a museum and grounds open to the public was the birthplace of Annie Laurie, the subject of the seventeenth-century poem and song.

Drumlanrig Castle is found just off the A76, a short drive north of Thornhill and is the home of the Duke of Buccleuch, an immense mansion rather than a fortified stronghold built by the first Duke of Queensberry in 1689. Apparently, the Duke only stayed one night in his new home deciding after that he did not like it. The interior is a repository of artistic treasures including Rembrandt's *Old Woman Reading* and Leonardo Di Vinci's *Madonna with the Yarnwinder*.

Sanquar is a staging post on the Southern Upland Way most noted for its Tolbooth, now a visitor centre and museum for the local region. There is also the oldest post office in Britain, still working today and in commission in 1763. Following the Mennock Pass on the B797 are the villages of Wanlockhead and Leadhills, once the centre of a metal mining industry that survived from the Middle Ages until early this century. **Wanlockhead**, at 1,380ft (421m), is Scotland's highest village with its cottages still reflecting the time when they were 'company' designed, built and owned. A museum dedicated to the lead mining industry shows the artifacts of the trade as well as the lifestyle of the miners in two converted cottages. There is a water-powered wooden beam engine nearby and also a narrow mine-shaft, the Loch Nell mine, that can be descended on a guided tour if you are not claustrophobic. Gold and silver mining was common here also and gold panning stills goes on today in some of the peaty burns that roll off the hills.

The area east of Dumfries is arable land with Annan being the chief centre of population. The main attraction on this part of the Solway's coast is **Caerlaverock Castle**, a solid chunk of thirteenth-century architecture. The most scenic route to get there is following the B725 along the mouth of the Nith. The archetypal, turreted castle was improved by the first Earl of Nithsdale in the seventeenth century who added a much-refined interior to its formidable façade before it was turned to ruin again by the Covenanters soon after the Earl's work was complete. A mile or so further on is the entrance to Caerlaverock National Nature Reserve, 1,400 acres (560 hectares) of salt-marsh and mud-flats, where legions of 'twitchers' spend hours in hushed concentration until a particularly scarce specimen comes in view of their telescopes.

Annan is by-passed by the A75 making it a quiet back-water with its town hall and a carved tablet built into its walls being the main piece of historic fascination. The Brus Stone was held to be part of a castle built by the Brus lords and is inscribed 'Robert de Brus', possible pertaining to be King Robert the Bruce. The celebrated community of **Gretna Green** is 10 miles (16km) on at the Scottish/English border. Until 1856, eloping English couples could cross the border and be united over an anvil by the local blacksmith. This 'trade' continued until 1969 as Scotland did not require parental consent for marriage after the age of 16. The Old Blacksmith Shop displays the anvil, photographs and documents from this period.

The upgraded M74 motorway, carries traffic north to Lochkerbie, Moffat and Langholm. For one of the best meals on crossing the border stop at the Riverside Inn in Canonbie near Langholm which also has some comfortable accommodation. The village of **Ecclefechan** was the birthplace of the essayist and historian, Thomas Carlyle. The Arched House, as his family home was called, is now a museum dedicated to this brilliant man of letters. His gravestone stands in a churchyard behind the cottage. Lochmaben on the A709 claims to be the birthplace of Robert the Bruce whose statue glowers down upon the main road.

Before the disaster that came upon it, **Lockerbie** was a simple little market town. Today, the memories of the Pan-AM flight that fell from the sky following the explosion of a terrorist bomb are irrevocably attached to the place. There is a Garden of Remembrance attached to the town's graveyard at the north end.

Surrounded by the oft-times stern Southern Uplands, **Moffat** is set only a mile or so from the main motorway. Its broad High Street is a touch 'continental' with a wide boulevard, divided by trees. In the late seventeenth and eighteenth centuries Moffat became a popular spa resort owing to its sulphurous waters that still pour from two mineral springs. Moffat is a good place to stop for a day or two with plenty of choice in B&B accommodation. Moffat Museum describes the towns important links with the sheep trade.

To the north of Moffat following the A701 there is a deep, natural basin that was once used by cattle rustlers to contain and conceal their ill-gotten gains called the **Devil's Beef Tub**. On the A708, the Moffat to Selkirk route, the **Grey Mare's Tail**, a 200ft (61m) water fall, spills over from Loch Skeen to join the Moffat Water. There is a short walk to reach the most impressive outlook of the falls and further, more strenuous walks up to Loch Skeen itself. From here the route carries on through the Borders towards Edinburgh. Most other areas are accessed by the M74 which carries on to Glasgow to the north or the M6 and England to the south.

Additional Information

Places of Interest

Alloway

Burns Cottage and Museum
On the B7024 just south of Ayr
☎ 01292 441215
Open: All year, June to August, 9am-7pm, April, May, September and October, 10am-5pm. Sundays 2-5pm. November to March, 10am-4pm not including Sundays.

Burns Monument
☎ 01292 441321
Open: All year, June to August 9am-7pm. April, May September, October, 10am-5pm, Sundays 2-5pm. November to March, 10am-4pm and not Sundays.

Land O' Burns Centre
Opposite Kirk, 2 miles (3km) South of Ayr
☎ 01292 443700
Open: All year, daily, 10am-5.30pm.

Wonderwest World
3 miles South of Ayr on A719
☎ 01292 445641 (Bookings)
Open: Daily - Day visits, 10am -7.30pm and a special evening pass is issued for night shows.

Arran

Brodick Castle Gardens and Country Park
1¹/₂ miles (2km) north of Brodick, Isle of Arran

☎ 01770 302202
Open: Daily, April to mid-October, 1-5pm.

Isle of Arran Heritage Museum
Rosaburn, Brodick
☎ 01770 302636
Open: Early May to September, Monday to Saturday, 10am-1pm & 2-5pm.

King's Cave
2 miles (3km) north of Blackwaterfoot on west coast
Open: At all times.

Lochranza Castle
North coast of Island of Arran
Historic Scotland ☎ 0131 244 3101
Open: April to September, Monday to Saturday, 9.30am-7pm. Sunday, 2-7pm. October to March, Monday to Saturday, 9.30am-4pm. Sunday, 2-4pm.

Machrie Moor Standing Stones
1¹/₂ miles (2km) east of A841 on Arran, follow Moss Farm Road South of Machrie
Historic Scotland ☎ 0131 244 3101
Open: All times.

Ayrshire
Ayr
Alloway Kirk
Alloway near Ayr
☎ 01292 441252
Tours by prior arrangement.

The Tam O'Shanter Experience
Centre of Alloway
☎ 01292 619400
Open: daily, April to October, 10am-6pm. November to March, 10am-4pm.

Girvan
Ailsa Craig Island
Firth of Clyde, off Girvan
☎ 01465 713219

Irvine
Magnum Leisure Centre
Large metal building near Harbourside
☎ 01294 278381
Open: All year daily, 9am-10pm.

Scottish Maritime Museum
Harbourside, Irvine
☎ 01294 278283
Open: April to October.

Vennel Museum and Heckling Shop
No's 4 & 10, Glasgow Vennel
☎ 01294 275059
Open: All year, Monday to Saturday, 10am-4pm.

Kilmarnock
Burns Monument and Museum
Kilmarnock
☎ 01563 522072
Open: Recently refurbished but as yet not open to the public. Phone for more updated information.

Dean Castle & Country Park
Off the Glasgow Road
☎ 01563 522702
Open: Daily 12-5pm.

Dick Institute
Elmbank Avenue, Kilmarnock
☎ 01563 526401
Open: daily, 10am to 8pm unless otherwise stated.

Kirkoswald
Culzean Castle & Country Park
On the A719, 12 miles (19km) South-west of Ayr
☎ 01655 760269
Open: April to October, daily, 10.30am-5.30pm.

Soutar Johnnie's Cottage
In Kirkoswald on the A77
☎ 01655 760603
Open: April to October, daily 12-5pm.

Largs
Largs Museum
Manse Court, Largs
☎ 01475 687081
Open: June to September, Monday to Saturday, 2-5pm.

Kelburn Country Park
South of town
☎ 01475 568685
Open: Daily, April to October, 10am-6pm. November to March, 11am-5pm. (Glen & Gardens only).

Mauchline
Burns House Museum
Castle Street
☎ 01290 500455
Open: All year, Easter to October, Monday to Saturday, 11am-12.30pm, and 1.30-5.30pm. Sundays 2-5pm.

Poosie Nansie's Pub
Just off Mauchline centre
Open: normal public house hours.

Maybole
Crossraguel Abbey
2 miles (3km) South-west of Maybole on A77
Historic Scotland ☎ 0131 244 3101
Open: April to September, Monday to Saturday, 9.30am-7pm. Sunday, 2-7pm. October to March, Monday to Saturday, 9.30am-4pm. Sunday, 2-4pm.

Tarbolton
Batchelor's Club
On the B744 7 miles (11km) north-east of Ayr
☎ 01292 541940
Open: April to October, daily 12-5pm.

West Kilbride
West Kilbride Museum
The Institute
☎ 01294 822987
Open: All year, Tuesday, Thursday, Friday & Saturday, 10.30am-12.30pm, 2-4pm.

Dumfries and Galloway

Ardwell
Logan Botanic Gardens
14 miles (22km) South of Stranraer on B7065.
☎ 01776 860231
Open: Daily, March to Oct, 10am-6pm.

Castle Douglas

Threave Castle
North of A75 3 miles (5km) north-west
of Castle Douglas
Historic Scotland ☎ 0131 244 3101
Open: April to September, Monday to
Saturday, 9.30-5.15pm,
Sunday,10.30am-4.45pm. October to
March, Monday to Saturday, 9.30am-
4.20pm. Sunday, 12.30-3.35pm.

Threave Gardens & Wildfowl Refuge
South of A75 and 1 mile (2km) west of
Castle Douglas
☎ 01556 502575
Open: All year daily, 9am to sunset.

Creetown

Creetown Gem Rock Museum and Gallery
A75 in Creetown, turn up opposite
clock tower
☎ 01671 820554
Open: Daily, Easter to September,
9.30am-6pm. Oct to Easter, 9.30am-5pm.

Dumfries

Burns House
In Dumfries, Burns Street
☎ 01387 255297
Open: All year, April to October,
Monday to Saturday, 10am-1pm,
2-5pm. Sunday 2-5pm. Closed Sunday
and Monday October to March.

Robert Burns Centre
Mill Road, Dumfries
☎ 01387 264808
Open: All year, April to October, Monday
to Saturday, 10am-8pm. Sunday 2-5pm.
October to March, Tuesday to Saturday,
10am-1pm and 2-7pm.

Globe Inn
Off the High Street in Dumfries centre
☎ 01387 252335
Open: All week, pub hours.

Old Bridge House
Mill Road, Dumfries at end of
Devorgilla's Bridge
☎ 01387 253374
Open: April to September, Monday to Sat,
10am-1pm, 2-5pm. Sun 2-5pm.

Dumfries Museum
The Observatory
☎ 01387 253374
Open: All year, Monday to Saturday
10am-1pm & 2pm-5pm. Sunday 2-5pm.

Caerlaverock Castle
Off the B725 9 miles (14km) south of
Dumfries
Historic Scotland ☎ 0131 244 3101
Open: April to September, Monday to
Saturday, 9.30am-7pm. Sunday, 2-7pm.
October to March, Monday to Saturday,
9.30am-4pm. Sunday, 2-4pm.

Caerlaverock National Nature Reserve
B725 9 miles (14km) south of Dumfries
☎ 01387 770275
Open: All year.

Ellisland Farm
Off the A76, 7 miles (11km) north of
Dumfries
☎ 01387 274426
Phone in advance to arrange a visit.

Sweetheart Abbey
New Abbey
South of Dumfries
Historic Scotland ☎ 0131 244 3101
Open: April to September, Monday to
Saturday, 9.30-5.15pm,
Sunday,10.30am-4.45pm. October to
March, Monday to Saturday, 9.30am-
4.20pm. Sunday, 12.30-3.35pm

Gatehouse of Fleet

Mill on the Fleet Museum
Near Tourist Information Office
☎ 01557 814099
Open: March to October, daily, 10am-
5.30pm.

Gretna Green

Old Blacksmith's Shop and Visitor Centre
Gretna Green just over the Scottish/
English border
☎ 01461 338363
Open: daily all year.

Kirkcudbright

MacLellan's Castle
Off High Street in Kirkcudbright
Historic Scotland ☎ 0131 244 3101
Open: April to September, Monday to
Saturday, 9.30am-7pm. Sunday, 2-7pm.
Closed October to March, Monday to
Friday.

Broughton House
☎ 01557 330437
Open: Easter then May to October, daily
1-5.30pm.

Moffat

Carlyle's Birthplace
Ecchelfechan off A74
☎ 01576 300666
Open: April to October daily, 12-5pm.

Devil's Beef Tub
A701 North of Moffat
☎ 01683 20620
Open: All year.

Grey Mare's Tail
Off the A708 10 miles (16km) north-east
of Moffat
☎ 0141 552 8391

Moffat Museum
☎ 01683 20868
Open: March to September, 10.30am-
1pm & 2.30-5pm. Sunday 2.30-5pm.

Newton Stewart

Newton Stewart Museum
☎ 01671 402106
Open: April to October, Monday to
Saturday, 2-5pm. July and August,
10am-12.30pm. 2-5pm. Sundays, July to
September, 2-5pm

Galloway Forest Park
10 miles (16km) north of Newton
Stewart on the A714
☎ 01671 402420

Portpatrick

Little Wheels
Portpatrick
☎ 01776 810536
Open: 11am-4pm.

Sanquar

Museum of Scottish Lead Mining
In Wanlockhead on B797, 8 miles
(13km) north-east of Sanquar
☎ 01659 74387
Open: Easter to October, daily, 11am-4pm.

*Sanquar Post Office, Britain's Oldest Post
Office*
Sanquar Main Street
☎ 01659 50201
Open: During business hours.

Sanquar Tolbooth
☎ 01659 50186
Open: April to Sept, Tuesday to Saturday,
10am-1pm and 2-5pm. Sunday 2-5pm.

Stranraer

Castle Kennedy Gardens
Off A75, 3 miles (5km) north-east of
Stranraer
☎ 01776 702024
Open: April to Sept, daily 10am-5pm.
Sunday 2-5pm, Nov to March 2-4pm.

Glenluce Abbey
Off the A75, 3 miles (5km) north of
Glenluce
Historic Scotland ☎ 0131 244 3101
Open: April to September, Monday to
Saturday, 9.30am-7pm. Sunday, 2-7pm.
October to March, Monday to Saturday,
9.30am-4pm. Sunday, 2-4pm.

Stranraer Museum
Old Town Hall, George Street
☎ 01776 705088
Open: All year Monday to Friday,
10am-5pm and Saturdays 10am-1pm.

Thornhill

Drumlanrig Castle
Off A76, 3 miles (5km) north of Thornhill
☎ 01848 330248
Open: May to September, weekdays
11am-5pm, weekends 2-6pm.

Maxweltown House
30 miles (48km) north-west of Dumfries
on the B729 near Moniaive
☎ 0184 82 385
Open: May to September, 2-5pm.

Wanlockhead

Wanlockhead Beam Engine
Village of Wanlockhead
☎ 01659 74387
Open: At all times.

Whithorn

St Ninian's Chapel
Isle of Whithorn, 3 miles (5km) south-
east of Whithorn
Historic Scotland ☎ 0131 244 3101
Open: At all times.

Whithorn Dig & Visitor Centre
45-46 George Street
☎ 01988 500508
Open: Easter to end of October, daily,
10.30am-5pm. Sundays, 1-5pm.

Whithorn Priory & Museum
Main Street
Historic Scotland ☎ 0131 244 3101
Open: April to September, Monday to
Saturday, 9.30-5.15pm, Sunday,10.30am-
4.45pm. October to March, Monday to
Saturday, 9.30am-4.20pm. Sunday, 12.30-
3.35pm except closed October and March,
Monday to Friday.

Useful Information

Emergencies
Ambulance, Police & Firebrigade ☎ 999
Ferry Services
P&O European ☎ 01581 200276
Seacat, Stranraer ☎ 01776 702255
Sealink ☎ 01776 702262
Rail
Dumfries Station ☎ 01387 264105
Stranraer Station ☎ 01776 6234
Airport
Prestwick International Airport
☎ 01292 479822
Weathercall for this area ☎ 01898 500420

Accommodation

Troon
Piersland Hotel **
☎ 01292 314747

Alloway
Burns Monument Hotel *
☎ 01292 442466

Turnberry
Turnberry Hotel ***
☎ 01655 331000

Glenlochrie House Farmhouse B&B *
Near Turnberry
☎ 01465 811242

Portpatrick
Knockinaam Lodge **
☎ 01776 810471

Newton Stewart
Creebridge House Hotel **
☎ 01671 402121

Kirkcudbright
Gladstone House *
☎ 01557 331734

New Abbey
Criffel Inn *
☎ 01387 850244

Dumfries
Station Hotel **
☎ 01387 254316

Near Dumfries (Clarencefield)
Comlongon Castle **
☎ 01387 870283

Camping

Sandihills near Dumfries
☎ 01387 780257

Tourist Information Offices

Arran

Brodick
The Pier ☎ 01770 302140
Lochranza ☎ 01770 830320

Ayrshire

Ayrshire Tourist Board
Prestwick Airport ☎ 01292 479000

Ayr
Burns House
Burns Statue Square ☎ 01292 288688

Ardrossan
Ferry Terminal Building ☎ 01294 601063

Girvan
Bridge Street ☎ 01465 714950

Irvine
New Street ☎ 01294 313886

Kilmarnock
62 Bank Street ☎ 01563 539090

Largs
Promendade ☎ 01475 673765

Mauchline
National Burns Memorial Tower
☎ 01290 551916

Millport
28 Stuart Street ☎ 01475 530753

Troon
South Beach ☎ 01292 317696

Dumfries and Galloway

Dumfries and Galloway Tourist Board
Bank End Road, Dumfries
☎ 01387 253862

Castle Douglas ☎ 01556 502611

Dalbeattie ☎ 01556 610117

Gatehouse of Fleet ☎ 01557 814212

Kirkcudbright ☎ 01557 330494

Newton Stewart ☎ 01671 402431

Stranraer ☎ 01776 702595

Kelvingrove Park ☎ 0141 221 9600

Fact File

15

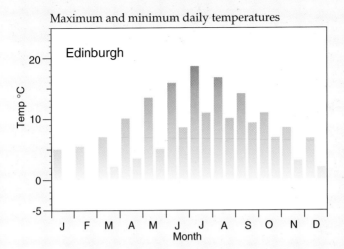

Maximum and minimum daily temperatures

Edinburgh

Scotland's northern latitude, in line with Norway, Labrador and Moscow should make it much colder than it is but the warming effects of the Gulf Stream allay this. Often the best weather is found in May and September. These are also the months that the north-west of Scotland are relatively "midge" free. For the rest of the summer months these tiny biting insects can cause fair distress if you are out in wooded areas or on the hills.

Climate

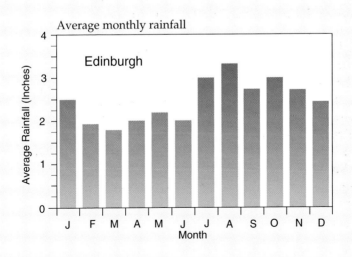

Average monthly rainfall

Edinburgh

Accommodation

Throughout Scotland there is generally a high standard of all types of accommodation including B&B's, guest houses, country house hotels, larger hotels, self catering cottages, youth hostels and camp-sites.

If you are travelling independently a useful tip is to call in at the local Tourist Information Office (listed at the end of each chapter) who will find suitable accommodation at short notice with their Book-A-Bed-Ahead scheme. This still depends on availability and in popular areas can occasionally lead to trepidation if most rooms are taken.

To help you plan your trip in advance, each area tourist board publishes guides to their region which list a wide range of accommodation including camp-sites and hostels. There is a 10 per cent booking charge on the Advanced Booking Service as well as the Book-A-Bed-Ahead scheme but this is deducted from your accommodation bill.

The Scottish Tourist Board inspects hotels and guest houses that are members of their scheme and grades/classifies them annually so this is a useful indicator to help your choice. Grades and classification are included in the guides and also indicated by blue oval plaques placed outside an establishment with information such as whether it is Approved, Commended, Highly Commended or Deluxe.

The accommodation is categorised by a star system found in the Additional Information section of each chapter as follows:

> expensive***
> medium**
> moderate*

Hotels

Hotels often offer restaurants, bars and leisure facilities all within the building which can be quite useful in Scotland. Special deals are also advertised in local and national press. Hotel chains such as Best Western, Consort, Mount Charlotte Thistle and Stakis (☎01800 262626) have hotels placed effectively throughout the country and are worth contacting through your travel agent.

Country House Hotels

This is one category of accommodation Scotland does better than most with individually designed rooms, log fires, home-made scones and jam in the afternoon and excellent dinners at night. They too, form themselves into marketing associations such as Pride of Britain, Connoisseurs Scotland and the Tartan Collection. Some of the member hotels are quite pricey but you are assured of a unique and comfortable stay.

B&B's & Guest Houses

Scotland's Bed and Breakfast and Guest House industry offers some of the best, budget accommodation available. It forms into a vast network of excellent and varied rooms, many now with en-suite facilities as well as television and coffee makers, all at very reasonable prices. Look out for the Scottish Board's grading system.

Self Catering Cottages

These are available especially in more remote areas for those that wish to enjoy a quieter or more active break such as hill-walking. There are companies that specialise in this type of accommodation such as Country Cottages in Scotland (☎ 01328 851155).

Youth Hostels & Camping
Youth Hostels represent excellent value for money as well as the camaraderie of close quarters with fellow travellers from around the globe. You are required to join the (SYHA) to use these facilities at a very modest fee and this can be dealt with at any SYHA establishment when you arrive. The SYHA address is 161 Warrender-Park Road, Edinburgh EH9 16Q ☎ 0131 229 8660.

Camping in Scotland varies wildly and is dominated by caravanners whose site facilities also allow tents. Most sites are well provided for with showers and washing-up facilities although others are simply a corner of a field. Wild-camping is possible especially in the north-west but permission should be sought from the landowner where possible.

Accommodation Agencies
Beyond the recommended establishments in the individual sections of this book, there are several agencies offering properties of all kinds throughout Scotland.

Holiday Cottages (Scotland)
  Limited
Lilliesleaf
Melrose
Roxburghshire
RD6 9JD
☎ 01835 870481

The Landmark Trust
Shottesbrooke
Maidenhead
Berkshire
SL6 3SW
☎ 01628 825925

Scottish Country Cottages
Suite 2d
Churchill Way
Bishopbriggs
Glasgow
G64 2RH
☎ 0141 772 5920

Scottish Farmhouse Holidays
Drumtenant
Ladybank
Fife
KY7 7UG
☎ 01337 830451

Scotland's Heritage Hotels
2d Churchhill Way
Bishopbriggs
Glasgow
G64 2RH
☎ 0141 772 6911

Scottish Tourist Board
23 Ravelston Terrace
Edinburgh
EH4 3EU
☎ 0131 332 2433

Scottish Youth Hostel Association
7 Glebe Crescent
Stirling
FK8 2JA
☎ 01786 451181

Crime

Like everywhere, some precautions should be taken in protecting your property such as leaving bags or cameras out of sight in the trunk of a car and keeping the passenger compartment free of other tell-tale signs that the car is being used for touring.

Currency & Credit Cards

The basic unit of currency in Scotland and throughout the UK is the sterling which is based upon 100 units or pennies. Coins in circulation are 1p, 2p, 5p, 10p 20p and 50p with 100p to the pound. There are £1 notes circulating in Scotland but the £1 coin is now more common. £1 notes have been discontinued in England. Scottish banks such as the Royal Bank of Scotland, Bank of Scotland and Clydesdale Bank issue their own sterling notes which are legal tender throughout the UK although occasionally you will find reluctance to have these accept should you take them to England.

Traveller's cheques are accepted in most city outlets but occasionally these might prove difficult to use in smaller establishments located in outlying areas especially if the cheque is more than £20.00. In the north or more remote west be sure to obtain cash especially before the weekend when banks are closed. Banks are open Monday to Saturday morning and in most cases later on Thursdays. Bureau de Changes are found in larger towns only and have longer opening hours than banks.

Credit cards are widely accepted with Visa and Mastercard the most established. Small hotels, restaurants and B&Bs in the north might not be equipped to accept credit cards so cash will be required. Filling stations almost always accept credit cards. Using your credit card to obtain money from a bank's outside cash dispenser is a simple and often cost effective method, depending on the exchange rate at the time. This avoids the double fee paid on obtaining and cashing travellers cheques. It is worth ensuring you know your pin (personal identification) number. Cash dispensers are found throughout Scotland.

Disabled Tourists

Scotland has not kept pace with providing facilities for disabled travellers but this is gradually changing and major attractions such as Edinburgh Castle as well as many hotels and shops now make access for wheel-chairs available. Intercity rail network and Scotrail are the most advanced travel organisations on this front with special facilities at most main stations and helpful staff to ensure disabled travellers are catered for. Public transport within towns has generally not recognized the need for disabled facilities. Car hire companies do have hand controlled vehicles but these are often in the higher priced categories.

'Disability Scotland' is an organisation that will provide a list of tour operators, hotels and guest houses, self-catering holidays, university accommodation and groups activities that cater for disabled travellers and this can be obtained from 'Disability Scotland', Princes House, 5 Shandwick Place, Edinburgh, EH2 4RG (☎ 0131 229 8632). The information is free to disabled individuals.

Drink

As a rule, Scots do not drink at home unless on special occasions and so Scottish pubs are the mainstay of social life as they have been for many centuries. At lunch time and between 5 and 7pm most pubs become eating places. They then stow away the menus and crockery to welcome a more alcohol-oriented evening crowd. Opening hours in Scottish pubs were extended some years ago, usually from 11am to midnight and this helped change the image from hard drinking to a more sociable environment.

Electricity

The electrical current throughout the UK is 240V / AC using a large 3-pin plug. An adapter is required for Australasian appliances but an adapter and transformer is needed for North American appliances making it less useful to bring appliances from these countries. Most hotels provide hair-dryers and irons but it might prove useful to buy your own hair-dryer in Scotland especially if you intend to stay in B&Bs.

Embassies

The are no Embassies in Scotland but British Embassies abroad include:

USA
3100 Massachusetts
Avenue NW
Washington DC
20008
☎ 202 462 1340

Canada
80 Elgin Street
Ottawa
Ontario, K1P 5K7
☎ 613 237 1530

Australia
Commonwealth Avenue
Yarralumia
Canberra, ACT 2600
☎ 062 270 6666

New Zealand
Reserve Bank Building
2 The Terrace
PO Box 1812
Wellington
☎ 04 726 049

Ireland
31-33 Merrion Road
Dublin 4
☎ 01 695211

Netherlands
General Koningslaan, 44
Amsterdam
☎ 676 43 43

Emergencies

To summon the police, ambulance or fire brigade ☎ 999 on any phone. There is no charge for this although it should be used only in emergencies.

Entertainment

Scotland's main forms of entertainment for the visitor is surely the scenery or the delightful characters you are likely to meet. Pubs, are the most popular form of evening entertainment while there are plenty of cinemas, theatres, bowling alleys, ice rinks and leisure complexes. Check with the local tourist information for a copy of their *What's On* publication. For traditional Scottish entertainment such as a 'Ceilidh', that is Scottish dancing to accordion, fiddle bass, drums and a variety of other instruments, look in the *Glasgow Herald* or *Scotsman's* entertainment sections. In the Lowlands, these are less frequent with centres in the Highlands or island such as Tobermory or Aviemore the more likely venue.

Festivals & Public Holidays

The only statutory public holiday in Scotland is New Year's Day. Bank holidays are frequent and include 2 January, the Friday before Easter, the first and last Friday in May, the first Monday in August, the 30 November and the 25 and 26 of December.

Besides banks, many offices close on these days but most retailers, accommodation and visitor attractions are open. All towns have local trade holidays which vary from district to district. Again, this does not usually affect tourist activities. Tourist boards often carry a leaflet entitled *Public Holidays in Scotland* and there is booklet printed by Glasgow Chamber of Commerce detailing local holidays. Write to them at 30 George Square, Glasgow, G2 1EQ.

Food

The culinary arts have lagged miserably behind the rest of the world in Scotland. Dishes like tatties and mince or white pudding suppers have formed a large part of the Scottish diet and led to the worst incidence of heart disease in the world followed by an equally bleak dental record. Today it is vastly improved. Year after year there are new and innovative restaurants opening to provide an ever-varying choice of good food. Pubs offering lunches and dinners have become prolific and are usually quite satisfying as well as inexpensive.

Health Care

Most travel agents offer health insurance along with your other travel arrangements and this is recommended. If you need to attend a doctor in Scotland many nationals of EC countries as well as others are treated free of charge under the NHS scheme. Countries such as the USA and Canada and several more are treated as private patients and a consultation with a GP will cost £30. Most surgeries operate an appointment system so generally speaking an appointment should be made. In emergencies patients will be seen as soon as possible.

Language

Apart from Gaelic which is spoken by around 70,000 people mainly in the Western Isles and Skye who all speak a lovely, lilting English as well, Scotland is an English speaking country. Some dialects may pose a problem for visitors but again, locals will switch to a softer version of their regional dialect when speaking to a visitor.

Road signs in the Western Isles are displayed in Gaelic but most good maps or instructions from the Tourist Information Office will avoid any problems. Buy a copy of the bilingual *Western Isles Leisure Map* from any of the outlets on the islands.

Maps & Brochures

Maps are always a good investment and the best for general touring purposes is the *Scottish Touring Map* published by the Scottish Tourist Board. It includes most of the important attractions and facilities in each area and is accompanied by a useful little book, *1001 Things to See in Scotland*. Every Tourist Information Office carries copious amounts of brochures and flyers on attractions in their own and other areas, mostly free of charge.

What's On Guides are useful indicators of events as well as places of interest in each town or region and can be obtained in the local Tourist

Information Office. Occasionally, free maps are available accompanied with advertising of tourist attractions, accommodations and local restaurants. Some newspapers produce a yearly publication such as *Welcome to the Highlands and Islands* published by the Highland News Group, available free at Tourist Information Offices throughout the north.

Measurements

The imperial system is used in Britain

2.2lb = 1kg (1,000 grams)
$1^3/_4$ pints = 1 litre
1 gallon = $4^1/_2$ litres
5 miles = 8 km
5ft = $1^1/_2$ m

Newspapers

For a broad view of what is going on is Scotland as well as the rest of the world, the *Glasgow Herald* or the *Scotsman* newspapers are the best buy. Local newspapers are useful for local information or events and special deals offered by hotels. If you are looking to take back a kilt or a set of bagpipes it might be worth looking in the classified sections of local papers for a second-hand version as these items are quite expensive new.

Foreign papers and magazines can be purchased in some shops in Edinburgh or the larger chain stores such as Menzies or W.H. Smith. The *European, Time* and *Newsweek* are quite widely available as are some American golf magazines etc. There are magazines such as *Scottish Field* or the *Scots Magazine* that visitors might find mildly useful although the features are written mainly for those that know the country well or expatriate Scots.

Opening Hours

Opening hours for shops and most relevant facilities are generally 9am-5pm as is the case with offices and other places of employment. Banks all have outside cash-points that can be used at all hours. Convenience stores open from 8am until late. Pubs are open 11am to midnight. Businesses in the north-west and especially the Western Isles are usually closed on a Sunday including filling stations and stores.

Passports

Visitors from all European countries except Poland, Albania and Bulgaria require only a passport and no visa. This is also the case for citizens of North America, Australia and New Zealand. Generally, a stay of 3 months is allowed but stays of a longer duration than 6 months will require a visa. There are no vaccination requirements.

Religion

Scotland's religion has past through many phases from the early Celtic foundations in Iona and Whithorn through the Reformation and on to a less zealous form today. It is broadly divided between Presbyterian and Catholic and visitors are free to attend services or mass at most churches.

Shopping & Souvenirs

Scotland's best buys are probably woollens, smoked salmon and whisky although the latter may be cheaper in your home country as taxes make spirits quite expensive in Scotland. Having said that the choice of malts is greatest here so it is probably worth purchasing some of the less exported brands. Some clothes items can be of a superior quality. VAT or Value Added Tax, is effected on most purchases with the exception of food and books but this can be claimed back on goods taken out of the country by non-nationals. Not all shops participate in this 'Retail Export Scheme' so look for a sign or enquire before purchasing.

Sports & Activities

Soccer

Football is Scotland's most popular spectator sport. Scots have an insatiable appetite for the game with huge crowds gathering at grounds around the nation once or twice a week from September through May to support their teams.

Walking

One of the best ways to enjoy Scotland is by walking or climbing over its many mountains and glens. Every part of the country offers some form of hill-walking or rambling and the rewards are plentiful. There are certain prescribed routes for the more serious walker while casual ramblers will find a host of pleasant walks.

Skiing

Skiing in the Cairngorms, the Grampians or Aonach is popular if a little unreliable. There are winters where the climate remains mild and not enough snow falls throughout the season. Poor visibility and rain can make it rather miserable.

Water Sports

White-water rafting, canoing and sailing are all available along the major inland lochs and rivers. Surfing may not be Scotland's main sport but the breakers around the north coast provide some of the best surf in Europe. Diving around the west coast and the islands is surprisingly popular in crystal clear waters with white shell sand. Usually freezing, the water contains many sights such as part of the World War I German fleet scuttled around Scapa Flow in Orkney.

Hunting, Shooting and Fishing

Hunting and shooting are popular on estates throughout the Highlands and Border uplands. This can be arranged through the local Tourist Information Office who will put you in contact with estate gillies or stalkers that can take you on to the hills for deer or grouse. The 'Glorious 12th' of August is the start of the grouse hunting season and rows of 'beaters' drive the birds on to the line of shot-guns. These sports can be expensive and attract a rather elitist clientele.

Fishing

Fishing is the most popular participant activity in Britain and Scotland has some of the best known salmon and trout beats in the world. The River Tay is considered by many to be the finest salmon river in Scotland with its source at 3,708ft (1,130m) on Ben Lui and it flows 117 miles (188km) to the sea on the east coast at Dundee. The Tay has a catchment area of some 2,800 sq miles (7,258sq km) helps to maintain good water levels from January to October.

The Tweed is most popular too, £1,000 per rod for a few days. The Dee is similar. Salmon fishing has been struck by the effects of over-fishing in Greenland and netting near the mouths of the rivers. Spring salmon enter Scottish east coast rivers as early as November and are well distributed throughout the system.

Fly fishing is very popular but instruction on how to cast properly is essential to be effective as well as stop you becoming exhausted after an hour. Courses are available throughout the country.

Telephone & Postal Service

The British phone system is highly efficient and poses little difficulty in dealing with it. The biggest problem has been the recent change in area codes and additions to rural numbers throughout Scotland. These changes have added a 1 to all area codes commencing with 0 and all 3, 4, or 5 digit numbers have been increased to 6. This means that some numbers you may see in older reference material will be out of date. However, a recorded message will inform you of the changes to the number you have dialled at no extra cost. Most of the numbers listed in this guide have been upgraded.

Useful Operator numbers on the British Telecom system are:

100 for the UK operator
155 for the International Operator
192 for UK Directory Enquiries
153 for International Directory Enquiries

The cheaper rate for making international call is 8pm - 8am through the week and all day Saturday and Sunday. To instigate a call routed through your own telephone credit card company dial 155, British Telecom's international operator and they will connect you. International reverse charge calls (Collect) are also available through 155. When dialling foreign countries from the UK start with 010 then the country code followed by the area code then the number. All country and area codes are found in the front section of British Telecom's telephone directory or by dialling 153.

01898 numbers, some of which are listed in this book eg Skicall or Weathercall, cost around 40 to 50 pence per minute depending on when you dial.

Tipping

In restaurants a 15 per cent service charge is often added to the bill so check this before you leave a further tip. With credit cards the final total is left blank to allow you to leave a gratuity. Taxi drivers, hair dressers and hotel porters are used to a small tip for their services. Otherwise, a tip is not compulsory but always appreciated especially if someone has given you particularly good service.

Tourist Information Offices

Scottish Tourist Board
Central Information
23 Ravelston Terrace
Edinburgh, EH3 4EU
☎ 0131 332 2433

London
19 Cockspur Street
Trafalgar Square
London SW1Y 5BL
☎ 0171 930 8661

Canada
British Tourist Authority
BTA Toronto
111Avenue Rd
Suite 450
Toronto, Ontario
M5R 3JB
☎ 416 925 2175

USA
British Tourist Authority
New York BTA North American HQ
40 West 57th Street
Suite 320
New York, NY.
10019-4001
☎ 212 581 4708
Fax: 212 265 0649

Travelling in Scotland

Airlines
Glasgow and Edinburgh Airports are the main air gateways to Scotland with good connections available to most outlying areas. Many visitors choose to see London then use the frequent shuttle flights from both Heathrow and Gatwick to Edinburgh, Glasgow, Aberdeen or Inverness. Shuttle fairs are competitive between operators and service is frequent. You do not have to book ahead with most shuttle services and tickets can be purchased on the day of travel at the airport or on board the plane.

British Rail
British Rail offers a variety of tickets to reach Scotland from the south and cheap fares can be had if you can book well in advance. The sleeper service from London is a useful way of covering the distance in comfort for an extra cost that is little more than a B&B. The present rail system, like that of so many other countries, is a shadow of its former self and there is still talk of reducing it further especially to the north-east and north-west. Many of the lines that served smaller communities have been converted to bicycle paths or walk-ways, even a hazard on a golf course.

Ferries
To explore the islands off the west coast or north to Orkney and Shetland you need to use a ferry or plane. Caledonian McBrayne offers good services to most of the Western Isles and P&O operate between the mainland and Orkney and Shetland.

Motoring
The most prevalent way of seeing Scotland is by car. The advantages of having your own transport are obvious including transporting your luggage right up the hotel door. Fly-drive tickets purchased in your home country are probably the most economical way of car-hiring as prices in the UK tend to be comparatively expensive. Internationally known car-hire companies are found at the airports and throughout most towns.

Vehicles use the left side of the road. Negotiating roundabouts or circles might be the most hazardous problem for visitors who have never driven in the UK or on the left. These are intended to slow traffic and provide a safe entrance or exit to or from a busy road.

Seat belts are compulsory in Scotland, both front and rear. Motorway driving is and speed limits on motorways might seem fast for North American drivers.

Parking a car in Glasgow and Edinburgh city centres is a taxing experience for everyone so if you have a hire car whilst visiting these cities leave it at your hotel and use public transport. This will prove cheaper in terms of parking charges and a lot less hassle. Other cities and towns are no more trouble than can be expected.

In more rural parts, hazards of driving can take the shape of sheep who, along with the rest of the Highlands, reckon they own the roads as well. With little consideration for other users they will saunter across to check out the grass on the other side of their sunbathing patio. There is a great sense of permanence driving on some Scottish back roads. Old dry-stane dykes, wood copses and hedgerows have often been standing for 200 years or more.

Useful Addresses

National Trust for Scotland
Head Office, 5 Charlotte Square
Edinburgh EH2 4DU
☎ 0131 226 5922

RSPB (Royal Society for the
  Protection of Birds)
17 Regent Terrace
Edinburgh
EH7 5BN
☎ 0131 556 5624
Own or run numerous Reserves
across Scotland

Association for the Protection of
  Rural Scotland
14a Napier Road
Edinburgh EH10 5AY
☎ 0131 229 11081

Scottish Countryside Activities
  Council
39 Clepington Road
Dundee DD4 7EL
☎ 01382 41095

Scottish Inland Waterways
  Association
139 Old Dalkeith Road
Edinburgh EH16 4SZ
☎ 0131 664 1070

Scottish National Heritage
Caspian House
Mariner Court
Clydebank Business Park
Clydebank G81 2NR

The Scottish Wildlife Trust
25 Johnstone Terrace
Edinburgh EH1 2NH
☎ 0131 226 4602

Wildlife

Wildlife is still one of Scotland's greatest commodities. Scots are used to seeing plovers, chaffinches, seals and deer. But for the visitor, they are often struck by the numbers of native birds and animals that can be easily spotted where, at home, they rarely come in contact with anything more than sparrows or pigeons. It is luck more than skill to spot Scotland's more rare species such as a golden eagle or lynx, confined mostly to the north-west Highlands.

Index